The publisher gratefully acknowledges the generous support of the African American Studies Endowment Fund of the University of California Press Foundation, which was established by a major gift from the George Gund Foundation.

January 2011

The Street Stops Here

Rebecca

To a fellow traveller
Through life's marvels &
mysteries

Patrick J. McCloskey

The Street Stops Here

A YEAR AT A CATHOLIC HIGH SCHOOL
IN HARLEM

Patrick J. McCloskey

Foreword by Samuel G. Freedman

UNIVERSITY OF CALIFORNIA PRESS

BERKELEY   LOS ANGELES   LONDON

University of California Press, one of the most
distinguished university presses in the United States,
enriches lives around the world by advancing scholarship
in the humanities, social sciences, and natural sciences. Its
activities are supported by the UC Press Foundation and
by philanthropic contributions from individuals and
institutions. For more information, visit www.ucpress.edu.

Photographs by Tamara Beckwith

University of California Press
Berkeley and Los Angeles, California

University of California Press, Ltd.
London, England

First Paperback Printing 2011

Library of Congress Cataloging-in-Publication Data

McCloskey, Patrick.
    The street stops here : a year at a Catholic high school
in Harlem / Patrick J. McCloskey ; foreword by Samuel
G. Freedman.
        p.   cm.
    Includes bibliographical references and index.
    ISBN: 978-0-520-26797-8 (pbk. : alk. paper)
    1. Catholic high schools—New York (State)—New
York.   2. Minorities—Education (Secondary)—New
York (State)—New York.   I. Title.

LC503.N5.M38   2008
371.071'27471—dc22   2007047490

Manufactured in the United States of America

17 16 15 14 13 12 11
10 9 8 7 6 5 4 3 2 1

This book is printed on Natures Book, which contains
50% post-consumer waste and meets the minimum requirements of ANSI/NISO Z39.48–1992 (R 1997) (Perma-
nence of Paper).

This book is dedicated to Stephanie and Piper,
and to everyone who opens it.

CONTENTS

WHEN I WAS A TEENAGER more than thirty years ago, an especially intense rivalry developed between two high school basketball teams in my corner of New Jersey. One was from St. Peter's, a Catholic school in New Brunswick; the other was from the public school in Perth Amboy. Because the teams played in different leagues, and because they perennially dominated that competition, St. Peter's and Perth Amboy met only in the heightened atmosphere of county or state tournaments. Though I went to neither school, I can still vividly remember listening to one typical cliffhanger of a game on the local AM radio station, and subsequently hearing from a friend who went to St. Peter's about the near brawl after the final buzzer among the exiting fans.

Something other than nostalgia for lost youth, though, summons these memories for me now, as I consider Patrick McCloskey's book *The Street Stops Here*. Even as a relatively insensate teen, I recognized the broader social implications of the confrontations between St. Peter's and Perth Amboy. St. Peter's was composed almost entirely of the children of the white-ethnic working-class, Italians and Irish and Poles and Hungarians. For their families, St. Peter's offered a refuge, and not coincidentally a virtually segregated one, from New Brunswick's descent into urban rot, a process so stunning in a city of just forty thousand that the *Washington Post* once reported on it. Perth Amboy High, on the other hand, was the receptacle for the blacks and Puerto Ricans who had migrated into that small, gritty port city at the same time its industrial economy was collapsing, leaving them the inheritors of despair. It is no wonder that basketball offered such a tempting vision of escape. One of Perth Amboy's greatest stars, a guard named Brian Taylor, had ridden the sport to Princeton University and then the NBA.

Around the immediate friction between St. Peter's and Perth Amboy hung the aura of America's tortured history of race and class. By the early 1970s, the years I recall, the civil rights movement had decisively turned its attention from South to North and from the de jure segregation of Jim Crow to the de facto segregation of economically separate communities and schools. As a bit of African American wisdom put it, "In the South, the white man will let you get close but not high, and in the North, the white man will let you get high but not close." Working-class whites, more often than not Catholics, formed the tense border between inner-city black poverty and suburban Protestant and Jewish affluence.

I say all this by way of making a point: I saw Catholic schools and racial minorities as mutually exclusive, even as intrinsically antagonistic. Nothing in my own experience as a student in the relatively recent past prepared me for the day when Catholic schools would serve large and growing numbers of African Americans and Latinos, of Baptists and Pentecostals and even Muslims, and, moreover, that those Catholic schools would be seen by those newcomers as their last best hope. Yet in my years as a journalist and author often specializing in education, I have seen that exact phenomenon occur. And it is the phenomenon to which Patrick McCloskey bears witness in this vivid and important book.

In a certain respect, the movement of the nonwhite, often non-Catholic working-class into Catholic schools should not come as a surprise. Rather, the trend represents an updating of the foundational missions of Catholic schools in the United States—to be a bulwark against bigotry, in that case the bigotry of WASP nativists against Catholic immigrants; to provide the ladder of upward mobility for a population otherwise condemned to low-wage labor; and, yes, to do the Lord's work amid fallen humanity.

In cities and inner-ring suburbs, where public education has too often failed to meet the immense needs, Catholic schools have compiled a track record of achievement at a strikingly modest cost. That story is as true in longstanding institutions such as Rice High School in Harlem, the focus of this book, as it is in the small, nimble start-ups of the Nativity and Cristo Rey education networks.

Such success has been achieved in the face of daunting obstacles, obstacles that endanger the future of urban Catholic education. The movement of newly affluent Catholics to suburbia has imperiled the financial stability of their former urban parishes. The severe contraction in the religious orders, which provided so many teachers and administrators to Catholic schools at essentially no salary, has driven up staff costs and eroded the literarily religious sense of vocation. Catholic schools in many cases grew complacent during decades of reliable funding from diocese or archdiocese and have only belatedly and amateurishly entered into the necessary field of high-stakes fund-raising. All these forces add up to a piercing irony. At the same time inner-city families are increasingly relying on Catholic schools, at the same time the nation's Catholic population is growing due to immigration, Catholic schools are closing down at a steady pace.

The purpose of *The Street Stops Here,* however, is not simply to illustrate the accomplishments of schools like Rice in neighborhoods like Harlem. In both implicit and explicit ways, this book also raises questions of public policy. One question involves the use of vouchers, paid for with tax dollars, by low-income families seeking alternatives to their miserable local public schools. Few issues within education have proven more polarizing than vouchers, in part because teachers' unions are ironclad in their opposition and in part because the libertarian wing of the conservative movement is only too happy to tether its anti-government agenda to the moral cause of inner-city children. No one who reads this book can ever see the vouchers issue quite so reductively again.

Even putting vouchers aside, there remains a second question, which is what public schools can learn from the Catholic school model. In many cities, public schools (often with widespread support from parents) already require modest uniforms, much as Catholic schools long have done. The pleated skirt or blue blazer, though, serves only as an external symbol of deeper elements of the Catholic school model—the use of a core curriculum; the commitment to traditional modes of teaching reading and math; the refusal to group students into different tracks according to supposed ability; the infusion of language about values and morals into the school.

According to one standard line of dismissive argument, Catholic schools out-perform nearby public schools because they skim the best kids. Yet the students at Rice High School hardly constitute a privileged cohort. Their scores on standardized tests, interestingly, do not exceed those of peers in adjacent public schools. But they do excel in graduation rate and college admission, the signs of a school culture that insists upon perseverance and brooks no excuses.

Simple-minded advocates of Catholic education, though, will not find this book to be an advertising brochure. McCloskey is an empathetic chronicler, and also an honest one. *The Street Stops Here* does not avert its eyes from the students who break rules, blow assignments, and even get kicked out; it recognizes the exasperation of teachers and the struggle among top administrators. By admitting to imperfection, however, this book makes the most persuasive case possible for what Catholic education has achieved and how its example can help improve public education.

The most startling part of this book, perhaps, is that no one until Patrick McCloskey wrote it. Because here, in the form of a compelling and deeply humane work of narrative, is an integral addition to the American national debate on race, class, and education, which is to say our collective destiny.

Samuel G. Freedman, June 2007

ACKNOWLEDGMENTS

THIS BOOK WOULD NOT HAVE been possible without Sam Freedman's encouragement, counsel, mentoring, editing skills, and unwavering faith. Nor would *The Street Stops Here* have been published without the expert advice and representation of my agent, Warren Frazier. Naomi Schneider, executive editor at the University of California Press, provided invaluable support and guidance. I gratefully acknowledge the generous support of the Smith Richardson Foundation, the William E. Simon Foundation, William F. Buckley, and the Lehrman Institute, and of Marlboro College for administrative help. I deeply appreciate the complete editorial freedom that these sources granted, since this project was rigorously nonideological from the start. Photographs were taken by Tamara Beckwith, who volunteered her time and highly professional talents. Several editors were essential to my development as a writer as I worked on this text, including Nancy Sharkey and Connie Rosenblum at the *New York Times* and Rich Shea at *Teacher Magazine*. Trina Daniel performed the final edits before submission. My children, Stephanie and Piper, patiently endured the obsessive nature of book writing and provided acute insights via their educational experiences. I was also cheered on—and tolerated—by my six brothers and sisters and by many friends, especially Larry Kelly, Amy McConnell, Lucinda Sloan, Deborah Devedjian, and Paul and Patricia Dole. A special thanks is due to Marilyn Spiro and Amy Rubenstein, who own and run Peter Luger's

Steakhouse in Brooklyn, N.Y. Finally, I'm grateful to the memory of Saul Poliak, who established the Poliak Center for the Study of First Amendment Issues at Columbia University. Saul '26, advised me to apply to Columbia's journalism school and would have been delighted to see a book result from his counsel.

Introduction

———

We are simply seeking to bring into full realization the American dream—a dream yet unfulfilled. A dream of equality of opportunity, of privilege and property widely distributed; a dream of a land where men no longer argue that the color of a man's skin determines the content of his character; the dream of a land where every man will respect the dignity and worth of human personality—this is the dream. When it is realized, the jangling discords of our nation will be transformed into a beautiful symphony of brotherhood, and men everywhere will know that America is truly the land of the free and home of the brave.—DR. MARTIN LUTHER KING, JR., 1963

THE MOST URGENT PROBLEM in American education today is the high dropout rate and low achievement of inner-city minority students. Tragically, this is also the most persistent problem. Despite the civil rights gains in the decades since Dr. King articulated the "dream," many disadvantaged African Americans and Hispanics have remained trapped in cycles of poverty, dysfunction, and despair, primarily because of academic failure. At the same time, the research shows that Catholic schools have become the saving grace for hundreds of thousands of the same inner-city students who fare poorly in the public system. Since the Catholic school model is also the only one proven to work systemwide, it offers a solution to this national dilemma.

A second crisis brings more urgency to this scenario. Catholic schools are closing at an alarming rate in the very neighborhoods where they're needed most, due to rising costs. At risk is a vital resource that fulfills the *public* mandate of providing a quality education to all children. In the public interest, it is imperative that the question of saving these schools be addressed, along with the question of applying the lessons of Catholic education to urban public schools.

This is not a voucher advocacy book, but a nonideological narrative inquiry into these issues based on the year I spent as a journalist-in-residence at Rice High School, an all-boys Congregation of Christian Brothers academy in Harlem.[1] Readers on all sides of the education reform and school choice debates will become intimately familiar with Rice's students and their families, and with its teachers and administrators, all of whom are dramatically affected by educational policy decisions. About 20 percent of Rice's students participate in a privately funded voucher program, so readers will experience the sort of school that participates in public programs, and be better positioned to decide about vouchers as public policy.

I first became aware of problems in American education in the process of choosing an elementary school for my daughter, Stephanie. We were living in Hoboken, New Jersey, just across the Hudson River from Manhattan, in the mid-1980s, and I couldn't help but notice differences in the behavior and outcomes of demographically identical students at local public, parochial, and private schools.

Having grown up in Canada, I found these contrasts shockingly odd. In Ottawa, my hometown, not only were public schools publicly funded, but so were Catholic schools, which I attended from kindergarten through high school. Many of my neighborhood friends were Protestants and Jews who attended public school. No academic or behavioral distinctions between the students in these systems were significant enough to provoke academic or journalistic inquiry.

After investigating the options in Hoboken, I chose Mustard Seed, a nondenominational Christian school for my daughter—not the local Catholic school, which was acceptable, but not as innovative or demanding. The experience was mostly positive, since Mustard Seed remained true to the origins of the progressive movement, relating learning to the students' real-life experiences and individual interests. Although the school was somewhat weak in grammar and science, basic skills and academic content were transmitted sufficiently well.

My curiosity and angst about education resurfaced when Stephanie entered high school. At this point, I was a single parent and consequently impoverished. We moved to a rented townhouse in Madison, New Jersey, so Stephanie could attend a high-scoring—and tuition-free—public high school. Despite the town's and the school's all-American idyllic appearance, this proved disastrous. By the end of October, my daughter was ready to drop out. Her grades fell from straight As to Cs and Ds, which elicited no concern on the part of teachers or administrators. Stephanie was an adolescent trying to make the difficult adjustment to a large school where indifference ruled, despite tax dollars paying for small class size.

In addition, neither of us was prepared for Madison's after-school culture.

"Dad, guess what the kids do after school?" Stephanie asked one evening just before Halloween.

"Tennis? Soccer? Football?" I answered, envisioning the expansive green fields and new hard courts. "Band practice?" I added as Stephanie kept shaking her head. "What?"

"Drugs and sex," she said flatly, but a cloudy intensity brewed in her eyes.

In an instant, her situation became horrendously clear. Of course lots of students participated in extracurricular activities at Madison High. But most, including her new friends, left school at 3 P.M. with nowhere to go—other than the one hangout for teenagers, a pizza parlor, that could hardly compete with temptation. These were the children of Manhattan stockbrokers and lawyers; they had cars, money, and, since their parents wouldn't return from work until 7 P.M., empty houses.

"Start packing," I commanded. "We're moving."

There was a spark of defiance in Stephanie that soon gave way to relief. Within weeks, we made our exodus and landed safely at West 107th Street and Amsterdam Avenue, on the fringe of Harlem. There were drug dealers sitting on our stoop 24/7, but that danger paled in comparison to the nihilism facing affluent kids in suburbia. Stephanie attended a small, alternative public high school that was progressive in style, but in practice this approach was reduced to ensuring that students enjoyed the experience of being in the building. In sum, it was an alternative to education; Stephanie did little work in class and less at home, but Manhattan afforded a wealth of Starbucks, clothing stores, and parks to hang out in and avoid serious trouble.

Meanwhile I searched for a better school. The city has several flagship public high schools, such as Stuyvesant, that operate at a high academic level. But my daughter's experience in the public system had been so discouraging that she'd lost the will to compete. Unfortunately there were few other attractive choices, and it became apparent that there were really two public systems: one comprised of a handful of elite academies, populated mostly by Asian and white students; and the other consisting of the vast majority of schools, mediocre to low-performing institutions serving mostly black and Hispanic students.

After finding out that Stephanie had been insulted regularly by black and Hispanic female classmates at the alternative school—she'd been called a "white bitch," among other racist epithets—I was reluctant to enroll her in another public school with a sizeable minority population. I didn't see this as an indictment of urban public schools in general, and the African American and Latino boys always treated Stephanie with respect. However, I knew that private academies guaranteed zero tolerance for negative behavior, regardless of their racial mix. Happily Stephanie was accepted at Saint Ann's, a secular academy in Brooklyn Heights, modeled after Bard College, a private liberal arts college in upstate New York. Instead of teacher- or child-centered classes, Stephanie attended seminars led by teachers with graduate degrees from top universities in the subjects they were teaching. From her first day, Stephanie's attitude and performance were transformed. She enjoyed courses in Russian history, creative writing, and filmmaking, as well as standard academic fare, and she scored well on the SAT without any preparation. In fact, Saint Ann's was rated first in the country by the *Wall Street Journal* for having the highest percentage of graduates enrolling in Ivy League and other highly selective colleges.[2]

At the same time, to afford tuition we lived in a cramped apartment in a high-crime area. After deducting $16,000 a year in school costs from my net income, we lived at about the same economic level as most families at Rice High School, several of whom, as I would discover, resided nearby. For my daughter, this was a tale of two cities—or worlds, more accurately. Every morning she passed by bodegas and Santeria outlets in our predominately Hispanic and Catholic neighborhood on her way to the subway. Forty minutes later, she emerged in the exclusive residential area of Brooklyn Heights to attend class with the sons and daughters of very wealthy and mostly Jewish families at a school founded as part of the Episcopalian confederacy of private institutions that, beginning in the eighteenth century, educated children of the mostly Protestant elite and sent them on to Ivy League colleges to be groomed to run the country.

I lived a similar dual reality that, although I didn't realize it at the time, was preparing me for this book. Like many other parents in the neighborhood, I was fighting through—and thus thoroughly appreciating—the difficulties involved in finding adequate schooling, paying tuition, and raising a child in the inner city. And like many of these parents, I was doing so alone and as an immigrant without family support, connections, or resources.

But I had an empowering advantage: a postsecondary education. And, in the summer after Stephanie finished her sophomore year, I started the part-time program at Columbia University's Graduate School of Journalism.

Almost immediately I became aware of how important Catholic schools had become to urban education. In an editing class taught by Nancy Sharkey, then the *New York Times* education editor, I pitched a story about parochial education in Canada. To my surprise, she let me write the article since she was fascinated that Canadian Catholics received public financing for their schools while a contentious argument over vouchers was erupting south of the border. A major component of this debate was the disagreement over the appropriateness of public funds going via vouchers to parochial schools. In Canada, Catholic schools in some provinces have been receiving public funds for over a century. This has not proven in the least divisive, civic values haven't suffered, and theocracy has not taken root. In fact, Canada has become more secular than the United States.

Back in the United States, the school choice controversy marked a profound shift in the education debate away from reform from within—after spending tens of billions of dollars on a myriad of failed "education reforms" over several decades—to change from without. The crisis in urban education had become so serious that coalitions of parents, politicians, and philanthropists were establishing both privately and publicly funded programs that placed disadvantaged minority students from chronically underperforming public schools in private academies. Most of these schools are Catholic, since their tuitions remain low and they are located in the same neighborhoods.

That urban Catholic education deserves book-length treatment became obvious as I reviewed the literature. With astonishment, I discovered that while the national graduation rate for white public school students is 78 percent, it's only 60 percent for African American and Hispanic girls, and less than half for minority boys. Focusing on big-city school districts, the true extent of this catastrophe emerges. Only a third of New York City's black and Latino boys finish secondary school. In inner-city neighborhoods, such as Harlem and the South Bronx, these proportions decline even further. In other cities, the results are similar, or often worse.[3] And any reported increases in graduations rates are suspect.[4]

Catholic schools destroy the unholy trinity of poverty, race, and academic failure that has become axiomatic in much of the public system. Since the 1960s, the academic efficacy of Catholic education has been well documented. James S. Coleman, a renowned sociologist, completed two landmark studies in the 1980s (his "High School and Beyond" and, with Thomas Hoffers, *Public and Private High Schools: The Impact of Communities*), showing, for example, that, in contrast to students at Catholic schools, children from single-parent families in public schools were twice as likely to drop out as public school children from two-parent families.

The Catholic school advantage has been consistently reconfirmed by experts since. In the late 1990s, Derek Neal, an economics professor at the

University of Chicago, dispelled criticisms of Coleman's studies that Catholic school students perform better because they're more talented or come from better families. Among other findings, Neal showed that the graduation rate for black and Hispanic students from urban Catholic high schools was higher than that for urban whites at Catholic or public schools.

It soon became clear that there was little need for more quantitative evidence. Missing was an immersion book that would yield an in-depth narrative account of a particular Catholic school during a particular academic year. The idea for such a qualitative exploration of parochial education took shape in Sam Freedman's book writing seminar at the journalism school in the spring of 1997. Freedman has written six excellent nonfiction books, including *The Inheritance*, a 1997 Pulitzer Prize finalist and named by the *Wall Street Journal* in 2007 as one of the "five best books about America."[5] He also writes a biweekly education column for the *New York Times*. His class was an amazing apprenticeship and so far has yielded forty-seven book contracts for its students since its inception in 1991.

The first task was to find an appropriate focus school. Initially I chose Bishop Loughlin Memorial High School in Brooklyn, since the students are predominately non-Catholic African Americans. It is also Rudolph W. Giuliani's alma mater ('61). As mayor, he often held Loughlin up as an example and demanded that the Board of Education initiate a program of "radical reform" modeled on the city's Catholic schools.[6] To begin turning lousy schools around, Giuliani strongly recommended that public school principals be given the same authority as Loughlin's principal, Brother James Bonilla. Catholic schools are site-based institutions, where principals have the authority to hire and fire teachers, and mold them according to the school's mission. Brother James would have made an excellent main character for a book, but several months after I reached an agreement to spend the next school year with him, he died suddenly of a heart attack.

The following spring, searching for a similar school with a strong leadership, I heard Brother J. Matthew Walderman, Rice's president, speak at a fund-raising event. I was struck by his passionate eloquence and realized that Rice High School would make the perfect focus school. The next week, I visited Rice and proposed writing a book based on the 1999–2000 school year. I explained that it would be an honest, accurate account, requiring complete access to students, teachers, and administrators. I also explained that I would need to interview family members of the students I chose to write about, since family issues play a crucial role in students' behavior and attitude at school. Since some parents might understandably express reservations about their sons spending time with an older male, often in unsupervised situations—for example, in an empty classroom conducting an interview—I asked that the school provide recommendations to parents when needed. Brother Walderman agreed to the project without reservation or condition. Paradoxically like most independent schools, Rice proved to be both a typical and an utterly idiosyncratic example of urban Catholic education.

I visited Rice several times during the spring and summer of 1999 to become familiar with students and staff, then returned at the end of August for the new teachers' orientation and began to immerse myself full-time in the school as journalist-in-residence. Most mornings I made the twenty-minute walk from my apartment at West 107th Street and Amsterdam Avenue to central Harlem, passing by the Malcolm Shabazz Mosque, where Malcolm X had preached, at East 116th Street and Lenox Avenue. Eight blocks north I entered Rice, usually before classes began at 8 A.M.

I sat in on several classes a day and attended school functions, teachers' meetings, and basketball games after school. I interviewed teachers and administrators regularly and visited students in their neighborhoods to get a sense of what they dealt with on the street. When I first came to Rice, it was obvious that the book's main character couldn't be Brother Walderman, whose administrative position precluded him from day-to-day involvement in the high school. Instead, the principal, a charismatic and complex visionary, was the obvious choice for the lead character, so I spent several hours a day with him.

In the evening, I returned home to make a summary of the notes I'd taken, usually two or three reporter's notebooks worth. I catalogued the audiotapes of the day's interviews and then transferred the digital videotapes of classes and events onto VHS cassettes for storage. The videotapes proved invaluable because students often spoke quickly in class, their idioms were sometimes difficult to decipher, and several classmates would add to a discussion in rapid-fire succession. By replaying the exchanges, I was able to examine the body language and facial expressions of students and teachers. All these efforts were dedicated to rendering the scenes in the book with accuracy, which would have been impossible had I relied solely on my notes, since I was not expecting to begin the writing for months.

In addition, I worked several evenings a week at Peter Luger's Steakhouse in Brooklyn to make ends meet and be available to go to Rice every weekday. Occasionally I freelanced for several publications and somehow also spent time with my daughter, who was in the twelfth grade that year. We went through the anxieties of the college admissions process at the same time as Rice seniors and their parents were contending with this frustratingly arcane rite of passage.

In many ways, Rice was a return to familiar ground. In the ninth grade at St. Pius X Minor Seminary in Ottawa, I was voted most likely to become a priest. But as much as I wanted to be ordained, my spiritual calling included having a family. For two years I attended a Catholic liberal arts college that was subsequently purchased by a secular university nearby, where I completed undergraduate and graduate programs in philosophy, with an undergraduate minor in English. By the time I started writing *The Street Stops Here*, I realized that there was a commonality to my schooling and my daughter's, especially at Saint Ann's, that constituted the fundamental viewpoint from which I approached the researching and writing of this book.

I believe that a liberal arts education with an academic curriculum is best for all students, unless severe learning disabilities make this impossible. "Certainly the college-bound need these studies," wrote Diane Ravitch, a New York University professor of education, senior fellow at both the Brookings Institution and Stanford University's Hoover Institution, and a former federal Assistant Secretary of Education. "But so too do those who do not plan to go to college, for they may never have another chance to get instruction about the organizing principles of society and nature, about the varieties of human experience. . . . They too need the knowledge and skills that will enrich their lives as citizens, individuals, and members of a community. . . . One of the great virtues of the academic tradition is that it organizes human knowledge and makes it comprehensible to the learner. It aims to make a chaotic world coherent. . . . Knowledge builds on knowledge, and we cannot dispense with the systematic study of human knowledge without risking mass ignorance."[7]

To many readers, this seems so obvious it hardly needs stating, but many education experts and officials, beginning in the early decades of the twentieth century, successfully fought to eliminate the liberal arts approach from much of public education. Large numbers of children were deemed unfit for higher studies—primarily the poor, immigrants, and African Americans—and instead were streamed into courses preparing them for the workforce and to adjust to their lot in life. This approach was not only highly prejudicial, but also proved utterly inadequate as the country deindustrialized. For the last several decades, public educators have sought to address these missteps with a parade of education reforms aimed at boosting outcomes and reestablishing the common school ideal that any child of humble origins could climb the education ladder. Although sometimes successful, for the most part these reforms floundered because they ignored the liberal arts approach.

Media reports often distort this basic reality. For example, in 2005 there was a much touted 20 percent gain in the proportion (rising to 60 percent) of New York City's public school students reaching proficient or above on the statewide fourth grade reading test.[8] But scores rose significantly across the state, indicating that the test was much easier. Catholic school scores also rose by 10 percentage points, maintaining their traditional 10-point advantage. Across the country, state and city tests are highly unreliable, since the results can be manipulated and proficiency levels vary greatly.[9]

A more accurate assessment was given within weeks by the National Assessment of Education Progress (NAEP)—considered the "nation's report card" by education experts because of its integrity—that biennially administers reading and math tests to a large sampling of fourth and eighth graders across the country. The results were as embarrassing as they were revealing. In big-city public school districts, proficiency levels for African American and Hispanic students in fourth-grade reading ranged from 7 to 16 percent in Chicago, New York, Washington, D.C., Los Angeles, and so on. These assessments were districtwide, meaning that reading levels in the poorest neighborhoods were significantly lower. In addition, girls outperformed boys by significant margins, so the proportion of disadvantaged minority males reading acceptably approached the statistical three-percent margin of error. Scores declined even further at the eighth-grade level, and outcomes were similar on the math tests.[10]

The 2007 NAEP results showed slight improvement on both the fourth- and eighth-grade levels, with gains in big-city school districts mirroring those in public schools nationwide. Overall urban minority levels at or above proficiency increased from 12 to 14 percent in fourth-grade reading, as a typical example. This could be important if the beginning of a consistent trend, but there is far to go. Without singling out disadvantaged African American and Hispanic males, proficiency levels for minority students on both tests and grade levels in large urban school districts were still in single digits twice as often as in the 20- to 26-percent range. In contrast, white and Asian students reached proficiency in the 40- to 60-percent range.[11]

Understandably, closing the black-white test score gap (more properly, the gap between whites and Asians on the one hand, and blacks and Latinos on the other) has become a major issue for public educators and politicians—and a major embarrassment since the gap has stubbornly resisted amelioration for decades. Yet mysteriously, these same officials have ignored Catholic school efficacy, despite the pressure to improve performance that the No Child Left Behind legislation has exerted. In the NAEP tests, Catholic school students averaged 46 percent proficiency in reading at the fourth grade and 49 percent at the eighth grade.[12] These rates were 15 percent higher than for white and Asian public school students, and included the scores of Catholic school minority students. It would seem prudent for public educators to consult their parochial counterparts, who readily share their hard-won lessons.

Determining why public educators choose not to adopt the Catholic school model at low-functioning schools lies beyond the scope of this book, but *The Street Stops Here* aims to help bridge the divide between the two systems. There is no intention here to disparage public school teachers and administrators, who often labor heroically in very difficult circumstances. Indeed, there are highly successful public schools, albeit few in number, situated in underprivileged neighborhoods.[13] For example, Frederick Douglass Academy, a public middle and high school in Harlem, as well as networks of charter schools, such as the KIPP Academies, get their students up to grade level and through high school on time.

What accounts for high performance at these schools is exactly what Anthony Bryk, an award-winning sociology and education professor, formerly at Harvard University and now at Stanford, described as the key to Catholic education's success: the common school effect.[14] All students, regardless of their ethnic background, social class, family problems, or future plans and regardless of their scholastic level entering high school, are taught basically in the same way. Other factors include a demanding curriculum, high expectations, discipline, school safety, a high level of parental involvement, a dedicated faculty, and a learning environment imbued with moral values.

Nineteenth-century educators in both the Catholic and public systems developed the common school approach, but it has been preserved—and improved, since there was too much reliance on rote learning—primarily at Catholic schools. Setting religion aside, the Catholic school model translates seamlessly back to the public system.

Concerning religion, contemporary Catholic schools make no attempt to convert non-Catholic students. Nor could the religion curriculum be described as indoctrination. The Old and New Testaments and Church history are studied at Rice, but more emphasis is put on faith as a way of life vis-à-vis morality and social justice than on Catholicism as doctrine. In fact, more African American graduates convert to Islam than Catholicism. Of course there is a Catholic dimension to Rice High School, and religious values are infused into the school's culture. On this basis, the reader can decide on the appropriateness of a Catholic school education for children who would otherwise attend failing public schools.

For Catholic parents, much has changed regarding the Catholicity of their schools; this book attempts to separate false stereotypes from today's reality. Of obvious interest is how a Catholic school operates with mostly non-Catholic students. Historically the small number of African Americans attending Catholic schools was the result of shameful—although not universal—bigotry. After the Civil War, little effort was made to convert blacks, as racism became entrenched, particularly among Irish Catholics, who played up their "whiteness" to the dominant Protestant classes, and exaggerated the otherness of African Americans and Chinese immigrants in order to become more acceptable in comparison.[15] Then in the twentieth century, serving only Catholic children functioned partially as a means of keeping the schools predominately white. This changed dramatically with the civil rights era. Now urban schools like Rice that once educated mostly Irish and Italian youngsters are dedicated to minority students. To be fair, there always were black and sometimes Chinese Catholic students at Rice and other Catholic schools, but their numbers were small.

Completing *The Street Stops Here* was delayed for several years as I struggled with a misdiagnosed illness with symptoms similar to chronic fatigue syndrome. By the end of 2001, I couldn't concentrate sufficiently for more than two or three hours a day, and usually was plagued with a migraine. This continued until 2004 when I finally met a physician who linked the symptoms to acute food sensitivities. Since then, I have recovered completely but slowly. I also worked full-time through most of this period to pay for much of my daughter's college expenses.

Fortunately for the book, but unfortunately for the majority of inner-city public school students, the nation's educational situation has not improved significantly since the 1999–2000 school year. As I write this introduction and complete the book's final update in February 2008, public schools still fail miserably in the same neighborhoods where Catholic schools succeed and at a lower cost per student by a factor of three or more. In fact, the situation has become increasingly dire. As recent reports show, the plight of young African American males, in terms of joblessness, earnings, nonmarital fathering, and all measurable outcomes, is deteriorating—and Hispanic males are not faring much better.[16]

The Street Stops Here has an unavoidable structural complexity since it attempts to capture an institution in story form. It would have been much easier to build the text around a single character and write about a year in the life of a Catholic school principal. Although much of the book follows this format, a school is an ensemble event that succeeds and/or fails because of what occurs between students and teachers in all classrooms simultaneously, and because of the interactions in counseling sessions, detention periods, coaching, and so on. As a result, the book occasionally takes the reader into scenes that are integral to understanding Rice High School, but aren't as tightly connected as in a novel or cinematic portrayal. It is also necessary to include contextual information to render what happened at Rice comprehensible. Likely there are readers unaware of the history of Catholic education, for example, without which the contemporary reality can't be understood properly.

Occasionally, I also include comments to clarify my viewpoint and background to enable the reader to better evaluate what the book presents. I leave ample room for the reader to make up his or her mind, but I unavoidably function as the vehicle bringing the reader into an environment that for most is far removed from their everyday experience.

The book's title I took from a sign that hung for decades over the entrance to St. Agnes High School when it was situated near Grand Central Station. That school moved to the increasingly affluent Upper West Side, while its countercultural slogan—"The Street Ends Here"—found its way to Rice several years after I was there. Unlike Rice's administrators, I had no qualms about stealing the slogan. Please be assured that the names of some of the students have been changed, mostly at my discretion, to protect the best interests of the young men and their families.

Should urban Catholic schools be preserved for the common good? Should the Catholic school model be emulated at public school districts? Let us go to Rice High School and see.

Chapter One

———

IN 1985 ORLANDO R. GOBER was the principal at St. Mark's, a Lutheran elementary school in Bushwick, Brooklyn, one of New York City's poorest and most crime-ridden neighborhoods. He was the school's first African American principal and, at thirty-one years of age, the youngest Lutheran principal in the metropolitan area—a distinction he'd held since 1977, when he became the youngest principal at any school, public or private, in New York City.

Every fall, Orlando organized class trips to give his mostly African American youngsters a memorable experience in nature. That year, he took forty-five fourth graders and their teachers on a three-day overnight camping trip to Highland Lake in the Catskill Mountains, a two-and-a-half-hour drive upstate.

On the afternoon of the outing's second day, Wednesday, October 30, Orlando took half the students, including nine-year-old Samantha Brown, on a canoe trip, while the rest went hiking. When it came time to switch activities, "I tried so hard to convince Samantha to accompany me again in the canoe because she was asthmatic," Orlando recalled. "I thought the walk up the mountain would be very exhausting for her." But Samantha insisted on the hike, and after a prolonged argument, Orlando gave in.

Over an hour later at 4:30 P.M., Orlando and half the students pulled their canoes on shore and talked about dinner. Meanwhile, the other youngsters trod down the mountain behind the camp with two teachers. They crossed the bridge that Orlando and his crew had canoed under minutes before and were almost in view of the campsite when Samantha suffered a severe asthma attack. One of the teachers and several students ran ahead, their echoing voices sounding an alarm. Orlando ran up the trail toward them.

By the time Orlando got to Samantha, she was drawing tortured breaths. Orlando dispatched one counselor to call an ambulance and another to retrieve the girl's medications that were neatly packed in her book bag at the camp's homestead. Orlando took Samantha in his arms and held her. He rubbed her face and hands as the temperature dropped through the forties. He held her close to keep her body core warm and prevent her from catching pneumonia.

When the paramedics arrived, Orlando insisted on riding in the ambulance with Samantha. He held her hand until the emergency room physician took her for examination at the hospital. Orlando wouldn't leave her side as the doctor examined her.

"Is she going to be all right?" Orlando asked several times.

"Didn't you realize that she was cold?" the doctor finally answered.

"We were up in the mountains," Orlando answered. "It was close to freezing."

"I'm sorry, but we're pronouncing her DOA," the doctor put his hand on Orlando's shoulder and said.

Orlando gasped as he realized Samantha had died in his arms, then he fainted for the first time in his life. Half an hour later, Orlando regained consciousness in an emergency room bay. Immediately he began to tremble at the thought of calling Samantha's parents.

Orlando decided to phone St. Mark's pastor first to ask him to be at the Brown residence for the dreaded call. Twenty minutes later, Orlando summoned enough courage to dial the Browns' number. He has no memory of the conversation other than fighting to maintain his composure as he related the afternoon's events. Mr. and Mrs. Brown drove to the hospital right away with the pastor to see their daughter's body. Orlando met them in the lobby and struggled to offer his condolences.

Orlando boarded the bus with his other students around midnight. He felt his mind and body go numb, and fell into a near comatose state on the ride back to St. Mark's, as the phrase "Up with 45 and down with 44" pounded relentlessly in his brain. When the bus arrived, Orlando stepped off in a trance. His father, St. Mark's maintenance man, had been told about Samantha and was waiting for his son. Without saying a word, Orlando collapsed into his father's arms and began to sob.

Arrangements had been made for a doctor to meet the arriving bus to examine staff and students. The physician advised Orlando's father to take him to the family house in Queens. Orlando crawled into his childhood bed and stayed there a week without showering, and he refused to eat. Orlando stared straight ahead, his near catatonic state broken only by uncontrollable crying. He suffered violent mood swings from guilt to anger, and then despair. Orlando felt unforgivably responsible for the young girl's death since he had allowed her to go on the hike.

Orlando pulled himself together to attend Samantha's wake and funeral, albeit under sedation. He found it impossible to converse with the girl's parents or her classmates. When he saw Samantha laid out in her school uniform, he went into hysterics.

After the services, Orlando sent a letter of resignation to St. Mark's and resolved to leave education, feeling utterly incapable of dealing with the possibility of losing another student. The school's board of directors refused to accept the resignation, insisting that he come back to work as soon as possible. The board considered his return a crucial therapeutic step for both principal and students. The board also notified the school's parents about Orlando's crisis. In response, many parents visited daily, along with Orlando's relatives and friends. "There was a tremendous outpouring of support," he recalls. They also brought food and prayed with Orlando, which began to assuage his guilt.

Within two weeks of Samantha's passing, Orlando was back at St. Mark's, although not functioning fully. Perhaps miraculously, it was Samantha's parents who saved Orlando's psyche from self-destructing. They visited him often and kept repeating, "Samantha lived a good life; it wasn't your fault." Samantha had convinced her parents to let her live normally and accept the consequences.

The Browns paid Samantha's tuition for the next four years, so that another child could take her place. Orlando created the Samantha Brown School Spirit Award to honor her, and on the day she would have graduated from the eighth grade, he presented her parents with her diploma.

"Many of my friends thought I would suffer permanently from massive depression, but it didn't happen," Orlando recounts. "They recommended medication and psychotherapy, but I relied on faith instead. At church services, I was brought to the front and prayed over. For weeks, the minister laid his hands on me; maybe it's unusual, but I felt a healing going on without chemicals."

After taking the dean of students' position at Rice High School in central Harlem in 1993, Orlando lost touch with Samantha's parents. Yet every October 30, he travels to the cemetery on Long Island where she was buried to honor her memory.

For months after Samantha's passing, "Up with 45 and down with 44" repeated in Orlando's mind as an unstoppable rhythmic refrain, and it branded his psyche with guilt. Fourteen years later, the phrase no longer sounds in his mind. Instead it has become the fault line beneath the powerful persona that he has built to lead inner-city children to education's Promised Land.

———

Orlando strides into Rice's cafeteria to address the new students at their orientation on Wednesday, September 8, 1999. His pumpkin-hued suit, black shirt and rust-tinted tie attract everyone's attention. The orange tones vibrate warmly against his dark brown skin, and Orlando exudes confidence and strength. He knows his presence can be intimidating, which is useful in establishing a leadership role, but he also wants the young men to feel welcome. Orlando smiles expansively and gathers his boys as if into a hug. At 8:28 A.M., he takes charge of their high school careers as both father figure and school administrator.

Orlando's suit has been tailored to fall gracefully over his six-foot, two-inch frame. He weighs 250 pounds, with a slight thickening at his midsection, but otherwise looks fit for a forty-six-year-old. Orlando projects a robust, invincible energy, and moves with studied ease, although not with the grace of a natural athlete. He never had the talent nor inclination to play sports. Instead he's buoyed by a righteous pride as the Rice chief elder.

In order to ensure that his entrance would be dramatic, Orlando had kept the door to his office off the school's foyer closed. For this first morning of the school year and only for this one time, he avoided socializing with students or answering questions from the many parents who accompanied their ninth graders to school to take care of tuition payments. Mostly he wanted to sweep into the assembly as if from a higher dimension to establish that he is the general in "the war against the culture of academic failure that affects most of the freshmen," as he says. Few perform at grade level in all subject areas.

One hundred and thirty-five pairs of eyes are riveted on their principal as he approaches the podium. The ninth graders, together with eight new upperclassmen, sit in complete silence on rows of plastic molded chairs, forming three sides of a rectangle centered around a six-inch riser that functions as a stage. Five pillars down the center of the room hold the acoustic-tiled ceiling about dunking distance from the green and black tiled floor. The students sway in their seats, as if rocked gently by the breeze slipping through clattering vertical blinds along the cafeteria's 124th Street side. Most of the young men wear their hair shorn close to the scalp, and all appear exceptionally well-groomed. Rice students are allowed to wear their hair as they choose, within reason. Typically, closely-cropped styles dominate in September, and by spring, a third of the students have let their hair grow long enough to be braided or sometimes worn as an Afro.

As Orlando steps onto the stage, he still hasn't decided what he's going to say to the largest freshman class in over a decade. He always trusts that God will inspire the right words to flow from his mouth.

"You are going to learn how to empower yourself, how to take charge of your own education," Orlando begins softly with what the new students will hear daily in various versions until it seeps into their dreams at night.

"You'll make the decision to be an A student, or a B student, or worse," he continues. "You—not your parents or your teachers." Young minority males who have never seen a black man running a white-owned institution lean forward to listen. The leaning may save many, for the idea of being responsible for oneself and capable of fulfilling that charge is both new and scary. Many have attended low-functioning public schools since kindergarten. When asked about the daily classroom experience, they all talk about the lack of discipline and accountability. Some recount using cell phones to talk to friends on the other side of a classroom, because it was too noisy to shout.

Orlando rubs a hand over wiry black hair that's been cut short and gives the impression of squaring the roundness of his head. Behind aviation-style glasses, his eyes are dark brown and, although opaque, twinkle as he launches into an explanation of his academic expectations. Not only is the passing grade 70 percent, that's merely a minimum requirement. As Orlando clarifies, a student's real passing grade is the measure of his potential, and each student here, he emphasizes, can make the honor roll.

Two-thirds of the new students inhale at once. This is a moment of challenge that they've never experienced before. Getting on the honor roll seems far too lofty a goal for youngsters worried about merely passing their subjects. Many of these freshmen scored low enough on Rice's entrance exam that they were required to attend a summer readiness program. After five weeks of remedial math and English classes, they know that Rice makes real academic demands, in contrast to what most experienced previously.

Although the majority of freshmen enter Rice with academic deficiencies, Orlando accepts few scoring below the fifth-grade level on entrance tests. Urban Catholic high schools don't have the resources to remediate students approaching functional illiteracy. Zoned public high schools must accept these youngsters since they are obliged to register students according to geographic area of residence. This accounts for some of the difference in outcomes. But the public system also has the resources, in terms of available funding, to deal with those who lag far behind. Regrettably, failed pedagogies, such as variations on whole-language reading programs and constructivist math classes, are still in vogue, contributing significantly to the problem.

To be fair, Orlando points out that students from inner-city Catholic elementary schools aren't always prepared for high school work either. Many students transfer in and out, depending on the parents' ability to pay tuition. In addition, tuitions are so low at urban Catholic elementary schools that five times less is spent per student, sometimes pushing the no-frills approach beyond its effective limit.

Orlando assures the young men that their teachers will show them how to succeed, and that he is always available to discuss academic problems and arrange tutoring. He addresses lingering doubts with the assurance that "All we have to do is call upon the presence of God; I can do all things through Christ who strengthens me." Orlando emphasizes "strengthens" in a vocal crescendo, and for a moment it seems that the students will respond by breaking into a chorus of "Amens." Orlando grew up in a Lutheran congregation, joined several evangelical churches, and then become Catholic after joining the Rice faculty. However, the preacher bred in Orlando's bones has taken little notice of his latest conversion.

Nor does Orlando miss an opportunity to proclaim his message. He wears two buttons on his jacket's left lapel, one reading "Rice Men, You Are Worthy. Believe It," and the other with the letter N stricken through with a red line. Orlando's first campaign when he arrived at Rice was to ban the word "nigger" (invariably pronounced "nigga") from the building, and hopefully beyond. At first, the students had trouble understanding why, since they heard the word used so often in the street, and sometimes at home, that they failed to see it as derogatory. The N-word hasn't disappeared completely from the students' vocabulary, but it's seldom invoked within the school walls and never in a teacher's presence. As a result, there's been a noticeable improvement in the camaraderie and civility among students.

About a dozen black men peer over Orlando's shoulders from various angles, as if trying to communicate with the new students. These are the patron saints of the civil rights movement: Frederick Douglass, Marcus Garvey, Malcolm X, Martin Luther King, Jr., Nelson Mandela, and so on. Their portraits float on white clouds in a blue sky on a forty-five-foot mural painted by a local artist and paid for by the class of '92. Most students don't know who these men are. They might have heard names like Booker T. Washington and W. E. B. DuBois at their grade schools during black history month, but they've inherited little curiosity about older black males. Sometimes the positive presence of fathers in their lives is a question mark; other times, it's an endless ellipse.

Orlando ends his talk by presenting each student with a Bic pen as a welcoming gift. All the pens have been engraved with Orlando's slogans, either "Attitude Is Everything" or "Believe and Succeed."

"Does any student have masking tape on his pen?" Orlando asks.

Three young men rise tentatively to their feet, unsure of whether the tape bodes well.

"On Monday, you'll get a free lunch on me," the principal announces.

A loud "Oooohhhhh!" rolls around the cafeteria as the three students smile broadly. When Orlando became the dean of students, he instituted rewards for good behavior after realizing that many students get into trouble partly because the detentions and "talkings-to" earn the attention they ache for. Now there's a behavior honor roll, a Student-of-the-Month Award for each grade, a "Goodfinder's" list for students who turn in lost property or books, and a bulletin board honoring "Responsible Men." Every marking period, Orlando throws pizza parties or shows movies to reward good grades and positive conduct. This year, he hopes to extend the practice to random groupings of students as a way of "affirming each one's intrinsic value" and encouraging positive feelings about the school.

Orlando smiles to signal the end of what amounts to his induction ceremony. He has effectively adopted the new students as Rice Men and sons. Orlando's boys file toward the stairwell holding the pens in their fists like wizard's wands—and perhaps they are. Writing instruments are history's most transformative invention, and learning to use one properly will profoundly change the lives of these young men.

The stakes are high. If a young man stays four years at Rice, he will graduate and be accepted into college, or perhaps choose a career in the military. If he does reasonably well, overt or subtle forms of affirmative action, together with need-based financial aid, will make it feasible to attend college. On the other hand, if a young man leaves Rice, he will almost certainly have to attend a zoned or otherwise low-performing public high school where less than a third of students graduate, and only a few of these go on to postsecondary schooling.

Ten minutes later in classrooms on the seventh floor, teachers direct the freshmen to their assigned seats, answer questions about their schedules, then usher them to the fifth-floor bookstore to receive a locker number and a lock. Many youngsters have never used a combination lock before, which produces one of the year's most amusing rituals: widespread fights between man and metal.

———

Orlando slips quietly back into his office after the orientation. He is pleased he was able to command the attention of fourteen- and fifteen-year-olds for almost half an hour—no small feat given their predilection for fast-paced video games. Orlando pads across the worn industrial carpet to his desk against the wall. As he waits for his computer to reboot, Orlando complains about his stuffy office. There's only one narrow window, giving him the choice between a small air conditioner or occasional scoops of fresh air, which he prefers. But today's humidity makes the room feel warmer than the seventy-two degrees outside.

The principal could install himself more comfortably in an office one flight up on the second floor, but here his door faces the foyer, making it easy for students to flow in and out from early morning into the evening. Orlando became an educator at eighteen to get involved with students. This is his seventh year at Rice, and his twenty-eighth as an educator. Last year, he became the first African American to head this or any Christian Brothers academy in the country. In fact, Orlando is the first black principal in the Roman Catholic Archdiocese of New York, which includes Manhattan, Staten Island, and the Bronx in New York City, and seven counties extending north to the foothills of the Catskill Mountains—with 2.5 million Catholics belonging to 402 parishes.[1] Orlando's installment was especially fitting for Rice, which has the highest proportion of black students of the archdiocese's high schools. He's also the first black principal at a Catholic school in the city, which includes the Diocese of Brooklyn and Queens.

After logging onto Rice's computer network, Orlando tweaks the returning students' schedules, which he will give out tomorrow. He started calculating class schedules last April, so he could present teachers with class rosters at their orientation at the end of August. Consequently there's no sense of administrative panic as the new school year begins. At Catholic schools, the principal is empowered to organize students and faculty according to what experience and common sense prove most efficacious, without cumbersome regulations or union rules to follow.

Ten minutes later, Orlando sighs deeply and closes his eyes. He prays for the strength to shoulder the responsibility involved in taking on the new students. Through observation, counseling, and feedback from the faculty, he will soon get to know each boy's academic, behavioral, and family issues. He will also become intimately involved in addressing their weaknesses and challenging their strengths. Already Orlando feels tired. Instead of taking his normal and badly needed summer vacation, he served on the grand jury in Manhattan criminal court for five weeks, while also teaching a Regents' global history course for students who failed the exam in June.

Predictably Orlando was chosen as jury foreman and presided over fifty-four cases. Most of the alleged offenders had been arrested on drug charges, while some were arraigned for violent crimes. Orlando was struck by the sense of hopelessness underlying "their big-shot attitudes." He said the defense lawyers obviously hadn't bothered to prepare the young men for the courtroom. They were dressed in hip-hop styles and spoke as if standing on street corners in their neighborhoods. Orlando's fellow jurors quickly lost sympathy and pushed to process each case as quickly as possible. Orlando slowed down the deliberations and confronted several jurors concerning what he considered their indifference to the alleged perpetrators. The young men looked so much like his students at Rice and were the same age or only a few years older. Orlando couldn't help but feel a sense of fatherly obligation, while at the same time he was overwhelmed with futility as the evidence against one after another proved convincing.

"The stark reality of seeing this parade of young African American male offenders was so devastating," he declared afterward. "These kids had been emotionally hurt and abandoned. The adults in their lives failed to guide them properly or reassure them that they could pull it together. Instead, parents and teachers made excuses, which crippled their willpower. There's definitely racism in society and a culture that makes you feel worthless;

that's a given. But we use racism as a scapegoat too often, instead of rising above it. People have to be held responsible for what they do."

With searing regret, Orlando felt compelled to recommend indictments for all the accused, knowing they wouldn't get the help they needed in jail. "The experience redoubled my determination to teach the young men at Rice the responsibility that's the heart of manhood, and the worthiness they need to feel about themselves," Orlando resolved. "God knows how many of our young men are just one step away from doing something terrible. I get phone calls all the time from students asking to come over to my house because something's going to happen on their block, and they don't want to be around." Several times a year, Orlando bails out a student, fortunately not for anything serious so far. Statistically, a black male has a one-in-three chance of going to prison in his lifetime, a rate more than six times higher than that for white males.[2] Without a high school diploma, jail becomes an expected event in the life of many African American boys.

Orlando also resolved not to waste time on what he considers pointless discussions, as one parent now finds out. A knock at the office door pulls Orlando back to the present tense. He rises with noticeable effort, then directs the mother of a prospective sophomore to the couch along the wall opposite his desk. Orlando asks her why she wants her son to attend Rice. The woman responds with a lengthy monologue about violence at public schools. Orlando asks about the young man's grades, to which the mother apologizes for her son's mediocre performance, blaming it on gang activity.

"We've been talking for twenty minutes now," Orlando finally says with obvious exasperation, "and you haven't asked one question about our academic program. I know safety's an important concern these days, but Rice High School was not built for the sole purpose of protecting your son."

Orlando pauses to give the mother a chance to respond, but she's dumbfounded. "I'm not going to waste your money," he continues. "Clearly Rice is not the right school for your son. You need to get your priorities in order before enrolling him here." The woman's face registers dismay and she begins to protest. Orlando stands and directs her curtly back to the foyer, then closes the door sharply behind her.

———

At 11:30 A.M., Orlando stands in the hallway between the main office and the stairs down to the front door. He shakes hands and chats with his boys as they're dismissed. Some take his hand and pump vigorously, while others seem confused by the simplicity of the gesture. Orlando doesn't know all their faces yet, and variations in size and physical maturity are striking. One appears prepubescent while the next looks almost like a man. Regardless of their stage of adolescence, Orlando has conferred Rice Man status on all the new students as fully initiated members of the Rice family.

An incident this morning showed that given their first opportunity, the students honor the Rice tradition. One freshman left his Walkman under his chair in the cafeteria when he went upstairs after the orientation. A classmate found the Walkman and brought it to the school office to become the year's first "Goodfinder." This pleased Orlando immensely, and he declared that "this affirms right away what we're doing."

On an amusing note, a freshman asks why the school was named after a type of food. Orlando laughs loudly and makes a mental note to ask the freshman religion teacher to clarify the point with his students.

Directly behind Orlando, and reaching about six inches overhead, is a large statue of Blessed Edmund Rice, set on a pedestal.[3] Rice founded the Congregation of Christian Brothers in Ireland at the beginning of the nineteenth century to teach the children of the poor. Playing out now in front of the founder's figure is the expansion of his legacy to include educating black and Latino students. The shiny white plaster representation watches over Orlando like a guardian angel, transmitting Edmund Rice's leadership role to an African American.

———

I sit on a bench in the foyer watching Orlando interact with the new students. I'm struck with both how familiar and fascinatingly exotic Rice seems. There's no mistaking that Rice is a Catholic school: religious icons adorn walls throughout the building, and of course there's an impressive array of sports trophies on display in the foyer. The students are neatly dressed and well behaved. There is no hint of the threatening chaos that characterizes many urban public high schools.

At the same time, almost all the students are black, which is a striking visual contrast to the Catholic schools I attended in Canada and to most of Catholic schools that middle-class Americans attend. As much as I cringe at the admission, I'm having trouble telling some of the students apart. Although I met the majority of freshmen during the summer session, now they're wearing uniforms and most have similar haircuts. Most likely I'd have less trouble at a predominately white school. Before going home, I'll ask for a copy of last year's yearbook to prepare for the upperclassmen who arrive tomorrow. The freshmen I'll get to know thoroughly within a few days.

Listening to the students, I'm confounded by some of their vocabulary and idioms, which are specific to urban minority teenagers, and some expressions are peculiar to Harlem and the South Bronx. For example, overhearing one freshman say, "My shorty's a dime," is bewildering. Fortunately several students at each grade level catch on and furnish translations over the next few weeks until I'm conversant. The freshman above is bragging about his girlfriend, a "shorty," by saying that she's a 10 on the beauty scale.

Behaviorally Rice students are more boisterous than their white peers; their positive energy, melodic speech patterns, and frequent laughter charge the school with an irresistible vitality. Most remarkable is something I sense but struggle to name. Finally I perceive the obvious: these young men have hope in their eyes.

Chapter Two

THE NEXT MORNING, THURSDAY, September 9, Brother J. Matthew Walderman gives the first talk at the orientation for returning students. As Rice's president, Brother Walderman's duties include fund-raising and budgeting, and he represents the school at official functions in Harlem and the archdiocese. In contrast to Orlando, he always prepares his remarks as a formal speech, and delivers virtually the same homily as he did yesterday to the new students at their orientation.

Needing no amplification, Brother Walderman moves the microphone stand aside and welcomes 203 upperclassmen back to Rice. They've all gotten to know him despite the fact that he no longer teaches, coaches, or has direct involvement in the day-to-day running of the school. Every morning, Brother Walderman stands outside the school, regardless of the weather, to personally greet every student. They appreciate starting the day with words of encouragement and often a short conversation about sports.

"When I see Brother Walderman in front of Rice on my way to work," the father of Andre Barrett, the varsity basketball team's starting point guard, says, "I know it's going to be a good day."

Brother Walderman is a powerfully built man about five feet, ten inches tall, with a shaven head that sits on thick shoulders like a helmet. He moves like a linebacker—who might tackle a student for bad grammar—but his warm, engaging smile belies the impression that he's overly strict. As usual, he wears a black suit with a Roman collar that has been darkened across the bottom of the small white rectangle, distinguishing him from a priest. Certainly none of the students notice, and few understand the difference between a brother and a priest, whether or not they attended Catholic elementary school. Like priests, brothers take vows of poverty, chastity, and obedience, and live in community just as do some clerical orders. Unlike priests, brothers are not ordained and so can't administer the sacraments of the Church.[1]

Brother Walderman is beginning his ninth year at Rice. He served as assistant principal for his first two years, then principal for another two. For the last four years, Brother has wrestled with the job of president, a notoriously difficult task for a religious educator since it involves overseeing all fund-raising efforts. Although gregarious by nature, Brother didn't join a teaching order to spend most of his time seeking donations from individual and corporate sources. His original vocation, for which he professed final vows thirty-five years ago, has been reduced, as he puts it jokingly, "to getting wheeled out for Rice functions." But with so few brothers left in the order, many of those who remain must provide leadership.

Until the mid-1960s, religious orders staffed their schools almost exclusively with their own members. Unintentionally, the Second Vatican Council (Vatican II), which ended in 1965 and produced the Church's most far-reaching social justice initiatives, also precipitated a mass exodus from religious orders that drastically reduced the presence of nuns, brothers, and priests in the classroom. Now only two of Rice's twenty-six teachers are Christian Brothers, and a third brother, who also runs the school office, teaches the Advanced Placement U.S. history class. Typically, religious orders now maintain their influence primarily through administrative control, and Brother Walderman's commanding personality made him a natural choice for president.

"This is what you are here for," Brother Walderman suddenly booms as he lifts a Rice High School diploma over his head. "You want to walk down that aisle at St. Patrick's as a senior and receive your diploma. This is your ticket to the next stop on the education train." Rice holds its graduation ceremonies at the historic St. Patrick's Cathedral in midtown at the end of May every year. The procession down the cathedral's aisle is the climactic event in a Rice student's career. More than merely graduating, Rice students look forward to seeing their families beam with pride at their accomplishment. Most matriculating students are the first member of their families to finish high school on time and go to college.

Even more important than getting the freshmen fired up is motivating the sophomores and juniors. Rice loses most of its students in these grades. The thrill of merely being in high school has faded and finishing seems, for many, light years away. The current juniors have lost 30 percent of their original classmates, and the seniors have seen 40 percent of their classmates transfer, mostly back to the public system. But Orlando's efforts to get students to perform better lowered the attrition among last year's freshmen to 10 percent. This rate needs to be reduced further, or another 10 percent will likely transfer or fail out before graduating.

"Over 5,000 men have gone through these halls and call this their alma mater," Brother Walderman reminds the students. "We have men who are CEOs, bank presidents, and college professors." Brother Walderman pauses for a beat. "People who are rap stars and in the National Basketball Association sat where you are right now when they were in high school." Several NBA players, such as Rod Strickland and Dean "the Dream" Meminger, went to Rice, and two graduates now in college have a legitimate chance. Regarding hip-hop, Darryl McDaniel graduated in 1981 and went on to found Run-DMC, one of the most successful rap groups. Hearing these names precipitates a reverential hush.

"So you should be asking: How can I inscribe my name on that list of heroes?" Brother Walderman reminds the students of the connection between education and success, even for those who dream of becoming celebrities. The key to accomplishment, Brother says, is captured in the Latin phrase carpe diem, which he translates loudly as " 'Seize the day.' Now everyone—"

"Carpe diem," the students mumble.

"Oh my Gaawd, get the vitamins," Brother Walderman exclaims, rolling his eyes. "What's the phrase?"

"Carpe diem," they call back three times at Brother's instigation until their decibel level earns his imprimatur.

"Seize the day. Seize the moment," Brother Walderman yells as his arms rise over his head. His hands open, and he seems to shovel air, or maybe it's the future. Brother continues softly, "Now's your chance to write upon that slate what you want the rest of your high school career to be."

Brother's message about taking advantage of opportunities is not merely an exhortation. "It doesn't matter whether you're an A student or a D student," he explains later, "we all have to be stewards of the gifts we're given and use those gifts for the good of others. To do this, students need a sense of structure. They have to be told 'no' sometimes; they need to be pushed, dragged, and cajoled—but with respect."

The pushing, dragging, and so on converts intentions into action, the ultimate result of which is the challenge Brother Walderman issues for the seniors to top last year's 99 percent college acceptance rate, and three million dollars in scholarships and grants. One of last year's graduates enlisted in the Marines, which Brother applauded and Orlando lamented because he mistakenly believes that minorities are overrepresented among combat troops.[2] At All Hallows in the South Bronx, the other Congregation of Christian Brothers high school in New York City, every senior got into college. Much to Brother Walderman's good-natured chagrin, the *Wall Street Journal* wrote a front-page article in April about the perfect acceptance rate at All Hallows.[3]

Brother Walderman steps down into the clearing in front of the podium. "You are called to be smart, but you are also called to be holy, to be good," he says as he paces from side to side, and then backward and forward in short, straight lines. "There are too many evil geniuses in the world."

Brother Walderman pauses for a few moments to let the students meditate on the idea that secular achievements, without proper spiritual guidance, often bring more harm than good. This is part of the larger reflection that transpires throughout the year as the students deal with what Brother refers to as "the schizophrenic demands of urban Catholic schools." On street corners right outside the school, there are men—some as young as the students—selling drugs and guns, and engaging in other gang-related activities. The code on the streets is strictly amoral, which Rice Men must deal with in their everyday lives without either succumbing or appearing self-righteous. In stark contrast, as soon as they walk through Rice's front door, they enter a thoroughly moral world where actions are evaluated in class discussions and private conferences according to traditional values. On the one hand, Rice students must present themselves on the streets as if the school were not making them "soft," as they describe wimps. On the other, they have to navigate Rice's demands as if the streets were not making them hard.

Brother Walderman marches the upperclassmen through his stock formula for success at Rice, the seven Rs—reading, 'riting, 'rithmetic, results, responsibility, respect, and reverence—as his arms rise over his head again and seem to translate the list into a sailor's semaphores. Focusing on reverence, Brother Walderman asks with passion, "Is there room for God in your life?"

A moment later he adds, "Genesis tells us that God created us in his image and likeness." This oft-quoted verse squirts by everyone's ears. Yet without it, Catholic education would have succumbed to various forms of academic tracking decades ago. According to Catholic teachings, each individual member of every generation deserves to be educated in body, mind, and soul because each has sacred value. Regardless of social status, natural intelligence, or utilitarian value, every child inherits civilization's cultural wealth. As far as possible, Catholic schools are charged with fulfilling this divinely ordained mission that seeks to integrate traditional liberal education and training in job skills into a religious framework.

"Ralph Waldo Emerson, one of our great poets, said, 'What you do speaks so loudly, I can't hear what you are saying,' " Brother says, then concludes with the Catholic school ethic of personal responsibility: "Deeds not words, gentlemen."

Brother doesn't expect immediate results from his speech. One of the few sayings that Edmund Rice left his followers has guided Brother Walderman's career and often provided consolation: "Have courage; the good seed will grow up in the child's heart later on."

Orlando walks triumphantly to the podium since he is welcoming back the students who performed better than he could have imagined last year, proving to the Christian Brothers and Rice's board of trustees that he was the right choice as principal. Orlando wears a lime-green suit as bright as a text highlighter, drawing attention to himself as always, but to promote his agenda: academics.

At the podium, he immediately challenges the students to exceed last year's record: a full third of the students made the honor roll. Thanks to their achievement, he says proudly, Rice has attracted so many students that there's a long waiting list—one of his most prized possessions. He plans to use the list as leverage to push for more of the programs and innovations, such as a math and science summer enrichment program, that he believes will make Rice competitive with prestigious Catholic high schools such as Regis High School.

After several minutes of fatherly banter about how much he enjoys seeing his sons again, Orlando reminds the sophomores, juniors, and seniors that "I stand firm. The issue here is excellence, and you all know what I'm talking about."

Moments later, he softens his voice, as if speaking to each young man individually, to say, "Let me tell you what you already know: You are loved and we say it unabashedly. The only thing that's missing from time to time is that you have to believe." In Orlando's experience, getting disadvantaged African American and Hispanic boys to trust they can succeed academically is his greatest challenge. They need constant reminders that they are appreciated in order to dare believe in themselves. Once they buy into the possibility of achievement, Orlando feels confident he can coach them on how to succeed.

After Brother's lengthy speech, Orlando chooses brevity and soon dismisses the upperclassmen. He makes his way to the front door where he shakes hands with his boys as they leave. The upperclassmen are noticeably more boisterous than the new students, but as visiting teachers and administrators from both Catholic and public urban schools often remark, they are more subdued than the young men and especially the young women at their own schools. Orlando's strong personality and his insistence on appropriate behavior have tempered Rice students without diminishing their spirit.

There are still many self-described "loudmouths," such as Linwood Sessoms, who called out, "Yo, dawg," to fellow seniors across the cafeteria when he arrived this morning.

"Wha'z up?" several classmates answered at normal volume.

Linwood pushed his way between a row of chairs and a gathering of juniors to the back of the room, farthest from the podium, where the seniors began congregating. Linwood's clean-shaven head and muscular body projected a menacing persona, until he flashed his trademark smile, revealing a perfect set of sparkling white teeth.

As the seniors arrived, hands slapped together, then pulled away; or palms grasped and arms interlocked, as if to arm-wrestle, and pulled chests together. Most of the returning students haven't seen each other since June; their neighborhoods tend to be subway stops apart, and the city provides free metro cards for public transportation only when school is in session.

After the orientation, Linwood clasps Orlando's hand and says, "Hey, Gobe." Many other seniors display the same informality, but the sophomores and juniors don't dare yet.

The upperclassmen congregate in the street in front of Rice, then move in grade-level groups up Lenox Avenue to the corner of 125th Street where they "chill" for an hour before drifting back to their neighborhoods.

The seniors say they can't wait for the year to be over, so they can get away to college next fall. But the truth is nothing frightens them more. The proverbial mean streets seem to offer more security than the unknown world outside where they will suddenly find themselves in the minority. Even those who choose black colleges will discover that most peers come from middle- to upper-class backgrounds and have little more in common with them than suburban white teens.

Inner-city students seldom venture outside their neighborhoods and develop suspicious outlooks as a result. To illustrate, Steve DiMattia, the forensics coach, tells a story about a student who calls him at home the night before a competition at Xavier High School in Greenwich Village because he's afraid to venture downtown from his neighborhood in the Bronx, which is one of the most dangerous in the city. In fact, his father was almost shot to death there after being robbed by a minority male he picked up in his gypsy cab. Like his classmates, this student worries about how dangerous a predominately white area of Manhattan will be, and almost imagines lynch mobs.

After Linwood shook the principal's hand, a new sophomore—who didn't attend yesterday's orientation to avoid being associated with freshmen—mumbles "Mr. Gober." At sixteen, Yusef Abednego isn't a novice to the grade. This is his third try, although his first at Rice. He spent most of last year on the streets selling drugs, but he wants to turn his life around. After hearing the principal's empowerment message, Yusef later says that this was the first time he felt filled with hope since the fourth grade.

After the last student leaves, Orlando heads back to his office to interview a mother and her son about admission to the eleventh grade. If the class wasn't so small, Orlando wouldn't consider the request. There are only 45 juniors, along with 52 seniors. Mostly as a result of Orlando becoming principal, the school attracted 106 sophomores and 127 freshmen. Although the total of 330 students strains the school's resources, in Orlando's view, an additional junior won't be burdensome. The young man seems less enthused than his mother, but the principal decides to give him a chance since the mother is a well-paid administrative assistant who emigrated from the Caribbean. During the interview, she talked of nothing but her son's academic future. Even if the young man fails to become inspired by his mother's vision, it seems clear she won't tolerate poor grades.

———

In the late afternoon, after several lengthy mentoring sessions with new teachers in his office, Orlando is finally alone. He closes his eyes. He has been wondering all day what changes summer brought for the fifteen- to seventeen-year-old returning students who spent much of their break hanging around street corners, housing-project playgrounds, and outdoor basketball courts with neighborhood friends. On the other hand, some students traveled to the South for extended visits with relatives, and most work at least part-time at jobs where they learn to take some responsibility. Growth or more trouble? Orlando asks and then prays for all his boys. He shudders to think about how many of the new faces, so innocent looking and hopeful on their first day, might become problem students.

The stakes are high for the principal as well as his students. When Orlando was installed a year ago, he completed Rice's transformation into a predominately African American school. From Rice's founding in 1938 into the 1950s, there were always a handful of black students who happened to be Catholic, but the majority of the students were ethnic Irish and to a lesser extent Italian. Since the Christian Brothers crammed over eight hundred students into classrooms averaging forty or more young men, they were always able to charge the lowest tuition in the city. Rice attracted students from lower-class white families in the immediate area in Harlem, and from similar areas in the Bronx, Brooklyn, and mostly in Queens.

Then demographic shifts in surrounding neighborhoods generated a growing minority student population. Many working-class black families could afford the tuition of $350 a year in 1963, when 20 percent of Rice's students were African American and still had to be Catholic.[4] Over the next decade, Hispanic young men started enrolling, so that by 1973 Rice was one-third Latino, one-third black, and one-third white.

These demographic changes were caused in large part by the suburbanization that encouraged and enabled large numbers of white families to leave urban centers—termed "white flight," it was also a reaction to desegregation and forced busing—while preventing black families from leaving as well, due to mortgage discrimination and other blatantly racist practices. As a result, neighborhoods around schools like Rice emptied, and black and Hispanic families took over the apartment buildings and Catholic schools left behind. Ironically, the current social-justice mission of inner-city Catholic schools was preceded and made possible by discrimination against the parents and grandparents of their current students. These prejudicial policies also necessitated this mission, since many black families weren't allowed to buy homes and build equity to pass on to subsequent generations, which accounts for much of the relative difference in net worth between the races.

Concurrent with white flight, several new Catholic high schools—rich in resources by Catholic standards—opened in Brooklyn and Queens, and competed favorably for the white students still commuting to Rice from these boroughs. Rice's population became increasingly African American, growing to two-thirds by the late 1980s, while the Hispanic contingent held at a third until the early 1990s. Today, Rice is 85 percent black, and all but two of the other students, both Filipino, are Hispanic. In fact, it's the only predominately African American Catholic high school in the New York Archdiocese.

The Diocese of Brooklyn, where the majority of the city's blacks live, has three Catholic high schools with predominately black populations, but only Bishop Loughlin has a majority of African American students. Students at the other two schools are mostly first and second generation blacks of Caribbean or African descent.

At Rice, as the percentage of African American students increased, the total enrollment dwindled steadily since families in the area were less able to pay tuition. Black flight took Harlem's middle and upper classes to the suburbs, meaning the neighborhood became less a cohesive community and more a refuge for poor, fractured families. When Orlando started working at Rice in 1993, there were only 369 students, mostly from disadvantaged, single-parent households. By 1997, enrollment bottomed out at 298 students, with a mere 64 young men in the freshmen class.

Meanwhile, tuition has shot up since 1963 by a power of ten, to $3,550 for the 1999–2000 school year, and will continue to rise. Tuition averages $5,000 at Catholic high schools in the city, making Rice one of most affordable private options, but still beyond the means of many families.[5] As enrollment fell, Rice lost money to the point where the Christian Brothers considered shutting it down at the end of the 1996–1997 school year. But more than did their other schools, Rice fulfilled the order's original mission of educating poverty-stricken boys from the streets. The Brothers decided to try one last and, in their view, desperate option—an administrative Hail Mary pass—and turned to Orlando for leadership. The board wanted to run an open search for a new principal, but Brother Walderman argued successfully that Orlando was the best choice given the circumstances—although much to the disappointment of some teachers and Christian Brothers. Orlando had become a very popular dean with the students and their parents, but he had also offended many colleagues.

"None of this was supposed to happen," Orlando chuckles, "since I was hired to be Rice's disciplinarian. But when interviewed, I agreed to take the position on the condition that my title would be changed from dean of discipline to dean of students. I did that intentionally, because I knew what the Brothers meant by 'discipline.' They expected me to be their hammer, so the parents couldn't claim it was racism. The Brothers didn't understand it at the time, but becoming the dean of students gave me a broader mandate." During his five years as dean of students Orlando counseled students and worked with their parents to solve problems, rather than rely primarily on handing out detentions for behavioral infractions and then expelling troublemakers.

In 1993, when he was first hired, the majority of the faculty at Rice was young, white, and male, and in Orlando's estimation, hostile to his approach. There was one black and one Hispanic teacher, and there were few women on staff. The white male teachers enjoyed strong friendships, socialized together, and "ran the school," according to Orlando. "I hate to say this, but they all wanted me to validate them," Orlando recounts. "The Christian Brothers wanted me to thank them for all they did in Harlem, and to do what I was told. But I came with my own set of qualifications, values, and expectations, and I wasn't going to plead for a job. Then the teachers wanted me to set them up as the great white hope. They expected me to play bad cop, so they would come in like the great father and save the students from my wrath." At faculty meetings, colleagues complained openly that he wasn't strict enough with the students.

Orlando took the offensive and accused fellow teachers and even the administration of holding attitudes that "bordered on racism." He berated virtually every faculty member for harboring low expectations for minority students. His allegations had some merit in that, for example, so few students made the honor roll that their names weren't even posted in the foyer—which he vehemently said was especially insulting, since the Brothers prominently displayed basketball trophies honoring city, state, and tournament championships. When Orlando saw how much higher the academic demands were at the Christian Brothers schools that were predominately white, he charged the Brothers with "institutional racism."

Orlando's racial attitudes were forged in the late 1960s when as a high school student he joined the Black Panthers. When the Panthers' organization collapsed several years later, Orlando decided to become an educator in order to "uplift my race and continue the struggle." He cultivated his militant persona and together with a thunderous preacher's delivery, became adept at quick and decisive victories in verbal strikes against colleagues. At Rice, as at previous schools, staff members found themselves targeted by Orlando for reasons both justified and imagined. Orlando incited so much anger and antagonism that he said he overheard Brother Walderman, then Rice's assistant principal, taking bets in the teacher's lounge on whether Orlando would make it through his first year. No one put money on Orlando, nor does anyone else remember this occurring, and Brother vehemently denies the incident. Most likely, Brother Walderman made a passing comment that was amplified in Orlando's mind, since he felt persecuted.

"It was hell during my first years," Orlando relates, "but eventually those who were against me left Rice or came around to realize that I must be doing something right." Grudgingly at first, Brother Walderman and others learned to respect Orlando's leadership abilities, and Orlando tempered his wrath. In truth, Orlando overstated his criticisms of the brothers and lay teachers. For decades, educational institutions across the country floundered in their attempts at schooling urban youngsters. Orlando neglected to give the Rice faculty credit for graduating so many, despite the difficulties. Over time, Rice teachers have learned that Orlando thrives on opposition, especially from whites, and if he can't find any, he will create it as a necessary foil. Teachers blessed with patience eventually discover that his initial approach is nine-tenths bluster and, once expressed, evaporates and a softer, more traditional Orlando emerges who is skilled at shepherding both students and faculty toward higher performance.

Brother Walderman became a strategic ally and recommended Orlando to the board of trustees to succeed him as principal. Orlando accepted the board's offer, promising to make a dramatic impact on Rice's academic achievement. The board believed this would make the school less attractive for several years while a market developed for Rice as a true college prep academy.

Instead there was an immediate increase in applications for admission. Word traveled quickly through Harlem and the South Bronx, from single mother to wife to grandmother, that here in our neighborhood is an educator who turns our boys into men by instilling a code of behavior based on personal responsibility. Many mothers have been abandoned by their husbands or partners, or see them only on visits to jail. The women fear their sons will turn into their fathers. News that Orlando would be in charge at Rice spurred a surge of interest. Last year's freshman enrollment shot up by two-thirds, and this year's freshman class added twenty-one students. Next year, Orlando expects Rice to have a total of four hundred students.

In his first year as principal, Orlando strengthened the school's traditional pedagogy, which combines academic basics and discipline with intensive one-on-one counseling. At the beginning, Orlando worried that his students would rebel when he raised the passing grade from 65 to 70 percent and promoted academics as more important than athletics. This was not an easy pitch at a school with a top-ranked varsity basketball team, but the young men responded positively to Orlando's in-class pep talks and constant exhortations to improve performance. The number of students on the honor roll, which requires an 85 average and no grade below 75, rose steadily every marking period until 105 students, a 500 percent increase, made it in June. Orlando would have felt triumphant with half that number.

Despite his confidence and dynamism, Orlando doesn't assume his success will continue. Instead he worries whether he can convince the new students to take their studies seriously. All summer, disturbing questions churned in his mind like Was last year a fluke? and Will the upperclassmen set a good example again? Orlando knows well there's more at stake than personal affirmation. If enrollment or standards falter, the Christian Brothers will withdraw their support. Although he and Brother Walderman have forged a working alliance, their personalities conflict often and strain their relationship to the breaking point.

A major quarrel erupted last June when Brother Walderman commented that winning so many basketball championships was more significant than getting over one hundred students on the honor roll. Orlando exploded angrily, railing against what he interpreted as a deeply ingrained racism. Brother Walderman apologized three times, saying he never meant to reinforce the negative stereotypes that Orlando despises. Rather, Brother was expressing his passion for sports and concern that Orlando was devaluing this dimension of Rice's culture that both keeps students in school and helps with enrollment and fund-raising. Eventually Orlando's rage subsided and their relationship returned to the "marriage" that both describe as difficult. They get along by avoiding each other as much as possible, and Orlando says he won't tolerate any interference regarding how he runs the school. Fortunately their offices are on different floors and they've agreed to air their differences in private, which amounts mostly to squabbling over expenditures.

For example, Orlando is pushing for a computer for every teacher in the classroom to make the Internet available to enhance lessons. Of course, Catholic classrooms are already outfitted with links to the ancient Catholic Internet: crucifixes above the blackboard and statues of the Virgin Mary high on pedestals in the corners that offer, via prayer, access to God's chat room. The official purpose of Catholic education has always been "getting into heaven before getting into college," as Monsignor Guy Puglisi, the Brooklyn diocese's superintendent of schools, says when he addresses students. Practically speaking, however, college preparation must take precedence; otherwise the schools would go out of business.

The religious mission of Catholic schools has been further complicated by the increase in the number of non-Catholic students, who now account for over 60 percent of Rice's population and 14 percent, nationwide.[6] As a Catholic convert, Orlando infuses essential elements of Catholicism into the school's culture, but emphasizes aspects of the African American gospel traditions that are familiar to his students. He firmly believes that nurturing an Afrocentric Christian spirituality is essential to their success. This would be jeopardized without him, he believes, since Rice would revert to the traditional religious instruction and liturgy that appeal to white Catholics.

Orlando also fears that if he were forced to leave, Rice's entire culture would slide back to the white male "machismo"—in his coinage—and the low expectations that he encountered seven years ago. In fairness, there were several excellent teachers then, and others who were adequate. But academic achievement wasn't valued as highly schoolwide as it is now. Orlando's major achievement has been to make it cool to be smart.

———

Listening to Orlando talk about his radical past makes me acutely aware of being an outsider not only vis-à-vis the African American community, but also because I've never figured out exactly how to be white in America. According to my upbringing, divisions don't fall between races, but between religious and linguistic groups.

For my forebears in Northern Ireland, religion was the fault line, and they were on the wrong side. Anti–Irish Catholic prejudice crossed the Atlantic with the Irish and persisted in Canada into my childhood. I asked my father why we lived in Ottawa, Canada's capital, rather than Toronto, Canada's New York, where opportunities seemed greater. He replied that Catholics had a difficult time finding a high-paying job there when he joined the workforce. Obviously this doesn't compare to what Orlando's family experienced, but it accounts for a different perspective.

My parents' only question about my first black girlfriend was whether she was Catholic. To marry a Lutheran would have constituted a mixed marriage in their eyes, while marrying a convent-educated Grenadian with chocolate skin meant that their grandchildren wouldn't look like lobsters on the beach—after Sunday Mass. The race drama that unfolded through the 1960s in the United States was so foreign to Canadians that in 1966 a TV anchor at a leading national channel announced that Malcolm the Tenth had been assassinated.[7] Orlando laughed heartily when I recounted this anecdote. I suppose if he had been born in Canada, he could have become Malcolm the Eleventh. My black girlfriend and I didn't marry, and it never occurred to me that Denise was "black" in the American sense, until I moved to the United States and became aware that although much has been overcome, the historical gulf between whites and blacks persists.

Religion gradually lost its divisive power in Canada. Catholic identity weakened, as did that of most Christian denominations, and intermarriage became common. But as the joke goes, although Christians are obliged to follow the Ten Commandments, six out of ten constitutes a passing grade these days. The dividing line that remains runs roughly between those who sincerely try to live according to a faith and those who, regardless of self-identification, have become thoroughly secular.

In the 1840s, my father's great grandfather immigrated to western Quebec near Ottawa. To this day, the main division among Canadians lies between Anglophones and Francophones. Although little antagonism remains—except when Quebec separatists threaten once again to break up the country—significant cultural and political differences endure. Regardless of religion or race, one's social identity, especially in Canada's capital, is defined primarily by linguistic group.

To understand Orlando in his own terms, I realize that I'll have to put on the lens of black-white racial consciousness that was integral to his upbringing, played a defining role in his people's history, and underpins Black Panther philosophy. Orlando's perspective has evolved since the 1960s, but the frequency with which he cites his militant origins conveys how much he honors that political coming of age.

The belief in a racial hierarchy is deeply ingrained in American culture and to the extent that slavery, conquest, and discrimination needed to be justified, this belief can be found elsewhere. In Canada, slavery was far less common and so easier to outlaw. Other means of creating advantages, as Anglophones did politically over Francophones from the late eighteenth century through to the 1960s, flourished instead.

What becomes clear is that race, just like religious and linguistic identity, is a historical construct. Biologically, there is far greater genetic variation within than between racial groups. In fact, "Some Europeans have more genes in common with Nigerians than do Nigerians with Ethiopians. . . ."[8] The few genes that affect skin color, hair type, and eye color, by which race is most commonly defined, are recent geographic adaptations and physiologically unimportant distinctions.

In America, race was a weapon honed to suppress blacks. The civil rights era transformed racial consciousness into a mechanism of defense and liberation. For Orlando, race has become his vision of black excellence via academics that is both revolutionary and traditional.

So far, Orlando shows little interest in where I come from, but I'm glad it's not Mississippi or Georgia. If one is an outsider, perhaps less shared acrimonious history is better. Like most Americans, Orlando has a vaguely positive impression of Canada. He knows that tens of thousands of escaped slaves went there via the Underground Railroad, but few stayed, so he hasn't much curiosity about the Great White North. The truth is that although slavery was illegal and the majority of Canadians were abolitionists, racism and segregation persisted. This was usually much milder than in the Deep South, but there were thousands of KKK members in Canada. For the most part, with the departure of American blacks after Emancipation, Canadians simply were spared the agonies of race relations, proving nothing about their moral superiority.

From our conversations, it's clear that Orlando assumes I'm a white liberal since I went to Columbia University's journalism school. As a result, he seems to think my views on race fall somewhere between innocuous and annoying and so need not be engaged. He assumes I fundamentally agree with his viewpoint and won't dare contradict it in any significant manner.

At this point, I'm not trying to propound a point of view, but to observe race as a social phenomenon and chronicle Orlando's perspective. Fortunately he's completely open about his thoughts and plans for Rice and has been since our first interview. His candor is striking; he tells me exactly how he feels about teachers, administrators, and parents shortly after every interaction.

———

In the early evening, about fifty parents and guardians of Rice's new students gather in the cafeteria for the second of three parent orientations. More than 80 percent are single mothers, and some rely on welfare. There are also aunts and grandmothers, as every year more of these act as primary caregivers, and there are two single fathers. All dare to envision the unimaginable: a son heading off to college.

"It costs us $5,800 a year to educate a student," Brother Walderman begins the session. "Since Rice's tuition is $3,550, every student here receives a $2,300 scholarship." Brother explains that his primary responsibility as Rice's president involves raising money from corporate sources and private individuals to cover that de facto scholarship, which amounts to $760,000 overall. He raised an additional $456,000 that will be distributed in two ways: first, evenly among two hundred families with financial need; and second, to about twenty-five students on academic scholarship, who must maintain an 85 average. In all cases, the amount per student accounts for half the tuition.

Brother Walderman knows well how most families struggle financially and tries to provide a soothing perspective by breaking the tuition down to $19.72 a day (based on an academic year of 180 days), and a mere $3.28 an hour (based on a six-hour school day). This is less, he points out with a smile, than the cost of a baby-sitter.

In comparison, as he points out, New York City's public schools will spend well over $10,000 per student annum, and this amount will double over the next several years.[9] The parents and guardians nod in agreement that Rice is both a bargain and a sacrifice. Many take second jobs or receive help from relatives since they typically work downtown as secretaries, retail sales clerks, or taxi cab drivers. Some work for the city as subway clerks or police officers. To see their sons become freshmen at Rice is a big deal in this neighborhood. Students have a chance to get out, not necessarily from Harlem (which is enjoying an economic rebirth), but get out from poverty and its attendant furies.

Brother Walderman ends his speech by introducing Orlando as the recipient of last year's Tri-State Principal of the Year award from WABC-TV. Orlando begins by telling the parents that he once sat where they are sitting now. On September 10, 1978, he brought his younger brother, Wylie, who teaches religion at Rice, for his first day as a freshman. Twenty years later to the day, Orlando was installed as Rice's principal. To underscore "God's blessings," Orlando points out that Rice opened on September 10, 1938.

"People expect that a school like Rice wins basketball games," Orlando says, gaining verbal momentum. "And you all know what I'm talking about. But what shocks many people is having Andre Barrett, one of the top point guards in the country, in the running for valedictorian with a 95 average."

Orlando reviews changes in this year's academic program. During the summer, parents expressed concern about the Regents, the series of standardized tests designed and administered through New York state's Board of Regents. Previously students could choose to take an easier set of competency exams, but the state's education department is making the Regents mandatory for graduation. This year's graduating class will be required to pass the English Regents, while next year's seniors will have to take the math Regents as well. In succeeding years, the state will phase in American history, global history, and science Regents exams. Also, though the passing grade is currently set at 55, but this will be raised to 65 over the next several years.[10]

News reports predict that the majority of city students—meaning most of the city's black and Hispanic youngsters—will fail the Regents on their first attempt and even on subsequent tries, which will worsen already appalling dropout rates. Bolstering this claim is the fact that over three-quarters of the city's freshman class failed the state's eighth grade math test last year, and two-thirds failed English.[11] As standards rise, minority students, and males especially, are arriving at secondary school grossly underprepared.[12]

Rice students have been doing well on the English and U.S. history Regents, but poorly in science, with only half the class passing on the first attempt, and worse in math, with only a quarter getting by. Parents have good reason to worry, but Orlando brushes away their concerns with a flick of his wrist, promising to get all students ready for the Regents. He emphasizes that the issue is not the state's demands, but rather convincing students to take responsibility for their own academic success. There's nothing on the Regents exams, he points out, that students shouldn't be learning anyway.

Traditionally Rice fostered academic achievement precisely because it refused to pity youngsters growing up in difficult circumstances. Stories from many graduates in the 1940s and 1950s attest that poverty and absent fathers were common. Men went away to war, sought work in distant locations, or died in combat, while alcoholism and disease claimed others. Rice families then, although mostly white, lived at or below the income level of contemporary Rice families, after adjusting for inflation.[13] Yet letters from state education officials during these decades, on file in Brother Walderman's office, congratulate Rice students for persevering in spite of their problems and scoring well on the Regents exams. One note advised the principal to ease up on academic demands, so that seniors could spend more time preparing for the transition to the work force. Some went on to college, but the majority couldn't afford it.

Orlando pauses to signal a change in focus, then raises his hand to stab the air as he articulates his frustration with what has become, in his experience, one of the most formidable obstacles to academic success.

"Stop coddling them," he commands, and all around the room, faces freeze. "Stop making excuses for them, and you do it all the time. You still wake them up in the morning and make their beds: Stop babying them! You still iron their shirts. You are not teaching them responsibility. Mothers, cut them loose."

One woman in a turquoise skirt and white blouse makes eye contact with another mother a few seats to her right, and both yield to a quiet, nervous laugh. Other women join them, careful not to antagonize the principal.

"Some mothers tell me, 'I already do it,'" Orlando continues. "Don't give any attitude to me. I'm telling you straight up: If you don't like it, too bad. I have twenty-nine godsons and raised four boys. All these young men are responsible. If they're out with the young ladies, they know how to treat them. Why do we have so many separations? Now women want for husbands because the young men are not trained at home."

Orlando's voice softens as he ends the parent orientation. "Stop crippling them. If the young men happen to fall, pick them up and brush them off, then let them keep on going. I say this every year because I see it so much. Let them grow up and be men."

———

Orlando and Brother Walderman constitute a fascinating and at times perplexing administrative team. Both are talented educators with complicated, forceful personalities. Not only their views but sometimes their recollections of events differ. For example, Brother contends that Orlando's complaints about "institutional racism" due to low academic expectations when he started as dean of students are unfounded. Honors assemblies were always held, Brother relates, and "most teachers were strict on academics." Brother points out that Felipe Lopez, beginning his second year in the NBA, earned six college credits (three in math and three in Spanish) before graduating in 1994 and entering St. John's University. In Brother's view, Orlando's issue is that many of the best teachers were also the ones who reacted negatively to his management style, so he tends to discount their competency.

Underlying Orlando's and Brother's sometimes differing accounts is a dynamic in which Brother gives Orlando as much leeway as possible for the benefit of his students. But Brother has to set budgetary limits and rein in Orlando's emotional exuberance, thereby becoming for the radical Orlando a white authority figure he sometimes feels compelled to cast blame on or to protest or rebel against. Instead of straightforwardly negotiating areas of conflict, the principal and president act out a drama that affects their perceptions of conversations and events.

The truth, as I experience it on the ground, is less about determining who's right than about seeing this relationship as a living paradox, a microcosm of race relations in America today.

Chapter Three

———

ON THE FIRST DAY OF CLASS, Monday, September 13, Christopher M. Abbasse stands at the top of the flight of stairs that lead from Rice's front door up to the foyer. As Rice's current dean of students, Abbasse fulfills his duties with enough strictness to establish that he is firmly in charge of behavioral standards from the first minute of the school year.

Every morning, Abbasse greets the students to "make sure they're dressed properly and to set a business-like tone for the day," he explains. "Otherwise they'll shuffle into cafeteria all disheveled, listening to their headphones, and talking on their cell phones." Instead of a school uniform, Rice has a dress code that mandates dress pants or slacks—not too baggy—and a shirt and tie under the dark green Rice sweater vest with the school's name embroidered in gold script. Today, many sport the warm-weather alternative: a white polo shirt with a small Nike logo and Rice High School in green cursive stitching.

With increasing frequency, as 8 A.M. approaches, the front door swings open to admit students arriving alone or in groups. They walk down neighborhood streets, hop off busses, or climb out of the subway station, commuting from as far away as Staten Island, although most live in Harlem and the Bronx.

Some young men saunter by Sterling Optical, a black-owned business, on the corner of 125th Street and Lenox Avenue where Carver Federal Savings

Bank, the first and only black-owned bank in the country, opened its first branch in 1949. As Rice High School comes into view, one block south, the new students walk with more purpose but without losing their cool—as much a teenage predilection as a survival skill on these streets. The building is a rectangular box that looks like an apartment building from the front and a former factory from the rear. It was erected in 1893, built as Harlem's first and white-only YWCA. The windows were replaced several years ago and give the building a refreshed look that is enhanced by new white mortar between the red bricks. Rice High School rises above its rundown neighbors, unmistakably the most vibrant building in the area.

Outside, it's only seventy degrees, but humidity thickens the morning breeze, and shirts cling to the backs of the approaching students. A short, muscular student wearing a plaid shirt and dark green tie skids past seven-foot, two-inch-tall Shagari Alleyne, as both freshmen cross 124th Street. The blur is Ricky Rodriguez, who is almost two feet shorter than Shagari and who attacks Rice's front door as if he were trying to beat the throw to first base. Ricky loves to play baseball and hopes to make the varsity team, although in his Bronx neighborhood, "running from" is more important than "running to."

Ricky springs up the one front step to grab Rice's door. Hanging over his head on the glass bricks above the door is a sign with green letters on gold proclaiming:

RICE MEN WELCOME TO SUCCESS!
You are worthy!

"Excuse me," a voice slams Ricky the moment his foot lands in the school vestibule. "Take off that hat before you come in the building."

"Sorry," Ricky answers and sucks his teeth—a habit he picked up learning to speak English at public school after immigrating from the Dominican Republic as an eight-year-old. Except for the occasional Hispanic inflection, Ricky could pass for a chocolate-hued African American. He swipes the black do-rag (a nylon skullcap with long tails that wraps around the head and hangs down the back) from his head and stuffs it into his book bag. From now on, he'll do it automatically as soon as he crosses Rice's threshold. This simple gesture concretizes Rice's educational prerequisite: discipline based on respect and reinforced by constant adult supervision.

Ricky smiles wryly up the stairs and holds his breath as he encounters Abbasse's deadpan stare. At six feet, five inches tall and 260 pounds, Abbasse makes an imposing gatekeeper. A trimmed beard covers the bottom half of his oval face, and his thick, dark brown hair is tied back into a ponytail that falls between his shoulder blades. His skin is pale, slightly olive, with few wrinkles, but the streaks of gray in the forty-two-year-old's hair and beard give away his age. Today, Abbasse wears black denim jeans, a green shirt, which matches his hazel eyes, and a charcoal tie—and looks more like a biker than an educator. Halfway up the stairs to the main level, Ricky exhales as he detects a twinkle filtering through the Abbasse's horn-rimmed glasses,

Working with students is Abbasse's beloved vocation. He grew up near Grand Rapids, Michigan, in an extended Lebanese American family, and was an honors student through public high school. But when Abbasse got to the University of Michigan, where he aspired to become a marine biologist, he missed class often, but never a party—until he was forced to drop out. Abbasse then worked at an office-furniture manufacturing plant for several years, before returning to school at Aquinas College in Grand Rapids. While majoring in biology and history, he happened to take an education course during which he "fell in love with teaching." Abbasse graduated in 1987 with a bachelor's degree in science and accreditation to teach high school science. He also gained a personal understanding of failing out that continues to help him counsel at-risk students.

Instead of going immediately into teaching, Abbasse pursued an interest in current events by working for over a year at the American-Arab Anti-Discrimination Committee in Washington, D.C., as the director of the Eyewitness Israel project. Until the end of 1989, he organized fact-finding missions to investigate the conduct of the Israeli military during the Palestinian intifada, which had begun two years earlier. Unhappy with the politicization of his reports, Abbasse accepted an offer to teach social studies at a public high school in Birmingham, Michigan, replacing his brother who was on long-term sick leave.

Then on Memorial Day weekend in 1990, Abbasse was visiting a friend in New York City when he learned about an opening at Rice for a science teacher. Abbasse interviewed the next week and was offered the position starting in September, despite some reluctance on the Christian Brothers' part to hire a Muslim, Abbasse recalled, because they had had negative interactions with members of the Nation of Islam. Over the next eight years before becoming dean of students, Abbasse taught virtually every subject offered at Rice. During his summer breaks, he completed a master's degree in the great books of Western civilization at St. John's College in Annapolis, Maryland.

Yet every year, Abbasse contemplates returning to public education as a teacher, since he self-identifies as "a proud product of public schooling" and claims to be a firm believer in the public system. But he knows he would lose the freedom and authority to treat discipline problems as he sees best, and instead would have to contend with a maze of rules and regulations, and much needless paperwork. Begrudgingly, he admits that his belief in public education is mostly nostalgia for a system that has changed radically in the urban areas where he has wanted to work since he graduated.

"I'm still at Rice because I love it," Abbasse told the teachers at their orientation just before Labor Day weekend. "We're empowered to nurture a growth process especially with Mr. Gober in charge. Rice is becoming what I think a school should be." He recounted attending a seminar at the University of Michigan earlier in the summer, sponsored by the National Endowment for the Humanities, on the contributions of Islamic society to Western civilization. "There were teachers from all over the world, and as usual they complained about how their students don't care and don't want to learn," Abbasse said. "But I don't think that's true; they just need to be prodded along. The seminar made me feel that we're doing a good job at Rice. If you take the time to teach students how to study and think, they respond. We give our young men voices in the school to deal with learning issues and problems with teachers. And we help them deal with their problems outside."

Abbasse went on to explain that Rice is small enough to function as a family in which new teachers will soon know all the students by name. It's also a family in the traditional sense that the adults in charge impose consequences for missteps. Being late even by one second after the bell rings, for example, earns an automatic detention. Five "lates" or absences warrant an in-school suspension.

With such a focus on acting correctly, neither Rice nor any Catholic school in the country needs the metal detectors that have been installed at entrances to New York City's public junior high and high schools. Although the same proportion of Rice students would be eligible for the free or reduced lunch program—the standard measure of poverty—as their peers at zoned public high schools (where violence is as common as it is underreported), they wouldn't dare bring a weapon to class.[1] For the most part, they won't even conduct fistfights on school property, instead settling disputes at Marcus Garvey Park, a block east on 124th Street. Still, fights are rare since Abbasse and Orlando emphasize what the Rice handbook states: "Any behavior, in or outside of school, that reflects unfavorably on Rice

High School will bring immediate expulsion." One of Abbasse's major challenges over the first weeks of September will be to impress this behavioral ethos on the freshmen before anyone faces the consequence.

Ricky nods his head at Abbasse's chest as he reaches the top of the stairs. Ricky is not sure what to make of the dean. It's reassuring to have a big man in charge to protect the smaller students from bullies—not that he'd personally ever need help, he says later. However, Abbasse's stern expression doesn't match the warmth in his voice, as he tells several students to hurry, since the bell's about to ring and they won't want to start the year with a detention. Like his classmates, Ricky doesn't yet understand that Abbasse's intimidating persona is a pedagogical tool more than an expression of anger. The dean wants to impress upon the young men how serious he is about Rice's code of behavior in order to protect them.

What Abbasse doesn't show is how endearing he finds the freshmen. For example, one youngster asked earlier if he could borrow a tie, since he couldn't find one at home to match his shirt. Almost all the young men enter the school with shiny eyes and few words, spoken softly. Abbasse savors their meekness, knowing it won't last long. There are twenty-seven more young men this year, whose budding manhood will more easily precipitate conflicts in the crowded hallways and cafeteria. There will be additional students in detention after school as a result, and more behavior problems to deal with later in his office. Abbasse worries that the dark circles that appeared under his eyes last June could return before Christmas.

Orlando worries about Abbasse's health too, since he's become "my right-hand man." Abbasse took over as dean with Orlando's recommendation when he became principal. That the two would work together so well as partners seemed laughably improbable seven years ago. Orlando says Abbasse acted as the "ringleader" of the teachers who tried to sabotage his tenure at Rice.

Abbasse did tell Brother Walderman that he thought Orlando wasn't the right fit for Rice, but that was the extent of his involvement in any conspiracy. Months later, Abbasse couldn't deny Orlando's success with the students. Eventually he started to talk with Orlando about school problems and discovered their common ground as educators. Then when Orlando found out that Abbasse is an "Arab American Muslim and so, less white than the others," as Abbasse says, "he warmed up and now calls me a close friend."

Once the students get past Abbasse's inspection, they walk along the side of the foyer past the school office, and then turn left under an archway mounted with posters listing the 105 names on last year's honor roll. This is Rice's Arc de Triomphe, which Orlando installed so students would have to pass beneath it every morning and at lunch.

A short hallway leads to the cafeteria, which shows wear from decades of use. The walls bear hundreds of scuff marks, particularly where students line up for lunch every day. It's been five or six years since paint brushes covered the expressions of teenage impatience. In stairwells and classrooms throughout the building, the impact of shoes, shoulders, and book bags on wood surfaces, tile floors, and drywall are as evident in their multiplicity as their restraint. All the nicks and scrapes are clearly accidental, and the building's well-worn interior has been washed and waxed to a welcoming shine.

——

At 9:15 A.M., Orlando stands in the doorway halfway through John Shea's freshmen religion period. The principal says nothing, instead letting his black-and-white checked jacket and red shirt with a gray tie adorned with redder flowers announce his presence. As arranged via e-mail, Shea leaves the room. Orlando marches to the blackboard, picks up a piece of chalk and writes "EMPOWERMENT" in large, round letters. A key component in last year's transformation of school culture was Orlando's practice of visiting classes so frequently that every student experienced his proselytizing regularly. This year, Orlando decided to start right away with the ninth graders to teach them his priorities as soon as possible.

Orlando points to the blackboard as he talks about the positive meanings of the root word, "power," and then delivers the mantra the freshmen will soon hear in their sleep: "If you empower yourself, then you're responsible for your learning. It's the teacher's job to teach and yours to learn. Believe it and you can do it."

Orlando writes the number 70 on the blackboard. The students all know that this is the passing grade at Rice, and Orlando knows they've heard him say it several times already. But he sees repetition as absolutely crucial to getting students to buy into his vision. Too many principals, he says, give a dramatic speech at the start of the year, then flee the scene rather than fight for their goals every day.

Pointing at the number, Orlando says, "If you get below this grade, you'll be put on academic probation, something you don't want." He finds that students really don't comprehend how grading systems work. Teachers and administrators seldom decode the numbers that are branded on their report cards. As a result, the youngsters tend to interpret grades as measures of how much teachers like them, instead of indications of what skills they need to improve.

"What about this number?" Orlando asks, marking 75 underneath. Without waiting for an answer, he continues, "The lowest grade in any class for you to qualify for second honors. But your average has to be at least 85." The principal quickly scratches an 80 on the blackboard and, below it, 90, then brushes chalk dust from his sleeve. "First honors requires a 90 average," he explains, "and no grade lower than 85."

"Can you get on the honor roll with most of your grades in the high 70s?" Orlando asks.

The ninth graders stare back in silence, not dumbfounded by the question, but enchanted by this most extraordinary character.

"Not very likely," Orlando answers for the freshmen. "The more grades you have in the 70s, the higher your others have to be for the honor roll."

Of course, no missionary gets far without wampum. Honor students earn a week without homework, a movie during a school day, or a pizza party at lunch—or all three if enough students make it. Even more enticing, every student who maintains a 90 average won't have to sit for midterms or finals in that subject. "A lot of brothers were able to stay home the whole week in January and then in June," the principal adds.

"Mr. Gober," asks Nelson Castellano, a fourteen-year-old who's repeating the ninth grade after being expelled for misbehavior from St. Michael's, a Catholic parish high school on West 33rd Street. Nelson stops twirling a clump of his hedge-like hair and almost sits up straight. "What do you get out of this?"

"No one's ever asked me that before," Orlando responds, then pauses for a rare moment of public reflection. "I get to say that I am the principal of a school where the students care about learning, especially when the outside community believes we're filled with Hispanic and African American young men who can't, or don't, want to learn. So we're going to break all those stereotypes, and I get to walk around to other principals and say that my school is equal to your school. That's the greatest high I could ever have."

For Orlando, the "outside community" refers at once to society at large, meaning whites in general, and more specifically, to Catholic schools such as Regis High School—a mostly white and elite Jesuit all-boys high school on Manhattan's exclusive Upper East Side—that he believes looks down on Rice. But insofar as Regis students and faculty hold a negative assessment of Rice, it's a long-standing view based more on class than race. When Rice was all white, it served Catholic boys on the lower socioeconomic rungs who were outperformed by their peers at Regis, Fordham Preparatory School, and other more middle- and upper-class Catholic high schools. When Rice became all-minority, the gap widened considerably, so Orlando has greatly enjoyed telling principals throughout the archdiocese about the high percentage of Rice students now making the honor roll. Nothing would please him more than to walk into the yearly gathering of his peers with objective proof—such as greatly improved SAT scores, or a high percentage of his boys passing AP exams—that Rice students are indeed second to none.

Orlando envisions transforming Rice into a Regis in Harlem. This is a lofty goal, considering that Regis has its own entrance exam that is at least as difficult as the one the city administers for admission to its flagship public high schools, such as Stuyvesant. But Orlando has no doubt he can get there and would direct any detractors, once he stopped yelling, to the eighty-five-year history (1870–1955) of academic prowess at Dunbar High School in Washington, D.C., as a prime example. Most of Dunbar's 12,000 graduates during this period went on to higher education, which was remarkable. Few public high schools serving whites established such a record.[2] Blacks, regardless of socioeconomic status, can perform as well as any race or ethnic group in public or private academies. Tragically during the era of desegregation, Dunbar lost its academic focus and soon became another failing neighborhood public high school, without achieving any racial integration as a result. Today the school is known for its sports accomplishments—a fate Orlando is determined to avoid at Rice. He is adamant that the road to the Promised Land for minorities and better race relations travels directly through a demanding academic curriculum. Otherwise there will always be an entrenched "outside community."

Ten minutes before noon, Kate Hebinck greets her fifth-period freshman English class, then bows her head to say a short prayer, as do most Rice teachers. Whether or not praying succeeds in invoking the divine, it creates a respectful silence, at least temporarily. Seven floors below, a jackhammer answers with its own litany. Consolidated Edison workers are digging a trench along 124th Street to repair the gas lines that will service a row of brownstones under renovation next to Rice. Soon, middle-income families will move onto a street that until recent years was serenaded nightly by gunfire.

Harlem is currently undergoing what has been termed its second renaissance. The first renaissance was the renowned literary and artistic movement that reached its high point from 1925 through the Great Depression. In recent years, dramatically reduced crime rates have allowed an economic rebirth. Billions of dollars are being invested in new businesses and real estate developments. Brownstones, two-thirds of which stood abandoned until the early 1990s, are being renovated at an astounding pace, and new apartment buildings, condominium conversions, town houses, and hotels are under construction. Supermarkets have located on 125th Street, and major retailers like Old Navy and the Gap are opening stores. Magic Johnson invested in a Starbucks at the corner of Lenox Avenue and 125th Street. Then he participated in the deal that resulted in building a Loews Multiplex movie theater near the famous Apollo Theater, which recently underwent a fifty million dollar renovation. All these establishments and many smaller ones hire locally, providing about six thousand badly needed new jobs.[3]

Some of the new housing is geared to helping working-class residents own a home. For the most part, the renovations and new condos are attracting more affluent families and young single professionals, a noticeable number being white. At this point, few poor Harlemites are being displaced since the development involves previously empty buildings and vacant lots. However, rents have risen steeply and property values are bound to keep increasing.

Even though Harlem is situated directly north of Central Park in Manhattan, the logic of its boom was delayed for decades by high crime rates and political apathy until the Rudolph W. Giuliani administration took on the gangs and drugs. At the same time, the area was declared an economic development zone by the federal government and benefited from lobbying efforts by Harlem's longtime congressional representative, Charles Rangel, and local politicians and businessmen. Tax incentives, development funds, and geography soon created a fertile environment for economic growth.

There are, however, two Harlems. One bursts with new hope, while the other has remained marooned on the edge of the mainstream for generations. The two Harlems intermingle on every major thoroughfare, as the entire spectrum of African American society can often be seen at a glance. Bankers brush shoulders with gangbangers—but proximity is not enough, nor is a low-wage job at a movie theater. The average household income in Harlem is about 60 percent of that in Manhattan as a whole. Certainly living conditions have improved in recent years, but for many, the Mecca of

Black America remains a "symbol of perpetual alienation."[4] Racism no longer effectively prevents the transition from lower-income to upper-income Harlem. Instead, the major obstacle is the difficulty children face getting a quality education, and the most pernicious hindrance on that road is exactly what Kate Hebinck confronts in all her classes: low verbal skills.

At twenty-nine years of age, Hebinck is beginning her second year at Rice and her fourth as a full-time teacher. She studied English and Spanish at Saint Louis University, a Jesuit institution in St. Louis, Missouri, and graduated magna cum laude. Hebinck then joined the Jesuit Volunteer Corps (JVC) and lived in community in Cleveland for a year and a half. The JVC arranged for social service positions for each volunteer. First, Hebinck worked at a residence for homeless women, then she became a caretaker for the terminally ill at a local hospice. "Everyone, including the volunteers and the dying, had a tremendous sense of family," she explains. "It was the most profound experience of Christian love I've ever had. The complete acceptance we practiced and received—as we tried to make the last days of someone's life better—was the love of our fellow humans that we should always have. I loved going to work."

Hebinck returned to Houston, her hometown, to complete a master's degree in education—with a 4.0 grade point average—at the University of St. Thomas in 1996. For the next two years, she taught language arts at a predominantly Mexican-American Catholic junior high school in Houston. Then Hebinck moved to New York City to join her fiancé, who had taken a job as a sous-chef at a two-star restaurant in Manhattan. She looked for a teaching position at an inner-city Catholic school, since she has spent her entire life in Catholic schools and believes that it's her mission to pass on the Catholic educational heritage to disadvantaged students. Hebinck's qualifications and sincerity prompted Brother Walderman to hire her immediately.

Again this year, Hebinck teaches English to all the freshmen, which translates into four regular English classes, one honors class, and a remedial reading class for students who scored lowest on the entrance tests. The top third of the freshman class knows how to parse a sentence, write complex sentences, and compose an acceptable paragraph. Many were placed in the honors class, and several were allocated to each of the other classes. These students lighten Hebinck's burden, tending to pull their slower peers along, while modeling proper classroom comportment. She prays their example will prevent the recurrence of last year's nightmare, when she often felt like the jackhammers outside, pounding at the base of a seven-story mountain as she tried to get through to her low achievers. This year, she wants to quickly eliminate the resistances to learning that years of low demands and the prevalence of the culture of failure have created.

Ricky Rodriguez looks up as Hebinck goes over the proper Rice heading on the blackboard. As carefully as he tries to copy it on a piece of loose-leaf paper, his pen yearns to make all the nouns plural. He crosses out the extra *s*'s and renders the heading that he will write, with his name and student ID number, on every assignment, test, and project for as long as he's a Rice Man:

Rice High School	# 098
Ms. Hebinck	Ricky Rodriguez
English	September 13, 1999

However, Ricky has little confidence he'll be able to remain a Rice Man for four years. Although his grades were in the 80s through elementary and junior high school, he's not sure he can pass all his subjects at Rice. After the summer readiness program, he knows the demands at Rice are much higher than those he previously encountered.

Ricky catches Hebinck's silhouette out of the corner of his eye as she paces up and down the aisles observing students, in some cases wrestling with pens that seem alien to their fingers. At five feet, four inches tall, Hebinck can only look down at many of the young men when they're seated. Hebinck instructs the almost two dozen ninth graders to copy a list of common homonyms from the blackboard. She then takes the class slowly through the mysteries of *we're, wear,* and *where,* and then *there, they're,* and *their.*

"This is mad tough," Ricky mutters to himself and scratches his head. He scratches out a "thier" and "thayre" in his notebook and begins again.

Hebinck brushes back her shoulder-length, dark brown hair and punctuates her repetition of correct usage with stiff karate chops, her right hand pounding her left. The upperclassmen have nicknamed her "Al Gore" for the relentless character of her delivery and for her dogged pursuit of the fundamentals of grammar and writing on their often reluctant behalf.

"What do we call what's written as one word but means two words?" Hebinck asks, moving on to another aspect of the English language that confounded the freshmen during the summer session.

No one raises a hand.

"It's a contraction," Hebinck sighs. Only fifteen minutes into the class, the students are showing signs that they are no longer listening. Hebinck tries to regain their attention with a spaghetti-arm demonstration. "Now watch this muscle. See how it's getting shorter. Contraction means to shorten, like 'can't' and 'don't.'"

The young men show some interest, if only to see how much muscle their new teacher can generate. She wears a sleeveless, yellow blouse and a black cotton skirt that reaches almost to her ankles. Her clothes hang loosely over a swimmer's physique. Hebinck's arm produces more definition than expected, which impresses the young men.

Beginning the school year with the teaching of fourth- and fifth-grade grammar, Hebinck will need an athlete's strength and endurance to push the students toward grade level. *My father used bring home video tape and he make me read them,* wrote one student in Hebinck's summer English class. As another example, Prince Youmans, who failed the ninth grade at public school, wrote: *I like basketball because it is fun to play and meet many different. I'm very good a it and sometimes you get thing out of playing well. Like, awards and medals, and other thing.*

By the end of the five-week summer session, which amounted to twenty-five hours of instruction in both math and English, Ricky began his last assignment: *The Relations between Latin America. one thing the united states ganed was the Panama canal.* As often as Hebinck corrected his compositions, Ricky invented new distortions. His public school teachers seldom pointed out mistakes, Ricky attests, preferring to let the students "creatively discover" correct spelling and usage, as if linguistic conventions floated around in the ether, eager to drop into minds unencumbered by knowledge. If Ricky's grammar, punctuation, and spelling—no matter how incorrect—hinted at a complete sentence, his teachers let the errors pass.

Hebinck knows well that many of her students stand at a crisis point. If they fail out and return to the public system, few will graduate precisely because they won't be able to raise their academic skills. If they stay at Rice for two or three years before returning to the public system, their odds of graduating increase significantly. But the first hurdle is the basics, without which dire consequences are sadly predictable, as T. Willard Fair, president of the Urban League of Greater Miami, illustrates at speaking engagements around the country.

Fair recounts a chance meeting with two men in an airport bar on his way to an engagement. He learned that the two men worked for the Florida state prison system and were responsible for planning future prison needs. Fair asked them how they determine the number of prison cells a community will need in fifteen or twenty years. At first, the men evaded answering, but several drinks later, they confided that they looked at the fourth-grade reading and math scores on statewide tests. The number of students performing below standard, even this early in a child's life, follows a strict correlation with the number of future inmates. The overwhelming majority of prison inmates, Fair notes, are functionally illiterate high school dropouts. As a growing number of black leaders contend, Fair proclaims that education is the civil rights issue of the twenty-first century.

Looking at the freshmen sitting quietly in rows wearing Rice uniforms, Hebinck has hope for their futures, but trepidation sets in every time she glances out the window to the streets below. Dozens of unemployed men hang out in small clusters, while others trudge back from the methadone clinic on 124th Street, half a block west of Rice. On the street corners, young men of high school age sell drugs.

Culturally it is difficult for inner-city minority youngsters to focus on academics, as one freshman illustrates. Eric McBride attended a junior high school in Harlem where he was threatened every day for trying to do schoolwork in class. His peers warned that they would beat him up after school if he dared to study and thus "act white." The young man invented circuitous routes from the school to his home in a housing project on what used to be the Polo Grounds, where the New York Giants and Mets baseball teams originally played. Eric says he had to work hard to get up to the fifth grade level and into Rice. But he begins the year staring off into space with sleepy eyes after fifteen minutes of class work. Eric has never had to pay attention for an entire forty-seven-minute period and seems unable to focus without being harassed.

Even decoding the Rice schedule challenges many of the freshmen. Hebinck has had to explain the six-day, rotating cycle several times, since the last period of one day becomes the first period of the next, and most classes reverse their order. One student asked if the six-day cycle meant that they had to come to school on Saturdays. There are eight regular periods a day, A through H, followed by the extended school period (ESP), which is an additional forty-minute period that integrates student clubs, Regents prep courses, and group guidance sessions into the school day.[5] Orlando is introducing ESP this year as an experiment, after observing that a large number of students leave right after school for part-time jobs or family responsibilities, missing the opportunity to participate in extracurricular activities.

About 80 percent of Hebinck's students fit the profile of the typical urban dropout. A full third had significant trouble completing assignments at the summer session and have forgotten most of what was covered. The middle third of her students stumbled through phrases on the way to forming reasonably complete thoughts, but fashioning a paragraph was a major challenge. They have a fragmentary grasp of basic skills, functioning about two grades below par, and have far to go to pass the English Regents in two years.

The good news, as Orlando pointed out during the teacher orientation, is that raising verbal competency leads to competency in all subject areas. Essay questions appear on all exams in the humanities from high school through college, and word problems form a significant part of math and science exams. So much depends on Hebinck's ability to drill her students in fundamentals and wake them up from accepting poor performance as normal for minority males.

The task of improving verbal skills is far more challenging than raising math scores, according to Adam Robinson, the co-founder of Princeton Review and a *New York Times* best-selling author (or co-author) of eight books on test preparation and academic excellence. Verbal competency, Robinson emphasizes, is acquired throughout a lifetime of reading, writing, and speaking—or not—and so is much more difficult to cultivate quickly.[6]

As class ends, Hebinck tells the students to write down the homework assignment, which consists of making up sentences using the homonyms that were discussed in class. She impresses upon the young men that there will be a 15 percent grade reduction if the assignment is handed in one day late, and 30 percent off for turning it in two days late. After that, students receive a zero.

Like many of his classmates, Ricky shakes his head since he's never heard of real penalties before. At his former schools, no matter what the teacher said, there was never a deduction for late work or consequence for substandard effort. At the student orientation, doubts about his abilities swirled in his mind, but Ricky tried on the idea that he could really choose to be an A student at Rice. Then at Orlando's in-class talk earlier today, Ricky listened intently as the principal preached about empowerment.

"I can do this," sounded in Ricky's mind, but he wasn't sure whether it was as a declaration or an inscrutable riddle.

Chapter Four

———

A FEW MINUTES AFTER THE sixth period begins on Wednesday, September 15, Orlando leaves his office and heads for the elevator. Usually he tours the school once a day, but he's been too busy so far. Anxious to see how the first week of school is unfolding, Orlando debarks on the seventh floor, then shuffles down the green-tiled hallway toward Winsom Rene-Campbell's freshman global studies classroom.

As Orlando approaches her open door, he realizes that the students have already figured out that this is her first year of teaching. Last year, she felt a calling to become a teacher and switched from a part-time MBA program to a master's degree in business education. Rene-Campbell believes she can uplift disadvantaged youngsters both academically and spiritually. As a practicing Catholic, she sees Rice as the perfect fit.

Orlando stands beside her door, barely able to hear her soft, elegant voice over the din of adolescent chatter, re-emerging cicada-like after its summer slumber. Worse, chairs and desk legs are being dragged back and forth as the boys flit from one conversation to another. Rene-Campbell tries to coax the young men to quiet down and remain seated, but they ignore her. Her musical speech pattern and impeccable manners inspire no fear. Rene-Campbell is a Jamaican immigrant who dresses in conservative suits or dresses, and addresses the freshmen as if they were business clients. Orlando makes a mental note to talk to Abbasse about monitoring Rene-Campbell's classes regularly and helping her learn how to become assertive. With five freshman classes a day and the global studies Regents exam to begin preparing students for at the end of sophomore year, Rene-Campbell must learn quickly.

Orlando does not see his boys as customers in a Catholic-school version of the service industry. The youngsters are still children—albeit often occupying large bodies—and teachers need to establish themselves vigorously as parents. In loco parentis may be an anachronism at public schools, but it is a vital component of the Catholic school model.

As Orlando ambles back down the narrow hallway, lined with student lockers, he hears Rene Bodie reading out an arithmetic problem in surprisingly shrill tones, given her melodic Caribbean cadence. Orlando winces; he'd love to replace her, but math teachers are difficult to find. Last year's freshmen complained that she could explain little beyond what the textbook stated and worse, taught disjointed lessons punctuated with rude remarks. Recruiting and retaining good teachers is one of the most persistent problems Orlando faces. Typically, about twelve of Rice's twenty-six teachers have to be replaced every year, meaning that entire academic departments have to re-invent themselves regularly and then have difficulty doing more than re-establish basic standards.

Rice hires many beginning and foreign teachers who often find managing urban minority students too difficult. However, most teachers leave Rice for financial reasons. The salary for new teachers is about $30,000 depending on qualifications, which compares favorably with the first-year pay of $31,910 at the city's public schools.[1] But after a few years, even teachers who previously fled the public system begin considering long-term career options as the discrepancy in pay and benefits widens every year. Nationwide, less than 30 percent of Catholic school teachers last more than five years.[2]

The city's sixty-three thousand public school teachers average about $49,000 a year, compared with about $37,000 for the eighteen full-time lay teachers at Rice.[3] Not only do public school teachers make a third more, soon that gap will increase dramatically as new contracts are negotiated.[4] In addition, public school teachers also have much better medical, dental, and pension benefits, and virtually impregnable job security.

Maintaining a core of competent teachers is obviously a challenge. Over the summer, Orlando had to hire only five new teachers and one new guidance counselor, which he attributes to the improvements in student performance and behavior that he nurtured last year. Unfortunately, Rice lost a sixth teacher when Charles Mauer, the eleventh-grade English teacher, resigned last Friday to accept an offer to teach at Stuyvesant High School, the city's flagship public high school. Orlando swallowed his disappointment at having to relinquish one of his best instructors and gave Charles his blessing. After all, Frank McCourt taught English at Stuyvesant until he retired to write his best-seller, *Angela's Ashes*. Orlando's displeasure was tempered with pride that one of his teachers was selected by such a prestigious institution.

But the major reason Mauer chose to leave Rice was Orlando's overbearing personality. Typically, new teachers are charmed by Orlando's personal magnetism and clear vision for the school. But he tends to continue micromanaging veteran teachers instead of giving them the professional latitude they've earned. Orlando fears losing control of his staff as they mature and naturally become more independent. Orlando isn't willing to recognize this as a character flaw. Without reflecting on his role in the loss of several quality teachers, Orlando plans to keep the teacher turnover low so that he can institute professional development programs instead of expending so much time and energy on giving new teachers basic training every year.

Orlando also intends to replace several teachers like Bodie, whom he considers "driftwood." Unfortunately for Rice and for Catholic schools nationwide, attracting quality replacements, especially in math and science, is difficult. Catholic schools have remained cost-effective because of the low salaries paid to teachers and administrators. This is especially true at the elementary level, where teachers average only $32,000 a year, a reflection of tuition as low as $1,800 at urban Catholic elementary schools.[5] In contrast, public school teachers are paid the same, whether they teach kindergarten or high school.

As public school districts continue to outpace Catholic schools regarding salaries and benefits, Catholic schools will either be forced to offer better compensation, which most can't afford or, failing to do so, suffer higher turnover. With twenty-six teachers on staff, it would cost Rice over $500,000 per year to catch up to the average public school salary, without including comparable benefits.[6] This would obviously throw Rice into a severe financial crisis with no alternatives but to close or charge much higher tuition and become an elite academy.

Orlando walks past Rene Bodie's classroom, then onto a balcony overlooking the gym on the sixth floor. At the far end, an impressive array of banners herald recent basketball championships. Rice's varsity team won city and state titles four out of the last six years, while the junior varsity team won two city titles, and the freshman team won one. *USA Today* perennially ranks the varsity team in the nation's top 20, yet Rice's athletic facilities would certainly be among the country's worst. The basketball court is only fifty-five feet long, instead of the regulation ninety-four feet. Brick walls stand less than arm's length from the edge of the court on three sides and earn the gym its euphemism, "The Brick Palace." Until the late 1980s, all of the Rice Raiders' home games were played here. In the early 1960s, Lew Alcindor (later, Kareem Abdul-Jabbar) led Power Memorial Academy against the Raiders and not surprisingly, won every game.

Power Memorial was the second of three high schools that the Christian Brothers founded in three contiguous brownstones on 124th Street, a block east of Rice across from Marcus Garvey Park. The first was All Hallows High School in 1913, which was moved to the Bronx in 1931. That September, Power Memorial opened in the same brownstones and then moved to West 61st Street, now the site of Fordham University Law School, in 1938. Rice opened later that year in the brownstones, then found its permanent home in the former YWCA in 1940. Rice was also the first American school named after the order's founder.

Large protective pads now cover the brick walls around the gym, and the freshman, varsity B, and junior varsity teams still play home games here. As usual, the pounding of a basketball on the parquet floor now mixes with squeaking sneakers and boyish yelps in a sophomore gym class. Orlando ignores the students to see if Lou DiMello, Rice's full-time gym teacher in his thirteenth year, is doing more than reading the newspaper. True to Orlando's expectation, DiMello sits on a metal folding chair with the *New York Post* at his feet. Orlando cannot understand why DiMello refuses to get the young men involved in physical activities other than basketball, which Orlando sees as reinforcing the stereotypes he despises. When Orlando first came to Rice six years ago, he objected strongly to how much the game was the focal point of school culture. "Everything was basketball then. Students would come to school with a basketball in their hand and no books," Orlando often says. "And it was okay with the teachers. What they were saying was that black guys don't need culture, music, art, or drama: throw them a basketball in gym class. Don't even bother teaching them calisthenics or different games, because they're inner-city kids and that's what they do."

Even as a teen, Orlando felt little attraction to activities at which blacks already excelled. He appreciated how basketball's discipline helped his brother, Wylie, post good grades at Rice and then get into St. John's University on an academic scholarship. But for most African American youngsters, Orlando sees the sport as a trap. Few make it a career, and the pursuit misdirects talent away from areas where there are clearly more opportunities. For all the winning basketball teams Rice has produced, only four players have made it to the NBA.

On the way home from summer school in July, Orlando was walking through Jackie Robinson Park in Harlem. A small boy bounced a basketball while his mother talked with friends. The boy dropped the ball and let it roll. One of the women on the bench picked the ball up and gave it to the boy's mother. The child ran over to his mother and knocked the ball out her hands. It rolled away and another woman chased it. The vignette repeated several times until the mother held the ball higher than the boy could reach.

"Gimme. Gimme," the boy yelled, then started to cry.

"How old is he?" Orlando asked the mother.

"Three," she replied.

"Why don't you give him a book to put in his hand instead of a basketball?"

"What are you talking about? He can't read."

"Yes, you're right," Orlando agreed. "But he can't play basketball either."

"Oh," the mother nodded.

Orlando walked away thinking that you've got to start with culture, and you've got to start early.

Quintupling the honor roll in a single year, he realizes, was more a cultural turnaround than a substantive gain as measured by objective tests. On the SAT, Rice students score well below the national average for both whites and blacks, averaging 800 as a combined score on the math and verbal sections.[7] This is lower than the 825 minimum required for a student to qualify for a Division I college basketball team. Low SAT scores are not unusual at urban Catholic schools, since all seniors take the test. Catholic schools certainly can't be accused of skimming the brightest students to achieve their impressive graduation rates.

Orlando takes the elevator down to the fifth floor. His shoes click on the glistening tiles in the hallway. The tenth, eleventh, and twelfth graders take classes here and on the floor below, and the fourth floor also holds two computer labs, administrative offices, and the teachers' lounge. The Christian Brothers have their residence on the third floor. Of historical note, Paul Robeson appeared in his first stage performance on the second floor, when the YWCA had a theater there. The basement houses the physics and chemistry labs, and a swimming pool that fell into disrepair several decades ago.

Orlando passes Dionedes J. Lopez's half-sized music room at the end of the fifth floor hallway. D.J., as she prefers, seems to be surviving her first days at Rice as the school's first music teacher. He's pleased to see that like most teachers, D.J. followed his directives on how to set up a classroom. She covered her bulletin board with yellow and green paper and put up subject-appropriate posters of Mozart and Billie Holiday, and also blown-up covers of *Playbill* magazine, advertising Broadway musicals. D.J. laminated printouts listing class procedures and school rules, and mounted them over the blackboard.

After graduating from Abilene Christian University in West Texas, D.J. taught music and choir at a high school there for two years. The twenty-three-year-old is thin, about five feet, five inches tall, and has attractively wholesome features. Her golden complexion and almond-shaped, dark brown eyes suggest her Mexican lineage. This is D.J.'s first experience teaching at an inner-city school and dealing with mostly African American students. Nor has she ever taught poor Hispanic students.

Although D.J.'s grandparents were impoverished immigrants to south Texas, they insisted that all their children go to college. As a result, D.J. grew up in a middle-class family with all the opportunities afforded by the American mainstream. But she never learned to speak Spanish, and lost the Catholic component of her Hispanic heritage when her family converted to an evangelical denomination.

For Orlando, instituting a music program was an essential part of his war on stereotypes. For financial reasons, Brother Walderman resisted the idea when Orlando started advocating it several years ago, but he agreed as enrollment rose. All the freshmen and sophomores take a semester of D.J.'s music course. Orlando also asked her to start a Men of Rice choral group.

"Who would think that black males in Harlem study music theory and appreciation?" Orlando asks rhetorically whenever he touts the program to visitors. Orlando considers himself God's sledgehammer, smashing false idols: the stereotypes about African American males that whites set up to both confirm and maintain superiority.

Inside D.J.'s half-sized classroom, the former teacher's lounge, twenty-two freshmen sit elbow to elbow. D.J. plays a Duke Ellington song on her portable CD player to introduce her students to their African American musical roots.

"We don't listen to that white music, Miss," one student says afterward.

"White is butt," remarks another.

D.J.'s mouth drops open in shock and she can frame no response. She realizes that she'll have to prepare several lessons illustrating the prominence of black performers, composers, and songwriters in the history of American music.

Meanwhile, Orlando trudges away feeling like Sisyphus in the middle of his uphill battle against the anti-intellectual attitudes that have infected so many minority youngsters. Reflecting on the incident later, Orlando says he shouldn't have been so surprised about the students' ignorance since whites have adopted elements of black culture throughout American history, but neglected to credit the source.

Fifty feet down the hall, Orlando stops beside the closed door to Jonathan Mason's classroom and watches through the window. Mason sits on a desktop in the middle of the room with tenth graders slouching in their desks around him. He seems to be hanging out with his "peeps" (slang for "peoples," or buddies) rather than teaching math. Mason's face tenses as he raises his voice to break up a conversation at the back of the room. He is having trouble adjusting, even after teaching the Regents' summer math class to the Rice sophomores who failed the exam in June. It was Mason's first teaching experience after moving here three years ago from Kansas City to complete an undergraduate degree at New York University. He failed to establish order in the classroom and instead succumbed to yelling at the students—the least effective way to institute discipline.

"This new teacher is wack, yo," several students told both Orlando and Abbasse afterward.

Steve DiMattia, the twelfth-grade English teacher, explained Mason's dilemma: "A big problem a lot of black teachers run into at Rice is that they rely on the power of their personalities. They tend to think that, 'the kids are going to get me because I'm like they are,' which is a huge pile of crap. In fact, it works in reverse." DiMattia remembers an African American teacher who was hired several years ago to teach computer science and math to seniors. He told DiMattia that the students were going to be "cool" with him because he was from the projects too. Within two weeks, the seniors had locked him in the computer room with his own keys. He wasn't hired back the following year.

Since then, Orlando has spoken several times to the teachers about the hierarchy of difficulty. He said that black men have the hardest time teaching black boys because so few black males have kept their promises to them. In addition, the young men have difficulty accepting a black male in authority since they're accustomed to seeing African American males as custodians or coaches in schools. When Kim Davis, the new eleventh-grade guidance counselor, began teaching the U.S. history Regents class at Rice in the summer, Linwood Sessoms immediately questioned his qualifications. Linwood wanted to make sure that Davis could teach him what he needed to know to pass the exam on his second try. But as Linwood admitted, he wouldn't have asked the question if Davis were white or a woman.

If a black male proves himself to the students, Orlando explained, he wins more respect and a closer relationship with the youngsters than is possible for the other teachers. Last year, Langston Jones, an African American and recent college graduate, dealt patiently with rude behavior from the freshmen in his global studies class. By November, the students competed to sit with him at lunch, after he impressed them with his familiarity with their favorite video games and stayed after school to play with them. Unfortunately for the young men, Jones took a high-paying job with a computer software company in the summer and did not return. Both Orlando and Abbasse believed that he would have become one of the school's best teachers and were sorry to see him go.

According to Orlando, white males have less difficulty than black males because white represents authority. Black females experience the easiest beginnings in the classroom since almost all the young men have been raised by African American women and are accustomed to their place at the head of the family. White females benefit from both color and gender, and tend to be accepted as authority figures more easily than men, but not quite as readily as black women.

As soon as Orlando was hired, he pushed Brother Walderman to employ more minority teachers, then aggressively pursued this when he became principal. Although Brother Walderman retained the final say regarding any candidate, Orlando made it clear that he wouldn't tolerate interference. He respected Brother's input, but seized the operational right to hire as he saw fit. When a position becomes available at Rice, Orlando places ads first in the *Amsterdam News,* an African American weekly published in Harlem, and in *El Diario,* the city's Spanish-language daily. Only if these measures fail does Orlando post a notice at the archdiocese office or place an ad in the *New York Times.* Now minority teachers constitute 60 percent of the faculty, including eighteen blacks and five Hispanics. Men still outnumber women four to one.

When interviewing a prospective teacher, Orlando says he pays most attention to the words the candidate uses to determine his or her commitment to education. "Teaching is an art and a profession," Orlando explains.

"I would be less inclined to go further with someone whose vocabulary revealed that they saw it as only a job." Secondly, Orlando asks questions "to get a sense of the teacher's spiritual base. I'm not looking for a Catholic, or even a Christian necessarily, but I want to see how they handled struggles in their lives." Thirdly, "I'm very interested in whether they like teaching and children. If they go on and on about the subject they teach, I give lower marks than if they talk positively about teaching kids and define their developmental stages."

Unfortunately Orlando's desire to balance the faculty with more blacks and Hispanics sometimes results in hiring less-qualified teachers, which undermines his academic vision for Rice. Before offering Mason the position, Orlando interviewed a white male who was as qualified academically and had just graduated from Iona College, the Christian Brothers' liberal arts institution in nearby New Rochelle. Orlando has often criticized Iona for not encouraging its graduates to teach at Rice but wouldn't consider this one—even though the young man was also a track coach, which would have fulfilled Orlando's longstanding desire to re-establish a track team. Mason, on the other hand, is completely unfamiliar with Catholic education, and he makes no secret of his plans to leave as soon as possible to become a college basketball coach.

In addition, Orlando communicated with Mason solely by e-mail during the hiring period since Mason was visiting Los Angeles. Orlando openly admits he chose Mason because of his race, and makes no apology. "Rice is an all-boys, African American school," Orlando said, "and the students need to see people like them teaching and in charge." But as important as hiring black male role models might be, the students gain nothing from incompetence. Worse, Mason resists correction. Orlando proposed that Olivene Browne, the most experienced math teacher, mentor him. But Mason balked when he found out that Browne would sit in on some of his classes and then offer constructive criticism. Orlando plans to confront Mason soon with his failings and has decided not to prolong the on-the-job training like he did last year when he allowed a verbally abusive Hispanic teacher to finish the spring term before firing her.

Orlando walks away from the door gritting his teeth as Mason shouts at another student. Orlando takes the elevator down one floor, then shuffles past Tim Hearn's classroom without stopping. The two educators hardly exchange greetings anymore. Hearn, who teaches eleventh-grade chemistry and twelfth-grade physics, is on a collision course with Orlando, despite being one of the most respected and popular teachers. The source of the problem is Orlando's demand that every teacher assign student projects this year. In addition, he has told the science teachers to perform more lab experiments. The labs were renovated four years ago with a $350,000 grant from Pfizer that Brother Walderman brokered through a Rice alumnus.

It seems reasonable to both take advantage of these facilities and assign projects, which the students enjoy. But Hearn refuses, saying his students lack fundamentals to the point where he has to concentrate considerable time on basic reading skills and arithmetic to cover the curriculum.

The tension between Orlando and Hearn arises mostly from the similarities in their personalities. Orlando operates like a medieval king more than an administrator, fiercely defending his domain from Brother Walderman's papal oversight, and demanding absolute loyalty from his staff. Hearn protects his fiefdom with the same fierceness, refusing to swear allegiance to Orlando. Every teacher who has challenged Orlando's authority over the last seven years left out of frustration or was fired. Orlando countenances no opposition, and interprets the same independent attitude that he displays vis-à-vis Brother Walderman as a threat. Hearn has had several run-ins with Orlando over the past few years and considers him a "blowhard." From a career perspective, Hearn has nothing to fear, since highly competent, state-certified science teachers are in great demand everywhere.

Remarkably Orlando is probably the only principal in a public or Catholic school in the city without a master's degree, although he will earn one in administration and counseling from Manhattan College next May compliments of Rice, which paid the tuition. To be fair, there's nothing an academic course could teach him about counseling young men; nor would education theory, notoriously thin academic gruel, offer much benefit. Traditionally, parochial schools make little effort to develop or follow pedagogical theories, instead keeping the methods that work and discarding those that don't. Orlando's approach is a synthesis of the practical built around his own insights and experience. Ironically, he's unwilling to give talented eccentrics like Hearn the same latitude.

Chapter Five

AFTER THE LAST CLASS ENDS at 2:20 P.M., several dozen upperclassmen stop by Orlando's office to say goodbye or discuss a problem. An hour later, the day decelerates, allowing Orlando to sit at his computer and finish a letter to parents. Five minutes later, Dwayne Carter, a senior, slips through the door that was left slightly ajar on purpose. Some students make appointments to discuss personal problems, but often they just drift in at this hour needing his undivided attention.

"What's up, Mr. Gober?" Dwayne asks. His hands are buried deep inside his front pockets. Dwayne lives nearby and went home after school to put on his hip-hop uniform. A billowing black T-shirt reaches almost to his knees, and a black do-rag and very baggy black denim jeans complete a fashionable outfit that allows him to maintain his cool while reaching out.

"Well, okay. How are you?" Orlando replies, looking up from his monitor.

"Chillin'," Dwayne answers.

Orlando stands slowly, then walks the three steps from his desk to the small round table he installed in the middle of the room to better facilitate conversation with students. Dwayne talks about family issues, not because he's seeking advice but to connect with Orlando. At the end of last year, Abbasse recommended that Dwayne not be allowed to return in the fall, mostly for behavioral reasons. Dwayne begged for reconsideration and Orlando said he could write a letter in his own defense. The letter failed to convince Abbasse that he would drop his "smart-ass" attitude with teachers, avoid detentions, and work to his potential. But Orlando was reluctant to dismiss one of his brightest young men—having recruited him as an eighth grade honors student—and decided to give him another chance.

Sadly Dwayne already shows signs of continuing his old ways. After the half-day schedule on Friday, all Dwayne's teachers complained to Abbasse about his attitude. When questioned, Dwayne told Abbasse that the half-day wasn't a real school day. Abbasse walked away convinced Dwayne won't make it through September. He told Orlando, who chided the senior sternly yesterday in the hallway. Today Dwayne is checking to see how close he is to the edge of the principal's patience.

Although there were sixty-three juniors at the end of last year, this fall begins with only fifty-two seniors. In June, Orlando asked twenty-five students from grades nine through eleven not to return in the fall for academic and behavioral reasons. He had warned students all year that he was serious about education, and he lowered the maximum number of allowable failures from three to two per year. Although most students responded to Orlando's call and pumped up the honor roll by a power of five, there still remained a small group who struggled with grades and earned regular detentions.

Dwayne's cousin, Desmond Carter, also a junior last year, was told not to return after failing three subjects. "I heard you say it all year," he told Orlando in tears, "but I never believed you'd really do it."

"I had to take a stand that let everybody know we weren't joking around," Orlando explained. "Those who failed out needed to learn to take responsibility that can happen only if there are consequences. Every one of those young men asked for his parents to meet me, so they could get back in. I asked them, 'Why Rice?' and they all talked about hating the street and having to go back there if they went to public school because that's the atmosphere. But I had to think of what's good for the school more than the individuals, even though many were very close to me personally and it broke my heart."

Satisfied that he still has some leeway, Dwayne bids his principal good night and saunters up Lenox Avenue. At the corner of 127th and Lenox, he stops at a bodega and squats on a concrete step beside the entrance, waiting for his "peeps" to show up. Ten minutes later, two young men arrive who, unlike Dwayne, do not carry book bags. Both are dressed in full hip-hop regalia with black and blue bandanas, indicating that they're Crips, members of the second most powerful drug gang, next to the Bloods.

Both Crips have eyes as hard as bullets behind turret-like eyelids. Dwayne trades "yo's" and handshakes that proceed from hand clasping to finger-pulling to fist-knocking. His friends mumble in a neighborhood code that's as languid as it is laconic.

"Word," Dwayne answers, and the three young men saunter into the bodega to conduct what have become regular transactions. Dwayne will probably forget about his homework again and wake up tomorrow to his fading resolve to salvage his future at Rice.

———

Meanwhile Orlando sends an e-mail to his teachers and another to his administrative staff. Just after 5 P.M., he hears another knock and Prince Youmans, a freshman, stands in the open doorway, rocking slightly from one foot to the other. He explains that he spent several hours chillin' with his half-brother, senior Hayward Washington, then happened to be in the neighborhood and dropped by to say hello. Orlando wonders what "in the neighborhood" means since Prince lives on West 155th Street in Harlem with his grandmother, while Hayward shares an apartment with his mother on 95th Street on the Upper West Side. Like many freshmen, Prince makes an excuse to establish a relationship with the principal.

"Rice be the only school like this," Prince says as he sits down on the couch just inside the office door, diagonally across the room from the principal's desk. Several yards of kinte cloth are draped over the aging couch to make it seem inviting and keep it functional.

"Like what?" Orlando asks as he strokes his moustache.

"Where guys don't be sayin' the N-word."

"You mean an African American school where students don't degrade each other that way?" Orlando takes pains to translate into Standard English.

"Yeah, I be talkin' to my friends and they sayin' no school does that," Prince replies.

Orlando nods and thinks: Now here's this kid coming into this culture from one full of that disgusting language; this is God's way of sending me a message about why I'm here. When Orlando started to preach abstinence from the N-word in 1993, Brother Walderman's predecessor told Orlando "to go easy on these kids because it's part of their culture."

"You mean 'Mick' is part of your culture because you're Irish," Orlando shot back.

The principal glared at him in shocked silence "that a black person would stare him down," Orlando recalls. "The Brothers were incredulous when I got the whole school to stop using that word without expelling or screaming at anyone. This will probably be my greatest legacy at Rice: that I changed the school's culture by systematically talking to the students." In fairness, the Christian Brothers and other religious teaching orders have a long history of changing both students' social and academic behavior. But what made Orlando's achievement remarkable was that he did it alone. Of course he had support from the staff, including the brothers, but Orlando was the prime and very forceful mover who earned the students' trust.

Meanwhile, Prince stretches his short limbs in an attempt to sprawl into teenage nonchalance, but can't quite lose the bear-cub look. He throws one arm on top of the couch's back pillow and leans against the worn chocolate-gray wood paneling. Directly over his head is an accurately rendered pencil portrait of Tupac Shakur that was presented to Orlando by a former student. The portrait has helped the principal earn a reputation as cool, which he has used with skill to disarm the natural teenage resistance to opening up about problems.

Prince talks about playing basketball for various indoor and outdoor leagues around the city, hinting at how much he wants to make Rice's freshman team. He then discusses what he considers a major problem: the restrictions his grandmother imposes on his freedom. Unlike many of his peers, Prince has a curfew and must keep his grandmother informed of his whereabouts after school. He complies but angrily resents the limitations. Mrs. Geraldine Crawford is the only one left to take care of Prince after he lost both parents to AIDS almost a decade ago. He both resists and cries out for her strong parenting. Although strict, his grandmother lacks the dynamism to corral Prince's temper and the psychotherapeutic skills to ease the bitter sense of helplessness that percolates beneath his easygoing manner. Inside Prince, ghosts fight with demons and he turns, as do many Rice students, to Orlando for salvation.

Orlando listens quietly as Prince's face flushes with hurt and rage; as yet he can't articulate his feelings or even mention his parents. Orlando lets the silent pause hang between them like a bridge under construction. During private consultations, Orlando sheds his aggressive persona especially with students from shredded families.

Orlando's parents are still alive and together; they provided well for their children, insisted on discipline, promoted their education, and took them to church regularly. Orlando dedicated himself to becoming a respected teacher and administrator to bring the benefits of his upbringing and experience to youngsters like Prince.

In the years since his own childhood, Orlando has witnessed the problem of race overwhelmed by the relentless disintegration of the African American family and the consequent breakdown of urban black communities. "Just being black exerts an external pressure, since we're not seen as American because we're not immigrants," Orlando explains. "We don't fit into the national mythology. Instead we're like property or Native Americans. Then we're always fighting to get into whatever this American culture and society is, because we don't have a built-in culture like immigrants have that we can collectively take and walk into the mainstream. We have no common language or dress. What's African in our heritage isn't even respected by us, really. When we talk about our roots, it's all about southern cooking and culture that developed within slavery and Jim Crow. Since we don't have roots that establish true self-esteem, we're more vulnerable; our wounds are more open."

The already fragile black psyche fractured easily when drugs were introduced into black neighborhoods beginning in the late 1950s, Orlando observes. Then welfare, the loss of jobs due to deindustrialization, and rising crime rates tore at the African American social fabric. "This caused the unraveling of the African American home," Orlando explains, "and created an internal psychological pressure far more destructive than the external problems of racism, since there was no one to give our boys emotional and spiritual stability."

To counter these forces, Orlando proclaims, "I represent my own people, so that they may be empowered to rise above what the world is giving them as crap, and above their own self-sabotage."

However, the two sides of Orlando's divine calling often come into conflict when dealing with students like Prince and Dwayne. Subconsciously Orlando still cradles Samantha Brown in his arms, utterly powerless to help. He swore he'd never lose another child, and every consultation with a troubled student revives these feelings. Orlando publicly camouflages this private pietà behind his highly demonstrative in-class proselytizing about academic empowerment, his exhortations in the hallways to display racial pride through behavior, and the motivational talks he gives to get students to believe in themselves.

But Orlando's leadership isn't directed merely at salvaging at-risk students. As he repeats often, he wants to make Rice into what it advertises: a true college preparatory high school. Dwayne and Prince are intelligent enough to meet the demands this entails, but both boys have hard-earned street reputations they believe can be protected only by being seen as cool by their classmates. On the street, "cool" is defined as disobedient, defiant, and indifferent to intellectual pursuits. Dwayne has spent eight of his nine lives at Rice in failed attempts at self-reformation, while Prince may not be given that many. Orlando is narrowing the road for the very students who need the most latitude. It pains him to do so, but the greater sorrow would involve the loss of the entire school's potential, which he will not tolerate.

For a year after Samantha Brown died, the thought of taking students on a trip threw Orlando into a panic. Eventually he learned to trust normal precautions again. An acute sensitivity to students with illnesses remains with him, as does "a more general fear of losing kids from dropping out. I spend much more time trying to keep students than getting rid of them, and I fall into a terrible depression whenever we lose one. I cling to them and they cling to me; they are my sons."

As the conversation ends, Prince says he feels at home at a school for the first time since he moved in with his grandmother. Orlando encourages him to study hard and stay out of the trouble that caused him to be held back twice already. Prince will be sixteen in January and wants to earn his half-brother's respect by graduating in four years. At seventeen, Hayward is a senior, and he's been warning Prince that Rice is his last chance. Hayward can't imagine Prince starting the ninth grade for a third time at a neighborhood public high school.

Orlando walks Prince to the doorway and gives him a hug, as if to stabilize the young man's resolve. Ultimately Orlando hopes he'll come to value himself enough to succeed. Prince walks away with a lightened step, filled with almost enough inspiration to believe.

———

As Prince exits Rice, I get up from the bench in the foyer and join Orlando in his office. Whenever a student comes in for a consultation, I offer to leave or take my cue from the student's body language. So far, students who are establishing a relationship with Orlando prefer to be alone with him. Dwayne had no issue with me sitting on the couch, but Prince was clearly uneasy about my presence.

Functionally, it doesn't matter since Orlando recounts what occurred in abundant detail and recalls essential parts of the conversations verbatim. Technically he's breaching confidentiality, but he says he feels this book is part of his legacy at Rice. I surmise that Orlando views his office as a confessional where healing and redemption transcend privacy, and he sees himself modeling how to be an inner-city principal for peers across the country.

At this point, I need to address a concern that some readers might have in light of the numerous recent priest sex scandals. Although Orlando is not a cleric, I could imagine suspicions arising about the nature of his relationships with students. He's an unmarried man who carries on intimate sessions behind closed doors with vulnerable young men, some of whom could be manipulated—and in a Catholic institution. At first, I had some anxiety since Orlando unabashedly hugs students when he feels there's a need and often puts his hand on shoulders to express paternal caring. However, after interviewing all the teachers and most of the students, I can say that there's never been a hint of inappropriate behavior in Orlando's seven years at Rice. Rather, the normal physical contact that a father would have with a son is an integral part of Orlando's paternal role with young men who've experienced little or no fatherly love. It's also true that he doesn't hug the students with functioning fathers, or grandfathers or stepfathers assuming that role. Orlando orchestrates his behavior according to his boys' needs.

Chapter Six

———

THE NEXT MONDAY, SEPTEMBER 20, Abbasse tells Orlando about the theft of a pair of sneakers from a book bag during one of Dr. Zachariah Saad's ninth-grade Earth science classes. Orlando sinks into the chair at his desk, as a righteous anger begins to roil. This is the third similar incident since the school year began. Certainly, the N-word is blasphemy in Orlando's world, but theft, which undermines the trust that girds a positive school culture, attains the rank of unforgivable sin.

At the end of the day, Orlando calls the students from the Earth science class to the cafeteria for a thirty-minute discussion about moral choices and manhood. He charges them with righting the situation and then dismisses them abruptly.

———

At the beginning of the first lunch period on Thursday, September 23, a dozen juniors appear at Orlando's office to tell him they hadn't had a teacher for the morning English class he has been teaching. After Charles Mauer resigned, Orlando decided to take over both eleventh-grade English classes since, he said, Rice's rotating schedule would make it difficult to find a part-time replacement. The truth is Orlando didn't want to look for a new teacher because the classes provide a captive audience for expounding his views on politics and race, which he finds especially tempting since the junior-year curriculum focuses on American literature.

This morning, Orlando covered Hebinck's class instead of his own because he wanted to talk to the freshmen about the N-word. Rene-Campbell was assigned to cover Orlando's class and supervise the completion of an assignment, but she forgot to check with the school office. The juniors proudly show Orlando the work they finished without adult supervision. Orlando shakes his head, both touched and amazed to see "teenagers acting like they're in the fourth grade, so unaware of the neediness they display for recognition."

Among the juniors is Sheldon Slade-Jones, a teenager with dark circles under his eyes and desire for fatherly attention in them. Orlando is concerned about how tired Sheldon is every day, but can only offer encouragement. After school, Sheldon does his homework on a park bench near his apartment building. Then he hangs out until 2 A.M. to avoid returning home to a mother who says she's "tired of him" and a stepfather who doesn't want him at home. There are also indications of physical abuse; more than once, he's come to school wearing a bandage because, he says, "I fell off my bike."

Every year there are students like Sheldon. Two years ago, another junior did his homework while riding the subway for hours every night. The young man waited until he knew his alcoholic father would have passed out before returning home, so he wouldn't be beaten.

The other side of staying out late is getting up early—in Sheldon's case, after only three hours of sleep, since he commutes from Staten Island. Orlando understands why Sheldon is so lethargic in class and gives him leeway. The principal says he'll never comprehend the boy's mother saying that she doesn't care who he hangs with at night or what he does at night as long as "he gets his ass out of here in the morning."

Fortunately, as Sheldon reassured Orlando, albeit with an unfathomable sadness, "I'm a good kid and stay away from troublemakers in the park."

Orlando sends the juniors back to the cafeteria with a broad smile and makes a point of putting his arm around Sheldon's shoulder before he leaves. The principal takes the incident as an affirmation that he is running the school effectively, and he is thankful that the juniors' display of responsibility frees him to focus on the new students.

"Relationship-building is the most crucial thing we've got going for us," Orlando comments, "and I love that part of the ministry. I give the young men what they need. I'm careful to stroke them and still hold them accountable—and I'm in awe of the way they respond. They don't challenge me even when I give them a swift kick. There's an enormous amount of respect on both sides."

———

After the extended school period (ESP), Orlando calls the entire freshman class down to the cafeteria. He marches in and yells at them to stop play-fighting and sit down. His mood-shift since they saw him in Hebinck's classes this morning exhorting them to adopt Rice's culture is startling.

"Can I go home?" Ephraim Yisreal asks as he twists a braid of hair.

"Why?" Orlando snaps.

Ephraim, a thin fifteen-year-old with a scar across his right temple, mumbles something about forgetting to take his medications. Ephraim suffers from a neurological ailment and has to take antiseizure pills at lunch to avoid becoming disoriented.

"Are you in the ninth grade?" Orlando demands.

"Yes."

"Then get over there and sit down," Orlando barks. His indifference to the young man's medical condition reveals the depth of his anger.

Ephraim walks to his seat in a daze, as Orlando commands: "Everyone stop talking right now and face me." Half the students are sitting with their backs to the principal. Several shift their chairs around, but most merely crane their necks in his direction.

"Do you understand English?" Orlando shouts. "Turn the chairs around." The freshmen comply and then stare up at Orlando with wide eyes.

Orlando kept the entire grade after school yesterday as well, since he thought they made too much noise on the way back to class after lunch. The boys were exuberant, but not disturbingly loud. Orlando lectured the freshmen for an hour, catching several daring to giggle and a few blasphemous enough to smirk as he talked. As a result, he called the entire class back today for another orientation in the bylaws of his domain.

"There may be one hundred and twenty-seven of you and only one of me, but if you are stupid enough to go up against me, you won't win," Orlando warns as he walks slowly around them, as if marking a perimeter. "You come from a whole variety of schools, but now you have to learn our rules. Some of you don't understand that yet; you ran wild at your last school. You had years of joking around, smirking and using the N-word, and you want to bring that filth in here!"

Some students look down at the floor; others pucker their lips in apology.

"Mr. Abbasse says your behavior today improved," he grants them, then quickly points out that the cafeteria is still littered with garbage.

Ephraim rocks slightly in his chair, wondering if he'll make it through the principal's feature-length scolding. He should have taken his pills after lunch, but they make him sleepy so he often waits until the end of the day. But if he waits too long he becomes delirious. Prince Youmans spots Ephraim's distress and makes a face, hoping to get him to laugh out loud. But Ephraim is too distracted to notice. Prince turns toward Nelson Castellano and mocks Orlando's wrath, but fails to budge Nelson from his scowl. Prince is alone in his irreverence today; his classmates are sufficiently intimidated by the power of Orlando's tempest to sit quietly and quake. Both Prince and Nelson have already received several detentions and are becoming known as troublemakers.

While Ephraim struggles for self-control, Prince fights his tendency to sabotage his academic efforts by not taking himself seriously enough. The loss of his parents so early in life resulted in a shattered ego and a diminished sense of self. He emulates his half-brother in short spurts, but soon collapses into playing the jokester for laughs. Nelson, on the other hand, plays out the drama of the abandoned child who gives up caring about himself. He refuses to work on establishing a positive reputation with his teachers, avoiding the possibility that he might be worth their efforts, since then he would have to accept his own worth, which can be very difficult for fatherless children and especially so for a youngster like Prince who has lost both parents.

Orlando turns into the middle aisle and paces between the rows of seated students like a drill sergeant reviewing his new, and wholly unsuitable, recruits.

"Don't come to me with excuses; I want action," he begins strongly, then a beat later explodes with: "Conform or leave! No fuss, it's simple. It's overcrowded here as it is. There's only supposed to be a hundred freshmen. Twenty-seven of you could go and it wouldn't bother me."

Virtually all the freshmen gasp at once. Orlando truly would prefer a smaller class, and the students sense that his threat is real.

Orlando takes several steps forward, then turns and smirks, "And I certainly don't want any parent letters about how my poor, precious child is being victimized."

Several ninth graders look up as if they're about to be abandoned.

"Conform or leave," Orlando repeats. Later, Orlando explains that he uses this phrase because it's "catchy and easy to understand. Mission statements should always be stated in a few words. I think the students know that by conformity I don't mean following society's values blindly, but that we have a system here of teaching responsibility within a culture that values each person. Each young man has to deal with things in this society as an African American or a Latino that others don't have to confront. To me, conformity means that we have to make sure everyone understands that when they leave Rice, they're going to face a hostile world, and it's our job to groom them to withstand it."

In effect, Orlando asks students to decide whether to buy into this version of empowerment. "You're not going to stay in a school that seeks to support you," he adds as the students fight impulses to fidget nervously, "and thumb your nose at what we're trying to do." Clearly Orlando has a very low threshold regarding what constitutes nose-thumbing.

Orlando explains the "leave" part, telling the students that "The State of New York says you have to be in high school, but it doesn't say that you have to be in Rice High School. Starting tomorrow, if I walk around the school and see you misbehaving, I'm going to pull you out of class and ask you to clean out your locker. I'll call your parents, refund all their money, and tell them to find you a new school on Monday. So if you're stupid enough to challenge me, I beg you, try me out."

The students sink into their seats, perhaps trying to present smaller targets for Orlando's wrath. He softens his voice and apologizes that the whole class has to be punished for a few. The same twenty or so freshmen who have been displaying immature behavior were making the most noise at lunch. Orlando's performance is a warning for these troublemakers and for other students who might feel tempted to emulate them.

Orlando stands still for half a minute, allowing an uncomfortable silence, before railing about the theft of a pair of sneakers. So far no one has returned them or talked to the principal about replacing them. For Orlando, the lack of a response strikes as much at the core of his community-building efforts as the incident itself.

"Rice is a four-year process," Orlando says. "In public school, they'll ask you at the end, 'Well, what have you learned?' But here at Rice, the question is, 'What kind of person have you become? Do you care about yourself academically, physically and spiritually? Can you function in society and care about others?' The important thing at a school isn't the computer rooms or the science labs, but what kind of climate we create, what we stress. This is the essence of what nonpublic schools do."

The freshmen stare back at the principal. Most are not sure what he's talking about, but make an effort to look like they do. Whether or not they've attended a parochial school, they've never heard an educator talk about morals with such conviction. Orlando takes the traditional Catholic view that human beings, rather than being born perfect and merely in need of facilitators, come into this world flawed and therefore need help overcoming their faults. In contrast, many Catholic school teachers are hesitant to impose their perspectives, accepting the romantic view of human nature that animates the teaching philosophy at most schools of education, even those at Catholic universities. Somehow children will learn right from wrong, as they're supposed to learn reading and math, through a child-centered process of creative and imaginative self-discovery. Orlando has nothing against this approach when it works, but in his experience most students need direction, meticulously and consistently applied.

Orlando's next ultimatum scares many of his boys more than "conform or leave." The Earth science class must "heal the wound that a member of our family has suffered" or they will be barred from the Rice Jam on the Saturday after next.

"Oh, man," Ephraim regains his focus and sucks his teeth. The dances were the main reason he chose to come to Rice. He has heard about them for years, as has every minority elementary school student in Harlem and the Bronx. Ephraim has been looking forward to his first experience in a darkened cafeteria filled with hundreds of girls.

"There have been more robberies in this ninth grade class so far than we had all of last year," Orlando suddenly yells. He paces back and forth increasingly agitated, shouts out the same statement again, and then a third time verging on hysteria, before he storms out of the cafeteria.

The freshmen freeze, not knowing how to react. Today is the first time they've seen Orlando erupt, and they realize that crossing their principal amounts to lighting a very short fuse on a very big bomb. Obviously the intensity of his lecture had more to do with the petty thefts than noise levels at lunch. With Orlando, moral choices aren't merely abstract discussions in religion class, but the most important questions the students must grapple with over the next four years.

After several uncomfortable moments, Abbasse steps forward to take charge. He calls out the names of the students with detentions and dismisses the rest, who slip quietly out of the cafeteria.

———

"I hold their feet to the fire, but while holding them, I massage them too," Orlando explains later in his office. He tends to lose himself in his own performance, arguably to the point of emotional abuse at times, but it is carefully staged. Orlando's first and most influential mentor, Lenchen De-Vane (whom he always referred to as Mrs. DeVane), gave him a book at the beginning of his career entitled *Man of Steel and Velvet*, a Christian account of manhood, after which his one-man "good cop–bad cop" routine is modeled.

"I really believe that God chose me to become an educator," Orlando says, "so I can uplift young people until I die." He remembers running home from his first day of school as a child and declaring, "Mommy, I know what I'm going to be when I grow up."

"What?" his mother asked, happy to see her son so excited.

"I'm going to become a teacher."

"Okay, sure you are, Robbie," his mother replied, calling him by his middle name. "Tomorrow, it'll be a doctor, and the next day a policeman. That's what you kids do."

"Yes, Mom," Orlando said, but he knew he would never change his mind.

Orlando's parents grew up in Fayetteville, North Carolina. After World War II, Orlando's father, Willie Gober, was discharged from the army and moved to Fort Greene, a Brooklyn neighborhood where, coincidentally, Orlando's mother happened to have moved—both on the same quest for a better life than the Jim Crow South offered. Willie and Evelyn were acquainted back in Fayetteville and happened to run into each other at a Laundromat in Fort Greene. They courted for a year, then married on January 28, 1950. Twin daughters, Vicki and Vivian, were born a year later, and Orlando joined the family as the first-born son on April 23, 1953.

Mrs. Gober hated the neighborhood and was determined to get out. Fort Greene had supported a substantial African American population since the 1840s, when free blacks worked as skilled craftsmen in the shipbuilding industry at the nearby Brooklyn Navy Yard. But with the decline of shipbuilding, the neighborhood crumbled. Even so, the only housing the Gobers could afford was in the Fort Greene public housing project.

"My parents came to New York to pursue the great American dream of owning their own house with a white picket fence," Orlando tells his students when they ask about his past. Orlando's father was a shipping clerk on the Bowery and took a second job at night, while his mother worked at a bookbinding firm. "They had good jobs for African Americans at that time and saved their money."

When Orlando was nine years old, his parents bought a single-family house in St. Albans, Queens. "It was a Mecca for African Americans getting out of the projects back then," Orlando recalls. "You could buy a home on tree-lined streets alongside Count Basie, Lena Horne, and all the big doctors. There was no picket fence, but we had a black wrought-iron gate and a yard on 202nd Street. We were making it." His three younger brothers— Dennis, Wylie, and Alphonso—were born after the family moved there.

Orlando attended P.S. 136 across the street, where he was always an A student. His sense of racial identity began to stir when he was ten years old and his parents took him on the 1963 civil rights march in Washington, D.C., that culminated with Martin Luther King, Jr.'s historic "I Have a Dream" speech. The next school year, Orlando fashioned a slogan for a current-events assignment about the ongoing presidential election campaign: Goldwater is Coldwater. Vote for Johnson. Hearing his classmates chant it provided Orlando his first taste of public recognition. Not surprisingly, Lyndon Baines Johnson won the election in a landslide.

As an adolescent, Orlando met Mrs. DeVane at Redeemer Lutheran Church in St. Albans when he became a volunteer teacher at her Sunday school program. There were almost three hundred children, and Mrs. DeVane ran the program as an academy, insisting that teachers prepare lesson plans and attend staff meetings. When Orlando taught her son, Tim, in a third-grade Bible class, Mrs. DeVane recognized his gift for working with youngsters. The two became close and Mrs. DeVane, who also taught at Orlando's elementary school but was never his teacher, began introducing him as "my protégé."

"Many are called but few are chosen," Mrs. DeVane said often. "Are you going to be a teacher, one of the chosen ones?"

Mrs. DeVane inspired Orlando to join the Future Teachers' Club at Andrew Jackson High School in Queens as soon as he became a freshman. He was elected president, and ran it like a corporation with dues and regulations. In his senior year, Mrs. DeVane recommended Orlando for a selective educational degree program at York College in Queens, where Orlando took academic courses at night and on weekends while he worked as a teacher's assistant during the day. Mrs. DeVane had him assigned to P.S. 136, where Orlando says that "she taught me everything about teaching from how to put up bulletin boards to classroom management."

One morning, a hyperactive third-grade boy threw a chair at Orlando after being reprimanded. The chair missed Orlando's head by an inch and left a large crack in the blackboard. Mrs. DeVane heard the noise, marched into the classroom, pulled the youngster out, and put him in her class.

"I hear you like to be a tough guy, Jay," Mrs. DeVane said.

"Yeah, yeah," he answered.

"And you like to throw chairs around the room."

"Yeah, yeah."

"Jay, you throw one chair in my room," Mrs. DeVane fixed him in her stare as if sighting a rifle, "and I'll break both your arms."

"Yeah, yeah, not a problem," Jay assured her. After getting into trouble every day in Orlando's class, he never acted out again.

"Mrs. DeVane simply would not tolerate bad behavior, so the kids didn't dare," Orlando recalls, acknowledging how closely he has tried to follow the same approach. "My push for academic excellence and empowerment comes from her; in many ways, I'm very traditional too."

Mrs. DeVane incorporated black history into the Sunday school curriculum and rooted her teaching in African American literature and poetry. She talked to Orlando about visits to Africa with her husband, a black professor at City College. In the late 1960s, Orlando was thrilled to see her join efforts to desegregate schools near Washington, D.C. Later in her career, Mrs. De-Vane founded an African American arts center for youngsters in Harlem. She also introduced her students to the classics of Western literature and taught them traditional European dances like the minuet. Mrs. DeVane saw the cultural treasures of civilization as her heritage; she taught Negro spirituals with the same energy and respect she accorded Shakespeare.

Mrs. DeVane was schooled in Afro-conservatism by her mentor, Mary McLeod Bethune—one of the nation's most important educators and most accomplished African American women—who in turn had been inspired by W. E. B. DuBois. Bethune was born the fifteenth of seventeen children in 1875 on a farm in South Carolina where her parents and several older siblings had come into the world as slaves. From childhood, Bethune was taught by semiliterate parents to view education as the key to improving the lives of African Americans. She worked hard, excelled, and won scholarships to Bible schools in North Carolina and Chicago.

After graduating, Bethune taught at mission schools until she opened her own college for African American girls in 1904 in Florida. In 1923, the school turned coeducational and became Bethune-Cookman College, which Mrs. DeVane attended. Bethune was determined not to leave "a single Negro boy or girl without a chance to prove his worth."[1] After defying the Ku Klux Klan over voter registration, she became a national spokeswoman for African American rights. Bethune founded the National Council of Negro Women and served in government agencies under four presidents. In 1936, she was appointed director of the Division of Negro Affairs by

President Franklin D. Roosevelt, becoming the first black woman to head a federal agency. Bethune is also remembered for the close friendship and productive working relationship she developed with First Lady Eleanor Roosevelt.[2] Coincidentally Mrs. DeVane served as the assistant principal at the Mary McLeod Bethune elementary school in Harlem. Unfortunately by then, all the values that Bethune believed in were seen by most students as "acting white."

Mrs. DeVane trained Orlando in the African American tradition of high academic achievement, which flourished in public education during the first half of Mrs. DeVane's career. She evaluated Orlando as "outstanding" after his first year's apprenticeship and put him in charge of his own class the next year, an unusual move considering he was only nineteen and a college sophomore.

"The one thing Mrs. DeVane couldn't do, and she admits it, was tone me down," Orlando says with a laugh. "She was so lady-like and dainty; she wore white gloves and frilly blouses, while I was this explosive volcano." Orlando recalls the dashikis and other traditional African dress he wore to school and of course his large Afro. He emblazoned T-shirts with BUY BLACK and imprinted others with a drawing of Malcolm X and Martin Luther King, Jr., that had a caption reading "Malcolm, Martin and Me." He also wore various protest buttons and so created his walking-billboard persona.

Throughout the civil rights era, Orlando attended numerous marches and was arrested three times at anti–Vietnam War protests in the early 1970s. A decade later, he was arrested a fourth time at an antiapartheid rally. "They were exciting times with a sense of commitment and brotherhood that's missing today," Orlando tells his students at every opportunity. "There was an energy there that pulled you along and made you feel good about who you were and what you were doing, and that you really could honestly make a difference. Today there's a lack of passion, not just racially, but all over. That's what bothers me."

From the first day of the school year, Orlando promoted student attendance at the thirty-first annual African American Day parade in Harlem, which took place Sunday, September 19. Orlando wanted the majority of Rice Men to march together since it was Rice's first appearance and from a public relations point of view, the parade offered an opportunity to make Harlem residents more aware of the school by impressing them with the Rice Men's comportment. Brother Walderman attested that a surprising number of Harlemites know little about the school beyond its basketball reputation. Many seniors snickered good-naturedly at Orlando's campaign, saying the principal really bribed the two hundred students who showed up by promising them the next day off from school.

For Orlando, the parade afforded an opportunity to introduce his boys to the activism that defined his own youth. "You'll be marching and singing songs," he told them. "The civil rights movement was carried very much on the backs of teenagers. I want you to understand that it was people your age who marched, faced the tear gas, and took the beatings. It wasn't just something in the history books, but a spirit that can always be renewed and made relevant to your lives."

At 10:30 A.M. Sunday morning, Rice students gathered just north of Central Park. As they waited for Orlando, they watched majorettes from high school marching bands practice. Whenever a group strutted by in sequined costumes, tights, and knee boots, the Rice Men competed with each other to get the girls' attention. They borrowed pieces of paper from teachers and made a show of coaxing phone numbers from the majorettes. The ritual was played good-naturedly by both sides, with the girls acting coy until the boys issued enough compliments to earn a response. But the truth is the majorettes weren't calling out valid phone numbers, and the boys admitted they wouldn't dare call a girl they don't know anyway.

Half an hour later, Orlando marshaled his young men up the Adam Clayton Powell Jr. Boulevard. Orlando's boys waved cheerfully at the spectators lining both sides of the street. The Rice Men stood out in their white school T-shirts and slacks—in stark contrast to the young men watching the parade, outfitted in hip-hop uniforms.

Orlando smiled broadly as his sons demonstrated that despite the stereotypes, Harlem does care about academics. The "larger community," he declared, tells "vicious lies" about African American males. Later he explained that white liberals, more than conservatives, are responsible for the idea that blacks don't want to get an education or aren't capable; they instituted social entitlement programs and low expectations at public schools that presuppose inferior moral character and intellect. Orlando says he would rather deal with outright bigotry.

Orlando cheered his students, and his enthusiasm moved them to join him in singing "Kumbaya," which was his way of saying, Wake up little brothers! Wake up! He hoped this would give them a taste of the Black Panther ideals that inspired him as a young man. Today's teenagers, especially those at the bottom of the socioeconomic ladder, do their marching mostly on the way to work at McDonald's or the Gap, making up the core of low-paid, service industry workers. Some help support their families, while most earn cash to participate in a different form of idealism: the romanticization of gangsta that requires just the right, and expensive, sneakers, clothing, and rap CDs. Today's teenagers, including most Rice Men, know little about predecessors who marched at great risk to free their nation from history. More accurately, they feel betrayed by the civil rights generation that left them poor and fatherless.

The African American Day parade ended with a feel-good aftertaste and little risk of an outbreak of political consciousness. Orlando expected to accomplish nothing more than plant seeds in Christian Brothers' fashion—as when the order nurtured a revolutionary agenda with students in Ireland during the struggle for independence from England. Orlando plans to cultivate his seeds throughout the school year, especially during Black History Month.

As Black Panther leaders met with violent ends or were sent to prison in the early 1970s, Orlando says that he and many others pursued teaching as the best way of continuing the struggle—only to realize that public education was more the problem than the solution. By 1973, Orlando was in the last year of his degree program when he asked for, and got, the lowest-achieving fourth-grade class at P.S. 136. There were thirty-four students, with the most advanced youngster reading at slightly better than the first-grade level. Early in the school year, Orlando called in sick with laryngitis. He was replaced by a substitute with the unfortunate surname of Fukes.

"They flipped Mrs. Fukes, went through her pocketbook, and threw all her money out the window," Orlando recalls. "One of the boys said, 'Mrs. Fuck, I have more hair around my asshole than you do on your head.'" Then all the boys climbed up onto the window ledge and urinated from the third floor onto the courtyard. Mrs. Fukes quit by midday. That afternoon, the principal called Orlando's house. His mother said he couldn't come to the phone because he was unable to speak, but the principal insisted.

"Do you value your job?" the principal asked without saying hello.

Orlando wheezed "yes" into the phone.

"Have your ass in here tomorrow or you're fired," she shouted, then hung up.

The next day, the school janitor led Orlando to his classroom. Rather than clean up the room the night before, Mr. Trincillo left the mess for Orlando to see himself. The children had torn apart every piece of paper and cardboard, and had destroyed the play store that Orlando built out of boxes to teach them math.

"I lined up every kid in that classroom and spanked them with the ruler I'd bound with rubber bands," Orlando recounts. "Then I went to their homes and talked to their parents." Even though the school was public, spanking was still permissible in the African American community, Orlando recalls. Parents would tell him to "save the eyes," which meant "don't hit the child in the face" as the only restriction.

Orlando's students behaved well afterward—a testament to the efficacy of consequences—which allowed him to create a learning environment that was so conducive to academics that his students raised their score on the citywide reading test from lower than the first-grade level to between the second- and third- grade levels.

The principal called Orlando into her office to tell him about the results.

"Why, that's fantastic," Orlando exclaimed.

"No, it isn't," the principal replied. "I want you to lower every score by one full point"—which meant a full grade level.

"What?" Orlando asked as if she'd slapped him.

The principal explained that the Board of Education had given P.S. 136 remedial status in recent years. As a nontenured teacher, she warned, Orlando would lose his position if he didn't go along.

"You mean if we keep these children dumb, we'll get more money?" Orlando asked.

"Now you've got it," the principal grinned.

Orlando felt outraged, especially that someone outside the community, a Jewish woman, was telling him this. Orlando refused to lower the test scores and filed a grievance with the district superintendent.

"But his name was Rubenstein," Orlando remembers. "So you can imagine how far I got." Orlando told the superintendent that he was quitting public education. But before leaving, he informed the parents about what had happened. They held a protest meeting and forced the school to report the correct scores. Orlando still felt betrayed and decided to leave anyway. "I was a rebel and didn't belong there. I'd taken down the American flag to fly the Panthers' red, black, and green flag instead."

Orlando took a teaching position at St. Mark's Lutheran Elementary School in the Bushwick area of Brooklyn and negotiated the starting salary up to $6,000, less than half of what he was making in the public school system. Orlando did not get along well with the mostly German American staff at this overwhelmingly African American school. One female teacher threatened to "knock the black off" him with an umbrella because he sided with the principal, the parish's black pastor, in a staff dispute. Orlando left for Grace Lutheran Elementary School in the Bronx at the end of the year. There he found sympathetic colleagues and, after two years and only twenty-four years old, he was asked to be principal.

Orlando moved to the Bronx, and as if the demands of running a school were not enough, he began taking in troubled youngsters from the school. The first was a student whose grandmother was too sick to care for him. The next year, Orlando legally adopted three young boys and enrolled them in his school. Their mother was a friend who suffered from a drug addiction.

Two years later, in the spring of 1979, Orlando was asked back to interview for the principal's position at St. Mark's. "So I hear you want to come back here," stated one of the two district church elders. St. Mark's enrollment had dwindled from over 300 to 89 students in kindergarten through the eighth grade since Orlando left five years before. The church council was contemplating shutting the school down.

"Excuse me?" Orlando said indignantly. The two men had asked him to consider returning.

"We'll give you two years to shape it up, or we'll close it down," the man with a German-sounding name said. He stood up, as did his colleague, and they walked out of the room.

"I'm not going to take this," Orlando cursed as he left. "They are nasty." Orlando returned home furious and called Ronald Fink, a mentor and the president of the Lutheran Church's Atlantic division.

"Don't take the job," Fink told Orlando.

"Why?"

"My boy, some ministries deserve to die."

"But there's people there," Orlando protested. "There's life."

"Take my word; you'll be committing educational suicide."

Orlando followed Fink's advice and turned the job down. Several weeks later, Orlando started dreaming at night about an old traffic light hanging from a wire over an intersection. The light flashed green. "It didn't say 'Go.' It just kept on flashing green until I woke up," he said. This happened every night for days until Orlando called back the pastor at St. Mark's and took the position.

Orlando's friends and colleagues implored him to stay at Grace, but he interpreted the dream as a sign from God. Orlando moved to Brooklyn to rebuild St. Mark's and within two years he had doubled the enrollment. St. Mark's won an award for the fastest growing school in New York State. Lutheran educators visited by the busload asking, as Orlando put it: "What's this black kid doing that works so well?" Orlando was only twenty-eight years old. Within five years, St. Mark's grew to over six hundred students and expanded to a second building. Orlando says he succeeded by applying what he had learned from Mrs. DeVane, plus adding in his father-figure role.

Orlando collected another dozen "godsons," as he called the young men he took in or counseled as students. Three brothers from a white Jewish family that had become Lutheran came under his care at St. Mark's. Sadly the parents were abusive, but not enough that Orlando could get custody.

Orlando found time for his own family by hiring them to work in his school. First, his father became the head of maintenance, and when his brother Wylie dropped out of college, Orlando took him on as a teacher. St. Mark's remained a twenty-four-hour devotion until 1982 when Orlando began a long-distance relationship with another teacher, Harriett "Scotti" Scott, whom he had met the previous summer in North Carolina through Mrs. DeVane. Three years later, Scotti's support helped him recover after Samantha Brown's death. Then in the summer of 1987, they married in Greensboro and returned to St. Mark's where Scotti taught for the next six years.

In the spring of 1992, Mrs. DeVane's son called to say his mother was sick and asking for her protégé. Orlando flew to North Carolina and sat by her bedside for several nights. She asked Orlando to play her favorite song, "Moon River" by Andy Williams, every evening at the customary hour she retired.

"Say, 'Goodnight Gracie,'" she asked Orlando when the song ended. Mrs. DeVane and her husband loved George Burns and Gracie Allen, and had watched their TV show regularly.

"Goodnight Gracie," Orlando said softly, holding her hand as she slipped away.

"Emotionally, I was devastated," Orlando recalls, then looks away. "My wife stood by me, but I was angry and really nasty, not a very good husband at the time." They separated and divorced. Scotti moved back to North Carolina, and Orlando made a clean break from his past. He interviewed at Rice where his brother Wylie had taught religion for the previous two years.

In September 1993, Orlando started at Rice as dean of students, still hurting from his personal losses. Partly as a result, he turned into the "explosive volcano" of his radical youth and fought with colleagues. He was also living by himself for the first time in his life and felt very lonely; not only was his wife gone, but his godsons had left for college or joined the work force. Orlando eventually made peace with the staff at Rice, but has no close friends among the faculty. He spends virtually all of his free time with students.

"We don't really have teachers like Mrs. DeVane anymore," Orlando reflects. "She knew all the angles of a lesson, and how to keep the kids actively involved. She knew how to ask thought-provoking questions. She wouldn't tolerate gum chewing, bad posture, or anything. A student had to raise his hand, could only speak when recognized, then had to stand to ask or answer a question." Orlando laments that the caliber of teachers has dropped significantly in his generation.

Even Rice's best teachers struggle through the day. Only the chemistry teacher, Tim Hearn, who Orlando is pressuring to conform or leave, comes close to Mrs. DeVane's competency, sense of order, and teaching style. Perhaps Orlando resents that her talents transubstantiated into a white host.

After witnessing the extent of Orlando's rage today, I worry about our relationship. When we discussed affirmative action recently, I held my breath. Orlando has mixed feelings since he recognizes that affirmative action programs presuppose and reinforce minority inferiority. At the same time, racial preferences in college admissions help Rice students both get in and get financed. I oppose affirmative action based on race, because I believe it is counterproductive at this point in history. For the most part, those who benefit are from middle- to upper-class families. This obscures the national tragedy that the vast majority of underclass and working-class minorities don't graduate or score high enough on standardized tests to qualify for selective colleges. But I support continuing affirmative action based on economic need.

Orlando examined me with intensity and then smiled enigmatically. I felt very uncomfortable, and this wasn't the first time I felt trapped with the proverbial tiger in a cage. Would he accuse me of being a racist—certainly some black leaders such as Jesse Jackson characterize my position as an attack on civil rights—and angrily throw me out of his office? The combination of his passionate opinions and volcanic temper didn't bode well. But we ended the discussion there, and he didn't react negatively when I subsequently expressed other opinions opposed to his.

As I began to learn, Orlando doesn't fundamentally care what I think. Nor does he expect me to agree with him, even though it surprises him sometimes when I don't. For Orlando the question is integrity. He can't stomach someone patronizing him or African Americans as a group. The more I speak honestly, the more he trusts that I'll portray him, his boys, and the school accurately, whether or not we agree on every issue.

All he asks of whites is to "get out of the way"; the responsibility for solving problems in the black community belongs primarily to African Americans. I'm just the scribe.

Still I worry that I'll say something that offends him. I feel Orlando's emotional volatility across the room, and I've never been sure of exactly what the black-white protocols are in America. I've noticed that white Americans avoid discussions of race with their black colleagues and among themselves. Even in the middle of Harlem, issues around skin color don't seem to exist among whites who defer to African Americans as the experts by virtue of that skin color.

This is partly for fear of job loss. A remark perceived as inappropriate, or any use of the N-word, might earn a black teacher a reprimand, but a white teacher would be fired. Also, there seems to be a general desire among the faculty and students to move beyond divisive aspects of race. Orlando is the only one to speak out as he does. Other African Americans here are more or less sympathetic to his views, but they see them as somewhat anachronistic.

I realize that Orlando can cut off my access to Rice and end the book project whenever he likes. Brother Walderman allowed me in without consulting Orlando, which usually spells the end of any initiative at Rice. Given their tenuous relationship and Orlando's uncompromising demand for absolute control over what happens inside the school, if he decides to banish me from the school, Brother Walderman wouldn't overrule him. Orlando would consider this an intolerable threat to his authority, and Brother wouldn't fire him over the issue.

As Orlando and I discuss his stern talk to the freshmen earlier, I realize that our temperaments are similar in that we say what's on our minds regardless of what others think. Orlando doesn't seek to hurt people's feelings, any more than my "piss and vinegar" Irish approach is meant to be harmful. So I wager that when we argue, for example about the extent of institutional racism in today's society, he'll respect my going for the truth, regardless of how mistaken or naïve he thinks my attempt. With Orlando, security can only be found in risk.

———

"May the spirit that lives within you continue to renew you, and have a blessed day," Orlando punctuates the end-of-day announcements a week later on September 30 with his usual benediction. Minutes later, he stands at the top of the stairs leading down to the front door, shaking hands with his boys as usual. He pulls several students aside to both encourage and admonish.

Fifteen minutes later, Orlando heads back to his office. He notices Donald Shetland, a tenth grader, standing motionless in the foyer, his unblinking eyes staring at the names on last year's honor roll. Orlando hasn't noticed Donald since school began, which surprises him. Last year, the young man had severe academic and behavioral problems, and Orlando doubted he would succeed. Donald's family is very poor, and his mother struggles to maintain her emotional stability. She was recently charged with child endangerment after Donald's younger brother was almost burned in an apartment fire while she was out. The boy was removed temporarily from her custody. The woman cares deeply about her children, but her ability to cope emotionally and financially is limited. Student Sponsor Partners (SSP) pays Donald's tuition, and might pay for his brother if Donald proves himself a good investment.

"Donald, how are you?" Orlando asks.

Donald continues to stare at the honor roll and makes no response. His feet seem to be growing roots in the tiles.

"What's wrong, Donald?" Orlando says with concern. "What are you looking at?"

"I'm picturing my name up on that list and I'm going to be there," Donald states quietly, then turns and walks out of the building.

Orlando feels his breath startle and take flight. "Now, that was a Rice moment."

Orlando spends the rest of the afternoon in private counseling sessions with several students discussing family problems. At 6:00 P.M., he e-mails several juniors who feel more secure about revealing their thoughts and troubles via the Internet. As dusk falls, Orlando's energy plummets. He is a diabetic who manages his condition poorly, always rationalizing that he has another student to salvage or a parent to call, instead of taking care of himself. He often forgets to eat lunch, then suffers from fluctuating blood sugar levels that partly fuel the intensity of his emotional shifts.

Orlando walks out of the school and turns north onto Lenox Avenue for his favorite evening destination: Sylvia's, Harlem's most famous soul food restaurant, at the corner of 126th Street. With his bagged take-out containers in hand, Orlando looks for a cab. Several speed by, so Orlando thinks about returning to Rice to call his car service, but he sees the M7 bus approaching. He lumbers on and then transfers at 145th Street. Ten minutes later, he enters his condo building near Edgecombe Avenue. A uniformed doorman opens the inner door to the lobby, and Orlando takes the elevator to the twelfth floor.

Two putty-colored steel filing cabinets greet Orlando as soon as he enters his apartment. Only a bachelor married to his work would install eight overflowing drawers of career archives just inside the front door, especially in a penthouse with a panoramic view. Orlando crosses the parquet floor to the kitchen and drops his dinner on the wooden table. The room's beige walls are turning yellow in the corners, or perhaps they're ripening. Wisps of dust dance in the wake of his footsteps, and paint peels from the ceiling.

Fifteen minutes later, Orlando lands heavily on his La-Z-Boy recliner in the living room and deposits his nemesis on the adjacent TV table: a reheated dinner of deep-fried, salt-laced Southern delights. To his right, two naked windows offer an unobstructed view of the entire east side of Harlem, glittering in the twilight. On the other side of the East River, a ribbon of headlights on the Major Deagan Expressway cuts through the shadows below Yankee Stadium, as commuters stream back to the safety of the suburbs. Baseball's holy temple seems to float above the entire South Bronx like a hot-air balloon. Orlando stares out the window and chews as he thinks about his 330 sometimes prodigal Rice sons. One freshman has already been expelled, and two others have transferred back to public school. All three students were replaced by late admissions.

"How many young men could be healed," Orlando laments, "if Rice had the resources for intensive small group and one-on-one counseling sessions?" As it is, the school has one full-time guidance counselor per grade, and both Orlando and Abbasse work with troubled students for hours every day. But Orlando still feels he's bailing water with a soup spoon, and worries about those he might lose this year. Most of the freshman teachers complain constantly about troublemakers such as Prince, Nelson, and Ephraim. If these students are expelled, they'll go to a public high school where guidance counselors typically handle five to ten times the number of students, with time only for major crises.

After dinner, Orlando remembers the incident with Donald Shetland as he leafs through the newspaper. He phones his longtime friend Lydia Colley, a relationship therapist.

"That was the statement for the first month of school," Orlando tells her, "and it affirms what we're doing. The most powerful thing was how calmly Donald said he's going to make the honor roll. All the students want to make it, but they don't always believe they can. You know, you can't measure the success of a school by test scores alone. It's the turnaround that's important, that shift in values. I hope and pray he makes it."

Orlando listens intently to Lydia's counsel about staying positive in the face of dysfunction's avalanche. After hanging up, he clicks on the television and looks for a rerun of *Golden Girls*.

Beside the wall unit, a bronze bust of Martin Luther King, Jr., stands on a waist-high pedestal. It was presented to Orlando by St. Mark's staff for saving the school. Orlando certainly shares Dr. King's "dream."

By midnight, exhaustion creeps from bone to bone, and Orlando pads his way to his bedroom. The room is long and narrow, and the walls are totally barren of décor, which makes it look more like a barracks. A single bed hugs the wall to the left. It's neatly made, as a tribute to his mother. "She was very headstrong, and we would fight all the time about my curfew or how exactly the bed should be made. She pursued everything with dogged determination and gave me my sense of purpose."

Orlando credits his father for his self-discipline and mental toughness. He will turn eighty in January and still refuses to see a doctor for a checkup. He taught Orlando to show up on time and "look at work, not as a job, but as a way to better humanity." The octogenarian manages a McDonald's in Fayetteville, North Carolina. Finally his wife got him to work only eight hours a day and smoke fewer cigarettes.

The only major conflict Orlando had with his father erupted when he announced at the end of high school that he wouldn't fight in Vietnam if drafted.

"I fought for my country in World War II," Orlando's father yelled. "Now it's your turn." In fact, his father and five of his twelve brothers fought in the war, setting the American record for the most siblings on active duty in the armed forces during wartime. Four brothers served in the Army, one in the Navy, and another in the Air Force, in both the European and Pacific theaters.[3]

However, Orlando refused to volunteer and swore he wouldn't go if drafted. His father fumed for years afterward.

Orlando hangs up his chocolate-colored suit jacket and pants in the small closet with his collection of suits in lime, pumpkin, black, rust and satin white. These bursts of color are the battle uniforms Orlando wears to his war.

Chapter Seven

———

FROM THE FIRST DAY, Rice's teachers have been implementing Orlando's pedagogical goals for the school year.

"We're going to go over some rules and procedures again," Kate Hebinck addresses her first-period freshman English class on Friday, September 17. "When you come in, you sit down, look on the blackboard for a note under 'Agenda' and begin to work quietly."

For three days at the August teacher orientation, Orlando preached a gospel of uniform behavioral expectations for all students in all classes. To accomplish this, he demanded that during every period for the entire first week of school, teachers instruct the students on precisely what comprises the school's behavioral expectations for them.

These fall into two categories. First, there are procedures for how tasks are to be accomplished: moving quickly from one classroom to the next without interfering with other students in the hallway; quietly taking assigned seats; placing their three-ring binders and textbooks on their desks before the bell rings to start class; how to ask questions in class; and so on.

Second, there are rules articulating behavioral limits, beyond which there are disciplinary consequences. While procedures are many and rendered in minute detail, Orlando insists that rules must be few in number and stated simply and clearly. Rules revolve around issues of respect. Acting rudely toward teachers or fellow students earns an automatic detention and often a conference with Abbasse. Disrespecting the school by arriving late earns a detention, as does forgetting the proper textbook. Teachers are supposed to give one warning if the offense isn't too severe, which students find confusing. They often complain that detentions are given without warning, but as Hebinck explained, warnings carry over from the beginning of the period to the end and usually from one day to the next. She told the freshmen that they can consider themselves warned for the rest of the year about cursing in class.

To illustrate this approach at the orientation, Orlando screened four of Harry K. Wong's eight videos on effective teaching and will show the rest at the weekly faculty meetings.[1] After teaching high school for seventeen years, Wong gave classroom management workshops across the country, one of which Orlando attended almost twenty years ago. In Wong's view, discipline is best established through the repetition of standardized ways of accomplishing classroom tasks and of dealing with fellow students and the teacher. Wong emphasizes that the normal tendency for teachers is to begin the school year with course content, then battle students when they misbehave. Wong advocates teaching and re-teaching how everything gets done in the classroom during the first days of the school year before introducing significant academic work. As the procedures become routines, the uncertainties that lead to most behavior problems evaporate, along with much of the need for detentions and other disciplinary measures.

Orlando advocated Wong's method last year but it wasn't mandatory. Teachers instituted the recommendations in varying degrees, producing different and often conflicting versions in each classroom. The students were confused and understandably found it difficult to buy into the new ethos. As well, the teachers who needed the most help—new teachers and veterans with less than charismatic personalities—tended to resist this approach the most, as if following it were an admission of professional failure.

In Orlando's experience, students crave structure, especially urban youngsters who experience chaos at home and on the streets. After years in failing public schools where discipline is anathema, they literally do not know how to act as serious students. Teachers, like parents, have a duty to separate youngsters from their own negativity. In response, students often tell Orlando that the willingness of adults to establish order proves they care. Even the worst-behaved students at Catholic high schools cite discipline and structure among the top reasons they choose to attend.[2] They also reveal that their problems with compliance revolve around difficulties taking personal responsibility, rather than being expressions of teenage rebellion. Only 1 percent of the students at the nation's thirty-one African American Catholic high schools are dismissed every year for severe disciplinary infractions. It is far more common for parents to enroll youngsters in Catholic schools because of behavioral problems at their former public schools.[3]

Discipline and order have always been pedagogical cornerstones of Catholic education. Religious orders of sisters, brothers, and priests all taught in the same didactic manner and tolerated no insolence. Graduates from Rice's early decades remember how unyielding the Christian Brothers were in their demands. From a practical point of view, discipline had to be imposed since classrooms were severely overcrowded by today's standards. At Rice, there used to be over forty students sitting in the same rooms now occupied by about half that number. It might also be true that imposed discipline is an essential factor in educating lower-class children, since so many grow up in home situations where self-discipline and academic interests are not nurtured even if they are encouraged.[4]

Catholic schools lost their traditional strictness when religious teaching orders were replaced by lay staff after Vatican II, producing a more relaxed school environment. The number of brothers diminished at Rice as they retreated from the classroom teaching to administrative chores and concerned themselves more with keeping the door open than with maintaining Rice's traditional classroom environment—a task that became more difficult as greater numbers of students with deeply troubled personal lives enrolled. When Orlando arrived, he was appalled by the behavior that was tolerated at Rice. The predominantly white staff, Orlando says, had fallen into the trap of thinking that little could be demanded of inner-city African American males. To be fair, there were instructors such as Abbasse and Hearn, who established oases of structure and high expectations.

Periodic attempts to re-establish the school's former strictness, and consequent academic prowess, inevitably faltered because today's youth also need counseling. Orlando helps his students deal with underlying personal and family problems, which in turn helps them learn how to act correctly, instead of acting out. In effect, he made it cool to be well behaved, as well as smart, and provided the means to do so. Similar transitions to a more holistic approach characterize most contemporary Catholic schools and are a welcome development.

In the classroom, Orlando is more inclined to establish order by force of will and charisma. But the possession of a commanding personality can never become policy. Most teachers struggle to assert themselves, and when they fail, resort to yelling at students and giving out needless detentions.

Hebinck has strong character traits, but lacks Orlando's magnetism. She hopes the standardized rules and procedures will help her overcome the low-level chatter that distracted last year's students from her lessons. Her first step is inscribed in perfect Catholic-school script over decades-old cracks in the blackboard's slate. Underneath the heading "Agenda," Hebinck has written out several grammar exercises to train the students to automatically begin class with work instead of conversations.

Sitting right in front of Hebinck is Ephraim Yisreal, whose long legs sprawl toward her as his head sinks to the back of his chair on the one-piece chrome and plastic desk. After every question Hebinck asks, he sits up quickly to call out, "Miss! Miss!" with unrestrained enthusiasm.

"Remember that if you want to say something, if you need my attention in any way," Hebinck enunciates loudly and avoids looking directly at Ephraim, "please raise your hand. That way I can see you."

Ephraim reclines to a deep slouch again, then mumbles, "Okay." His right leg shoots out, sending an unlaced ankle boot halfway between his desk and the blackboard. Hebinck steps over the boot as she walks to her desk in the corner. She ignores Ephraim's antics but appreciates his ardor.

Before class, Ephraim sauntered into Hebinck's room with his shirttail almost completely pulled out and the top two buttons of his shirt open. Ephraim's tie hung loosely around his neck like a noose and his shoelaces trailed behind him like streamers. Hebinck told the young man to go back into the hall to pull himself together; he returned a few minutes later but only half-composed. She wondered about his state of mind.

Ephraim fears he won't be able to control himself on a consistent basis, or even remember the rules. He has a long history of behavioral problems at both public and Catholic elementary schools, and Rice allows far less leeway. According to the student handbook, it takes only four detentions to earn a suspension and three suspensions warrant expulsion. Ephraim hasn't gotten a detention yet but has received several warnings for dress code violations, calling out in class, and forgetting textbooks.

Hebinck was very curious about the four-inch, crescent-shaped scar across Ephraim's right temple. She likes his oddball personality and would much rather work with his tendency to over-engage in class than with the passivity and childish play that characterize many of his peers and sabotage her lessons. While other teachers complain about Ephraim's lack of restraint, Hebinck sees it as a positive quality that merely needs to be channeled properly, although she's not sure exactly how.

One problem she faces with all her students is "flying blind." Neither

Orlando, Abbasse, nor the guidance counselors inform teachers about a student's family situation, behavioral history, or personal issues. The administration guards confidentiality, which means that students spend most of their time with teachers who know little about their problems, yet the teachers are expected to deal effectively with their behavior. Further, Rice is not a neighborhood school where students know each other from childhood and might volunteer information about classmates. Rice draws mostly from Harlem, Washington Heights, and the South Bronx, an area with about 1.5 million residents, and a wide range of elementary and regional junior high schools. Few freshmen attended the same junior high school as their classmates.

Hebinck turns her students' attention to the mystery of apostrophes, as revealed in the column of words she inscribed on the blackboard, illustrating singular and plural possessives. Halfway through the list, Ephraim suddenly lets out a loud cough that Abbasse hears from the hallway. The dean spends a significant portion of every period touring the school to monitor student behavior. Abbasse steps into the doorway to see Ephraim cough again, and watches as Ephraim bends his neck over so far between his legs that his nose almost touches the floor. Ephraim rears his head, bringing himself almost to an erect position before collapsing into another foghorn cough. The rasps send his peers into unrestrained laughter.

"Sorry, Miss," he says with a sheepish smile when he finally catches his breath. Several teachers had told Abbasse about Ephraim's cough, and he makes a mental note to call the boy's mother.

———

Fifteen minutes into the first lunch period on the following Tuesday, September 21, Abbasse's roar parts the waves of noise in the cafeteria. As the dean of students, he supervises the freshman and senior lunch, and then the sophomore and junior lunch during the following period. About a third of the freshmen and several seniors stand in line waiting to buy lunch. Four women—friends and employees of Olivene Browne, the eleventh- and twelfth-grade math teacher, who also supervises food preparation—dish out the day's hot meal of meatloaf with mashed potatoes and kernel corn, for the usual three dollars. All the students take lunch in the cafeteria since they're not allowed to leave the building until the end of the day.

"Sit down now and be quiet," Abbasse booms again at the freshmen around the rows of banquet tables nearest the kitchen. In accordance with the Rice pecking order, the freshmen eat at the least desirable tables, and the seniors take the tables closest to the windows that open onto 124th Street. The seniors also claim an adjacent raised platform with its couch and chairs, and hold court.

Moments earlier, Abbasse was talking with a teacher on the other side of the room. His well-conditioned peripheral vision detected ninth graders throwing bits of garbage and crumpled paper at the half-dozen classmates who work the clean-up crew in exchange for a free lunch. Every day, students who can't afford to eat make a point of arriving early in the morning to be the first to ask Abbasse for a clean-up job and lunch pass.

Abbasse seldom raises his voice to conduct a group lesson. Normally his presence is enough to command a reasonable adherence to behavioral protocols. He doesn't expect perfection, but has no tolerance for students embarrassing less fortunate classmates.

Troublemakers attract Abbasse's personal attention, often in the form of a practical joke. After hearing about Prince's clowning around from several teachers, for example, Abbasse asked him to take a note to John Shea's classroom on the seventh floor during lunch yesterday. Prince climbed the stairs and delivered the message, which Shea read, made several notations on, then asked Prince to return the note to Abbasse. When Prince arrived back downstairs, Abbasse studied the note as if Shea had sent him a state secret. He jotted several sentences on the piece of paper, folded it back up and asked Prince to get it back to Shea right away. Fifteen minutes later when a winded Prince was asked to make his fourth trip, he caught on. Abbasse guffawed as Prince opened the note to discover that it was covered with indecipherable scribbling. Abbasse winked and walked away, leaving Prince to ponder the prank's meaning.

"Don't mess with me," Prince called out.

"Exactly the point," Abbasse replied.

A dance has developed between Abbasse and Prince, because Abbasse genuinely likes the freshman and wants him to succeed. The dean singles Prince out for jibes and jokes that the freshman responds to good-naturedly.

After dealing with the students who mocked the clean-up crew today, Abbasse surveys a more civil cafeteria. Ricky Rodriguez scoots under his chin on the way to the vending machines. Abbasse spots a beeper hanging from the young man's belt. Ricky senses the dean's radar pinging him from behind and tries to slip the beeper into his pocket.

"Mr. Rodriguez, you can't wear that here," Abbasse says, stopping Ricky in mid-stride.

"But I needs it. I might have to pick up my sister from school. My Moms gonna beep me," Ricky explains rapid-fire. On his way to school from the Gun Hill area of the Bronx, Ricky walks his ten-year-old half-sister to his aunt's apartment, and later the aunt takes Stephanie to the local public school. Ricky's mother usually picks her daughter up after school, but sometimes doesn't finish her shift at a Spanish-speaking diner in the Bronx on time, and calls Ricky.

"You know beepers aren't permitted in the building," Abbasse shakes his head as he replied. "At least be a man and stand up for your convictions, instead of trying to hide the beeper."

"Oh, man, but my Moms," Ricky protests.

"She can call the school," Abbasse says.

"That's not fair," Ricky yells.

"C'mon. Hand it over then," Abbasse barks, exceeding his daily quota of patience for trouble from students.

"What?" Ricky whines and clicks his tongue.

"Hand it over now, then go sit on the bench in the foyer," Abbasse commands, sending Ricky to Rice's penalty box. "Cool down and we'll talk about it."

Beepers and cell phones are useful ways for parents to track and communicate with their children. Unfortunately drug dealers make optimal use of the same technology. Perhaps more importantly, the ban on beepers and cell phones helps keep the students focused on schoolwork, rather than fielding calls from girlfriends. Abbasse usually confiscates the devices for the day. Students are allowed to carry them in their book bags, as long as they are turned off and kept out of sight.

"If you weren't trying to be so slick, I'd give it back to you right now," Abbasse tells Ricky in the foyer at the end of lunch.

"Peoples gonna get hurt if they gets in my way," Ricky threatens. "I mean business. I hurt peoples at my old school."

"Yeah, right," Abbasse scowls since he is almost twice the freshman's size. Abbasse gave Ricky his first detention, then booked an appointment to talk afterward, since the freshman was giving off warning signals.

—————

Two days later, on Thursday, September 23, Abbasse approaches Dr. Saad's Earth science class as the period begins. Ricky is dutifully copying the Agenda question from the blackboard at his desk in the middle of the room. Most of his classmates ignore the soft-spoken teacher and keep talking.

Dr. Saad stands tall and thin, with a trimmed beard framing his bony features. As always, he wears a suit, which accords with his formal manner and the fact that he's the only staff member to have earned a Ph.D. The ninth graders, however, have only a vague inkling of what a doctorate degree is. Instead of giving Dr. Saad the respect that children in his native Sudan would normally offer, they take advantage of his inability to impose order.

Abbasse stands in the doorway for several minutes until the room quiets as students take notice. Abbasse calls three by name, telling them to turn around, face the teacher, and stop chatting. Several times a period, especially at the beginning of the year, Abbasse monitors every classroom in the school—a significant physical demand on a man his size, considering that he walks the hallways on all seven floors and mounts the stairs, both up and down. "I walk by and poke my head into problem classes," he explained later. "Nine-tenths of the battle as the dean of students is letting the kids know you are there, and they check themselves. Then you're left with only the problem students to deal with." This early in the year, Abbasse looks for the patterns that will help him determine which students and combinations of students create disturbances, and which teachers are having trouble. "I try to defuse situations before they become a problem. Teachers get to know I'll show up, so they feel a comfort zone and the kids feel the same way. They like to know they can push the envelope a little but get checked before getting into serious trouble. Most don't want to become hard core."

This is Dr. Saad's second year, but Abbasse sees no improvement in his classroom management skills. It's a common problem among African- and Caribbean-born teachers, since they grew up in societies where teachers are treated with reverence. Their first years at Rice tend to be difficult and few remain long.

As Abbasse leaves to continue his classroom tour, all the freshmen are taking notes, or at least pretending to do so, and Dr. Saad resumes his monologue about the anatomy of a cell. Ricky Rodriguez turns a page in his three-ring binder and continues to write.

Durrell Holford, a muscular youngster who sits across the aisle, watches Ricky for several minutes. He reaches over to flip the cover of Ricky's binder onto his writing hand.

"Yo, stop that," Ricky snaps at him and sucks his teeth.

A sarcastic smile wrinkles Durrell's rough-hewn features. He hunches over in his seat and pretends to work. Two minutes later, he hits Ricky's binder again.

"Motherff . . . !" Ricky mutters. "Don't do that. I hurt you."

"Yeah? I smack you good, son," Durrell fires back.

Durrell's challenge reminds Ricky of his first days at middle school in the Bronx when bigger students tried to push him around. After lunch one day, an upperclassman grabbed Ricky's baseball cap as he walked to his locker.

"I'm the hallway monitor," the larger boy said, "I'm gonna keep you' hat and you can't take it from me, yo."

Ricky pushed the boy and as they scuffled, he snatched back his hat. Students in nearby classrooms heard the noise and ran into the hall. Ricky looked up and saw "mad people itchin' to see a fight." Ricky's assailant swung at him and missed as Ricky ducked, countering with an uppercut. The boy went down hard, establishing Ricky's reputation and making him instantly popular. Afterward, the dynamics of "popular" and "tough" intrigued Ricky. He observed how his classmates wore baggy clothing, talked back to teachers, refused to do homework, broke school windows, and beat up weaklings as ways of intimidating their peers and gaining adulation. Ricky focused on maintaining his own "rep" and hung out with the cool kids. Then during Christmas vacation of his eighth grade year, he realized that despite the sacrifices his single mother was making to provide for him, he was heading nowhere—or worse—with his friends. He decided to change his behavior and "make my Moms proud."

Ricky was born in Santo Domingo, one of several children his father sired in different liaisons. Ricky's parents separated shortly after his birth without marrying. When Ricky turned four, his mother immigrated to the Bronx, leaving her son with his grandparents while she worked in a restaurant and saved money to send for him. Four years later, without seeing his mother once, Ricky finally joined her here. He spent the next year at home, missing school since his mother believed they needed to get to know each other again. The following year, Ricky was assessed at the fourth grade level at P.S. 41, his local public school, even though he had completed the grade back home. Ricky is still angry that he fell two years behind (although he's only fourteen) and very disappointed that the bilingual program he was forced into prevented him from catching up.

In addition to the pressure Ricky feels because of his academic shortcomings, he has to keep his grades up and stay out of trouble to maintain his privately funded voucher. After Christmas in the eighth grade, Ricky started doing his homework. Since he'd always treated his teachers with respect, they offered additional tutoring. When Ricky's marks improved, his science teacher took him aside to recommend he apply for a privately funded voucher from the Student Sponsor Partners (SSP) program to go to Catholic school.

"She told me I was smart and if I stayed in public school, I would get my head mixed up," Ricky recalls later. "She said at Catholic school, I could get away from the girls, get more work done, and maybe win a scholarship for college."

Ricky was accepted into SSP, but if he fails out of Rice, there's no guarantee he'll be given a second chance at another parochial school. Ricky's mother, a single parent with two children who earns about two hundred dollars a week as a waitress, certainly can't afford tuition. By Dominican standards, Ricky's father is considered affluent, but he sends very little money.

Ricky promised himself to walk away from conflicts at Rice, so he wouldn't end up getting kicked out. But from the first day of school, Ricky's intensity and diminutive size have attracted challenges. He's muscular enough to be considered a worthy opponent and short enough to inspire confidence in adversaries. Several students regularly give Ricky a shove or call him a name, hoping he'll react.

Durrell reaches over and flips Ricky's binder shut again, adding an insult: "You ugly."

"Shut up before I hurt you," Ricky blurts out. "You stupid!"

Durrell stands up and turns his broad shoulders toward Ricky, swaggering across the aisle, confident he can flatten him. Ricky's street instincts wind up like a spring. A calmer voice inside reminds him that he'll be expelled if he gets into a fistfight. He pictures the look of disappointment on his mother's face, but Durrell's smirk slaps him hard.

"Okay, let's fight," Ricky yells as he jumps to his feet.

"Let's do it," Durrell shouts back.

"Ricky and Durrell," Abbasse calls from the hallway. "Get out here."

Abbasse heard their squabble shortly after returning to his office across the hall, then arrived in time to prevent a serious incident. He reprimands both boys and sends them to see Father Sam Taylor, the tenth grade guidance counselor. Abbasse feels they need to talk to an older male, rather than with Mrs. Eunice Lewis, their ninth grade counselor, about fighting. Father Taylor meets them on the stairwell on his way down. He sits Ricky on the steps and asks him why he's getting into trouble so early in the year. Ricky blames Durrell, but Father Taylor points out that he didn't have to respond. Ricky thinks about it and agrees, but complains that Abbasse's punishment is too severe. Ricky is banned from playing the next five games of the base-ball season, the only ones remaining until spring.

"Why's Abbasse on my back?" Ricky mutters to himself while Father Tay-lor talks with Durrell. "Why can't he leave me alone and give me space? I'm trying to do well."

Later at 3:15 P.M., Abbasse dismisses the two students from detention, which consisted of standing quietly in the cafeteria for forty-five minutes. He tells Ricky and Durrell to meet him upstairs. Abbasse keeps an orga-nized filing system with every student's family history and the details of every detention given for behavioral reasons—but only in his mind. His of-fice is pure contrast. Papers are piled like haystacks on his desk. Behind his chair, yellowing documents seem to be in the process of escaping from a World War II–issue filing cabinet. Along the opposite wall, cardboard lost-and-found bins overflow with shoes and clothing.

After Abbasse speaks with Durrell, Ricky marches into his office to say he wants to transfer to another school. "Peoples gonna get hurt if I stays here," he seethes.

"Cut the crap, Ricky," Abbasse counters. "You're looking up at most of the students here."

Ricky recounts several fights at his junior high school where he beat up bigger boys.

"How much bigger?" Abbasse asks.

"I don't trust nobody," Ricky shoots back. His neck muscles look like steel cables and his skin turns an intoxicating burgundy. "I'm going to put somebody in the hospital."

"One more word," Abbasse warns.

"Just kick me out!" Ricky jumps up and screams. "A'ight. Just kick me out!"

Abbasse leans forward to tell Ricky to sit down. According to the street code that socialized the youngster, a man never backs down—an ethos that often escalates minor conflicts into violent confrontations. Worse, Ricky's temper is acting like an accelerant on its own.

"I can't deal with this place, man," Ricky says. "You always on my back, yo."

"I'm trying to get you to follow the rules," Abbasse explains warmly, trying to turn the confrontation into a conversation. "Every place has rules, Ricky."

"This school gots too many," Ricky exclaims.

"The National Baseball League has a whole book full," Abbasse reminds him. "How are you ever going to make it to the pros?"

"I don't care, yo," Ricky answers, then switches to Standard English to articulate with precision. "I'm used to being myself at public school. There were girls there, and I didn't have to worry about getting a 70, or rules about behavior and dress code. We have to talk a certain way at Rice. Damn, we have to watch out for the N-word and be on time. There I could show up when I wanted and say whatever. At Rice, there's demands every minute and I don't know how to handle them all."

"You can do it, Ricky," Abbasse assures him.

Ricky stares at the floor for a long moment and then says, "Nobody cares about me."

Abbasse asks Ricky about his relationship with his mother. The young man says she's very strict and is keeping him on a virtual lockdown after school. Like many single mothers in high crime neighborhoods, she's afraid Ricky will get involved with gangs or with girls. Ricky bucks her restrictions but acknowledges that she's also the only person he trusts.

Then he talks about his father, who lives in the Dominican Republic and makes promises to call or visit his son but never does.

Abbasse listens quietly. He reached the same conclusion as Orlando that the missing father's legacy fuels most behavioral problems and that it is almost impossible to get an estranged father to deal properly with his son.

"Nobody loves me," Ricky blurts out, then seems to deflate as the last of his emotional energy dissipates.

Abbasse gives Ricky a minute to recover, then counsels him on how to get emotional distance on his inner dynamics, so he can maintain control in a crisis, which he warns will recur often as long as Ricky reacts so easily.

"You can walk away if someone confronts you; you can tell a teacher," Abbasse reminds him. "You can come and get me or Mr. Gober."

Ricky nods.

"You have to rein in your temper, or you're not going to get anywhere in life, especially not at Rice High School," Abbasse speaks slowly, letting the words sink in. Abbasse points out that the rules are not arbitrary but instead protect students from each other, and enable them to graduate high school and go on to college.

"So that's the point of Catholic school," Ricky says.

"Bingo," Abbasse leans back in his chair, feeling optimistic about Ricky's future for the first time since the beeper incident.

"It's mad different from public school," Ricky says, holding his head in his hands and pondering. "There I could get away with everything."

"That's the problem most freshmen have."

"Now I understand," Ricky nods, "but it's so boring, yo."

"Why?" Abbasse challenges. "Do you think learning is boring?"

"Yes. Well, no," Ricky answers, then thinks about how eager all the teachers are to help him with his schoolwork. He decides against transferring, knowing that few boys like him graduate from his neighborhood public high school and go on to college—and now he knows why.

Abbasse repeats that if any student swings at another and connects, whether at Rice or elsewhere, even if the other student initiated the confrontation, he would be expelled. "Ricky, you'd have a hard time getting into another Catholic school, and you'd lose your voucher."

Ricky thanks Abbasse and heads home, realizing that the dean was not "on his back" out of spite but to prevent him from making an irrevocable mistake. Previously Ricky always saw himself forging his own path. Not only was he essentially fatherless, but he had no older male role model. Ricky's mother doesn't speak English and seldom ventures outside Hispanic areas of the Bronx. She wants him to go to college and become a professional, but she can offer little guidance about how to negotiate the obstacles in his path. But now, an older male in the person of the dean offers counsel that Ricky values. He is still smarting from the loss of the rest of the baseball season, but accepts it and the idea that misbehavior warrants consequences.

Abbasse exhales with relief as Ricky leaves. The dean finds the young man's intensity taxing, but he is pleased at the outcome of the meeting. "Having the guys come to my office to talk about problems over the last few years has helped calm the school down. When I started teaching here a decade ago, there were a lot of tough kids since Rice had become 'the school of last resort' for a student who couldn't get into any other Catholic school."

Together, white and black flight had cut Rice's population to less than half, and admission requirements had been lowered to keep the school open. Increasingly Rice students came from poor, single-parent families in Harlem and the South Bronx, and they tended to have more academic and behavioral problems. At the same time, the better-qualified minority students attended the many public high schools that into the mid-1980s were still a viable option. Rice became a catchall for troubled young men with little interest in academics. Fights were commonplace, and the smell of marijuana lingered in stairwells. The neighborhood around Rice was also disintegrating, and only a determined effort by the Brothers kept the school open.

The graduation rate was still over 90 percent during these difficult years. Certainly, academic and behavioral standards were lower, but the students met the state's requirements, and there were no severe beatings, knifings, or shootings. Fights were broken up quickly, and there were never any weapons involved. Rice's basketball program became one of the best in the country, sending many young men to Division I colleges on athletic scholarship.

However, the school was definitely on a downward spiral until Orlando arrived. As Abbasse observed, "This year's troublemakers and last year's are immature, in contrast to the near-thugs we used to deal with."

———

Abbasse stands up to leave and then remembers how oddly Ephraim Yisreal has been acting in class. Abbasse phones Ephraim's mother, Vicki Williams, and talks with Marvin Smith, her common-law husband, as well. Both display a genuine interest in helping Ephraim succeed at Rice. Marvin isn't the father of any of Vicki's three children, but he's been working on establishing close relationships with the two still living at home. Parental support is crucial, in Abbasse's view. If he can call an adult in charge at home to reinforce what he's trying to accomplish at school, he feels there's hope. If not, Abbasse is inclined to follow the disciplinary process more strictly and expel a student according to Rice handbook protocol.

Just before Ephraim was born in 1984, his natural father, who was married to and living with Ephraim's mother, joined a Moorish Jewish congregation in Harlem. Vicki converted shortly afterward to what she describes as an African version of Judaism. When Ephraim was born, Vicki chose his name from the Old Testament and wrote an eccentric spelling of the name of the Hebrew nation for his surname on his birth records at the hospital. Ephraim's younger sister, born the next year, was given the name Geburah Yisreal. Vicki says the hospital staff should never have allowed her to choose "Yisreal" as a legal surname, but it was processed without incident.

Last January, Vicky received a phone call from Ephraim's school in the Bronx. She expected to hear about another behavioral incident. Instead, she was told that her son had just suffered a grand mal seizure in class. Without warning, Ephraim had slipped from his desk and begun shaking uncontrollably on the floor. His classmates watched in horror as foam oozed from his mouth and his eyes rolled up, exposing the whites in what looked like a death stare. Paramedics rushed Ephraim to the hospital in time to save his life. A CAT scan revealed that Ephraim was suffering from a genetic condition that causes clogging in the blood vessels that supply oxygen to the frontal lobe.

Looking back, Ephraim's mother remembered how often her son inexplicably banged into walls as a child or fell down as if he were drunk. In fact, the youngster was bruised so often his teachers and family friends suspected that Vicki was abusing him. By three years of age, Ephraim could make talking sounds but formed few words, let alone complete sentences. His mother took him for speech therapy, where Ephraim made significant progress, yet by kindergarten at the local public school, his verbal skills still lagged behind those of his classmates. An evaluation process at the end of his first-grade year recommended that Ephraim be placed in a special education classroom. Vicki refused, knowing well that special education is urban public education's "black hole," especially for minority boys with minor learning disabilities and behavioral problems. Only about 12 percent of the city's special education students graduate with either a local or Regents diploma. A local diploma entails passing all the required Regents exams with a grade of 55 to 64, while a Regents diploma demands 65 or better. For students contemplating a competitive college, a Regents diploma is usually required, but a shockingly low 0.004 percent of special education students earn one.[5]

Reacting immediately, Vicki took Ephraim out of public school and enrolled him at St. Aloysius in Harlem for second grade. The youngster's conversational skills and reading comprehension improved significantly, but he often misbehaved in class. His outbursts pointed to an emotional festering, the source of which Vicki knew only too well. Shortly after Ephraim's sister was born, their father abandoned the family and has maintained only sporadic contact with his children since then. Worse, he would make promises to come by and take his children to the zoo or to buy them sneakers, then not show up. In class at St. Aloysius, Ephraim acted out his rage every time his father reneged on a pledge. Vicki had to put Ephraim back into public school for several years where his behavior deteriorated, and finally he failed the seventh grade. Vicki transferred him back to Catholic school, this time to Our Lady of Mercy in the Bronx, where he lasted only a year, and then moved him to St. Augustine for the eighth grade. Catholic schools often ask students to leave, but unless their behavioral problems involve drugs or weapons, arrangements are usually made to transfer the youngster to another Catholic school. This practice allows the child a new start, and since it usually works, lets Catholic schools claim a lower expulsion rate than public schools.

The year at St. Augustine's passed without serious incident until the seizure sent Ephraim to the hospital in January. Within days of beginning treatment, Ephraim's hypersensitivity to his medication precipitated an autoimmune reaction known as Stevens-Johnson Syndrome, which manifests as skin lesions and severe inflammation. Ephraim's skin turned shades of maroon as a rash covered most of his body. All his joints began to swell and his face puffed up. Ephraim was put on oxygen and fed intravenously, as internal swelling made breathing and swallowing very difficult. By early March, Ephraim's condition became chronic, and he descended into delirium.

One feverish night, Ephraim had a vision in which he stood on the rooftop of an anonymous apartment building in a public housing project looking at dark clouds racing across a starless sky. A voice, somehow both all around and passing through him, said, "I am not ready for you yet." Later, Ephraim told his mother that these were the words of God, which surprised her since Ephraim never talked about his dreams or religion. Ephraim's fever abated suddenly; his skin turned back to its usual shade of milk chocolate, and his limbs shrank down to normal size. Then just after Memorial Day, surgeons opened his skull to repair the ailing blood vessels, leaving the large scar on his temple. Although Ephraim was supposed to attend Rice's summer program, he had to stay home to recuperate. He also had to start a regimen of antiseizure medications.

Abbasse hangs up and makes a note to talk to Ephraim's teachers about giving him leeway. He'll also explain that Ephraim's loud coughing fits began in childhood, starting not coincidentally right after Ephraim's father left the family.

As Abbasse made his calls, it became obvious how far Rice extends beyond its walls. Although Abbasse is chiefly responsible for ensuring that negative street influences don't infiltrate beyond Rice's front door, like Orlando he is deeply engaged with students' personal and academic problems, which means reaching out to family members and sometimes to pastors or coaches at leagues outside Rice. There are also consultations with the Student Sponsor Partners program and other sponsors who act as mentors, and with parole officers and lawyers when a student gets into trouble—albeit rarely—and with girlfriends who become pregnant or whose involvement jeopardizes a student's academic career.

At 5 P.M., after several more phone calls to the parents of students with behavior issues, Abbasse leaves his office feeling satisfied with the school year's beginning. So far he has seen more cohesion among the faculty as the application of standard procedures establishes common practices and a common language, presenting the teachers as a united front. The new teachers seem less lost than in previous years, and behavioral infractions are both less egregious and fewer than he expected given the larger number of students.

Abbasse lumbers down the hall to the elevator, and five minutes later catches a cab to the Aviation Bar on Third Avenue and East 92nd Street where he joins several Rice teachers, including DiMattia, Hearn, and Ed Flood, a global science teacher who's starting his thirty-seventh year at Rice. They talk about surviving the year's first dose of school, but mostly perform the Catholic ritual Abbasse knows best: seeking absolution in oblivion.

Chapter Eight

———

THE GIRLS LINE UP FOUR deep from Rice's front door around the corner and down Lenox Avenue to 123rd Street. It is 7:45 P.M. on Saturday, October 2, and the first Rice Jam is jammed. Many more teenage girls are queuing up than can be accommodated. Edgardo (Ed) Marrero, Rice's public relations officer, stands on the front steps with a bullhorn, as beads of sweat dapple his fleshy face. He says that two thousand young women surround the building, and imagines a riot. Already the cafeteria is three-quarters full, and Orlando will halt admission as soon as the room reaches its maximum.

Parents still pull up and discharge their daughters from late-model cars and SUVs. One mother yells that she'll be back at 11:30 P.M. to pick up her teen. "Rice has the best dance," another girl from Cathedral High School in Manhattan says as she approaches the line. Her expression changes as she rounds the corner and looks down Lenox.

Several police officers from the local 23rd precinct, including Officer Duane Lee (who graduated from Rice in 1988), stand on the street. They set up barricades earlier to help keep the crowd confined to the sidewalk. During the week, Rice is Officer Lee's beat. He hangs out with the students in the cafeteria, library, and gym, and also volunteers as an assistant coach for the junior varsity basketball team. Tonight he can't believe the number of teenage girls but doesn't foresee any disturbances. He estimates close to seven hundred young ladies and predicts that the approaching thunderstorm will disperse those still outside after the doors close.

Rice Jams have become famous among minority girls at Catholic high schools in Manhattan, the Bronx, and Brooklyn. A whisper would have attracted enough young women to the year's first Jam, but the seniors on the dance committee felt insecure about their public relations abilities and so promoted the dance at public schools as well. Tonight, they're too giddy from watching their efforts prove successful to feel sorry that the majority of the girls who bought tickets won't be allowed in.

For the young ladies, the Jam offers a chance to meet a Rice Man— maybe even a star basketball player. A young lady might land a boyfriend who's going to college someday. At least, the young man will have enough money to actually take a girl out, so the young ladies believe, since his family can afford to pay tuition. And if romance doesn't blossom, Rice Jams certainly deliver temptation.

Orlando sees the dances as an integral part of the school's culture. "Only the Rice brothers can get in so they feel special. The 'only-us' thing gives them a sense of camaraderie," Orlando says. "The Jams also show the regard Rice has for its students. Most schools won't do them anymore, but we respect the fact that they are young people who want to have a good time. We give them a safe environment where they won't be hustled, or get held up or knifed."

All week, however, Orlando has been feeling "uneasy in my spirit for the first time about a Rice Jam." He worries that one of the freshmen troublemakers will do "something stupid like start a fight." When Orlando first came to Rice, a student was caught with alcohol at a dance, but this has been the only incident during his tenure so far. The students know the principal would cancel the next Jam if contraband was found. But storm clouds have gathered on Orlando's intuitive landscape and he quakes.

On Friday, Orlando ended the morning announcements saying "all the young men who show poor behavior or inappropriate dancing at tomorrow night's dance will be removed and barred from all future Rice Jams." Ephraim hears the principal's warning and rolls his eyes like cue balls since he's already lost the right to go. Ephraim and several other freshmen have enough detentions that the next one earns a suspension. Hoping to avoid upping the disciplinary ante so early in the school year, Abbasse instituted Saturday morning detentions for repeat offenders, which won't count toward a suspension but are designed to make an impression. The young men will spend tomorrow morning cleaning up a vacant lot across the street from the school, and they are banned from future Rice Jams until their behavior improves.

Since the front doors opened half an hour ago, Orlando has been standing by the entrance to the library in the foyer watching the mothers on the hospitality committee hang up the girls' jackets and sweaters on portable racks in the school's foyer. Once inside, the young ladies peel off outer layers to reveal their budding femininity, seemingly oblivious to any sense of propriety. The mothers smile pleasantly and shake their heads. Orlando commissioned Marrero to deal with the crush of females outside and made sure the dance committee would greet the girls once they were inside the building to direct them to the cafeteria. Orlando turns and pads his way into the library, where he assigned himself the job of watching over the coats belonging to Rice students.

Orlando wears a Kelly-green nylon gym suit with Rice High School stitched over his heart. He paces the room and responds in gruff monotones when students come to retrieve a do-rag from a coat pocket or drop off a sweater. When not in the spotlight, Orlando's personality tends to retreat inward, turning pensive and shy. Tonight, he also feels tired, his legs ache, and his feet are sore. Tomorrow he resolves to take time to soak his feet.

Ten minutes later, Orlando reluctantly checks out the cafeteria. As soon as he steps past the coat racks in the foyer, teenage girls surround him on all sides talking loudly and taking no notice of the power of his presence with the boys. Orlando seems to hold his breath as an alien wave of femininity carries him toward the dancing. He passes Kawone Williams, who stands at the entrance leading to the cafeteria, and nods at the senior as if calling for a life jacket.

"Hi, great to see you," Kawone pays no notice to his principal's discomfort. He focuses on a tall, shapely girl behind Orlando. Her eyes seem to turn on at Kawone's greeting, and her hips swing more aggressively. She slinks past him as her lips wrinkle in an alluring but silent answer.

Kawone is acting as the main host tonight and "talks up" the young women as they enter the dance floor. Another girl approaches with a backless tank top that might have been spray-painted over her breasts.

"Yo, go home and put on some clothes," Kawone yells.

She stares straight ahead as Kawone launches additional playful barbs.

Kawone wears a white do-rag and a hooded sweatshirt over black semi-baggy jeans. He insisted that all the dance committee members wear hoodies so they could recognize each other at a distance. Rice Men are excused from the school dress code for the evening, but hooded sweatshirts are always banned, since they're considered gang gear, except for the dance committee. Many of the young men sport baseball caps, mostly on backward. The majority of boys have tied do-rags under their caps in spite of the humidity. Most are garbed in long, loose T-shirts hanging over baggy pants, which flop over loosely tied boots. Many wear earrings and gold chains around their necks. Most boys have spent weeks assembling a personal version of urban battle attire for the evening.

Kawone flashes a smile as another young lady, wearing pants so tight she can hardly flex her knees, passes by. Kawone is enjoying his high from the Jam's popularity because it will make Rice's unofficial record book, of which he is the custodian. Kawone's older brother came home after every Jam during his four years at Rice, climbed into the bunk above Kawone, and recounted the evening. Kawone knows exactly how popular every dance has been since 1993 and can rank tonight's event with authority.

After enjoying, or enduring, Kawone's salutations, the young ladies saunter, strut, and slink into the cafeteria. Several steps inside, the room darkens toward pitch-black, and silhouettes roil in waves to hip-hop's relentless rhythms. Faces bob eerily in the half-dozen puddles of violet light around the cafeteria. Onyxx Echeverria, the student council president, installed dark fluorescent tubes, trying to recreate a dance club atmosphere. Onyxx counted on the girls wearing light-colored outfits, through which every detail of their lithe figures radiates, as the dancing makes them perspire.

Orlando wades into the umbrage. Linwood Sessoms brushes by in pursuit of a tall, well-proportioned girl. The senior draws near and coos: "Hey babe . . . how you doin'? You look great." Linwood continues his sales pitch to the point where he usually asks for a phone number, but she turns suddenly and heads to the ladies' room. Linwood keeps talking as he follows, almost getting through the door before a chaperone, one of the grandmothers, jumps up to grab his arm. Linwood retreats with a so-what? look. He's the only male in a household of women but doesn't bother explaining. He steps aside and waits for another chance to add to the list of phone numbers he'll show off later to his peeps.

A new rap song pounds through the loudspeakers in percussive thrashings. Clusters of girls dance together as Rice sophomores snake through their groupings single-file, dancing, shaking, and hopping up and down. Meanwhile dozens of Rice Men pair off with new female acquaintances and begin to dance, seemingly morphing into Siamese twins. Other couples retreat into the dark along the walls where Orlando does most of his patrolling. The principal interrupts one groping duo after another with insistent taps on his boys' shoulders and a litany of "Cool it!" and "Break it up!" Several times, he almost slips on a greasy film from the night's humidity and the sweaty spray of four hundred gyrating bodies.

In the middle of the cafeteria, a freshman swivels his shoulders and hips as he closes in on a shapely, cherub-faced girl in tight jeans and even tighter tank top. A laser-quick look from the boy meets an eye flicker from the girl and she edges toward him. The bass pounds from bulky speakers and male voices howl, "Spank the nigga'," followed by a syllabic gyre, then again: "Spank the nigga' . . . Spank the nigga' . . ."

The boy slips behind the girl as he brushes the tail of his white do-rag from his shoulder. The girl bends over, keeping her knees straight, and sways gently.

"Spank the nigga' . . ."

The boy presses his crotch into the girl's buttocks, and they twist and churn with increasing vigor.

"Spank the nigga' . . . Spank . . ."

His fingers dig into her pelvic bone, and his head rolls back drinking in the MTV-style romance. With the last "spank," the young couple disentangles, then they walk away from each other without exchanging a word, or even a look. As the next song begins, the young lady looks bored, standing beside her girlfriends, while the boy grooves on with his classmates. Within minutes, they are both engaged in the same impersonal ritual with other partners.

Brother Bill Sherlog comes to the cafeteria entrance and peers into the gloom. Instead of his usual black cassock, he's wearing white chinos and a white golf shirt. With his brush-cut, boyish face and diminutive frame, he looks like a high school student—from the 1950s. He walks ten feet into the crowd and catches the attention of a junior who is churning at a young girl's posterior. Brother Sherlog sighs deeply, then walks another ten feet into what, for him, is a shrouded nightmare. Five minutes later, he retreats to the relative calm of the entranceway where Brother James DePiro, in his first year at Rice as a math and religion teacher, rolls his eyes at his peer. Both brothers are in their late thirties and recall a very different experience as teenagers.

Brother DePiro takes a deep breath before diving into the crowd where he catches sight of Shagari's immense silhouette grinding genitals with one of the shortest girls at the dance. Brother DePiro suppresses a painful laugh. One moment it looks like Shagari might drive the young lady through the floor, then he picks her up and almost sticks the girl on the ceiling. Brother

DePiro slips out of the cafeteria moments later and flees back to the Brothers' residence for the rest of the evening, while Brother Sherlog remains to monitor for the rest of the Jam.

Brother Walderman never ventures near the Rice Jams, instead leaving the building for the entire soirée. He has expressed his dismay to Orlando, but hasn't demanded drastic changes—yet. In the view of Al Widziewicz, the seniors' guidance counselor, the Christian Brothers have always been more brotherly than patriarchal as an order. As such, they are open to outside influences, such as Orlando's, and gain the benefits. But they are also vulnerable to his excesses and in this case, his surprising timidity in the face of pop culture's excesses.

For the most part, it's the ninth and tenth graders who do the dancing. "They don't have any inhibitions, and it's the freshmen's first high school party," Kawone says later. "They don't care what you think of them. But we have standards and peer pressure; we have reps. We're putting it on, so we just hang back and chill."

Orlando readily admits he doesn't like the way his boys dance but says the way they carry on at commercial dance halls and private parties is even worse. He knowingly allows what the brothers, parents, and outsiders would consider shocking behavior. It is a concession he believes he has to make to the deeply eroticized pop culture in which his students have been steeped since childhood. They are subjected to an overwhelming amount of sexuality in music videos, TV shows, movies, and advertising, with little parental supervision. It is hardly surprising that sex at parties is both common and casual, and that the girls often act as aggressively as the boys. Orlando has at least four teachers on duty to prevent mock intercourse from actualizing, which he believes is the best he can do, without making sexuality instead of academics his prime focus.

"At outside parties," Orlando explains, "they're smoking weed and drinking beer or liquor, then having sex in the corner. Young people need to socialize and here they have a good time. Sometimes they get carried away, but we stop them from going too far, and I don't want to alienate them from Rice."

Even so, the dancing is antithetical to official Church teachings. Beginning in the nineteenth century, Catholic school students received their primary instruction in faith and morals by reading and memorizing the Baltimore Catechism. Nothing is clearer than the imperative that sexual foreplay and intercourse are reserved for marriage, and that sexual misconduct, as any sin, must be avoided in "thought, word, deed."[1] Few Catholics actually believe these teachings anymore, and sexual mores are no longer taught with the same ferocity as when the nuns were in charge. An even laxer version is now common at schools with predominately non-Catholic students, where the focus is on preventing pregnancies and sexually transmitted diseases.

Orlando adds that he doesn't know how to gauge student behavior in Catholic terms and has no idea what a "Catholic environment" is anymore. However, neither does anyone else. The Church refuses to deal with modern sexuality and so neither justifies its conservative stance convincingly nor offers a comprehensive alternative. Catholic educators are more inclined to pay lip service to Church teachings, while conveying a far more secular view in their actions and attitudes.

"I could stop the dances and it wouldn't bother me at all," Orlando maintains. "It's not that I'm compromising, but over time, I'm getting tougher on the music they play and on their behavior." He spends too little time inside the cafeteria to effectively monitor the Jam himself, instead delegating most of the policing to the seniors. "They would take a kid who brought booze or was undressing a girl outside and smack him around. They're very protective and know the Jams are a privilege, not a right."

The Rice Jams generate about eight thousand dollars in revenue every year, an attractive incentive to keep them going. A quarter of the receipts go toward the school's operating expenses. Orlando uses the rest to help finance incentive programs and student activities. For example, the proceeds from the spring Jam pay for a significant portion of the senior prom.

Meanwhile, Orlando walks around the cafeteria's periphery, peering into the darkest corners to make sure none of the couples are misbehaving. After another chorus of "break it up" and "that's enough," Orlando returns to the front of the room. Abbasse stands twenty feet away, manning a side door where he screens the Rice Men for contraband and makes sure no boys from other schools crash the party. Rice students are guaranteed admission, unless they've been disqualified for behavioral reasons, and don't have to line up with the girls at the front door.

"In my ten years here, I've found alcohol only once and never had drugs or weapons," Abbasse says later. "It's remarkable, given how packed the room is and how competitive the guys are, there's never been a fight over a girl. Maybe more surprising these days, we've never had girls fighting each other."

Prince arrives with his half-brother Hayward Washington and presents a two-liter bottle of Mountain Dew to Abbasse as an appeal for mercy. He, like Ephraim, was banned for having too many detentions. Prince hopes his offering will have an impact, which it does, but only on Abbasse's sense of humor. The dean of students begins, punctuates, and ends every day at Rice with cans of Mountain Dew, and makes sure the vending machine in the cafeteria is stocked at all times. Abbasse accepts Prince's bribe with a laugh but remains the implacable gatekeeper, sending the young man back into the street. Prince pleads with Abbasse and half an hour later is still putting on his best pouts.

"What part of 'No!' don't you understand?" Abbasse asks as Prince puts on a puppy-dog face, which proves just as ineffective. The freshman hangs his head for a few moments, then looks up wistfully at the crowd of girls swelling around the door. Once again, Marrero bellows through his bullhorn for the young ladies to get back in line, but they crowd in closer, as the sultry evening seeps into twilight.

Several other Rice students from the morning's DT crew show up, all with large bottles of Mountain Dew. Abbasse congratulates them for a "nice try" but refuses entry without Orlando's permission. The students know that Abbasse is tough, but occasionally he relents. Not one attempts to convince the principal.

Five minutes later, with no more Rice students waiting to get in and Prince finally convinced to leave, Abbasse heads to the office for a break. Orlando stumbles after him, almost falling again on the slime-slicked floor. Larry Smythe, a dance committee senior, crosses behind Orlando; his hands fly out, expecting to catch the sliding principal. Orlando rights himself and grunts in gratitude at Larry. Earlier the two had a run-in.

An hour and a half before the dance, Orlando inspected the cafeteria and spotted Larry's girlfriend, whom he'd brought to help out with the set-up. Orlando scowled, admonishing Larry that it really wasn't fair to all the girls who had already started to line up outside. Partly, Orlando was angry at this infringement on the letter of his law. But he'd also missed both lunch and dinner. It's not unusual for Orlando's energy level to plummet and his irritability to spike with low blood sugar.

Larry was tempted to debate, but he knew better than to argue when Orlando was upset. More important than being right was maintaining his close relationship with Orlando, who has been helping him deal with his strict grandmother, his absent, drug-addicted mother, and recently his incarcerated father. Larry lived in the Bronx with his grandmother until last month. She loves and cares for her grandson, but according to Orlando, is "a southern lady who sets high and uncompromising expectations that Larry aspires to meet but sometimes falls short." Larry appreciates the reasonably affluent lifestyle she provides, but feels he's in a constant battle for independence. Several times a year, the quarreling became so intense that Larry appealed to Orlando, who called the grandmother into his office to work out a truce. Larry's grandmother is driven by the fear that he might follow his parents' example.

Larry is one of Orlando's brightest seniors but an underachiever. He was one of few to score over 1000 on the SAT yet fails to make the honor roll as part of his rebellion against his grandmother's pressure. The revolt corrupts his capacity for self-discipline, a classic result in Orlando's view. That "mom or grandma doesn't understand" is a common theme among the young men. They don't feel that they can talk to females about manhood issues and resent female attempts at imposing authority. At the same time, they often fail to become their own authority.

Taciturn with other faculty members and classmates, Larry trusts Orlando and wants to emulate his career path. He plans to return to Rice after college as a teacher, but predictably his grandmother pushes him to aspire to a more respectable—that is, lucrative—profession.

Currently Orlando is counseling three other seniors who fight with their mothers, but to the point where the principal feels "they really could strangle them." One mother came to see Orlando a week ago and showed him the bruises her son gave her. "I told him straight up that if you lay your hands on your mother again, I will see to it that you're put away, and not by your mother, but by me." Larry has never threatened physical retaliation, but his anger has fueled several confrontations with other students. None were witnessed by teachers, saving Larry from being expelled.

Larry's relationship with his girlfriend became problematic several weeks ago. Her father had given him permission to move in, so he could get away from arguing with his grandmother and concentrate on schoolwork. Earlier today the two males had a blowout over sleeping arrangements, which Larry found very upsetting.

Assured that Orlando has regained his balance, Larry heads outside for a break from the sauna-like cafeteria. A few minutes later, he stands at the edge of the tide of females cresting at the front door. He can't believe the Jam is such a success, as a few pretty heads turn and take notice. Larry is tall and handsome with a slim, muscular build and hair longer than most of his peers, although not long enough to constitute an Afro.

Larry sees Kawone squeeze through the front door and stand beside Marrero, who for the last fifteen minutes has slowed down admissions to a trickle. The cafeteria is almost full, and he wants to postpone announcing the dance is closed. There seem to be more girls waiting to get in than when he first opened the doors. Marrero paces nervously back and forth on the front step.

Several minutes ago, Kawone left his post inside to take his turn helping fellow dance committee members with their most important task for the evening: "weeding out the ugly chicks." Several seniors cruise the crowd picking out the most attractive young ladies, whom they pass from one dance committee member to the next, all the way to the front door, where Kawone or another accomplice lets them inside. The trick is to open the door quickly and scoot the girls through when Marrero is distracted. The ritual is taken seriously by the seniors, who consider it a big-brother service for the underclassmen. Several juniors are being trained in selection rites for next year's dance committee.

"Doll, I don't like your attitude," Kawone tells one overweight young woman with a loud voice and the six-dollar ticket price clenched in her hand. She presses her fist against Kawone as he eyes a slim, pretty girl standing beside her.

"You, yeah you there," Kawone winks at the attractive Hispanic. "You can come in."

"I been standing here fo' a hour," the large girl snaps back, blocking the other girl from advancing.

"Don't come here and disrespect my school," Kawone booms. The heavy-set girl leans forward but allows just enough leeway for the Hispanic girl to squeeze by. Kawone whips the front door open, whisks her through, and then laughs at the big girl's cursing.

Two other young ladies with thin frames and full smiles slip forward.

"Focus, now! Focus! This ain't no animal house, yo," Kawone yells as they scoot by. Another senior, standing guard inside the front door, steps out to block the two girls. They turn to Kawone with pleading looks, and he can't help but smile back. Kawone nods to his classmate to let them enter, then turns back to deflect the large girl's fierce glare.

Officer Lee has been standing by the front door in case the girls press in too closely. He catches Kawone's eye, and they both joke about the dance committee's brashness. Marrero hears bits of their conversation and warns Kawone to be careful.

"Ain't nothin' goin' to happen," Kawone tells Officer Lee when Marrero turns away. "The girls know that it's all in good fun. It's not like they come here all ladylike. I almost got slugged a few times."

Meanwhile, senior Joe Carrington has been worming his way through the back of the crowd orchestrating a scam that's anything but "good fun."

Together with Linwood and several juniors, he has been singling out less attractive girls who realize they are being passed over by the dance committee scouts, then offers to get them inside for twenty dollars each or fifty dollars as a group rate. Now that admissions have stalled, girls are offering up to one hundred dollars for passage inside.

One frustrated young lady grabs at Linwood's oversized T-shirt.

"Any of y'all touch me and I'm going to punch you in the mouth, yo," Linwood snarls. "Anyway, you ugly; you not getting in."

Larry laughs at Linwood's act as Joe joins Larry for a few guffaws about the hustle. Marrero happens to spot them talking and slapping hands. He sees Joe counting money as Larry nods his head. Marrero knows the seniors are funneling girls inside, but he's confused since he doesn't realize there are two different groups with different agendas. He has heard girls complaining about having to bribe their way in; now he believes he has confirmation of the con and the ringleaders.

Joe saunters away from Larry to exhort his team to speed up collection efforts. It is getting more difficult to sneak their customers past Marrero, and Larry just informed him that the cafeteria is packed. Soon the door will be closed for the evening, and the cash flow will stop. Perhaps Joe needs the money to help out the young woman who recently bore him a child and whom he forgot to invite to the dance.

"No one else will be admitted," Marrero announces five minutes later, "unless people inside leave." This is really an indirect way of saying the dance is closed since no one's going home for several hours. But the girls pack even closer around the front door. At the same time, Joe approaches the door with several young ladies in tow and realizes he won't be able to get them through. Instead of refunding their money, he slides by his boys on the steps and escapes inside the school. His clients try to follow but "accidentally" bump into Joe's peeps, who close off the path behind him.

As the girls continue to push toward the front door, Marrero worries that some might get crushed. His raises the bullhorn and announces that the Rice Jam is officially closed. Hundreds of young women yell back in protest since many bought tickets. Marrero leaves the disappointed crowd to Officer Lee and his fellow officers, since he's bursting to run inside and tell Orlando about Joe and Larry.

Ten minutes later, Orlando sends Marrero to summon the two seniors. He escorts them back to the library, and in a barrage of shouts and flailing hand gestures, Marrero accuses Joe and Larry of shamelessly hustling the girls for money. Joe saunters before Orlando, smoothly maintaining a defiant attitude, while Larry treads quietly behind with burning eyes and tight, shallow breaths. Orlando studies his seniors for a moment. He has no concrete proof of Marrero's indictment and knows he exaggerates.

"Make sure it doesn't happen again," Orlando says sternly, "or I'll kick you off the dance committee. Now get out and go home!"

Orlando takes a breath before intending to lecture them on how their criminal ploy disgraced the school and shamed him personally. But before Orlando says a word, Larry swings his fist, catching Orlando's jaw squarely. His head snaps back, and he staggers a moment looking at Larry, completely stunned. Orlando's mouth drops open, and his lips fumble with syllables.

"Calm down, Larry," he finally says.

But the words enrage the senior more, and he lunges again at Orlando as Marrero and Joe watch in disbelief. Meanwhile Kawone and Onyxx look on from the foyer in frozen amazement, while senior Darren Elmore, who was talking with them, leaps over the table and bowls his way through the coat racks. As Larry cocks his arm to strike a second time, Darren bursts through the library door and tackles him. Darren slams his classmate to the floor and holds him there.

"Get Larry out of here," Marrero yells, now safely taking charge.

Darren pulls Larry up from the floor in a bear hug and hauls him across the foyer into the main office. Once inside Larry pounds on the door as Darren holds it closed from the outside.

Students rush out of the cafeteria to join the excitement.

"Get back inside," Kawone commands. "The show's over."

"What happened?" everyone asks.

"Come on, now, go back to the dance," Kawone yells. "It's all right."

The students continue to stream into the hallway as Kawone yells louder, but no one pays attention. Darren leaves Onyxx to hold the office door shut and joins Kawone. Without saying a word, Darren spreads his arms open, catching half-a-dozen bodies in his wingspan. He pushes them back toward the cafeteria, stemming the tide of curious teenagers, and sends them back onto the dance floor.

Dance committee members gather in the foyer dumfounded that Larry, one of Orlando's closest sons, would attack him.

Orlando teeters softly into his office holding his jaw, then sits down.

Kawone takes up his position in the middle of the foyer and tries to reassert the evening's former jocular tone. "How did you get out of the house lookin' like that?" he booms at a young woman retrieving lipstick from her jacket at the coat check. "Put some clothes on."

"Kawone," Orlando says softly from his doorway about ten feet away.

"Yes, Mr. Gober," Kawone answers, expecting a reprimand.

"You're doing a great job."

"Oh, thank you."

"But one thing," Orlando adds, "you're far too loud and you're making my head hurt." Orlando walks over to the main office door and peers through the window at Larry, who sits against the far wall, curled up almost in a fetal position and sobbing uncontrollably.

Outside, a slate sky finally releases its own tears. The young women still standing in the street huddle together and sprout a few umbrellas, but no one leaves or even takes cover under the scaffolding at the tenement across the street. About a hundred of the girls have congregated around the side door to the cafeteria. A dozen climb the six feet of brick wall to the windowsill running below the cafeteria's windows. Several succeed in pushing up the windows from the outside and climb in, where they're welcomed by Brother Sherlog, who escorts them back outside again.

The young ladies nearest the cafeteria door start banging on it. Inside, Emory Goode, the dance committee chairman, talks with Kawone and Darren about Larry. Annoyed at the ruckus, he stomps over to open the door and yells, "Get back. The dance is full."

Wet hands reach up and grab Emory's thin frame. He screams for help, alerting Darren, who spots Emory's hooded silhouette being swallowed by the throng. Darren races over and grabs his classmate by the waist just before one young lady yanks hard on his sweatshirt jerking Darren forward too and almost dragging both boys into the crowd. Darren reaches for the large flashlight hanging from his belt and raises it over his head. Still being pulled forward, Darren swings wildly—connecting several times until the girl clutching his shirt finally releases her grip. Darren pulls Emory back inside, then slams the door.

Darren examines the long fractures on his flashlight with satisfaction until he suddenly exclaims, "Shit, my hat."

"What hat?" Kawone asks.

"My brother's hat. It must've fallen off," Darren answers glumly. He was wearing an NYPD baseball cap, his only remaining physical connection with an older brother who drowned last year. Tragically, Darren's other older brother died in a car accident the year before.

When Officer Lee hears about Larry's fight with the principal, he offers to drive him to his grandmother's apartment. No one considers pressing charges, since the incident is seen as a domestic disturbance that will be dealt with within the Rice family.

For weeks after the Rice Jam, students and staff speculate about why Larry attacked Orlando. He had become even closer with the principal after his father was jailed. Larry told Kawone he had always maintained a good relationship with his father and followed his advice even though they didn't live together. "But why should I listen to him anymore?" Larry asked, expressing his sense of betrayal. "He's become a criminal." Perhaps Larry was taking out his repressed anger and hurt on Orlando, his surrogate father. When Orlando told him to get out, Larry later said he took it to mean he was being expelled from Rice, instead of merely being sent home for the evening. Larry panicked as his only safe refuge seemed to have been taken away, and then he struck out at Orlando.

The principal shrugs off the incident as more of a call for help from one of his sons than a violent attack. "Anyway, I've had bricks, bottles, and bats thrown at me," he says afterward, framing the experience in civil rights terms. But Orlando certainly was surprised, never thinking for a moment that he would be the object of the disturbance he had been fearing all week. Unfortunately, the event was public, so he would have to expel Larry.

———

The following Tuesday, October 5, Larry returns to apologize to Orlando, who now knows that he wasn't involved in Joe Carrington's scam. Orlando laments that Joe got off with only a reprimand because no one corroborated Marrero's observations. Most of the teachers blame Marrero for putting Larry on edge and wish it were him who was being forced to leave. Marrero was moved to the public relations post this year because he was an insensitive guidance counselor the year before. Orlando is not pleased with Marrero's performance at the new job and has decided not to rehire him next year.

Larry confesses he would have to leave Rice regardless, since he's receiving threatening phone calls from former students and fears for his life. This afternoon, he's heading down to apply to Lasalle Academy, a Lasallian Christian Brothers' school on Manhattan's Lower East Side. Orlando promises to recommend him for any school he chooses.

Orlando reminds Larry about the "one strike and you're out" predicament facing inner-city youths. He hopes this incident will save him from a more disastrous scenario. With drugs, guns, and gangs so ubiquitous on the street, the slightest misstep can turn deadly or result in incarceration.

The consequences of an arrest are often worse for a poor black teen than for a youngster from an affluent family, who likely will have competent legal counsel and will usually receive more lenient treatment for a first or even second offense.

"It only takes one mistake," Orlando tells his boys repeatedly. "It only takes one mistake."

Unfortunately, Larry's personality renders him susceptible to a disastrous blunder. As Linwood attests, Larry usually remains aloof but "suddenly he clicks and breaks niggers." Last year, a transfer student looked to establish a reputation and started "fronting" with Larry, since he appeared passive in the face of jibes from his friends. Larry took it quietly for several weeks. His boys already knew him to be a skilled fighter. The new student, however, failed to understand that his meekness signaled confidence, not fear, and he certainly failed to sense the anger that was quietly accumulating beneath Larry's serenity. Then one day, the new student insulted Larry in class and received a soft reply that they would settle the matter later. After the bell rang ending the period, Larry walked calmly up to his classmate, flattened him with one blow, and then walked just as calmly away. Fortunately for Larry, the teacher had already left the room. Also, fortunately for both boys, the conflict ended there without peeps from either side escalating the fight after school.

Rice students walk a thin line between self-defense and self-destruction. Linwood says that teen boys from other high schools often try to pick fights with Rice students on nights out. They inspire resentment from public school peers since their school is both one of the top basketball schools in the country and an academy where minority boys go on to college. Every year, several Rice students are attacked on the way home from class or from a jam. After the third rendition of "Who Let the Dawgs Out?" ended the jam on Saturday night, Linwood disappeared into the storm with a dozen of his classmates, one of whom always carries a gun after dark "in case some niggers try and jump us."

Two days later, Larry's girlfriend visits Orlando to apologize for Larry's behavior and her part in exacerbating the pressures in his life. Orlando is heartened by her sincerity and her support for Larry's plans to finish college. He'll be all right, Orlando says with guarded hope. Most Rice students who leave in their junior or senior years graduate from a public high school. The Catholic school "insistence on persistence," as Brother Walderman and many principals put it, usually has become ingrained by then.

Chapter Nine

————

"I'M A FIRM BELIEVER THAT we can find answers to all our problems in the Bible," said Kim Davis, the juniors' guidance counselor, to the eleventh graders. Like all the counselors, Davis has at least one ESP class a week with his students, during which he leads discussions about issues affecting their personal lives and academic careers.

It's Tuesday afternoon, October 12, ten days after the Rice Jam, which Davis missed to attend his own wedding. On the following Monday, he heard graphic descriptions of the event from several teachers and was appalled. The behavior of Rice students contrasted starkly with the more gentlemanly approach to male-female relations at the African American Catholic high school in New Orleans he graduated from only ten years ago.

For days, he has been grappling with how to approach sexuality and the moral imagination with his students. "The dances don't sit right with my soul," he remarked in his office as he prepared today's lesson. "It's very important for young men of color to realize the importance of strong family relationships. African Americans love to talk about community, but we also tear it down because we miss what God intends for relationships."

Da'mar McBean responds to Davis's assertion about the Bible as a source for solutions. "What are we talking about? We're confused over here."

"We're talking about the family you'll create some day. There's a right and a wrong way to do it," Davis explains to the blank expressions around the room. "Whenever you do anything outside the nature of God, you create dysfunction."

"Like what, cloning or somethin'?" asks Allan Sanders, a seventeen-year-old who Abbasse suspects might be selling drugs to other students.

Davis shakes his head. After working the last three years as a guidance counselor at Strake Jesuit College Preparatory high school in an upscale neighborhood in Houston, Texas, he is not used to having to spell out his views, phrase by phrase, in order to be understood.

"A'ight, we're talking about God and everything, a'ight?" asks Omar Nichols, an eighteen-year-old who projects a rapper's defiant attitude to cover for his family's poverty and his limited wardrobe. "What if there's three girls and the girls don't know they're being played 'cause two of them is doin' adultery?"

Davis stops pacing at the front of the classroom as he considers how to decode Omar's non sequiturs. Davis wears a blue shirt, dark tie, and crisply pressed brown dress pants. He stands about five feet, eight inches tall with closely cropped hair and a slightly stocky build. His bright, determined eyes shine like beacons toward upward mobility, albeit from the humblest of family origins. Davis's father was forced to quit school in the sixth grade to harvest crops and help his parents raise his thirteen younger siblings. Davis's mother grew up with more opportunities and became a schoolteacher, completing her master's degree in education when Davis was a child. She conditioned both father and son to the value of excelling at school.

"My father didn't know the difference between a B and a D," Davis recalls later. "But when I brought home my report card, my mother would have a private conversation with him and explain what the letters meant. Then my dad would come and say: 'You did all right in this subject, but this other grade isn't going to cut it.'"

Davis gives up on fashioning an answer for Omar. Instead he reads a passage from Genesis that best articulates what he believes God expects:

The Lord God then took the man and settled him in the Garden of Eden, to cultivate and care of it. The Lord God gave him this order: "You are free to eat from any tree of the trees of the garden except the tree of the knowledge of good and bad. From that tree you shall not eat; the moment you eat from it you are surely doomed to die." The Lord God said, "It is not good for the man to be alone. I will make a suitable partner for him."[1]

"I'm not tryin' to get on you, Mr. D.," Da'mar interrupts, "but is this religion or is this God?"

"This is God."

"I'm saying, but how does it relate to us?"

"You need a foundation for whatever you do, and that, I think, is God," Davis responds. "The standard I live by is: God, family, community, and self. That's my hierarchy and understanding it can help you guys get through what you're experiencing and help you work to your potential."

Several students chat loudly at the back of the room, despite Davis's disapproval.

"If you keep up the talking, you'll be copying lines soon," he takes several steps toward the offenders and warns. Davis allows lively discussions, but also demands order. The juniors have accorded Davis almost immediate respect, which is unusual so early in a teacher's first year, especially for a black male. But they look up to him as a role model and can't help but feel the intensity of his beliefs.

Davis grew up in a Catholic family in New Orleans. He went to the local public elementary school, where his mother taught, through the sixth grade. Then his mother "tricked" him, he relates with a laugh, into attending a Catholic junior high and then high school where she believed he would receive a better moral and academic education. Davis says he "had a thing for clothes" at the time, which allowed his mother to convince him that since Catholic school requires a uniform, he would be wearing his own clothes only on the weekend, making his friends think he had a larger wardrobe.

After graduating from Brother Martin High School in New Orleans, Davis majored in political science at the University of St. Thomas in Houston and planned to go to law school, then pursue a career in politics. As an undergraduate, he worked on several city and statewide Democratic campaigns, including former New York City police chief Lee Brown's successful bid to become Houston's mayor. But a more appealing vocation emerged as Davis devoted evenings and weekends to the Boy Scouts, and displayed a talent for counseling youngsters. After graduating, he decided to put off law school and political aspirations to pursue a career in counseling, fulfilling a commitment to social justice that his Catholic education and interest in the civil rights movement had nurtured.

Davis became an admissions officer at his college alma mater, and during three years there, also took on an advisory role for incoming African American students. At the same time, he completed a master's degree in educational counseling. The next three years took him to the Jesuits' Strake College Preparatory high school, where he worked as the development officer. Most Strake students are from white upper-income families and Davis thoroughly enjoyed working with them, but he was grateful his job also included promoting the school in the suburban African American community.

Then last year, Davis's fiancée was offered a marketing position with Colgate Inc. in New York City. Davis lobbied for her to accept and immediately started looking for a guidance counselor position at a predominately African American high school in a disadvantaged neighborhood here. He was thrilled when Orlando offered him his dream job at a Catholic, all-boys high school in Harlem, which, as Davis says, is "the African American cultural Mecca." Davis also teaches an elective course in economics to the seniors, in which he tries to impart the basics of money management and investment strategy—tools he considers essential for children of the poor.

The juniors finally quiet down, and Davis resumes his lecture: "So God places Adam in the garden and gives him the job of cultivating and protecting it. He doesn't want man to be alone, so he creates birds and so on. But none of them are suitable companions, so he puts Adam to sleep and makes Eve from one of his ribs."

Conversations perk up again at the corners of the classroom, not out of disrespect but because it's the ninth period of the day and many of the students are too large to sit comfortably in the desks.

"Listen, this is important. We're talking about what's wrong with the African American community and how to fix it," Davis raises his voice in exasperation. "Don't disrespect those who are trying to take part in this discussion. I'm not here because I make a million dollars or get praise. I feel strongly that God placed me here to work with y'all. So the bottom line is I'm not going to allow anyone to break the covenant I made with him."

The students quiet down. Invoking divine inspiration is not unusual in the African American community where evangelical denominations have historically constituted the social and spiritual core. As a result, black Catholics are far more likely than their white counterparts to publicly express a personal relationship with God, and this precipitates a sense of reverence, at least momentarily.

"Now look to the second part of the parable," Davis drawls. "Adam bites the apple even though he knows the consequences."

"What apple?" one student calls out.

"Man, why would he bite it, yo?" another asks and sucks his teeth.

"The point being: you have an extra added responsibility as a man," Davis explains. "It's through Eve that sin enters the world, and it's the man's job to make sure certain things don't happen in a relationship."

"But the woman tricked him," Shayne Howze whines. His mother is a public school teacher who complains vehemently every time her son earns a detention, usually for mouthing off. Abbasse says that she calls and argues rudely for Shayne's rights, failing to understand that the students' rights revolution largely bypassed parochial schools and has had a less corrosive effect on discipline, which is the reason she's sending him to Rice in the first place.

"You can put blame wherever you want." Davis stands confidently at the front of the room. He believes in establishing authority through the calm strength of his presence.

"I'm sayin' their relationship is fifty-fifty," Shayne responds. "If the girl does something wrong, it's her fault. Why should the man take full responsibility?"

"But you're the man and it's your responsibility to protect the relationship from sin," Davis argues.

"Owwww," cascades around the room in mocking tones, then the juniors break into a good-natured laugh.

"I'm a firm believer that a man's primary role is that of protector," Davis maintains a serious tone to keep the discussion from disintegrating. "Adam was lax and let sin into his home."

"Aren't women capable of protecting, too?" Shayne demands.

"It's not that women are weaker and more sinful, but it's the man's role to protect, including morally. The woman's natural role is to be more nurturing," Davis explains. "If the man doesn't do his job, then a woman becomes more vulnerable and so does the family. African American women have been forced to stretch and stretch to become protectors. They've carried our community far too long and done an exceptional job. But we'd be in much better shape, regardless of whether marriages work out, if more brothers would take up their responsibilities. We've got a lot of males out there, but not many men."

Last night, Davis hosted a college night with Widziewicz, the seniors' guidance counselor, in the cafeteria. Both spoke to the juniors, the seniors, and their parents about the college application process. Afterward Davis talked with many of the mothers and observed that "the majority of single moms send their sons to Rice to become men, to get the male role models they lack at home and in the neighborhood. What's wrong with a lot of our boys is they want to be men but don't know what it means. My father clearly defined things that made me a man and led me through steps across the manhood threshold. Every Saturday morning, we were up at 6 A.M. to clean and garden. Since the front yard was on display, it was his baby. When I was very young, he said, 'You can't push the lawn mower yet. You're not ready.' So I went from raking leaves and sweeping to cutting the back yard, and then I took the big step when he finally said, 'Okay, you can cut the front yard now.' "

Davis grew up in what began as a new development in suburban New Orleans but became a high crime area as the city tore down urban housing projects and replaced them with scatter-site housing. Poor, broken families were transplanted to Davis's subdivision, which soon became contaminated with gangs and drugs. "Without fathers, our kids don't have clearly defined steps towards manhood. So it's like *Lord of the Flies* and they're learning from each other. They think becoming a man means stealing a purse. Well, I never saw my father hit some old lady and steal her purse."

Shayne squirms at the thought that men have special moral responsibility. "But girls can kick you mad hard," he counters.

"And sometimes they can rape you," another junior suggests. It would take a young lady the size of a defensive end to force him into a compromising position.

"I'm not excusing Eve's behavior," Davis replies. "But the bottom line is you're the man, and you can't tell me that you don't expect more out of yourself."

"I don't," Shayne protests.

"So what's your point?" Davis asks with exasperation.

"Ladies have more rights that we do," Shayne complains.

"You are expected to be bigger and stronger," Davis responds. Later Davis speaks in his office about how men no longer understand how they're supposed to act. "The biggest fault of the feminist movement," he says, "was not educating men on how to be a man in relation to the changing roles of women. Men have become very insecure."

Sadly for contemporary young men, this insecurity seems a small price to pay for feminism's tendency to give them what men, on a superficial level, have always wanted: sex without responsibility. Then later in life, stripped of their traditional role as protector and provider, the young men become predatory—nibbling at the carnal version of the tree of knowledge—both contributing to and suffering from their own irrelevancy. "Many children now grow up to acknowledge no source of love, authority, or guidance apart from the mother, whose men come and go like seasonal laborers, drifting through the matriarchal realm with no prospect of a permanent position."[2] Many juniors have seen their fathers both reduced to, and embracing, the role of sexual sharecroppers. Several juniors allude to their own serial promiscuity and blame it on how "slutty" the girls behave.

"People think it's hard to find girls with class," Jermaine Anderson offers as he waves a small black book over his head. "This is my chicktionary."

Everyone including Davis responds with a belly laugh.

"A lot of my Nubian brothers," Jermaine continues, "think you get girls by disrespecting them. That's not how I got these forty names and phone numbers."

"If a woman wants to be a lady, she has to respect herself," a classmate points out, shifting the responsibility back to the female.

"I met this girl who lets me get away with stuff, so I do it," Shayne admits.

"Some girls be liking that. They let boys take advantage and talk down to them," Will Adams points out, talking hesitantly for the first time this period. Will is another boy abandoned by both parents to his grandmother and, as a result, wears a permanently beaten expression. For the third year in a row, he has enough detentions for acting out in class in the first few weeks of school to risk expulsion. Abbasse has already warned him he'll be given less leeway this year. Will's not sure how to believe in himself without the constant attention that getting into trouble brings.

"Why?" Davis asks dumbfounded. The girls he knew growing up didn't allow themselves to be used easily, if ever.

"Low self-esteem," Will explains, admitting as much about himself as about the girls he's met. "They got problems at home and let people walk all over them."

"Many women won't listen to good advice," Jermaine interjects. "I get discouraged."

"Men love to cheat," a husky voice calls out from the back of the room.

"Yeah," Jermaine rolls in his seat as he laughs. "This used to be my motto: Triple B—Bag, Bone, and Bounce."

The room erupts in applause. Jermaine springs to his feet and exchanges high fives with his buddies.

"I haven't found the right girl yet," Will offers in melancholy tones.

"What is the ideal woman?" Davis asks.

"A virgin," Jermaine states unashamedly. "A girl no one's had before; if someone else got there first, then no."

Davis is astounded again by the contradictory attitude about members of what has become for these young men the opposing sex. Almost all say they want to marry eventually and raise a family, and contend adamantly that their future bride must be a virgin. She must also cook, clean, and be prepared to take care of children. On the other hand, the boys are looking for every opportunity to have sex and consider their partners to be ho's and bitches. The virgin-prostitute dichotomy is hardly original and is at the root of the New Testament in the persons of the Virgin Mary and Mary Magdalene.

In Widziewicz's assessment, "Without dad around, Rice students win the Oedipal battle easily, but then assert their independence and authority in self-serving and immature ways. Women become either saints in the boy's consciousness or exist solely to be used. You see this with the Rice Jams in that they won't bring serious girlfriends here to be exposed to all the degrading play-sex."

Before coming to Rice, Widziewicz worked as a counselor for sex offenders in New Jersey and earned state certification as a psychiatric social worker. He sees "the mother-son bond becoming too close for mental health for many of the young men here. It was so obvious at the college night. They talk to their moms as if she's their best friend."

"What if the young lady wants her man to be a virgin?" Davis asks and shakes his head again.

"I lie," Jermaine retorts firmly.

"What if she lies too and then you find out?" Davis presses. "The trust is broken, but you're saying it's all right for you to lie."

"Yeah, of course," Jermaine blurts out.

His classmates agree, and Davis is too appalled to think of a counterargument.

"A friend asked about taking a virgin: Do they bleed then and there?" Will asks.

"It doesn't always happen," Davis answers flatly. "Some have hurt themselves in a bicycle accident, for example."

"A girl I met called me and said, 'You popped my cherry. Why did you do that?' " Will admits. "I feel so dirty."

As a traditional Catholic, Davis would recommend confession, the sacrament where guilt and repentance lead to spiritual reconciliation. But not only is Will a non-Catholic, this entire approach has been abandoned by most parishioners. Until Vatican II, confession was a vibrant part of the Catholic approach to personal responsibility. Today, priests are seldom available for the sacrament since sin and guilt have gone out of fashion, and the Church has failed to articulate where secular therapy leaves off and religious forgiveness and redemption take over.

"Guess I want a girl I don't have to gas. A girl I can tell the truth to," Steve Gouin, a handsome junior, adds in a deeply resonant voice.

Another student asks Davis if premarital sex buys a ticket to eternal damnation, and everyone jumps back into the discussion at once.

"Can you go to hell for that?" Shayne repeats what young men at parochial schools have always considered the most important moral question.

"I don't think anybody can really know," Davis answers with a dodge, not wanting to aid the eternal quest for loopholes.

"Everyone was born like with sexual desire, know what I'm saying," Da'mar calls out.

"Everyone has to fulfill their sexual desires somehow, but let me say this about premarital sex," Davis replies, looking for a way to frame a response to a largely "unchurched" audience. (The Christian Brothers and the religion teachers use this term often since they see little distinction in religious training—meaning virtually none—between many of the students who say they are Catholic and those who claim other denominations.) "If you continue to read about Adam and Eve, the Bible says there's a point where a man will leave his parents and 'cleave to his wife' and they become one. The word 'cleave' is interesting because it's stronger than hold onto or take her hand. What happens when you involve yourself with premarital sex is that you're unable to handle the responsibility, so the cleaving process can't take place."

"That's not the truth," Allan Sanders stammers loudly. "Now think about it. Mary was pregnant with Jesus at what age?"

"Fourteen," Da'mar answers. The Bible is no stranger in his household. Da'mar lives with a grandmother who suffers from a serious heart condition and prays for her grandson, whose temper hides a growing fear of losing her. Already Da'mar has come close to starting several fistfights that would get him expelled.

"See what I'm sayin'?" Allan exclaims. "What's the difference between Mary and Joseph, and teenagers today?"

"Joseph had a job so he was able to have a relationship," Davis counters. "A man has to take care of business first, and for you that means getting an education. If you don't, why expect anything great? The definition of insanity is doing the same thing over and over the same way and expecting to get different results. As long as the African American community operates outside of what God intends, we have no right to get upset about how life turns out."

As a doctrinal issue, Davis believes that premarital sex is a sin. "I'm a Catholic boy," he says later with a laugh. But the most important point he wants to get across to his students is that sex has consequences, although he admits, "the idea seems laughable in today's world."

The Rice Jams are orgies with clothes on, in his view. The dancing lacks grace and certainly corrodes tenderness and enchantment. Yet amid the tangle of limbs, the girls are looking for romance and the boys ache for chivalry. Despite the graphic nature of their encounters, the boys are still embarrassed by a kiss. Face-to-face is personal and very little of it goes on, even in the dark corners. Between songs, the girls shy away from the boys and act coyly, knowing instinctively that words and promises can touch the soul. For both genders, it has simply become easier and, in the absence of strong parental guidelines, more socially acceptable to follow the hormonal tribe.

The boys claim that they'll make the transition to courtship and marriage when they grow up, as if maturity is the inevitable result of long-term promiscuity. Instead, it has had disastrous consequences for the African American community. Despite recent decreases in childhood poverty due to welfare reform, a third of black children continue to live below the poverty line, compared to 9 percent of white children, and many others are not much better off.[3] The two most important causal factors of high child-poverty rates are welfare dependence and single parenthood—not race—with the latter producing much of the former. Black and white children raised in identical circumstances show identical probabilities of living in poverty. Instead, "Welfare dependence is extremely rare among married-couple families but is relatively common in single-parent families. Indeed, residing in a single-parent home could be considered almost a necessary precondition to long-term welfare dependence. Welfare dependence . . . is 1,700 percent more common among children residing with never-married mothers than among children born to married couples where the marriage has remained intact."[4]

Over 85 percent of black children were born to married couples in 1940. Now almost 72.5 percent of African American children are born out of wedlock, with the percentage rising in the inner cities (and generally in the South) to well over 80 percent, compared to 24 percent for white.[5] Single parenthood proves so damaging, especially among minorities, because fathers often abandon their children, and many mothers have low math and verbal skills that trap them and their children in poverty.

Traditionally, the male role was minimal when children are young, but older males took over the maturation process of adolescent boys with a series of initiation rites that transformed them into men. These rituals have largely vanished from contemporary society, which constitutes one of the main reasons boys have so much more trouble growing up than girls.

Then with little or no father presence, boys turn to gangs that offer rites of passage to a misguided version of manhood. Strengthening the role of fathers in the African American community has always made sense, because before the civil rights movement, extra nurturing was required for young men excluded from achieving success, power, and dignity by racism. Since then, many have been excluded from the mainstream by the breakdown of family, community, and public education. So strengthening the father role is just as important now, as Orlando labors to accomplish.

Davis fulfills more of a big brother role, exhorting the young men toward responsibility, so they can rebuild the African American family. The traditional sexual mores that he believes in passionately are taught more as preferable alternatives in religion classes at Rice than as moral imperatives. In accommodating non-Catholics, the Catholic view has lost much of its authority. For example, one brother apologized recently to his students for prayers at a liturgical service, saying they might offend non-Catholics. The students looked back at him with stunned expressions. They'd never encountered political correctness applied to religion at their churches, nor on the TV ministries that their mothers or grandmothers watch.

In religion and other classes, the students are encouraged to air their opinions candidly, and in discussions about sex, many defend casual encounters. Teachers argue for accountability, but most fail to present abstinence—the Church's official position—in a comprehensive, convincing manner. As Linwood and other students readily admit, they're looking to adults to set limits; their arguments for promiscuity are really pleas for boundaries.

The brothers teach by example in leading celibate lives. But this invalidates what they have to say about premarital sex in the eyes of the students who, both Catholic and non-Catholic, have been acculturated to see abstinence as merely the lack of sexuality, instead of a spiritual choice or a component of courtship and marriage (for example, during a partner's illness). The students conclude that the brothers are not men in the same way they are becoming, and so their teachings are suspect.

The brothers say that sexual intercourse is a sacred union, expressing a deep connection with God. In the juniors' religion class last week, Brother Sherlog corrected a student's graphic characterization of sex to describe lovemaking as a prayer. But little is said about self-control, as if African American culture were so invested with casual sexuality and the resulting high rates of single parenthood and poverty that promoting behavior changes aggressively would be intrinsically offensive.

The strongest appeal for sexual restraint comes with warnings about sexually transmitted diseases. At several student gatherings last year, and at one last week, Orlando emphasized that AIDS is the leading killer of young blacks.[6] A recent letter from the Centers for Disease Control and Prevention to public health officials across the country read: "the latest HIV/AIDS data demonstrate the continued severity of the HIV/AIDS epidemic in the African American communities. Although African Americans make up less than 13 percent of the U.S. population, they account for approximately half of the more than 1 million Americans currently estimated to be living with AIDS."[7] Blacks also constitute half of the newly diagnosed cases and 61 percent of those infected under twenty-five years of age. African American men are eight times more likely to be diagnosed than white males, and African American women are almost twenty-four times more susceptible than white women.

Rice students brag about having "sex in the raw," and many have only vague ideas about how to avoid contracting HIV. Freshmen ask with trepidation whether they can get AIDS from kissing, but then abandon caution as soon as they find a girlfriend. Orlando and others counsel strongly to act sensibly, but only Davis argues forcefully for abstinence until marriage as the solution for teenage pregnancy and STDs—a remedy that works if adopted, for obvious reasons.

Over half of teenagers engage in sexual intercourse before the end of high school, producing 750,000 teen pregnancies every year, 82 percent of which are unintended.[8] Five or six Rice students father a child every year, and just as many of the pregnancies they initiate end in abortion. Almost all the pregnancies and abortions involve juniors and seniors, suggesting high rates of sexual activity since there are only ninety-eight students in the eleventh and twelfth grades. Orlando is able to convince the student-fathers to provide as much support as they can without dropping out. But this is hardly sufficient for the mother and the child.

Clearly a comprehensive approach to sex education is called for. Not informing students thoroughly about safe sex is highly irresponsible. But given the high rates of STDs, especially among minority youth, using condoms can hardly be termed safe. Regrettably in Davis's view, "Rice doesn't mount much of a fight against promiscuity, and teaches neither restraint nor safe sex. Catholicism is watered down here." In New Orleans, the Catholic high schools have gone through the same transformation, Davis remarks, especially those serving predominately African American and non-Catholic populations. Regardless of the specific religious community in charge, the high schools are generically Christian with a Baptist flavor and a residual Catholic identity.

Rice students attend Mass twice a year, and there are prayer services several times throughout the school year. As well, several teachers begin their classes with a short prayer, and Orlando injects biblical quotations regularly into his interactions with students. With Brother Walderman greeting students in the morning and Orlando punctuating their day with "Have a blessed day," Christianity pervades the atmosphere and culture. Certainly the commitment to educate large numbers of non-Catholics expresses Catholic values, as Father Andrew M. Greeley, the renowned sociologist at the University of Chicago, points out.[9] But the strong sense of identity that characterized Catholic education prior to Vatican II has faded here and at most Catholic schools. Almost all the teachers are laity with no training in how to transmit Catholicity in the classroom. As well, a growing proportion of the staff is non-Catholic, as are more than half the teachers at Rice, compared to 25 percent in 1993.

A significant part of the problem, far beyond the control of the Christian Brothers, is that there is no consensus anymore about what it is to be Catholic. Most Catholics are liberal in practice, while Church teachings tend toward a conservative stance. Unresolved issues, especially regarding sexuality and the role of women, have been officially ignored for so long that they are now as much a part of the religion as its dogma. When Pope Paul VI overrode his own commission's recommendation to accept artificial birth control and issued his famous encyclical in 1968 banning contraceptives, the hierarchy lost touch with most American Catholics. As Rudyard Kipling once observed: "Nothing is ever settled, until it's settled right." Attendance at Mass fell by a third, and Catholics' use of contraceptives increased to match that of other Americans.

There are really two Catholicisms: the official edition that few accept in toto, and the "cafeteria" version that, although much maligned among the Church's hierarchy, predominates among parishioners. Most Catholics, including teachers, simply disregard Church teachings they don't agree with, which means Church dogma is no longer transmitted with passionate conviction. Since this predicament isn't discussed openly, students intuit a lack of sincerity that becomes a general impression, rather than specific to particular teachers regarding particular issues. Given how anachronistic Church teachings about premarital sex are from the mainstream culture's point of view—which overwhelms children via the entertainment industry, advertising, the Internet, and so on—the added lack of certainty of faith on the part of teachers completely undermines students' regard for the traditional approach.

In the Rice yearbooks from the 1950s and 1960s, photos show students in shirts and ties dancing close to, but not pressing against, young ladies in dresses that corresponded to the actual size of their bodies. These young men and women were no more angelic than today's, but for the most part they were kept within boundaries of traditional morality, which formed the bedrock of both the white and the African American communities.

Historically a strict moral code has been crucial to mainstreaming every ethnic and racial group, precisely because it keeps families together, despite the inevitable moral stumbling of individuals. This is not a prescription for the self-fulfillment of parents, but it is immensely beneficial for children and their ability to climb the socioeconomic ladder. A Stanford University study showed that Asian American students perform well academically not because of some genetic advantage—the inverse formulation of Charles Murray's bell curve—but because they work harder. The study's most salient point was that extremely high rates of marriage provide Asian children with at least one parent at home to supervise after-school hours and homework.[10]

Chapter Ten

———

AT 7:40 A.M. FRIDAY, OCTOBER 22, Orlando walks toward the cafeteria to start the day right with breakfast. He crosses paths with Dwayne Carter, whom he expelled last week after the senior talked back impolitely again to a teacher in class. Normally the incident would have drawn a suspension, given the number of detentions Dwayne already had accumulated, but Abbasse decided on "shock therapy" and recommended he leave.

"Kids used to say, 'I've got your back' and the teacher or principal knew that trust had been established and the student would do anything for you," Orlando says later, explaining his decision. "Every time Dwayne gets into serious trouble, he makes a show of contrition and tells me he's got my back, but it really means 'I'm going to take advantage of the trust you're putting in me.'"

The better teachers think expelling Dwayne was a mistake. They don't have much trouble with him and see substantial potential. It's the weaker teachers Dwayne doesn't respect, but that's no excuse.

How much patience to extend students is a running argument at urban Catholic schools. Brother James Bonilla, the principal at Bishop Loughlin Memorial High School in Brooklyn until his death two years ago, was often at odds with the dean of students and teachers who urged him to kick out habitual troublemakers. Prior to Loughlin, Brother James spent eleven years as a teacher and administrator at a Catholic detention center for juvenile delinquents in Philadelphia. He firmly believed that the best way to deal with problem students was to keep giving them chances, saying it's better to have students deal with the consequences of misbehavior vis-à-vis detentions and suspension—and hang onto them—than expel them, since they are the ones least likely to graduate from a failing public high school. To minimize the impact of disruptive students, Brother James had them visit his office almost daily and recruited them to play on the intercollegiate handball team that he coached.

Orlando shared Brother James's view when he was the dean of students. But the more he pushes to upgrade Rice's academic profile, the more he's inclined to resort to "shock therapy." As well, Orlando takes misbehavior more as a personal betrayal than when he was dean and didn't see himself as Rice incarnate.

Dwayne greets Orlando warmly with a complete lack of acrimony that's common among the expelled at Rice. Like many, Dwayne plans to visit the school regularly and maintain a relationship with both Orlando and Abbasse. He appreciates the chance he was given to return in September and takes his expulsion in the spirit it was intended: as an important life lesson. Dwayne heads upstairs to confer with Widziewicz about his best public high school option.

Orlando takes several steps toward the cafeteria, then spots a black woman standing by the sports trophy case.

"Can I help you?" he asks.

"I'm waiting to see Mr. Gober, the principal, about my son," she replies.

"He'll be with you in a moment," Orlando says and resumes his errand. He returns a few minutes later with his breakfast, then directs the woman into his office.

"Where's Mr. Gober?" the woman asks.

"Have a seat; he'll be right in," Orlando answers flatly, then points the woman to his couch. He puts his tray on the table in the middle of the room, then walks back to the school office to ask Brother Matthew Maistre a question.

Several minutes later, Orlando returns. "Now, what's your son's name?" he asks as he takes the seat at his desk and turns on his computer.

"You're Mr. Gober?" the woman asks, incredulous.

"What did you expect?"

"Well, I thought, uh, well . . ."

At least a dozen times since becoming principal, Orlando has re-enacted this vignette. "My people have such a hard time believing that a black man could be in charge."

During the summer, Orlando was cleaning his office while wearing a T-shirt and jeans. A salesman arrived and asked to see Mr. Gober.

"Yes, one minute, please," Orlando said as he sat down at his desk to make a phone call.

"Should you be doing that in the principal's office?" the salesman asked.

"Yeah, I should," Orlando shot back, "because I am the principal!"

The man turned shades of pink through scarlet.

"You just lost whatever it is you came for," Orlando smirked. "Have a nice day."

The salesman called back every day for two weeks to apologize, but in vain.

———

Minutes after the doubting mother leaves the principal's office, Linwood Sessoms knocks on the door, and Orlando waves him in. Linwood flops onto the couch and launches into a description of the fight he had earlier that morning with his father. Like many students, Linwood doesn't visit or hang around Orlando's office unless he's going through a crisis but then always seeks out the principal.

"Why did you fight with your father?" Orlando asks.

"My dad asked me to do something and I laughed," the senior recounts. "Then he came up to me real close and said, 'Did you hear me?' " Linwood says he answered with a smirk.

" 'So you think you're a man now?' " Linwood's father responded, shoving his son several times, then took a swing at him but missed. Fortunately, Linwood's mother was standing nearby and grabbed her husband's arm before he could swing again. Although a foot shorter than her husband, Sheila Sessoms does not lack physical presence; she untangled her men, ungluing their stares.

"He's real big, but I wasn't scared," Linwood emphasizes. Linwood's father is about four inches taller than his son and built like a heavyweight boxer. He could easily toss Linwood around, so Orlando cautions the senior about the better part of valor.

Linwood is upset because after the confrontation, his mother asked him to spend this weekend at her sister's apartment in the Bronx to avoid another incident, while she's visiting family in North Carolina.

"Why should I have to leave my own home?" Linwood asks Orlando, asserting his claim as the de facto man of the house. "Now he wants to play daddy. Where was he when I was a little boy? He didn't have a relationship with me and now he's trying to make up for lost time. But he treatin' me like I'm twelve years old."

"That doesn't mean you have to act like you're twelve years old," Orlando points out. "Do you think you're a man now?"

"Well . . . yeah," Linwood stammers.

"Remember: We are male by birth and men by choice," Orlando replies. The motto is on a sign on the bulletin board beside his desk. Orlando repeats his slogans relentlessly to counter both the perverse reality of the streets and its idealization in hip-hop culture.

"All his daddy days are gone," Linwood reiterates, reluctant to acquiesce too quickly to Orlando's advice. He wants to be prodded into accepting it.

Orlando nods, allowing Linwood to contemplate his underlying dilemma. Six months ago, Linwood's father was released from jail after serving a two-year sentence for a drug-related offense. His numerous incarcerations hurt his son deeply and sparked his long history of behavioral problems at school. Orlando realizes that Linwood could easily slide back into his old patterns and recognizes his plea for help—all the more poignant after his remarkable turnaround last year.

After being released from prison, Linwood's father moved in with his own father, also in Bronx, on his wife's insistence, since he had become a virtual stranger to his own children after three prison terms in twelve years. He took a job as a sheet metal worker and promised to stay clean and go straight. To rebuild family trust, he visits several times a week.

When Mrs. Sessoms made plans to go away this weekend, she asked her husband to stay over to mind Jennifer, their sixteen-year-old daughter who's been rebelling lately. Mrs. Sessoms fears Jennifer will follow their youngest daughter's example; the year before last, Mary started hanging around with classmates involved with gang members. Mary failed the seventh grade, then continued to misbehave, scaring her mother to the point where she sent her to live with the eldest sister, Lolita, a senior at the State University of New York in Oneonta. Mrs. Sessoms even signed over legal guardianship of Lolita to avoid paying the $3,500 per year she would otherwise be charged for Mary to attend the public school there as an out-of-district student.

Mrs. Sessoms is determined that none of her children follow their father's example and that they all finish college. She enforces strict rules about who her children can associate with, where they are allowed to go with friends, and how late they can stay out. Linwood stays within bounds for the most part, and emulates the tenacity his mother displayed in finishing her bachelor's degree in educational psychology at the College of New Rochelle last year. The degree qualified her to become the director of a child-care center in East Harlem.

Unfortunately Linwood adopted his father's tendency to settle disputes with aggression. Linwood grew up during the crack wars, when drug dealers fought for control of the fast-expanding drug trade with such violence that homicide and incarceration rates hit the highest levels ever. Linwood's father dealt drugs, then became a user. Although he was arrested more than sixty times, it was mostly for possession and robbery. He was never charged with a violent crime but earned a reputation as a "serious dude," as Linwood puts it.

Since the ninth grade, Linwood has heard Orlando talk about what it takes to become a man, delivering much the same message as his pastor, Elder Percy Hicks, that the real fight involves exercising self-control instead of aggression, and that schooling is the key to success. Mrs. Sessoms insists that all her children attend Sunday morning and afternoon services at New Bethel Way of the Cross Church of Christ, an Apostolic congregation in Harlem. She's been a member of this evangelical congregation since childhood and meets her mother and other family members there every Sunday. The pastor makes a point of including the young men in the service and praises their participation.

However, Linwood didn't start heeding the pastor's or the principal's advice until last fall when Orlando gave a pep talk to students who had failed one or more subjects in the first marking period. Orlando delivered a passionate sermon with scriptural references to the effect that his young men were capable of doing quality academic work but didn't yet trust the connection between effort and achievement.

Linwood had failed English with an overall average in the mid 70s. Throughout elementary school and his first two years at Rice, Linwood seldom posted failing grades, but his overall performance was mediocre. He never allowed himself to believe that excellence was within his reach. He wasn't in serious danger of failing the eleventh grade, but the next day when Orlando spoke to him privately in his office, he took his message personally for the first time.

"Mr. Gober, do you really think I can make the honor roll?" he asked with intense interest.

"If you believe you can, you will," Orlando answered.

"But do you believe I can?" Linwood asked.

As Orlando studied Linwood's face, the young man's history at Rice hung between them.

"Linwood was still a pain in the ass when he started the eleventh grade," John Shea, his freshman religion teacher, remembers. "He seldom paid attention or did his work properly." Linwood was suspended several times a year for disrespecting teachers and for fighting with students. He warned his Spanish teacher to watch what she said to him or she could get hurt. Several teachers recommended that Linwood be asked to leave. Fortunately for Linwood, Orlando was well acquainted with his family situation and behavioral history in elementary school. Despite Linwood's continuing propensity for angry outbursts, Orlando recognized his progress and let him remain.

Linwood Dockery Sessoms III was born on August 29, 1982. By kindergarten, he was the third of five children with two sisters on either side. Linwood's father worked for New York City's Parks Department until Linwood was six years old, then trained as a sheet metal worker. The family lived, and still does live, in a three-bedroom apartment in the Bronx River Housing projects, in the borough's geographic center. At home, Linwood was called "J.R." to distinguish him from his father. The nickname stuck, but the need for it vanished as did his father.

On Linwood's kindergarten report card at a nearby public school, the teacher wrote starkly: *His behavior must improve.* During the first grade, his teacher's comments read: *Linwood's recent academic progress has been marred by his extreme anger and his problems focusing on formal academic tasks.* So Linwood's behavior reflected his father's deepening involvement in taking drugs and in illegal activities to support the habit. Linwood had always been proud that his dad, noticeably the only African American in the photo of his graduating class, had attended the city's Aerospace Science Academy High School in Queens. His father's departures were very disappointing.

At the beginning of the third grade, Linwood's frustrations surfaced, and he ran home to ask his mother, "Who invented school?"

"Well, I don't know," Mrs. Sessoms answered.

"Mom, who made up school?" he demanded angrily.

"Linwood, why do you want to know?"

"Because whoever it was, I want to kill him," Linwood declared, then stomped away. In class, he was rebelling against any imposition of authority as an obvious childish protest against his father's frequent convictions and absences. As a result, Linwood's mother was called to school several times a month to deal with her son's behavioral issues.

When Linwood was in the fourth grade, his father was convicted of a drug offence and sentenced to six months in jail. Predictably, Linwood escalated his discontent, this time threatening to shoot his teacher after being disciplined. The teacher had Linwood suspended from school and even reported the incident to the police. "You'll never do anything in your life," he told the angry nine-year-old, who for the rest of the year hardened his outer shell and did his best to fulfill the prediction.

Linwood was reprimanded for acting out regularly in class and was suspended so often for fighting and talking back to his teacher that he was referred for professional evaluation. The school district's special education committee gave Linwood an "emotionally disturbed" classification, which allowed him to continue taking regular classes as long as he went to a psychologist for counseling.

At year's end, Linwood's psychotherapist wrote: *Linwood is an intelligent youngster who has been coping with great psychosocial stressors this year. Changes due to his father's status within the family have had significant bearing on his ability to maintain himself productively in the classroom.* The therapist recommended he be put on Ritalin, but Mrs. Sessoms refused to comply. She did not want to see the light in her son's eyes go out, no matter how mischievously he acted. Mrs. Sessoms was working part-time at a daycare center where she often saw children become more manageable through drug therapy—and dull, since Ritalin and other drugs are often overprescribed and in effect perform a frontal lobotomy.

Despite his behavioral problems, Linwood consistently posted good grades. No matter what transpired during the day, Linwood's mother insisted he do his homework and study for tests, enabling him to maintain an 80 average. He even won the award for perfect attendance in the fourth grade, perhaps to spite his teacher. But Linwood's results on standardized tests made it clear that, although he was doing his schoolwork, he was too preoccupied with troubles at home to learn much. Near the end of second grade, Linwood took the citywide math test and scored in the 61st percentile. But in the third grade, Linwood fell to the 29th percentile where he remained for the rest of elementary school. He did significantly worse on the reading test, ranking in the 15th percentile in the fourth grade, then slipping to the 9th percentile in fifth grade.

That year Linwood successfully fought off charges that he'd "mooned" his female classmates in the schoolyard. If found guilty, he could have been forced into special education. When Linwood admitted to operating as the lookout for a group of friends who pulled down their pants, he was suspended instead. In May, Linwood's teacher sent a note home to his mother, which read: *Linwood had the nerve to tell me to "shut-up" during lunch after*

I pulled him out for annoying the boy behind him in line. The other boy was pushing him around to tell him to leave him alone. Linwood denies this accusation, yet I had my eyes on him the whole time. As a result, the pressure on Linwood's mother to put him into special education increased. She stubbornly refused, knowing that few youngsters designated as emotionally disturbed graduate; in fact, only 4 percent do so.[1]

Across the country, black students are three times as likely as whites to end up in special education, but not because there are three times as many black children who should be classified as "mentally retarded" or "truly emotionally disturbed."[2] In a system with no effective means of establishing discipline, some special education classifications are used as ways of dealing with difficult students.

To avoid special education, the best compromise Linwood's mother could negotiate was an alternative middle school. However, the school she found, New Direction on West 117th Street in Harlem, turned out to be less "alternative" than a pilot project for troubled students. As muscular as Linwood was, at average height, he felt intimidated. "You always had to watch your back at New Direction. If there was a fight, you might get cut, or you had to worry about someone waiting for you after school," Linwood recalls. Fortunately he survived the sixth and half of the seventh grade without a major incident, which allowed his mother to negotiate his transfer to Booker T. Washington, an integrated junior high school on Manhattan's Upper West Side.

But by then, hormonal influences added turmoil to Linwood's emotional cauldron. As well as acting up in class, he got into trouble for mooning a group of girls at recess. "I was trying to be the toughest guy in the school and a mack, a girls' man," he laughs with embarrassment.

"Linwood's teachers couldn't control him," remembers Hayward Washington, a classmate at Booker T. and at Rice. "His friends would dare him and, to be down, he'd throw things at some girls and get hyper."

As the eighth grade began, Linwood told his mother he wouldn't go to a public high school. He said he'd get into fights that would be increasingly violent, and he'd drop out. But with her husband still in jail so often, Mrs. Sessoms was functionally a single mother with five children. She was still a student at the College of New Rochelle and so hardly in a position to pay Linwood's tuition for a private or parochial school. There are programs such as Prep for Prep that offer scholarships for high-achieving minority students to prestigious private schools, some charging over $20,000 a year. However, Linwood's academic talents fall in the normal range, and he certainly would not have gotten into any of the city's competitive public high schools like Stuyvesant either.

That fall, a Student Sponsor Partners representative came to Boys Harbor in East Harlem where Linwood's mother worked part-time and enrolled all her children in after-school programs. Linwood saw the Student Sponsor Partners' privately funded voucher and mentoring program as a life preserver. At first, Mrs. Sessoms was surprised to hear her son say he wanted to go to a Catholic school, since Linwood was raised a Baptist, but she had no objection. Linwood insisted his mother complete the SSP application immediately, then he mailed it in. Mrs. Sessoms admired her son's determination and was thrilled when SSP accepted him. Linwood made Rice his first choice because "I used to hear all the girls in my neighborhood talk about Rice parties and the Rice Men."

Linwood's joy soured within his first few weeks as a freshman after seeing how structure defines the school day at Rice. He wanted to leave. Fortunately, Linwood's SSP sponsor convinced him to stay and motivated him to work hard enough to pass. At the same time, however, Linwood reverted to old behavioral habits. In his sophomore year, for example, Linwood complained vociferously that his math teacher had given him too low a grade.

"Mrs. Browne, she playin' me," he told Orlando after being thrown out of class.

Orlando answered that his problem wasn't with the teacher but rather his own unwillingness to take responsibility for his grades. Orlando knew Linwood's father was in jail again, but would not let him use that as an excuse. Several suspensions later, Linwood began to see that what he disliked about Rice was in fact what was good about it.

"All there was to do was learn, especially with no girls," Linwood said, finally realizing the futility of his antics. "And the same rules apply inside the school and outside. If you get into a fight on the outside, you face the same consequences. So you feel secure at Rice and don't have to worry about anyone. It helped me concentrate."

"Yes!" Orlando yelled at Linwood, at the end of their consultation last year, answering his question about whether the principal thought he could make the honor roll.

"Then I will!" Linwood replied, seeing the future as a blueprint. "Thank you, Mr. Gober, for caring about me."

Orlando says his most difficult task is convincing students "to believe that they can do it." His boys have difficulty seeing the causal connection between effort and outcome, which might be rooted in the decades of racial discrimination during which even highly educated blacks were denied professional status and everything else in white society. Seeing effort as futile overshadowed the aspirations of many and weakened their capacity to try. It often takes Orlando years to convince a young man to accept the possibility that hard work brings results, and then additional counseling is often needed to persuade him that the equation applies specifically to him.

"Twice a month, Mr. Gober would come into class and talk about what school's for," Linwood remembers. "He must have told us, 'You can do it. All you have to do is believe,' dozens of times in my first three years at Rice. Finally it got through and I wanted to do it."

Desire, however, translated into only minor improvements in grades and behavior until a crisis struck the Sessoms family a few weeks later, which Linwood writes about it in the college essay he's been working on:

My mother always said she would be there for me through thick and thin. . . . But this year I experienced something unimaginable. . . . I almost lost my mother . . . [she] was rushed to the hospital earlier that morning after having a terrible attack on the brain . . . my eyes became filled with tears. I put on my coat, not knowing what to do or what to say. . . . I started to pray to God asking him not to let my mother die. She's everything in my life, even more. . . . I finally reached an agreement with God that if he was to make my mother okay, I would try my best in school, doing all I could. After getting to the hospital, the doctor's explained that she was close to death but had made it. They explained to me that the surgery was successful and that my mother was going to be fine.

While Mrs. Sessoms was recovering several weeks after the Christmas break, Linwood heard Orlando give a pep talk to eleventh graders about improving grades and getting on the honor roll. Linwood recalled his promise to God and the promise he'd made to his principal. He decided to work as hard as it took to make good. At home that evening, Linwood told his mother about his bargain with destiny and she suggested that "the only way to get on the honor roll is to study on the weekends." Until then, Linwood claimed Saturday and Sunday as "my time." Monday mornings he would get up early and try to get his homework done.

"I'll give you $150 towards that leather jacket you want to buy if you get on second honors," his mother offered.

"No way, mom," Linwood answered. "You're going to pay for the whole thing because I'm going to get on first honors."

Linwood studied on weekends and posted a 92 average in the spring, making first honors as promised. At the same time, he started going to church more often, attending prayer meetings on week nights in addition to mandatory Sunday attendance. The biggest surprise came when Linwood also made the behavior honor roll, perhaps a more difficult achievement for him. Orlando was so pleased at both accomplishments that he made Linwood the eleventh grade student of the month in April.

Fortunately for Linwood, "he was allowed to make mistakes," Orlando later reflects, "without us saying, 'Well, look, you screwed up. Now get out.' Students have a grace period here."

However, as Orlando raises the standards at Rice, it is questionable whether the Linwoods in this year's and future classes will be given as many chances. After expelling so many students at the end of last year, Orlando set a tone that clearly indicates less tolerance. While Linwood had already made his turnaround, many new students begin their career at Rice with missing fathers or, like Linwood, with fathers "in the system." All these young men carry a deep hurt that feeds rage of varying intensities. School is the safest place these youngsters have to play out their inner dramas. On the street, the consequences can be deadly. Unfortunately this often puts their tenure at Rice at risk.

To his credit, Linwood's father did reach out to his son from behind bars. Two years ago, he sent him a card reading:

Favour is deceitful, and beauty in vain:
But the woman that Fears the lord
She shall be praise until the end.
Give her the Fruits of her hands;
and let her own works praise her in the gates.
LOVE YOU ALLWAYS MY ONLY SON

Sessoms signed the card and wrote his inmate number underneath. Linwood was touched, but more by his father's continuing absence than his sentiment. When his father finally got out of prison earlier this year, Linwood argued with his mother that she should not let "that nigga' back into our house." Linwood believes it is only a matter of time before his father will betray the family again by getting arrested for using drugs or by robbing someone and making family members vulnerable to retaliation.

Linwood looks up at Orlando after reflecting on his choice to fight with his father. He admits he's angry with his mother for letting his father back into the household. He resents her request that he spend the weekend with his aunt since it undermines his position as the dominant male.

"But not as the dominant man," Orlando points out, then advises him to avoid falling back into blaming his father for his own actions.

Linwood promises to respect his mother's position as the head of the family, a common difficulty for maturing males who assume the "man of the house" role in the father's absence. He agrees that his mother's plan makes sense, then walks upstairs to class, thankful Orlando helped him overcome his wounded pride and do the right thing, which was his plan.

———

In between the second and third periods on the following Monday, October 25, Linwood knocks on Al Widziewicz's fifth floor office door. He barges in without waiting for an answer and interrupts a conversation with another senior about how to finance his college education. In general here, Puerto Rican families are significantly poorer than African American ones, and this young man is no exception. Worse, his father promises repeatedly to fill out financial aid forms, but then fails to do so. Widziewicz is beginning to suspect the father is jealous of his son's opportunity to go to college and subconsciously sabotages it. The young man might be eligible for need-based grants and financial aid programs, but will soon miss the application deadlines and his chance at a postsecondary education.

Usually Rice parents express gratitude effusively, as the mother of one of last year's graduates did yesterday. She called to say that the financial aid package worked out with Manhattan College was enabling her son to attend the school. As a low-income single mother and uneducated immigrant, she couldn't believe that her son could attend a private liberal arts college. She wept at the miracle as Widziewicz ended the conversation gracefully.

"But the shadow side comes out humorously," Widziewicz recounted after a recent evening session about the college application process he had held for parents of the juniors and seniors. "Every year, I tell the parents that all the scholarship and admission application forms require a self-addressed, stamped envelope. They always look at me like I'm from Mars, and then say they can't understand why anyone would send a letter to themselves."

"Yo, Mr. W.," Linwood announces, "I need to gets some info about the University of Buffalo."

"Linwood, please make an appointment next time," Widziewicz pleads but can't help letting a smile spoiling his attempt to look stern. He finds

Linwood's zeal refreshing compared to the passivity of many of his classmates, who wait for Widziewicz to initiate each step in the college application process.

Linwood has been researching postsecondary schools on his own, and writing and rewriting his college essay, following Widziewicz's input, since the first week of school. After making the honor roll last year, Linwood decided to buy into the rest of Orlando's vision and go to college. He took his first step in June with his year-end math project in which he determined that electrical engineering provides his best career option given his interests and aptitudes. He mapped out a salary trajectory starting around $35,000 that rose to six figures at the managerial level. Like his classmates, Linwood is determined to take care of his mother and "make her proud"—with emphasis on determination, since he struggles academically.

Linwood's first attempt at the SAT last year spelled out his problem. He posted a combined score of only 530 with 200 on the verbal section—the lowest possible score, meaning he got every question he answered wrong. He'll have to get his combined score up to over 900 to get into the schools he applied to, and as important, in order to qualify for the scholarships and other financial aid components, he needs to get both his tuition and room and board covered. Fortunately for African American and other designated minority groups, poverty is not nearly the barrier it is for disadvantaged whites and Asians. In addition, there are scholarships, such as New York State's Higher Education Opportunities Program, which target disadvantaged minorities who, like Linwood, score below the minimum acceptable SAT scores for various universities. The program provides remedial tutoring as well as financial aid.

Urban Catholic high schools such as Rice can hardly be accused of skimming the brightest students. Two seniors posted a mere 500 combined score on the SAT last spring, and several others scored about 600. Widziewicz finds these low scores disturbing, in his view belying Orlando's optimism that Rice can become a true academy. Widziewicz applauds the cultural shift to valuing scholarship but describes the actual steps as preliminary at best. The highest SAT score so far this year approached 1200, with only one other score over 1000.

The average combined score for the thirty-five seniors who took the test at the end of last year was only 793, with an even split on the verbal and math sections—about average for Rice students and their peers at African American Catholic high schools across the country.[3] Religiously affiliated schools, which are mostly Catholic, posted a mean combined score of 1047.

The large gap reflects the overwhelming presence of white students—at 69 percent, compared to blacks at 7 and Hispanics at 11 percent—in Catholic high schools nationwide, with a relatively small proportion of minorities.

The citywide average for public schools was 904, and nationally the mean was 1010.[4] In fairness, all the Rice seniors take the SAT, compared to only about a third of the city's graduating class—otherwise public schools would score significantly lower than Rice. In fact many schools with similar demographics already do, and only a quarter of graduates take the SAT. Similarly the national mean for African Americans was 856, and for Latinos, 913.[5] Again, most neither graduate nor take the test, so these scores represent only a small proportion of minorities.

The Catholic school advantage isn't so much about scores, which obviously aren't stellar, as the fact that the students stay in school long enough to graduate. They are also encouraged strongly to continue their education. As Linwood and many of his classmates from public school attest, teachers, administrators, and guidance counselors there seldom if ever talked to them about the possibility of going to college, let alone how to get admitted and financed.

All the boys Linwood grew up with attended large zoned high schools. As far as he knows, none are still in school. "They all dead or in jail," he remarked last week, as he stood outside his apartment building surveying the courtyard's benches, which were occupied by young men he'd known since childhood, "or selling drugs like them."

Currently Widziewicz's most pressing problem is convincing the seniors who need to better their scores to retake the SAT in November or December. Several have avoided taking it altogether, and Widziewicz is speaking to each about overcoming fears. One senior, Shawn Patterson, has a serious learning disability that limits his reading and writing abilities. He passes by listening carefully and memorizing lectures. Despite dozens of spelling and grammatical errors in Shawn's essays, writing standards are low enough at Rice that he receives a passing grade. Widziewicz worries whether the young man will make 500 as a combined score and can do little to help. Rice doesn't have the resources for students with disabilities, but Shawn's mother won't allow him to go to special education classes at public school, saying that it's more important for him to remain where he's safe and motivated.

Shawn is determined to go to college, a lofty aspiration considering the obstacles he faces. What Widziewicz usually struggles with is Rice students aspiring below what their already weak scores indicate. Those in the 900 range, for example, tend to apply to colleges where an 800 would suffice, mostly because they limit their alternatives to schools where they feel comfortable, meaning mostly African American and not academically challenging. Last week, Widziewicz took fifteen seniors to Marist College, a co-ed Catholic institution about an hour north of the city. The school offers a quality education in a somewhat Catholic environment where the SAT scores of entering freshmen average over 1100. When the seniors were taken on a campus tour, it became apparent that Marist actively pursues inner-city minority candidates. But several Rice seniors remarked there were too few black faces at Marist to inspire interest. What they were really saying was that the predominance of white and Asian faces meant that they would be outmatched academically, or at least that they didn't want to risk finding out.

Last year, Widziewicz worked hard to get the salutatorian a full scholarship to Notre Dame. The university even paid to fly the young man to Indiana for a campus visit, but he decided to go to a less demanding college with more minority students instead of facing the uphill academic battle he thought he would have to wage at Notre Dame. In truth, he ended up at a selective Jesuit university that was arguably as rigorous, but he *believed* it would be easier because of demographics. In Widziewicz's view, the mindset of Rice seniors is very similar to that of ethnic white Catholic students at parochial schools into the 1950s. They instinctively avoid environments that don't replicate their familiar ethnic village and where they might be embarrassed both socially and academically. Recently, Widziewicz talked to a senior with entrepreneurial interests about applying to a university with an international business program. The young man asked if the degree would help him fulfill his lifelong goal of becoming the manager of the Laundromat in his neighborhood.

"You might want to consider a wider world," Widziewicz exclaimed in an uncharacteristic show of emotion.

The senior shrugged and promised to think about it.

On the other hand, Widziewicz has to ensure that his students aren't overmatched, although this is more a matter of resources than the achievement gap.

Selective colleges aggressively pursue talented minority candidates and admit many with significantly lower SAT scores. At 1170, Aaron Ashe sits on the cusp of Ivy League eligibility. His second or third try will almost certainly qualify him for a highly competitive college and might garner a full scholarship. This sounds like a set-up for failure, since his white and Asian peers average 300 points higher.

The African American college dropout rate is 58 percent—48 percent higher than for whites—and higher for black males. But these rates vary dramatically from 5 percent at the most elite institutions to 93 percent at the University of the District of Columbia, which is 80 percent African American.[6]

"High dropout rates appear to be primarily caused by inferior K–12 preparation and an absence of a family college tradition," concluded the *Journal of Blacks in Higher Education*. It is no coincidence that the University of the District of Columbia is fed primarily by students from one of the worst urban public school systems in the country.

William Bowen, the former president of Princeton University and co-author of *The Shape of the River,* considered the bible for those who favor race-based college admissions, now calls for class-based affirmative action for the poorest applicants, regardless of race. Speaking at the University of Virginia, Bowen said that decades of race-based admissions policies have not resulted in a significant increase in the number of students from poor families getting into the most selective colleges.[7] This is hardly surprising since the vast majority of disadvantaged students are trapped in low-performing K–12 schools.

For minority students who qualify, the highest-ranked and best-endowed schools respond by expending enormous resources helping them make up academic ground, if necessary. As a result, at some highly reputable schools, such as Smith and Macalester Colleges, blacks outperform whites, with an 87 percent graduation rate, compared to 83 percent. But again, few of these students come from neighborhoods like Harlem. Most were born into middle- to upper-class black families with at least one parent with a college degree.[8]

Although graduates are accepted into selective colleges every year, no Rice seniors have scored high enough on the SAT to qualify for an Ivy League college since 1995, when twin brothers were both accepted on scholarship to Columbia University's engineering school. Unfortunately the twins both dropped out in their junior year, saying they couldn't handle the cultural differences; they felt intimidated because so many of their classmates had traveled extensively, owned laptops, and went home to upscale communities. Perhaps the mental and moral tenacity of previous generations has been lost. It is hard to imagine the pioneers of the civil rights movement dropping out because their white peers owned more stuff. These crusaders risked their lives to integrate schools and colleges. On the other hand, perhaps the twins' failure points to the success of the civil rights era, since the problems they faced were of class, not race. They didn't have to carry the burden of their race on their shoulders and so didn't have to become heroes—albeit, unfortunately for them.

At colleges in the mid-range to lower tiers, where remedial and support resources aren't as available, dropout rates increase. At Morehouse College, a historically black college with an all-male student body, SAT scores average 1050, making it almost as difficult to get into as institutions with higher test-score thresholds but using race-based admissions. Morehouse has a long and esteemed history graduating accomplished scholars and men of unrivaled accomplishments, such as Dr. Martin Luther King, Jr. But Morehouse doesn't have Yale's mentoring capability. Thirty-six percent drop out, versus 11 percent at Yale. Most historically black institutions fare worse, with dropout rates at Howard University at 44 percent, Clark Atlanta University at 66 percent, and Texas Southern University at 86 percent, for example.

The problem for minority seniors who are choosing among colleges below the top tier is to find ones that match their skill levels and provide as much academic support as possible. Gauging a student's character also plays a significant role. Linwood refuses to be intimidated by higher-scoring peers and is applying to several predominately white institutions, including the University of Buffalo and Hofstra University. He says his work ethic will make up for what he lacks in college readiness. Normally Widziewicz would caution a student with Linwood's results, but he trusts the senior's confidence and will power.

After school, Linwood works as a counselor at Boys Harbor where an administrator has a personal connection at the University of Buffalo and has offered to help Linwood with admissions, financial aid, and getting into a remedial program to catch up. Linwood has also applied for several small scholarships through Boys Harbor, among other sources, aggressively exploiting every possible source of support, since he wants to use his own money to buy a car.

Linwood finds the University of Buffalo attractive because it is far away from New York City and everyone he has ever known. "I need a different atmosphere to see if I can change myself and become a different person," Linwood says later. "I want to be anonymous next year to help me become calm and level-headed." On the other hand, Linwood fears being so far away from his mother where he can't protect her from his father and his "business associates." Linwood is also applying to colleges nearby like Hofstra University on Long Island. Family considerations weigh heavily on the conscience of many Rice seniors, who worry about younger siblings and their mothers' ability to pay the bills and deal with the 'hood alone.

Linwood continues to stand in Widziewicz's doorway, oblivious that he is interrupting a classmate's crucial counseling session. Widziewicz frowns with as much displeasure as he can muster, but as usual Linwood misses the meaning. Almost every day, Linwood pushes his way into Widziewicz's room with a question or a request for help in filling out application forms. And every day the guidance counselor reprimands him, but in such a mild-mannered way Linwood thinks he's joking. Widziewicz books Linwood an appointment for third period tomorrow, and then almost has to order him to go to class.

Widziewicz insists on appointments, partly to establish order and maintain confidentiality, but mostly because one-on-one sessions enable him to establish a relationship with each student. "I'm a personalist," he explains. "I begin the year with the fact that I want to treat each student as an individual masterpiece." Widziewicz sets psychodynamic goals for each young man without the student suspecting how much, as a Jungian-trained therapist, he is orchestrating the growing rapport. "I evaluate each student from a psychological and spiritual perspective to discern his pathology, his emotional and psychic needs, his goals, and his soul's code." Determining the appropriate list of colleges for each student and leading him through the application process is only the outer core of Widziewicz's perceived mission.

He also plans to help Linwood "cultivate an observing ego this year" instead of the puffed-up version that he believes Orlando relies on, "so he can stand outside himself and learn to reflect on and evaluate his choices before charging ahead"—which is exactly what Linwood says he needs to do without realizing how Widziewicz is influencing him in coming to that realization.

There is an unmistakable pastoral dimension to Widziewicz's counseling. He was educated entirely within the Catholic system, attended a seminary, and earned a master's degree in theology from Catholic University. In fact, Widziewicz looks like a priest. He stands well over six feet tall, exuding a meditative stillness rather than a formidable physical presence. Widziewicz's hairline receded over a high, round forehead two decades ago, when he was in his early twenties, leaving him with a permanent monastic appearance. His skin is pale, almost translucent, and stretches over sharply chiseled features that reveal his ascetic persona. Not surprisingly Widziewicz married a former nun.

Last year, Widziewicz orchestrated a 99 percent college acceptance rate and was honored by the seniors at graduation for establishing close relationships with them in only his first year at Rice. The one student not admitted to college chose to join the Marines instead, a far more demanding alternative than most postsecondary programs.

Widziewicz's gray-green eyes watch Linwood's shadow slip through the door as he slams it shut. Linwood isn't angry; rather the growing understanding that next year he'll be a college student fills him with both trepidation and glee that crackles like an electrical charge.

———

Like most students, Linwood was cautious about opening up to me at the beginning of the school year. Orlando informed the students at the orientations that I was writing a book about Rice.

"But I didn't totally believe it," Linwood said later. "Maybe you were working for Mr. Gober, and I didn't want to say anything that would get one of my classmates suspended or expelled." Linwood explained that "it wasn't cool to be opening up to a stranger, especially a white guy. It's not that race is such a big deal, but like my classmates, I was more hesitant. We didn't grow up around whites, and the only ones we knew were at Rice or other schools. They were all teachers and principals, and I wasn't close to any of them. We related more quickly to Mr. Davis because he's young and African American, and talked to us about our music and what goes on in the 'hood."

I make no effort to "be down" with the students about rap music or hip-hop culture. I ask questions about why this appeals to contemporary teenagers, but I don't personally like the music and could never pull off relating as Davis does. Instead I came to school every day, and after several weeks it became clear to Linwood and his peers that although I was taking notes, I wasn't passing information on to Orlando or Abbasse. By October, the students were comfortable with me in class and acted as if I wasn't there. In interviews, they began opening up about their private lives.

For Linwood, the turning point came when I took him for lunch a few weeks ago. He appreciated being allowed out of the school and avoiding cafeteria fare for a hamburger at the local diner. "I'm with that," he said, and we talked at length. I also visited his neighborhood, met his family, and interviewed his mother, who gave me the records she'd meticulously kept of Linwood's academic career since kindergarten.

Chapter Eleven

───

ORLANDO STRIDES INTO HIS FIRST-PERIOD English class twelve minutes late on Wednesday, October 27. He was delayed by a meeting with a parent about her son's behavioral problems. The mother arrived at 7:30 A.M. intending to bully the principal into siding with her against Abbasse, who she feels is being too hard on her first-born. Forty minutes later—after one of Orlando's passionate sermons on personal responsibility and high standards—the woman slid quietly out of his office. She resolved to deal directly with Abbasse next time.

Orlando passes under the ebony crucifix above the blackboard wearing a suit the color of grape juice and a collarless black shirt. He gives the eleventh graders one of his best disapproving looks, and they turn down their volume. They know Orlando's serious, but they also know him well enough to sense when he's overplaying himself for effect. Today, they can get away with low-level chatter.

By Orlando's own admission, his administrative and counseling duties allow so little time for class preparation that he "wings it every day." Instead of bringing the teacher's edition of the juniors' English textbook and its study guide back to his office to prepare, he leaves them in a file box on the teacher's desk in the classroom.

Orlando lifts the textbook and opens it slowly as he formulates today's lesson. He looks out the window, perhaps praying for inspiration, then tells the students to take out the instruction sheet on main characters that he handed out yesterday.

"You have there some character traits such as gender, race, and physical appearance. These are character traits about people, used to describe their character," Orlando begins in monotones so uncharacteristic of his speech pattern when not teaching. "Now in all works of reading in your textbook, you have characters. If there are no characters, there's no story. But character and characterization are two different things. Today you are going to write about a character. Think about someone you know well. You can't just say 'I know Jermaine Anderson.' You need to what?"

Jermaine stirs at the desk right in front of Orlando. He gathers his long legs together and almost sits up straight, but makes no attempt to answer.

"Expand," Allan Sanders calls from the back of the room as he works his thick glasses like binoculars.

"Embellish with details," Orlando corrects. "What can we say about a person's physical appearance, likes and dislikes, favorite recording artist? Take a minute to think, then take out a sheet of paper and write a paragraph on the character traits of the person you are writing about."

"Do you have to know the person's last name?" Dana Burton, a polite preacher's son, asks.

"Certainly," Orlando replies.

Meanwhile Aston Lindhart, who's only fifteen years old, hunches over his desk near the door. His score on the preparatory SAT (PSAT) last year indicated he'll score better than 1300 on the SAT in the spring. His mother wanted to send him to a private prep school this year, but his grades were too low. Both Orlando and Abbasse believe that Aston is simply too lazy to make the honor roll, but the young man's body language screams boredom. Aston has no patience for Rice's academic pace. He should be in a baccalaureate program or attending a demanding prep school and preparing to apply to an Ivy League college. Aston's neatly folded copy of the *New York Times* sits on the shelf under his desktop. After school, he works part-time designing and managing Web pages. As Orlando repeats his instructions, Aston shifts the increasing weight of his head from his right hand to his left and takes a pen out of his shirt pocket in slow motion.

"If the main character is 'Martin,' for example, we already know he's the main character since the show's named after him," Orlando refers to the TV sit-com *Martin* that most of the juniors watch regularly. "See if you can ID other major characters."

Aston stares blankly at the empty blackboard.

"Gina," Seve Sprouil volunteers, working hard to look cool, since his main extracurricular activity is playing classical violin. He has no illusions about his chances of becoming a professional musician, while many of his classmates who can't sing or play a musical instrument contemplate fame in the music business, albeit as rap artists.

"Yes, she plays his fiancée," Orlando over-enunciates as if Seve had just offered a profound literary insight. The principal then asks different students to read the definitions of minor, multi-faceted, and static character aloud from the photocopy and provide examples of each from *Martin*.

"As I said in summer school, you always want to relate what you are studying to your own environment because it helps learning," Orlando concludes twenty minutes later. The truth is that Orlando deliberately slows down to make his thin academic material last the entire period, at which point none of the students are awake enough to ask what "environment" the principal is referring to. Beyond the fact that most of the characters in *Martin* are African Americans, their upper middle-class TV lives bear almost no resemblance to those of Harlem and South Bronx residents.

As the period mercifully ends, Orlando assigns James Baldwin's short story "The Rockpile" as homework and announces a quiz on Monday. The ringing bell fails to rouse Aston from his trance, while Jan Vincent (J.V.) Agay, another high-achieving junior, stirs lethargically from his nap. Gregory (Greg) Vazquez, a white Hispanic with a choirboy persona, looks over at Mark Wilson, a handsome dark-skinned youth with a serious demeanor. Both boys scribble furiously in their notebooks, while classmates record the homework assignment in slow motion. As partners on Rice's forensics team, Greg and Mark have become best friends and competitors. Every week they compare their grades to see who has gained or lost slight advantages.

When Steve DiMattia and the other English teachers heard that Orlando was taking over the eleventh-grade English classes, they became concerned. Orlando has taught religion classes every year since coming to Rice and gained a reputation among his colleagues as a gifted administrator. DiMattia fears that a substantial number of juniors will fail the English Regents exam under Orlando's tutelage. Intelligent students like J.V., Greg, and Mark will certainly pass. But most students pretend to do the assigned readings they will need for the Regents without fear of being exposed, since Orlando is likewise pretending to prepare for class—which they sense. They will be able to pass Orlando's class with little effort, but DiMattia worries how well they will perform on the Regents' essay questions that presuppose a working knowledge of a wide range of literature from their three years of high school English.

This will be the first year the English Regents is required for graduation from all high schools in New York State. As a result, critics of higher standards predict a significant increase in the percentage of urban students failing to graduate. They also forecast a steady deterioration in the graduation rate, as additional Regents are phased in over the next several years and the passing grade on all tests is raised from 55 to 65.[1]

Orlando agrees with the plan to raise academic standards via the Regents exams, initiated in the mid-1990s by Richard P. Mills, the state's commissioner of education. Orlando firmly believes that higher standards will ultimately increase the number of minority graduates and force all schools to do a better job of preparing them for college.

"Even if a student fails the Regents, he can take it again that summer and then the following January," he points out. "There's no excuse for not getting all students through before graduating. And what are we here for anyway? Asian kids with parents who don't speak English have no trouble passing it, so why should our kids fail?"

For several weeks, Orlando has been planning to go over the Regents' test prep material that Charles Mauer assembled last year. Instead he's been spending an hour or more answering student e-mails about personal problems every evening, which also tires him emotionally. He makes a mental note to prepare this weekend, so he can begin drilling the juniors on Monday.

———

At 3 P.M., the teachers gather for their weekly faculty meeting in a fourth floor classroom, and Orlando is late for the first time. The teachers talk freely as they did regularly when Brother Walderman was principal. He initiated brief discussions on relevant issues, then left the meeting to let teachers vent their frustrations and talk about problems among themselves. In contrast, Orlando stays in the room to control all faculty interactions.

Today's unsupervised conversation begins with complaints about the workload. "With so many students, it's exhausting to keep up with all the tests and quizzes we're supposed to give," Rene Bodie complains, voicing what many teachers feel is one of their most vexing problems. Orlando expects grades to be reported in all five grading categories on a weekly to biweekly basis, multiplying the volume of work while diminishing its educational benefit. Teachers with freshman and sophomore classes have over a hundred students, making the marking of even a short quiz into a time-consuming affair. They are inclined to make the quizzes shorter and easier.

Another teacher describes the ongoing ordeal of having to prepare lesson plans for three grade levels with only one free period a day. Two teachers in the same predicament say that they have to cut back on tests and projects, but they are apprehensive about Orlando's reaction. All the teachers agree that the workload is even heavier than last year, when it was difficult enough to teach five or six classes a day and perform lunch duty. This year Orlando added the extended school period, which amounts to working another full period without compensation but with significant aggravation since discipline is poor. Orlando instituted ESP to benefit the students but never considered the effect on his teachers. ESP has no grades and therefore inspires disobedience from students.

The mention of discipline problems strikes a sensitive chord with most teachers, who share stories about how rude some students have recently become, as a result of Orlando's empowerment message. "The kids come into my classroom and ask about grades in an accusing tone," Steve DiMattia laments. "If I give a test one day, they expect results the next."

"Linwood told me I wasn't doing my job two weeks ago because the projects weren't marked right away," adds Brother James DePiro.

"Sometimes 'empower' gets confused with 'enabling,'" Widziewicz comments, "and puffs up egos." He worries that students will make similar demands at college and create negative impressions with their professors. Widziewicz points out that two important virtues are not appreciated under Orlando's reign: docility and humility. The Latin root for "education," Widziewicz adds matter of factly, is *docere,* also the root of "docile," indicating that being passive and receptive are critical components of learning.

Several teachers recount incidents where students were brazen enough to threaten them for giving low grades, intimating that they would use their pull with the principal to get the teacher fired. The warning, many teachers feel, is not as preposterous as it sounds after witnessing Orlando favoring students in confrontations.

"The message from the principal is that teachers are accountable even when students don't do their job," Brother DePiro complains. As a former high school principal, he expects more support for teachers.

"Do you feel validated as a teacher?" Widziewicz asks from a desk at the back of the room.

"Sometimes by the students," Steve DiMattia responds.

"By the administration?" Widziewicz presses.

"Once in a while, but Orlando's often condescending," Brother DePiro says.

Orlando pushes the teachers so hard to conform to his rules and profess faith in his vision, Widziewicz says, that working at Rice is sometimes like joining a cult. Teachers resist the indoctrination and consequently become targets of Orlando's ire—as all the veterans have seen and many have experienced, including Orlando's brother Wylie Gober. So far this year, Orlando hasn't publicly criticized any staff members, but no one wants to risk it, especially since it usually occurs in front of students. To be fair, Wylie Gober contends that despite the embarrassment, Orlando made him a much better teacher.

But as Widziewicz points out, Orlando sometimes tends to focus on minor details, such as whether teachers are following his decree to file student work in accordion folders at the back of the classroom, with the same intensity as more important issues. No one can predict when he'll fixate on the minutiae of one of his directives and suddenly criticize a teacher. "Orlando relates extremely well with children and terribly with adults," Widziewicz observes. "He treats grown-ups like children because he doesn't trust them. No wonder he has no adult social life."

Orlando usually starts faculty meetings with a Bible reading, or a long extemporaneous prayer, then a gives a pep talk about pedagogy interlaced with variations on the theme of "woundedness" and the African American male. The teachers don't disagree with Orlando's messages and consider his push for standard procedures a success, but they're tired of hearing his credo infused with threatening overtones directed at potential heretics. Great teachers, DiMattia points out, are not conformists; Orlando sometimes confuses stewardship with control.

The teachers feel they can't openly voice concerns without recrimination, believing for example that Orlando would take complaints about ESP as organized opposition and a personal betrayal.

"Who has challenged him here?" Widziewicz asks.

Silence answers. Maurice (Mo) Hicks, the varsity basketball coach, wanted to talk back last week. Orlando denied admission to a seven-foot Puerto Rican youngster Hicks had recommended. Hicks was imagining a twin-towers varsity team with Shagari, and another city and state champion. Brother Walderman would have taken the youngster in and considered it a coup, but Orlando dismissed the request, saying firmly that the freshman class was full and he wouldn't make any exceptions. For Hicks, it was pointless to try and reason with him.

"Orlando's really a borderline personality," Widziewicz offers as a diagnosis. "He has brittle defenses and sees things in black and white, and teachers are either saints or saboteurs. Some days I think he's great, but on others it's like being in a sick family. Everyone's afraid of how daddy's going to react."

Widziewicz lauds Orlando's expertise as a teacher mentor and his visionary gifts. "But he doesn't create community. He doesn't bring us together as adults in a cooperative enterprise," Widziewicz says. "We need to sit down and talk about real issues without fear. But everyone's petrified. His depressive side comes out, and he gets down on people, then he becomes messianic and declares, 'God has told me what I should do. I'm not answerable to Brother Walderman or the board of directors, only to him.' His bouts of paranoia are disturbing. Orlando seeks the adulation of the kids and fears the criticism of everyone else. He looks for people who are out to get him and imagines we're all in a conspiracy. He also gets upset that teachers are tired of his preaching, but he does preach. What he needs is a good mirror."

How Orlando organized the school demonstrates his insecurity. He abolished department heads as a way of eliminating rivals and reducing his most experienced teachers to the same official status as newcomers. With no effective opposition, administrative meetings usually consist of the same "Orlando-lectures-and-everyone-agrees" format as faculty meetings. As well, the administrative systems Orlando put in place can't operate without him, since they exist mostly in his head. Orlando takes care of all the scheduling, report cards, and correspondence himself. Instead of training Brother Maistre, a very intelligent and well-organized administrator, and providing the school with backup in case he becomes ill, Orlando shares some responsibilities but only with Michael DeWitt, a senior. Michael inputs the scheduling, grades, and other data into Orlando's computer. He's the only one who understands how it's organized and poses no threat since he's a student and completely under Orlando's authority.

Hebinck sits quietly at the back of the room listening to her colleagues' complaints. She finds Orlando's personality intimidating, but she's never had a professional problem with him. Her teaching issues revolve around getting the freshmen to quiet down and do their work. Orlando has consistently praised her efforts and advised that she persist in her demands. Recently he suggested that since contemporary youngsters, reared on video games and music videos, are so immature, they should be treated like elementary students and spend their first year at Rice in the same classroom with teachers rotating. Hebinck was relieved to realize the idea was Orlando's way of pointing out that the fault was not hers.

Abbasse remains silent as well. After arguing often with Orlando during his tenure as dean of students, Abbasse eventually became a staunch ally. He knows Orlando's faults well and isn't reticent about enumerating them. In fact, he still has a drink after work every week with Dino Murphy, the English teacher Orlando fought with most during his first years at Rice. Murphy, who Abbasse praises as the best teacher he's ever met, harbors nothing but scorn for Orlando. With several other teachers—all white males Abbasse describes as highly competent—Murphy battled Orlando's racial agenda and was his most vocal opponent. Orlando believes that Abbasse acted as the "ringleader," but Abbasse disputes his leadership role.

Although Murphy and Orlando couldn't look more dissimilar—the leprechaun squaring off with the bear—their personalities were mirror images. Both are visionary iconoclasts who couldn't tolerate opposition. Unfortunately, Orlando questioned Murphy's integrity, instead of seeking resolution and accommodation for the school's sake. "The students did better with Murphy because he rigidly willed them," Orlando said to diminish Murphy's success, implying that he was a closet racist. "It was part of Murphy's macho approach; he didn't give them any credit. It wasn't because they had half a mind."

Eventually Murphy tired of Orlando's implacable bias against him and took a teaching position at Frederick Douglass Academy, also in Harlem. Several other teachers migrated there because of difficulties with Orlando, and the principal at Frederick Douglass was always eager to take them on Murphy's recommendation. To determine the truth of Orlando's assessment of Murphy, I observed him teach several classes at the Frederick Douglass Academy. There wasn't a hint of racism or condescension in his approach. He was very entertaining, knowledgeable, and clearly adept at motivating his students.

Abbasse considers the loss of these teachers from Rice a significant blow, but he also says it was avoidable. Instead of responding to Orlando's tendency to challenge white males whenever he perceives an affront to his authority, Abbasse chose to talk honestly and calmly to Orlando about his issues with him. Instead of reacting angrily, Orlando answered in kind. The two worked out their differences and now consider each other indispensable partners. Murphy and the other teachers could have adopted this strategy in recognition of the difficulties that African Americans in leadership have faced and continue to encounter.

———

Ten minutes later, Orlando bursts into the faculty meeting beaming with joy. "We are blessed by God's grace every time we enter a classroom and touch the future. God calls us to his ministry. Amen," he lauds at the end of a shorter than usual opening prayer and calls the meeting to order.

Orlando clears his throat, mostly to quell his own excitement, and announces that Rice has been chosen as a Vanguard school, a major honor amounting to $750,000 in college scholarships each year for five graduates. His smile brightens even more as he adds that his proposed summer enrichment program might also be getting financial support.

This morning, Brother Walderman called Orlando to a meeting with officials from the National Action Council for Minorities in Engineering (NACME), the American Association of Black Engineers (AABE), Brooklyn Polytechnic University, Virtual Gold, Inc., and the 59th Street Con Ed power station. Orlando strode into the second floor meeting room across from Brother Walderman's office as if into alien territory. The hall used to be the Christian Brothers' dining room when more than thirty Brothers comprised the school's entire staff. Orlando was annoyed, thinking this would be another of what he describes as Brother Walderman's long-winded conferences in which representatives promise generous support but fail to deliver. Orlando suspects the real fault lies with poor follow-up on Brother Walderman's part.

Orlando's cynical attitude derives mostly from his own stereotype that whites are born with access to money, so Brother Walderman's failure to convert every contact into gold is a sign of indifference or incompetence. But to Orlando's surprise, Brother swiftly introduced each representative, who promptly announced his or her organization's part in Vanguard, a comprehensive mentoring and scholarship program that not only prepares minority high school students to get into college but also provides academic and big-brother support all the way through to a science-related career, especially in engineering.

Eva Graham, NACME's director of new program development, said NACME will fund Vanguard's scholarship component, which includes tuition and room and board, to top engineering schools such as the Rochester Institute of Technology and Texas A&M University. NACME is the leading privately funded source of scholarships for African American, Latino, and Native American engineering students, providing support for nearly 15 percent of minority graduates in engineering with a retention-to-graduation rate of 80 percent—more than double the national average for minority students.[2] Since the 1970s, NACME has played a major role in increasing the number of minorities graduating with engineering degrees yearly from a meager five hundred to over four thousand, a percentage gain from less than 1 percent to about 12 percent of the nation's total.[3]

Tutoring for Rice students will be provided by AABE engineers, and by graduate and undergraduate students from Brooklyn Polytech, which also offers to train Rice teachers to conduct math and science classes for juniors and seniors that will earn them college credit at Polytech and other science and engineering colleges, similar to the Advanced Placement program. The classes will also be open to Rice students who aren't chosen for scholarships but show an interest and sufficient aptitude.

Virtual Gold will provide Vanguard's sexiest element. As a pioneer in the developing field of data mining, Virtual Gold created the database program that most NBA teams use to analyze their opponents as a regular part of game preparation. Rice students will be able to log onto the Virtual Gold Web site and make the same scouting reports as the pros. Mastering the Virtual Gold program requires math and computer proficiency that the program develops, while hooking youngsters on the joys of quantitative analysis as a career path.

In addition, the manager of the 59th Street Con Ed power station will assign engineers to mentor Rice students preparing to qualify for the Vanguard scholarships.

Brother Walderman found out about Vanguard after having lunch several weeks ago at the Waldorf Hotel with two of Rice's board members, Stephen Fitzgerald '63, an IBM vice-president, and Joe Murphy '52, the chairman of the Country Savings Bank. Brother Walderman showed them a recent newspaper article that he had clipped in anger because it demonstrates the bias in the media favoring public schools. The article lauded an electronics superstore's donation of a mere six computers to a public school. The same week, a Rice alumnus gave the school twenty-five computers, which precipitated not a word of print even though Brother Walderman had press releases sent to all the city's major media outlets. Instead of lamenting further, the three men decided to look for a sponsorship deal the media couldn't ignore. A few hours of research uncovered Vanguard, a fledgling project, and Brother Walderman offered Rice as a pilot school.

Vanguard assessed the school's academic potential as an inner-city institution with the program's target demographics and accepted.

Orlando listened quietly, trying to catch his breath as each representative articulated his or her organization's contribution.

"I'm speechless," he finally told the assembly, "and I'm not usually at a loss for words." He did manage to say how much Vanguard will dovetail with his own plan to replace summer school with an enrichment program focusing on math and science. All the representatives agreed to consider support, and after realizing that the scholarships amount to three quarters of a million dollars a year, Orlando took their response as more than lip service.

As if on cue, Brother Walderman interrupted to praise Orlando for Rice's academic turnaround last year and add weight to his request for funding for the enrichment program. Orlando returned the compliment, a rarity since the two educators often disagree over the practicality of Orlando's expansive plans.

"It's heartwarming that major players like yourselves are saying to Rice students they're worth it," Orlando thanked the Vanguard representatives. "As we get students involved in Vanguard, others will become interested and that's how a school's culture changes."

Orlando finishes his account of Rice's selection by Vanguard to the faculty, obviously buoyed by the prospect of his dream of Rice as a "school on par with any other" becoming a reality. Sadly, while Vanguard offers an opportunity for young men with at least moderate talent and skill levels from a troubled, poverty-stricken neighborhood to go to excellent universities for free, many of the youngsters who could someday qualify for this and other programs refuse to apply themselves to school work, as evidenced in the student failure lists for the first marking period that ended last week, and which Orlando now hands out.

He asks the teachers to break into groups according to the grade level they teach to discuss students with multiple failures. Over a third of the student body failed at least one subject, and 20 percent failed two or more. Orlando announces that 113 students made the honor roll, but the achievement rings somewhat hollow in context.

Chapter Twelve

——

KATE HEBINCK LEAVES THE FACULTY meeting and follows the other ninth-grade teachers down the hall into Tim Hearn's classroom with a dour expression on her face. It seems that the day will never end, and tomorrow, Thursday, October 28, she'll have to endure parent-teacher conferences until 8 P.M. Hebinck sits at a desk to the side and lays down the failure list without glancing at the names; she put the majority there and feels guilty for showing little improvement from last year's freshman class. The ninth graders account for half the failing grades overall and 60 percent of the students with multiple failures. A full quarter of the freshman class have ended up failing English and another 20 percent, like Ricky Rodriguez, barely passed and are in serious danger of failing the next marking period. Most of the freshmen who failed English also failed at least one other subject as well, with three-quarters failing three or more. This makes Hebinck feel responsible for their academic shortcomings in all areas.

Remarkably, all of the Student Sponsor Partners' ninth graders, whose tenure at Catholic school depends on performance, did relatively well, with about half the failure rate of their peers. As Ricky Rodriguez said, "I didn't do so good, but I'm scared to fail out. My sponsor's spending big money, and he'd be pissed. Then where would I go?"

The weekly grade postings Hebinck compiled for the first marking period clearly reveal why so many freshmen got into trouble. For example, over seven weeks, Shagari Alleyne showed the typical pattern, scoring 100 on each of two quizzes and on an in-class assignment and a "homeworks," as the students say. The level of work is rudimentary to the point where virtually all students should be getting As—if they do their work. But Shagari earned four zeros for homework he didn't bother handing in, which reduced his final average to 50—a full 20 points below the passing grade—and he failed one other subject.

Nelson Castellano averaged 83 on the tests and 90 on the quizzes, yet his final grade was 51, again due to missed assignments. Ephraim Yisreal followed the same schizophrenic pattern, as did almost all the failing students. Hebinck's only surprise was that she motivated Prince to hand in enough work to get a 70, an astonishing achievement, considering that he failed all his other subjects.

A close look at Prince's record shows that he completed assignments and had passing grades until the first week of October. Then a childhood friend he hadn't seen for several years arrived at Rice as a sophomore. Paris Lane, already seventeen years old, had just been released from a juvenile detention center where he was consigned for the last year on drug-related charges. Prince started hanging with his charismatic pal after school instead of doing homework.

After-school habits account for the missed work of many students. Ephraim wanders around Times Square with classmates, frequenting video game arcades and record stores, or he goes back to his neighborhood and hangs out with friends. He returns home by 6 P.M., when his mother arrives from work. By the time dinner's over, Ephraim says he's too tired to do homework, but then watches TV or surfs the Internet on his computer for hours. He has both in his bedroom where they easily upstage textbooks.

Nelson failed four classes including English, primarily because he lacks supervision at home and, as a result, has acquired little self-discipline. His mother works in the evening as a subway clerk and doesn't return to their Bronx apartment until 10 P.M. This allows Nelson to hang out with friends and play basketball or video games, instead of doing homework. He says he brings his books home and starts working, but soon gets distracted when a friend comes by.

Shagari skipped homework assignments despite knowing that just one failure would prevent him from trying out for the varsity basketball team on November 8. Now the seven-footer won't be able to play until the end of the next marking period on December 3. Orlando bars all students who fail any classes from all extracurricular activities, including the chess and investment clubs that meet during the Extended School Period.

The freshman teachers sit in a circle with Eunice Lewis, the ninth-graders' guidance counselor, at the front of the room acting as chair. Since the summer session, she has arranged at least one meeting in her office with each young man to establish a relationship. She also teaches an ESP guidance class to half the ninth graders and often observes freshman classes as she patrols the hallways. Most of the chronically failing freshmen have trouble focusing on their work in class, fluctuating between falling asleep at their desks and hyperactive distraction. Some have grades as low as 12 out of 100. Fortunately for them, Orlando won't put any grade lower than 50 on report cards. He wants to allow for turnarounds that would become mathematically impossible with accurate grading. On the other hand, the additional leeway enables some students to postpone applying themselves. Many seem to need to fail several times before buying into the value of education.

The teachers first discuss the students who top the list for both academic and behavioral problems.

"They're not coping, but it's not a Rice issue," Lewis says firmly, her melancholy Caribbean cadence rippling through the room's glum atmosphere. She's trying to make the teachers feel better about the value of their efforts and the true limits of their responsibility. Every year, she reminds them, there are young men who are determined to fail out because they hate Rice's structured environment, and, as well, because often they are overwhelmed with personal and family issues.

"All those who aren't doing well in my class aren't putting any effort into it," Dionedes (D.J.) Lopez, the music teacher, echoes Hebinck's experience. "And believe it or not, Prince is falling asleep."

"I wish he'd fall asleep in my class," Rene Bodie comments and all the teachers laugh cathartically with her.

"It's a small class," Lopez continues. "Prince doesn't have enough people to bother so maybe he's bored."

The truth is Prince now has a girlfriend who goes to St. Jean Baptiste, an all-girls Catholic high school on the Upper East Side. They keep each other up late at night talking on the phone or meeting privately for more hormonal exchanges.

"He's in my G-period class and I have problems with them," says Ed Nunez, the new Spanish teacher, voicing the struggle he's having as a first-year teacher. According to Abbasse, Nunez's classroom management skills are typically minimal for a recent education-school graduate. He has trouble grasping the logic of Orlando's standardized procedures and falls back into yelling at disobedient students and expressing his frustrations, which only empowers the troublemakers. "They throw around paper all the time and I believe he's the one who starts it, but I can't catch him."

"I caught him today," Winsom Rene-Campbell offers with a note of triumph. "He couldn't believe I saw him."

"Now they're throwing pencils and making scotch-tape balls," Nunez continues in his slightly Hispanic accent tinged with a New England rounding of vowels. He's a first-generation Puerto Rican who grew up in Boston, then moved recently to New York. "They have this one big ball. So it's him."

"The students know who's doing it, so keep them after," Lewis suggests.

"I've done that. They're my detention class," Nunez responds. "But they haven't cracked yet."

"If they throw anything in my class, I pick it up and throw it back," Bodie says defiantly. "Believe me, they stop; they don't want to get hit. Anyway if I hit the wrong one, too bad."

"Yes, they make a ball and when I turn around they throw it around the room," Dr. Zachariah Saad, the Earth science teacher, adds. He strokes his beard like a college professor and speaks in a hesitant baritone that suggests he might be considering the event from the viewpoint of quantum mechanics. But the students consider him a drone and play around out of boredom, entirely missing what a valuable resource he could be.

Regarding Prince, most teachers concede there's been a slight improvement in his behavior over the last two weeks. Hebinck talked with his grandmother, and both Abbasse and Orlando have taken him aside for pep talks. After another detention pushed him over the limit for his first suspension two weeks ago, Abbasse asked his half-brother Hayward Washington and Andre Sweet, Rice's power forward, whom Prince idolizes, to have a talk with the freshman about his behavior. The two seniors took Prince out to the street after school and slapped him around. "That's not what I meant," Abbasse told them afterward, suppressing a laugh. "But you made your point. It's up to him now." However, since he failed all but one of his classes, no one's betting on a serious turnaround.

"Prince is certainly more talkative after lunch," Bodie observes.

"It's all that sugar," Hebinck comments.

"The students go to the vending machine and eat a lot of candy," Nunez says.

"Maybe it's that juice," Lopez suggests. The cafeteria staff uses a powdered mix to make a sugar-saturated drink.

"Lunch is also their social time. They get involved in conversations and get so riled up," Hebinck says, still too despondent to phrase her explanation eloquently. Relationships often develop between students who don't live near each other. With only three minutes allotted between periods, lunch is often the only time they have to reconnect.

"I'm glad we're having this talk because I'm like, 'What is going on?' " Nunez exclaims. "Every day after lunch, I think it's me."

"Ephraim's still a problem in my class," Lopez says, noting that he failed music, a difficult achievement.

"His average is about 85 in my class, but when he goes to the blackboard to write, he makes his letters so huge," Nunez says shaking his head. "I don't understand, he takes the entire board, and he's always such a clown."

"Where does he sit?" Hebinck asks.

"In the back."

"Move him to the front and put him right in front of you, not on the side," Hebinck suggests. "Works for me."

Several other teachers complain about Ephraim's antics. They show little patience for and less curiosity about what fuels his odd behavior patterns. Hebinck is surprised no one asks about his scar or whooping cough. The scar is disappearing under a healthy burst of hair, but Ephraim battles drowsiness if he takes his medications or disorientation if he skips them, becoming "a complete space cadet" according to Nunez, who doesn't understand the problem. Hebinck is the only teacher who has called Ephraim's mother or consulted with Abbasse.

"Now what's with this Jahman McKenzie?" Nunez asks. "He has a 90 average but he's very childish. When I give him a detention, he literally cries about it."

Other teachers relate stories about Jahman's "motor mouth." Not only does he talk constantly out of turn and instigate others to misbehave, but he can never resist responding to a classmate's prank or jibe no matter the consequence. He has become an easy mark for other students, who delight in manipulating his reactions into a detention. No doubt his baby face and waist-length dreads, usually tied back and hanging down his back, have made him a target for teasing all through his elementary school years, and the same is happening here. Jahman has developed a counterattack response that won't be tolerated at Rice, especially since it extends to talking back defiantly to teachers whenever they try to correct him. Abbasse can't figure out why Jahman resists following the classroom rules after he's explained them to him personally in detail several times. Jahman is one of the most intelligent freshmen and made the honor roll with ease. He certainly understands that challenging his teachers when he's clearly in the wrong leads to perdition at Rice, but he can't resist temptation. No doubt he's projecting the anger he wants to direct at the bullies onto his teachers.

When Abbasse talks to his father, a Jamaican immigrant who also wears his hair in long dreads, he finds total agreement about the need for discipline. But Jahman's behavior shows no improvement after several conferences with both father and son, which Abbasse finds discouraging. Both he and Orlando have taken a dislike to Jahman and view his recalcitrant behavior as arrogant. Unfortunately, Orlando's impatience with brighter students, such as Dwayne Carter, Aston Lindhart, and Jahman—who by public school standards are well behaved—and his failure to orchestrate sufficient intellectual challenges for them undermine his efforts to upgrade Rice's academic respectability.

Lewis makes a note to talk to Jahman next week in the hope that her more motherly approach will work. She reads further down the list of students with academic and behavioral problems and sighs: "Another big concern is Nelson Castellano."

"Oh yeah," the teachers moan in chorus.

"He seems like he doesn't care," Lewis observes.

"I feel his apathy is a sign that he doesn't believe in himself," Hebinck explains. "Even when he does his work, it's incomplete."

"He doesn't follow instructions," Bodie adds.

"I had him in summer school," Hebinck continues. "He's a smart kid, but didn't try to attain his potential. Maybe he needs to be put in honors classes because he's not being challenged. But will he rise to it? Now he hasn't got the motivation to do what's assigned."

"Mostly he sleeps in my class," Rene-Campbell says. To be fair to Nelson, she does little to encourage students to pay attention and stay awake.

"He didn't misbehave in my class at first," Hebinck adds, "but now he's very sarcastic and tries to get the class to laugh. He seems to feel that he's gotten a bad reputation and there's no way to change it."

"He has defenses," Lewis concludes, in effect writing Nelson off in her mind. She has a clear sense of the limits of the school's responsibility and a less-than-aggressive commitment to reaching out to lost souls who most need a pull in the right direction.

" 'Everybody's against me,' " Hebinck voices Nelson's persona. " 'They're going to blame it all on me, so why try?' "

Like so many of his classmates, Nelson has no older male at home to talk to or imitate. He's being socialized almost entirely by peers, and a steady diet of rap music and videos on MTV (Music Television) and BET (Black Entertainment Television). The unrelenting deluge of sexual and violent imagery primes teenagers for failure, and those without fatherly guidance are more susceptible. So far Nelson has resisted the antidote: bonding with Orlando, Abbasse, or one of the teachers. However, he seems drawn to Abbasse and certainly sees him often in detention or in conferences about his attitude in class.

The problem is that Nelson has no incentive to grow up since his mother will continue to reward his immaturity by buying him whatever he desires, and she will continue to allow him to run wild after school. If he's asked to leave Rice, he'll transfer to a zoned public school and hang out with other lost boys all day too. The catch is that Nelson secretly cherishes the prospect of success that Rice offers. He really wants to graduate in four years and go to college, he says. He plans to own his own business, buy a house, and raise a family far from the urban version of a rundown trailer park, which he now inhabits and despises. That Nelson has far fewer behavioral problems with his male teachers, Widziewicz remarks, is often typical of students who project more of their painful longings for a father figure than anger onto older males. Sadly, neither Lewis nor any of the teachers offer suggestions that might help Nelson establish a catalyzing connection with Rice.

The meeting ends with the new ninth-grade teachers feeling better about the problems they've been experiencing. This was their first opportunity to share anxieties, since Orlando monopolizes faculty meetings with his own agenda. If he had sat in on this forum, his mere presence would have silenced the more insecure teachers who needed to confess their tribulations.

Hebinck slogs dejectedly back up to her classroom on the seventh floor to collect her coat. By 4:30 P.M., she's walking slowly down 124th Street beside Mt. Morris Park, a block from Rice, on the way to the subway. More shadows than leaves fall from the darkening trees as Hebinck ponders her day. Unlike the other freshman teachers—with the exception of Shea, who has established a successful rapport with students—she's not merely trying to survive the year. Hebinck wants to achieve mastery. She sees the problem clearly, but what's the solution?

She considers that a homework clinic might work, and decides to ask Orlando tomorrow. It seems that many students literally don't know how to open a book and do homework on their own, never having done so at their previous schools. Hebinck knows she'll have stay at school an hour later every day, then still spend two or three hours marking assignments and preparing the next day's classes at home. But she'll do whatever it takes since teaching is more a ministry than a job for her.

But Hebinck no longer loves going to Rice, nor has she since last spring when the stubborn defiance of a core group of students wore on her desire to teach in an urban school. She hoped to avoid repeating the same slow, painful grind, but this year's freshmen are worse. Now Hebinck yearns for escape and contemplates her plan to marry her fiancé next summer and perhaps spend the next two years in France. Her betrothed is a chef who recently received an offer to work at a top restaurant in Lyons. Were she pleased with her progress, she would stay at Rice and visit her new husband during holidays. But she's grown so tired of the daily battle to control her classroom that she's decided to look for a position teaching English as a second language in France.

The difficult position that contemporary teachers find themselves in is captured best by Brian Copeland, the tenth-grade biology teacher. At the parent-teacher conference the next day, he says, "You see it coming through the door when the parents arrive. They've abdicated their responsibilities and put their kids up for adoption at school. Then they want to come back and play best friends instead of doing the hard job of caring and disciplining. So we're supposed to do it all."

Chapter Thirteen

———

ON THE FOLLOWING TUESDAY, NOVEMBER 2, Orlando stands in Brother DePiro's doorway ready to commandeer the last half of his third-period religion class. The principal approached Brother DePiro yesterday about wanting to talk to the seniors. Brother didn't complain about the loss of class time. He has been trying to give the seniors a sense of Church history and Catholic teachings before they graduate, but is becoming very frustrated.

"In the ninth grade, you covered the Old Testament and in the tenth, you studied the gospels," Brother DePiro told them in the first week of school. "Last year, you were introduced to the concept of morality and to Church history. This year, we're going to discuss the basic principles of Catholic Christianity as they apply to social justice and to faith." But again yesterday, Brother DePiro was dumbfounded by the seniors' capacity to forget what they've been taught. He began a lecture about fifth-century bishops gathering for the first Council of Nicea to draft the earliest version of the Nicene Creed, the Church's fundamental credo, when Linwood interrupted and asked earnestly, "What's a bishop?" Instead of analyzing the doctrinal issues at stake at the council, which were crucial in the development of modern Christianity, Brother DePiro had to review basics.

The problem is that there is little incentive for Rice students to retain information from religion class, since merely showing up and handing in elementary-level work is sufficient to pass. Linwood got an A for submitting an assignment three weeks ago that read:

> This . . . deals with the discussion of sex and how our youth are getting more interested in unprotected sex which cause's diseases that have not yet been cured. Also sex before marriage has become a very major issue in our society today, many people have been committing adultery and fornication which has been killing the purity of there virgin wool and also is killing with diseases.

The sad fact is that graded on a curve, Linwood's work deserved top marks.

Brother DePiro often laments that little Catholicism is taught at most Catholic schools anymore, even those with a majority of Catholic students. He hoped to lead his seniors through an academically rigorous inquiry into Catholic theology, but slowly has allowed his class to become a lax discussion seminar, like the religion classes in other grades where personal opinions rule. Ironically the decision to build an independent Catholic school system was made in the 1840s in significant part to prevent Catholic children from forming individual opinions about Scripture—and by extension, dogma and morality—as was encouraged in Protestant-oriented schools at the time.

"Brother, was Joseph, Jesus's father, a Catholic?" Linwood then asked.

Brother DePiro chuckled, both incredulous and painfully amused. He briefly recounted how Christianity developed out of Judaism, and how the differentiation between Catholic and Protestant occurred centuries later. He also explained how Catholics interpret the Bible symbolically, in contrast to the more literal rendering of the Protestant sects that most of the students belong to. Brother DePiro thought this would stimulate passionate arguments, but students answered with the usual chorus of yawns.

Brother DePiro nods to Orlando, then walks quickly out of the classroom without giving a homework assignment. He's resigned to simply surviving until June when he can request a transfer to another Christian Brothers school.

Orlando stands in the doorway, straightening his orange tie and seemingly aligning its geometric pattern with the sharp cut of his dark brown suit. Then he steps slowly across the front of the room like a polished actor. Finding center stage, Orlando pauses dramatically before speaking.

"This is the beginning of the end, and we need to talk about what's important for graduation," he intones, initiating his preemptive strike against senioritis that every year corrodes the academic focus of the graduating class. With students paying so much attention to the college application process, they lose interest in completing homework, projects, and studying for tests. "I'll start with number one: academics; number two is academics; and number three?"

"Yeah," the seniors respond jokingly.

"That's right, and number four would be: academics," Orlando laughs as he lumbers down the center aisle, surrounded by half the graduating class at desks arranged in a forum. He'll address the rest of the seniors tomorrow.

Andre Sweet sinks back into his seat looking bored but paying close attention. Sweet, as everyone calls him, is a six-foot, eight-inch power forward who's being recruited by some of the best basketball college programs in the country. Orlando has already told him that if he doesn't make first honors this marking period, he won't be allowed to play for the varsity team. Orlando said he's grown tired of Sweet working well below his potential and making only second honors. Sweet wants to go to Duke University where most starters make it to the NBA. On one hand, he feels relieved that Orlando is pushing him. Duke's coach, Mike Kryzewski, has the best basketball program in the country and wants his players to stay for four years. Over 90 percent graduate, far more than at most basketball powerhouses. Kryzewski won't tolerate poor academic performance and Duke is a demanding school.

However, Sweet is not accustomed to working hard. Getting onto first honors will force him to complete all his assignments on time. He'll also have to put more effort into his math and physics classes, since neither of his teachers, Olivene Browne nor Tim Hearn, make it easy to average over 90.

Sweet would never show it, but Orlando makes him quake. The principal really would make the senior sit out the season, even if it cost Rice another state championship, and cost Sweet his athletic scholarship.

"Last year we got tough and raised the passing grade from 65 to 70 percent," Orlando reminds them. "We didn't have 'mad failures,' like so many people, including many of you, said. On the contrary, if you raise standards, people measure up."

Linwood's eyes glaze over since he doesn't need prodding about his work ethic.

"Remember, there's no summer school next year for failures," Orlando continues, jolting several seniors who'd forgotten this change, to sit upright. "If you fail even one class, you won't graduate in May, and you'll have to retake the course at a public school." The idea that a student can learn in five weeks what he couldn't comprehend in forty strikes Orlando as ludicrous and a form of social promotion. Before he took over, about two-thirds of the student body would retake one course, if not several, every summer. As a result, Rice generated a substantial profit, which in Orlando's view showed that it had an institutional interest in tolerating failure. Orlando's textbook thumping last year reduced the number in summer school to less than one hundred students. Over Brother Walderman's pragmatic objections, Orlando was willing to take the next step toward the purity of his vision, even if some of his boys don't graduate on time. Next summer, there will be no classes for subject failures, but students can take Regents prep classes if they fail one or more of the state exams.

About a dozen seniors have failed the U.S. history Regents twice already, and Orlando reminds them they need to pass it in January. Actually, passing U.S. history isn't a state requirement yet, but Orlando insists that it is one of his graduation requirements. Orlando also reminds the seniors they must complete the required sixty-five hours of Christian service before graduating.

Orlando understands how much his young men want to walk down the aisle at St. Patrick's Cathedral to receive their diplomas in front of parents and guardians, who see sons from their neighborhoods matriculate on time so seldom that the event is as important as college graduation in an affluent area. Orlando looks forward to standing at the podium at St. Patrick's watching the procession approach the altar. Every diploma he hands out that evening anoints both the student's efforts and his mentoring. After losing almost half of their classmates since the ninth grade, the seniors don't take graduation from Rice for granted. Technically none of their former peers dropped out since they all transferred to other high schools. Some moved, as parents lost jobs or as families changed configuration; others left because they longed for the ease of public school or preferred a co-ed environment. But most failed too many subjects to continue or refused to conform to Orlando's strict behavioral standards. He will mourn the absence of these young men on graduation night too, for he had established close personal relationships with many of them.

"Last year, we had almost twenty seniors in the Gimme Five Club," Orlando intones, referring to what he set up to encourage seniors to apply to enough colleges that they would be accepted at five or more. Some students got into twenty without considering whether they had gained any qualitatively different alternatives, but the competition pushed everyone to get into at least one postsecondary institution, except the senior who enlisted in the Marines.

The students don't ask Orlando any questions, nor do they talk to each other. They've learned that even seemingly benign queries or comments can precipitate emotional eruptions. These were more common last year as Orlando established his regime, and so far no one risks inciting him.

Orlando pauses a moment, then launches into his main teaching homily for the day: "The story goes that there was a young brother who'd been saving up for a party like the Rice Jam. He purchased his outfit about two weeks before and then saved up $125 for the sneakers he wanted. But the first store didn't have his size, so down 145th Street he goes to the next one. This guy has his size, but unfortunately the wrong color, so onto the third store he journeys where finally he's blessed. This store has his size and color, but charges $150 for the sneakers. What does he do?"

"Go to another store," Linwood answers with characteristic determination.

Orlando nods an "all right," then looks in Sweet's direction and asks, "What would you do in his place?"

"Negotiate," Sweet answers.

"Okay, what about you?" Orlando surveys the back of the room.

"Pay the money," Ray Jones interjects.

"All right, the point is you would have to make a decision," Orlando explains, "and whatever you decide, it's going to cost you something: time or money or aggravation."

The seniors shift uncomfortably in their seats as Orlando opens his Bible.

"Suppose one of you wants to build a tower," he reads from St. Luke. "Will he not first sit down and estimate the cost to see if he has enough money to complete it?"[1] Orlando pauses a moment. "If you want to build a wardrobe for the Rice Jams, or if you want to build your skills as a basketball player, Jesus says it's going to cost you if you want to succeed, and he's not talking just about money. This brother said he'd dicker with the guy to get the price of the sneakers down. If you can do that, it's a talent."

Since the school year began, Orlando has been praying for guidance about how best to reach his students this year. "Finally, the Spirit came and told me to go into each class to talk from a biblical point of view, then I recalled the verse from Luke," Orlando explains later. "The Spirit always comes to me as a voice. I knew I was going to become the principal two years before anyone considered the possibility. I was taking a shower and the Spirit said: 'You will have this, but I want you to stay faithful; I want you to humble yourself to me and feed my lambs.'"

Orlando paces back toward the blackboard. "You guys stay late in the afternoon and come in on weekends to play ball," Orlando revs up his preacher's cadence. "Now nothing—get it into your heads—nothing comes to you without putting in the time. So my question to you is: Is it worth it?"

Silent nods of consent, at least regarding the value of working hard to improve basketball skills.

"It's my job to be the role model," Orlando softens his voice. "You see me sitting in my office at 8 o'clock in the morning when you get here. Then at 8 o'clock after basketball practice, I'm usually still there. So is it worth it for you to sit up late every night doing your homework instead of watching TV or talking on the phone to girls?"

With daily assignments, regular quizzes, and term projects, in addition to preparing for SATs and revising college essays, the seniors have a substantial volume of work this fall. Widziewicz characterizes much of it as "busy work" without much intellectual challenge, but it requires consistent effort. The seniors complain about the workload and are often up late doing homework, especially those with after-school jobs or who play on the basketball team.

"If you want to graduate and go to college, you're going to have to sacrifice," Orlando heads for an emotional crescendo. "Don't stop working until June because I will not tolerate senioritis. So count the cost and see if it's worth it to you." Orlando's voice cracks like a whip.

Instinctively the seniors hold their breath and remain still. Joe Carrington quickly grows uncomfortable in the reflective silence and mutters, "I'm goin' to U.C.L.A., Gobe."

"What's that, Joe?" asks Orlando, impressed with Joe's sudden aspiration. So far, he has refused even to take the SAT, saying he plans to go to a community college and study "whatever."

"Goin' to U.C.L.A.," Joe drawls with a smile.

"I didn't know you wanted to go to California," Orlando replies.

"California, no way," Joe quips. "You find me at da University at da Corner of Lenox Avenue."

The seniors erupt into laughter, and Joe earns a deep frown from the principal. Joe's speech patterns are rigorously street, as if he's always trying to prove he's black. His dirty blond hair and fair skin indicate mostly Caucasian genes. After school, Joe hangs with his peeps on their street corner and never tires of reminding his classmates that he's down with all the local drug dealers.

"Don't fall for what the world tells you because you're Latino or African American. They say you can't do it," Orlando roars, shaking his head. "That's a vicious lie, even if we don't always speak Standard English. And don't fall for the idea that getting on the honor roll, or graduating and going to college, is 'acting white.' If that's true, then acting black or Hispanic means you're dumb. You've got to believe."

While Orlando accepts Black English and other aspects of contemporary African American culture that deviate from the mainstream, he completely discounts the argument that the resistance to "acting white" is justified as a political rejection of the values of the oppressor or as a strategy to deal with the fear of failure. Orlando hosts a student rap contest every year in which "spitting" in Standard English would sound ridiculous, just as Black English or any dialect is inappropriate on the Regents exams.

———

Minutes after the school day ends, Jose Mateo, a junior, sits in Orlando's office talking about a recent fight with his father. The man drinks heavily, then argues with his son, sometimes beating him. Out of desperation, Jose conferred with Orlando last year. He also sought advice about how to deal with girls since several were vying for the handsome Hispanic's affection. He obliged all of them and felt guilty.

Perhaps one of the most important dimensions offered by a parochial education is the constant use of the verb "should." Despite the intellectual paucity of many religion classes, students become accustomed to asking and being asked what they should do in moral situations.

Instead of simply taking advantage of all the young women who throw themselves at him, Jose wants to live up to Orlando's constant exhortations to treat them properly. Jose listened intently when the principal coached him in the art of choosing the right partner by shifting his focus beyond physical attributes to examining character.

Several weeks ago, Orlando unexpectedly met Jose's mother on the street near Rice. She told him about the custody battle she is having with her husband, and how upset she is that Jose is living with his overly permissive father.

"My baby's hanging out until three o'clock in the morning with friends and girls and it's so dangerous," she sobbed.

"First of all, he's not your baby," Orlando reminded her, "but don't worry, we'll get through it."

Orlando talked to Jose the next day, expressing sympathy for the inner turmoil his parents' problems were causing, but focused as always on the young man's responsibility in the situation. Jose's schoolwork wasn't suffering yet, but Orlando warned that his noticeable fatigue in class would soon impact his grades. More importantly, he pointed out that hanging out on street corners at night associates him with drug dealers and with young women who are likely candidates for pregnancy. Jose promised to repent and the next day appeared more alert in class. He has maintained his poise since.

Today, Jose admits he has been back on the street the last few nights, avoiding his father, who attacked him after getting drunk.

"I'm the reason my father's an alcoholic," Jose blurts out.

"His drinking isn't your fault," Orlando corrects.

"My father tells me again and again I'm the reason he drinks," Jose replies as tears stream down his cheeks. The man blames his son for his own career failures, as if it is Jose's fault he didn't finish school. Remarkably, the father blames Jose for the two older sons' dropping out as well. When Jose's father saw his report card last week, he became enraged that Jose made the honor roll again. "You make me sick. You think you're smart," his father yelled before stomping off to a bar.

Orlando reassures Jose that his father's jealous rage has nothing to do with him.

"Mr. Gober, how would you feel if you were the reason your father's a drunk?" Jose asks, oblivious to Orlando's comment.

"First I'd see whether or not that's true," Orlando answers.

"But he tells me all the time," Jose sobs.

"It's not your fault," Orlando puts his arm around the young man and tries to heal another father wound. "The next time he says so, tell him: 'You're a drunk and that's your life, your choice—not mine.'"

"He'll hit me."

"That's the least of your problems," Orlando advises. "Besides, you can go live with your mother, even though it's farther away." He reassures Jose several times to help renew his emotional strength. Ten minutes later, Jose leaves and Orlando calls his father. Mr. Mateo apologizes for hitting his son, but then goes on to describe Jose as a "terror" at home who never listens. Orlando asks whether it's more accurate to say that he's provoking his son's negative reactions. Jose has never had a behavioral problem at school, even as his parents drag him through a contentious divorce. Jose's father ignores Orlando's question and blames his son again for driving him to act badly.

Mr. Mateo's been drinking all afternoon, Orlando concludes, and ends the conversation. "Jose is the latest example of a young man with enormous potential being crippled by his father," Orlando declares as he hangs up.

"He really believes all this negativity about himself and he's going to have trouble overcoming it."

Orlando turns back to his computer and sinks into his seat as he stares at a long list of e-mails from students. Some of the juniors submit assignments electronically, but most are from students about personal issues. The responsibility for so many lives weighs on Orlando, the burden noticeably heavier at the end of the day, when he feels alternately like St. George the Dragon Slayer, his patron saint by birthday, and Sisyphus. There are remarkable turnarounds like Linwood's, but then wrenching losses like Dwayne Carter's that fill Orlando with a sense of futility.

Almost every day another young man comes to the principal about problems Orlando then has to analyze in order to give specific advice. Once the process starts, Orlando mentally keeps track of the student's behavior, paying considerable attention to modulations in mood and attitude, which usually signal trouble. To some extent, he does this for everyone, but more intently for those in consultation, the number of which will grow to a third of the school's population by Christmas.

———

By the time Orlando gets home, exhaustion permeates every cell. At least he's not coughing much anymore. Shortly after becoming principal last year, Orlando caught a cold that never completely went away and flares up periodically. He thought it was a reaction to his office's air conditioning and lack of ventilation. After a tiring summer with grand jury duty and only a short break before school began again, Orlando felt his cold symptoms worsen through September. By the second week in October, Orlando's cough worsened to the point where he could no longer suppress it in class. He finally dragged himself to his doctor and found out that he had pneumonia. One lung had collapsed, and the other was filling quickly with fluid. Reluctantly Orlando took several days off to rest and allow the antibiotics to do their job.

It doesn't help that Orlando skips meals regularly at school, then gets home at 9 or 10 P.M., often with unhealthy take-out dinners. His blood-sugar levels fluctuate wildly at times, fueling emotional highs and lows, and making his diabetes more severe. He admits he should have consulted his physician months ago, but says he was raised to be a crusader and ignore his own discomfort. "I'm the oldest boy in the family and my mom and dad put so much emphasis on succeeding for the race and for the family," Orlando explains. "They drilled this into my head so much I felt I had the weight of the whole African American race on my shoulders. So I saw my illness in purely psychological terms as merely another obstacle to over-come." It is no coincidence that Orlando mounted a large poster in the foyer beside his office reading: I CAN, I WILL, I MUST! He views taking care of his own physical and mental health as self-indulgent.

Orlando is trapped in this cycle because, as Widziewicz remarks with compassion, the role of Jesus the martyr has become integral to his psy-chodynamics. After counseling students all day and into the evening, he works late and on weekends to catch up on administrative duties. On Sun-days, he arranges his schedule for the week, not a simple task with all the in-class talks he gives and the many meetings with parents and teachers as well as obligations such as the monthly meeting with the board of directors. Orlando e-mails the schedule to his administrative staff, then drags himself home for a feeble attempt at rejuvenation for the coming week. He's drowning in administrative trivia, but insists on micromanaging every de-tail. Anything less than a superhuman effort frightens Orlando because he would risk repeating the Samantha Brown incident—not literally, but the loss of any student resonates with the tragedy.

More than a quarter of New York City's public school principals leave their jobs less than two years after their appointments. They cite mounting stress from pressures to improve student performance on top of the peren-nial problems of establishing order when regulations conspire against en-forcing consequences for student misbehavior. Nationwide, a growing principal shortage will become acute as the majority will soon reach a me-dian age of fifty and become eligible to retire five years later.[2] Orlando could easily become a consultant for public or private schools struggling to serve minority students, or he could find a higher-paying principal's job at a sub-urban public school where problems would be less severe and support staff would take care of most administrative duties.[3]

With Rice's increasing enrollment, Orlando asked Brother Walderman to fund an assistant principal's position next year. When the school adopted the president-principal model in 1995, they eliminated the assistant princi-pal's job. But now Orlando feels overwhelmed, and next year the student population will shoot up by fifty students. However, Brother Walderman balks at the proposal, seeing the increased revenue as a step toward solvency rather than a means for easing burdens. Orlando's overpowering personal-ity gives Brother no indication that his core energies are depleting. There are more costs to count than those in a ledger book, and this applies equally to Orlando, who hides significant liabilities from the overall accounting.

Chapter Fourteen

ORLANDO'S EYES OPEN AS A wet wind rattles his bedroom window on the following Monday, November 8. At exactly 6:00 A.M., he picks up the phone and dials.

"Are you up?" Orlando asks and sits on the edge of his bed half an hour before sunrise.

"Yeah," Yusef Abednego, a sophomore, grunts softly. "Okay, dad, see you at school."

Half an hour later, Yusef knots his dark green tie as he walks down the dark hallway of his first floor apartment. The bare wooden floors are worn beyond memory of varnish and list toward the early decades of the twentieth century. Yusef pushes the sagging front door open and slips out of his narrow, two-story building in the Soundview area of the South Bronx across the Bronx River from Hunt's Point, which in turn faces Riker's Island, the city's jail, in the East River. Instinctively, he inspects the street corner to his right toward the Bruckner Freeway where he still sells crack cocaine occasionally, despite promises to his mother and himself to stop. There's no one there, but soon the junkies will prowl. Yusef might work the corner after school one night this week, where he can make about $150 per hour. He also timeshares purveying rights on two other street corners in the neighborhood, pushing heroin and marijuana, but far less often as a Rice Man.

According to Yusef, it's only the old-timers and white youths, venturing by car into the area, who buy crack and heroin anymore. In contrast, Yusef and his peers smoke weed, and some of his friends flirt with Ecstasy. But few of them do hard drugs or drink, or indulge in the infamous "forty and a blunt"—a forty-ounce bottle of malt liquor consumed while smoking a massive joint made from a hollowed-out cigar. The result is as intoxicating as any narcotic. Self-control has become a prime virtue for Yusef and his peers after seeing so many of their parents and older siblings suffer the ravages of the drug wars. Indulging in marijuana in controlled quantities won't get them completely wasted or turn them into psychotic killers. Nor will they be using needles that transmit HIV.

Yusef wears a checked white shirt today under his Rice vest. His hair is closely cropped beneath a white baseball cap and do-rag. The sixteen-year-old stands an inch or two shy of six feet tall, depending on whether he's slouching his shoulders as he walks. He has a wiry build that contributes to his boyish look, but there's no naïveté in his eyes. One moment, they check out his surroundings like surveillance cameras; the next, they seem to ponder deeper meaning like a philosopher.

Yusef walks up Colgate Avenue, then turns right under the elevated subway tracks and follows Westchester Avenue. Two blocks later, he passes by Wheeler Avenue on his right. Halfway down the block is a two-story apartment house numbered 1157, the same as Yusef's, where Amadou Diallo was mistaken for a rape suspect last February 4. As Yusef walked nearby with fellow gang members, he heard the eight-second, semi-automatic burst that propelled nineteen of the forty-one police bullets into, or right through, the wallet-toting African immigrant. The sound of gunfire was familiar to their ears and evoked no curiosity. They headed quickly in the opposite direction, believing that a drug dispute had turned violent. People get "popped" regularly in this neighborhood, Yusef attests, and the shooters "aren't like the cops; they don't know shit about aiming a gun."

Yusef takes the subway south. By 7:30 A.M., he sits alone in Rice's cafeteria eating his usual breakfast of scrambled eggs, sausage, and a roll for $2.50. Afterward, he spots Orlando walking toward the kitchen area to pick up his food. Yusef jumps up to intercept his principal.

"I don't know why I said what I did this morning," Yusef explains, perhaps the longest sentence he's spoken since September. "Guess I was thinking about the raffle tickets." Orlando organizes an annual raffle to raise money for school events. Students and their parents compete to sell tickets and please their chief.

"What did you say?" Orlando asks.

Yusef's jaw drops slightly and his eyelids become slits.

"Oh, I was just kidding," Orlando recovers quickly as he remembers that the youngster referred to him as "dad" earlier. "But why did you say it?"

"I don't know," Yusef shrugs.

"Well, thank you so much," Orlando says as he turns to face the young man directly.

Yusef's face brightens. A rare smile sweeps across his face and accompanies him upstairs to his first class. Although this is Yusef's third attempt at the tenth grade, he was a good student throughout elementary school at St. John Chrysostom in the Bronx, within walking distance of his house. Yusef wasn't raised Catholic, nor did he attend church regularly, but his mother, who grew up in the U.S. Virgin Islands, wants her children to receive a viable education. She economizes and lives in shabby accommodations so she can pay tuition for Yusef and his younger brother Kareem, like she did for their older sisters, Iyashia and Rasheeda.

Yusef started secondary school at All Hallows, the other Christian Brothers high school in the city, which is predominately Hispanic and directly across the Bronx from Yusef's apartment. He felt uncomfortable there from the first day. Many of his new classmates cursed at and made jokes about him in Spanish. He was not Hispanic and not from the neighborhood. To some extent, Yusef was forced to relive the same drama that Irish Catholic immigrants subjected African Americans to in the last half of the nineteenth century. The Irish stereotyped blacks (and Chinese) mercilessly so as to appear more acceptable themselves to mainstream society. After all, one's own downtrodden group can't be so bad if another is made to look worse.

Eventually Yusef befriended a fellow black with a Hispanic parent who translated the insults. Yusef ignored them for several weeks. He had made up his mind to focus on schoolwork and avoid fights in high school. He wanted to make his mother proud and her investment worthwhile, and the tuition at All Hallows was twice that of his elementary school. "All through grade school, I was a bad-assed kid," Yusef confesses later. He had been the smallest student in his class since kindergarten and always picked on by other boys. "People I have a beef with, I see them after school. I'm not big at all. But what I do is fight bigger guys. I got beat up at first, so I had to learn how."

Yusef's new classmates continued to throw gum and pens at him in class. Yusef resisted his natural impulse to retaliate until November. "Then I told one guy to stop throwing stuff, but he did it again. So I got up and punched him in the face right in class." Yusef recalls. "You've got to hit big guys first and no talking, no talking. Just do what you've gotta do. They start talking, and I hit 'em straight in the face with all my might. I ain't with that wrestling, don't like that wrestling."

Yusef was punished and developed a reputation that attracted more confrontations, which he sidestepped for the rest of the year. Traditionally Catholic schools don't immediately expel students for fighting if no weapons are involved. Orlando pushed Rice to zero tolerance to set an academic tone and break the stereotype that minority youngsters are prone to violence.

As the tenth grade began at All Hallows, Yusef's classmates renewed their efforts to goad him into physical conflicts since he had become a measuring stick of toughness and had no peeps in the school to back him up. In Yusef's neighborhood, if someone goes "poppin' off at the mouth" or if a stranger walks down the street "looking tough, grilling people with they eyes, all that's unnecessary and we confront that person. That's not keeping the rule. If you was walking with your boys acting tough and then when you're alone, you act like a little girl, I don't think you're really real about yourself and how you portray yourself. So we'd catch him by himself and smack him around a little bit. I do it alone or with my boys, either way."

To assist, Yusef packs a steel meat mallet, which he pulls out if a rival indicates that he is packing a gun or a knife. "I got my gun too, but I'd rather smack you up first. A gun's the last option. You've got to know what you're doing before you do it. You've got to see all the consequences."

By Christmas, Yusef grew so tired of the jibes that he transferred to James Monroe High School, a zoned school within walking distance of his home. He was still determined to graduate and go to college to study business management. Unfortunately Monroe was one of the worst secondary schools in the city; two years before, its students posted the lowest scores on the statewide math exam. Not surprisingly, the on-time graduation rate is an abominable 23 percent. Yusef's description of the classroom environment illustrates its corrosive impact on learning: "You can't hear the teacher giving the lesson with all the kids talking, hittin' on the girls, and listening to their Walkman."

Yusef quickly made new friends, but they were all Bloods. Several months later he joined the gang. "We all chill, so I was gonna' to be labeled a Blood anyway," he rationalized. Yusef won't talk about the initiation ritual, but three cigarette burns form an equilateral triangle on his shoulder, signaling gang affiliation. Several other Rice students wear the same burns. Yusef swears he never cut anyone as part of the initiation or later—except in self-defense. "I didn't shoot no peoples either," he says proudly, but won't talk about his mallet in detail.

Yusef claims that drug dealing and its inevitable violence were not the gang's main focus. Not everyone pushed, and no one was pressured into it, he says. "It's about being a unit. Even though we have no father figures around, we had each other. When our moms couldn't really explain stuff to us that happens in the streets, we could talk about it in a group."

It's important to note that street gangs are not the same as drug gangs, although the two overlap. In past generations, most gangs were turf-based and defended their neighborhoods and themselves from other gangs and ethnic groups. The influx of illegal drugs and handguns, starting in the 1950s, transformed many street gangs into serious criminal enterprises. Then the 1980s saw the arrival of crack cocaine, giving dealers a cheaper, highly addictive product. Sales grew exponentially and gangs armed themselves heavily to wage war over lucrative street corners and other distribution outlets.

To some extent, major Los Angeles drug gangs moved eastward and fueled the escalation. However, many street groups here that call themselves Bloods or Crips simply started wearing gang colors and used the names without real affiliation or major involvement in the drug wars. Most of Yusef's fellow Bloods were merely teenagers looking for the identity, companionship, and social status that comes with street gang affiliation. They did not buy a Bloods franchise. Some sold drugs on a small scale while others, Yusef admits, enjoyed jumping civilians and robbing them, then giving a beating for "fun," especially if the victims were white. Neither the drug dealing nor the assaults were part of a criminal plan since, like most street crews, Yusef's lacked the cohesion and discipline required to become a corporate-style drug gang. Their only association with hard-core criminals was the loose series of connections made to buy drugs for their retail sales locations.

For Yusef, the violence of fellow gang members amounted to "breaking the rule," which is one of personal authenticity. Yusef reminded "my niggers to keep it real" and, at times, felt compelled to articulate the message with his fists.

At Monroe High School, Yusef began meeting with his new friends before school at a nearby street corner to smoke weed. He made it to class on time most mornings and often sat through several periods. But around noon when the high wore off, Yusef cut class, sometimes walking out in the middle of a period. He would often go to the gym, play basketball, and then walk home with a female companion to an empty house.

Yusef's mother works full-time as a clerk at surrogate court in the Bronx. Like many Rice students, Yusef doesn't know much about what his mother does, nor does he have any interest in finding out, since her income is low. Yusef's younger brother was beginning his freshman year at St. Raymond's, a Lasallian Christian Brothers high school in the Bronx, and his sisters no longer lived at home.

Fortunately, Yusef didn't impregnate any of his fellow students. Amazingly—or perhaps not, given the low expectations at zoned schools—Yusef didn't earn a single reprimand for his daily absences from teachers or administrators. At schools like Monroe, as long as a student is accounted for on the daily attendance roll and doesn't cause a major behavioral problem, he or she is virtually free to go anywhere and do anything.

After neglecting to open his textbooks or complete assignments all year, Yusef skipped his final exams in June. The next September, he transferred to Adlai E. Stevenson High School, about a half-hour bus ride away, hoping the change would help him focus on academics. But Stevenson is another large zoned high school warehousing almost four thousand minority students. The four-year graduation rate is only slightly better than Monroe's, and Yusef soon fell into the same routine. Worse, he lost interest in basketball and his connection with coaches, who were encouraging him to study. Again, Yusef failed to take any exams at the end of the year. The following September, Yusef didn't register for school. He worked part-time at a midtown McDonald's as a stock clerk and cashier for six months, then joined his uncle's demolition crew. On days off, he entertained more female guests in his bedroom. At night, Yusef continued to hang out with fellow Bloods and sell drugs, finding it hard to give up the easy money since he could make a week's salary in a few hours, then enjoy spending it.

At the same time, Yusef had was losing all feeling, other than the sense that his brain was crystallizing like the powder he sold and would soon blow or get blown away. Yusef saw many of his friends get locked up or shot down. Others fled the neighborhood because of an outstanding warrant or a serious threat from another drug crew. Yusef's mother bore her disappointment stoically, which he both respected and longed to alleviate. So he restricted his drug dealing to one night a week and continued to work physically demanding, low-paying jobs out of an abiding sense that he would go completely straight soon and please her.

After Yusef's mother suggested for several months that he apply to Rice, he finally agreed to call the principal for an appointment. When Yusef arrived with his mother, he was surprised to discover that Orlando is black.

To Yusef's ears, the principal sounded white, since he enunciates clearly and speaks in grammatically correct sentences. Yusef was even more surprised to see Tupac Shakur's portrait on Orlando's wall, which immediately made the principal cool and relaxed Yusef as he sat beneath it on the couch. He talked candidly about his high school career and about wanting to make a turnaround.

"Go home and think about it," Orlando ended the interview. "If you're serious, you call me back—not your mother—and we'll talk."

Something about Orlando's big, easy movements reassured him. Yusef phoned the principal the next week, took the entrance test, and was accepted on a "wing and a prayer" in Orlando's view. He concluded that Yusef wasn't yet "a hardened street kid." Because he was without a father and had a history of poor decisions, Orlando predicted based on experience, the odds of Yusef persisting at Rice weren't great. But then Orlando is more a risk-taker than a calculating gambler.

Yusef said Orlando promised to look out for him "in case I slip up." The well-seasoned sophomore began dropping by the principal's office to talk about the "stuff" he longed to share with an older male. From his first day, Yusef felt positive about Rice. "I saw more faces like me and the kids were mostly friendly and joked around," Yusef remembers. In the first marking period, John Spinale, Yusef's global studies teacher, noticed that his grades were low and offered private tutoring after school without charge. After virtually no academic work in three years, Yusef found the readings difficult to understand and appreciated that Spinale, and in fact all his teachers, cared enough about him to reach out.

To avoid the possibility of conflicts with his new schoolmates, Yusef kept to himself. Eventually he made several acquaintances, playing basketball during gym class and at pick-up games after school, with the students who have been preparing for varsity tryouts after class today. Despite Yusef's unobtrusive persona, a larger classmate challenged him in the gym's locker room a few weeks ago, hoping for an easy victory and the consequent inflation of his reputation.

"I smack you up," Yusef cautioned the tenth grader, then walked over to close the locker room door. "I'm telling you straight up, I ain't with all that talking."

The bigger youngster kept taunting Yusef, who absorbed several insults before his fists answered with swift precision.

"I'm not with that bully shit," Yusef voiced as he stood over his classmate. "I'd rather be cool with you than bully. If not, fuck it. I'm not playing no games." Yusef shook his head and walked away wondering why people act harmful: "There ain't no point."

Two weeks ago, Yusef stood in Orlando's office doorway just before the school day began and asked for a favor.

"A favor?" Orlando answered with surprise.

"My mom's goin' home to the Virgin Islands for a while," Yusef explained.

"Okay," replied Orlando, still puzzled.

"Could you call me every morning at six?" Yusef asked. "I'll probably be up anyway, but . . ."

"Sure," Orlando shrugged, deciding to go along.

That afternoon, Yusef came back to Orlando's office saying he'd hurt his ankle in gym class and it was starting to swell.

"Why don't you put an ice bag on it?" Orlando asked.

"Where would I get one?"

"Mr. DiMello has them."

"Could you get one? My foot's sore," Yusef pleaded.

"You're not crippled," Orlando shot back, then realized what Yusef was doing. The principal's voice softened to say, "All right, I'll go."

At the end of the day, Orlando stopped Yusef in the foyer and asked him about his ankle.

"Oh, much better," he answered and bounded out of the school.

Halfway through today's second lunch period, Orlando ambles into the cafeteria to get his food. He spots Yusef's table and walks over. Yusef immediately thanks him again for calling in the morning while his classmates call out "Yo, Mr. G." and "O.G."

"Your uncle lives in the same house," Orlando asks, "so why doesn't he come downstairs from his apartment and wake you?"

"I don't trust him. I don't trust easy, that ain't me," Yusef answers.

"But you asked me to call," Orlando reminds him.

"Yeah, well I trust you," Yusef almost smiles. The opaque pupils of his eyes begin to lighten to the translucency of ancient amber, revealing mysterious prehistoric seeds. The first clusters of cells that develop after conception eventually form the lens of the human eye. These cells are never replaced, so humans spend their entire lifetimes literally looking through their own embryo, which is formed by the joining of their parents'—and their peoples'—genetic material. But the possibilities contained therein, for Yusef, have remained obscure. He hasn't seen his father since he was six years old and hardly knows him. The man moved back to the Virgin

Islands and never visits, calls, or invites his children there. To his credit, he sends money but otherwise has abandoned his children. Yusef's mother struggles bravely to do her best for her children, and as a result, hasn't focused on a career that would provide a professional example. For the first time, Yusef glimpses his own potential in the glow of the principal's attention.

"Okay," Orlando says softly and walks away thinking, "Here's another one looking for healing from the father wound." Orlando describes the "father wound" as "the single greatest risk to the survival of our young people; it drives all of their relationships. I can be really hard on these guys and they'll get angry, but the next day they're right back."

And they are glad to be back. Yusef's mother told Orlando her son feels very grateful that he was allowed into Rice. Yusef admits a deep appreciation, saying, "Actually I did a show. I asked Mr. Gober to wake me up because I felt like I wanted a father a bit. He really took the time and that kind of grew on me a little—a lot in fact."

———

Later that week, on Thursday, November 11, Orlando holds a teacher workshop in the cafeteria to help his staff better understand the social and psychological forces affecting his boys, especially those on the edge like Yusef. Orlando believes that many teachers have little comprehension of what the young men struggle with at home and in their neighborhoods. Only Hicks, the basketball coach, Father Taylor, and Brian Copeland, a science teacher, were raised in circumstances similar to the students. Both Hicks and Father Taylor grew up in Harlem, attended Catholic elementary school, and graduated from Rice. Copeland grew up in an African American area of Brooklyn and went to public school. All three come from intact two-parent households and find contemporary situations to be more treacherous and complex than what they faced.

Today is Veterans' Day, but no one complains about giving up the holiday without pay since Orlando's workshops always prove beneficial. He introduces the keynote speaker, Geoffrey Canada, forty-seven years old and the CEO and president of the Harlem Children's Zone (HCZ). Founded in 1970, HCZ has fifteen centers throughout Harlem serving 7,500 at-risk children and their parents with educational, social service, and recreational services as components of a comprehensive community- and family-building initiative. Canada believes, and HCZ demonstrates, that taking this holistic approach helps get students on grade level, stay in school, and go on to college or enter the workforce.

A crucial part of inner-city youngsters' at-risk status is their exposure directly and indirectly to violence. Canada begins his address referring to his first book, *Fist, Stick, Knife and Gun,* which details how his neighborhood in the South Bronx—like many urban minority areas nationwide—devolved from a tough quarter in the 1950s into a lawless principality ruled by gangs and drug lords by the 1980s. Fights were common in Canada's childhood, as they are today, but rivals settled disputes—mostly concerning the male pecking order—with their fists. Even the weaker boys learned to fight back because "having heart" earned respect from peers, whether or not a fight was won. The only mortal sin was cowardice when confronted by a bully, and the beating taken was a badge of honor.

In retrospect, the era seems almost a golden age to Canada, despite the severe poverty caused chiefly by racial discrimination. Fights were more a rite of passage than today's homicidal warfare. Tragically, drugs seeped into the inner cities sparking "an urban arms race," in Canada's assessment. Sticks replaced fists, which in turn were supplanted by knives that soon became toy-like in comparison to the increasing presence of handguns. With the evolution of violence's hardware, the idea that a fight should be fair became laughable.

"Now a young man shoots somebody for looking at him the wrong way," Canada observes.

Canada remembers the presence of adults in the community through the 1950s. Grown-ups or older boys usually stopped a fistfight before it caused permanent damage. Misbehaving children would earn a reprimand from any adult in the vicinity, and the elderly were treated with respect. The same boys who regularly scrapped with each other would help carry an old lady's groceries upstairs. The African proverb—it takes a village to raise a child— was still a working principle, although at many public schools the staff failed to protect youngsters during or after school, foreshadowing the collapse of moral authority in the community. Drug lords carved out fiefdoms, while welfare, drug addictions, and other forms of dependency gained sway over people's inner compasses.

As drugs became more ubiquitous in the 1960s and 1970s, junkies began mugging anyone, including the weak and elderly, to get money for a fix. Physical assaults became more vicious and random. Grown-ups feared young males and retreated from the streets, leaving teenagers increasingly vulnerable to being preyed upon by other boys. They were also increasingly likely to join a gang for protection and belonging, which heightened their aggression and made them part of the problem. Urban centers became increasingly ghettoized as young men ruled the streets, and violence and drug use alienated the entire disintegrating community from the rest of society. Culturally, a mythology of failure developed into orthodoxy, stigmatizing the behaviors that had previously allowed generations of immigrants and a significant portion of minorities to enter the American mainstream.

Another reason thugs were able to take over inner-city neighborhoods so easily was the flight of the black working- and middle-class to the suburbs. The success of civil rights legislation and the increasing affluence of working-class African Americans opened up residential and career opportunities only dreamt of by previous generations. In the *Atlantic Monthly*, Nicholas Lemann observed that "Suddenly most of the leaders and institutions (except criminal ones) left, and the preaching of assimilation by both blacks and whites stopped. What followed was a kind of free fall into what sociologists call social disorganization."[1] By the 1970s, the unraveling was beyond control as crime, unemployment, and illegitimacy rates spiraled. Not only were children increasingly abandoned by their fathers, but in effect they lost their entire village and its elders.

By the 1980s, crack and handguns flooded inner-city streets with disastrous results. Canada cites a report showing that during the eleven-year period leading up to 1991, the number of children killed nationwide by guns exceeded the number of American fatalities in the Vietnam War.[2] Over 50,000 U.S. servicemen and women were lost in Vietnam in the eleven-year period ending in 1972. Urban children, Canada emphasizes, live in an unrelenting state of war.

Homicide and all violent crime rates peaked in the early 1990s during the crack wars. Then crime rates fell 22 percent in all categories across the country. In New York City, the decrease was phenomenal. Homicides declined from horrific levels—2,262 in 1990 for example—50 percent above the big city rate, to 629 in 1998, a number unmatched since the 1960s. Including homicide, major crimes declined by 60 percent from 1990 to 1998, and continue to fall, making New York the safest big city in the country.[3]

Criminologists and police officials attribute this partly to the effective dismantling of large, corporate-style gangs and the successful prosecution of dealers and repeat offenders, putting many violent criminals in jail for lengthy sentences. Narcotics squads switched from futile efforts to deal with the city's 12,500 drug locations simultaneously, to concentrating on one troubled neighborhood at a time.[4] The new practice first targeted the blocks right around Yusef's house where "the Hole," one of city's most notorious narcotics outlets, operated. It was literally a hole in the wall of an abandoned building where New York police arrested one dealer after another, only to find new ones there the next day. Finally the city's police department concentrated enough resources on the surrounding blocks to root out the gang's upper echelons. Citywide, the NYPD has put hundreds of drug gangs out of business and curtailed the availability of crack that was fueling the explosion of violence.

This shift in policing strategy was instituted throughout the department. After decades when successive mayors ignored crime and often discouraged cops from doing their jobs, the Giuliani administration initiated a proactive approach. "The mayor made us realize what every aggressive cop knows," says Detective Sergeant Lou Savelli, who founded the NYPD's first citywide gang unit, "that aggressive enforcement works, and the day we let up is the day people start getting killed again."[5]

This proactive approach is termed Compstat, which involves precise computer mapping of crime incidents and weekly meetings at police headquarters where precinct and other unit commanders examine, and are held accountable for, crime statistics and police operations. The push from above for lower rates not only of major crimes but also minor violations and quality-of-life offenses, is relentless—which, Savelli attests, is exactly why it continues to work.[6]

Another key element has been the adoption of the now famous "Broken Windows" policy, based on the contention that "a broken window left unfixed is a sign that nobody cares and leads to more damage; similarly, disorderly conditions and behaviors left untended are signs that nobody cares and lead to serious crime, abandonment of neighborhoods to criminals, and urban decay."[7] Broken Windows enabled the police to restore order in many housing projects and high-crime neighborhoods, and snag fugitives with outstanding warrants for violent offenses.

The Broken Windows program bears a striking resemblance to the Catholic school ethos. Attention to strict codes of behavior and dress almost completely eliminates major problems. Much of what Orlando accomplished as Rice's dean of students was a reinstitution of this traditional approach. Considering the large percentage of police officers who attended Catholic schools, it seems strange that Broken Windows took decades to emerge.

But the consensus among criminologists, beginning in the 1960s, was that "to deal with crime one must deal with the social 'causes' of crime—

poverty, racism, and social injustice; minor offenses like prostitution and aggressive panhandling are victimless crimes; police order-maintenance activities constitute a 'war against the poor and minorities'; behaviors called disorderly are really expressions of cultural diversity that challenge middle-class mores; and finally, individual rights eclipse community interests on virtually every dimension short of imminent violence."[8]

Regrettably, decriminalizing minor offenses erodes crucial layers of restraint in society. "Crime rates soared when our courts began to concern themselves with such things as the unhappy childhoods of violent criminals or the 'root causes' of crime in general. Those who paid the highest price for these excursions into cosmic justice were not the judges or the theorists whose notions the judges reflected, but the victims of rape, murder and terrorization by hoodlums."[9]

Reversing this trend involved exactly what NYPD's Street Crime Unit accomplished, playing an assertive role in the 75-percent reduction in the city's firearm homicides since 1993.[10] Four members of this unit were involved in the tragic Diallo shooting. Professional activists and attention-seekers denigrated these officers without appreciation for what they had achieved at great personal risk. "The truth is people in these neighborhoods get it, even if they don't like everything that happens," Detective Sergeant Savelli says, "although if you watch the media, you might think we don't get along."

In recent years, police efforts such as those of the Street Crime Unit have helped save the lives of thousands of youngsters like Yusef, whose gang affiliation makes him a likely murder victim. Still, NYPD's treatment of African Americans hasn't been perfect. Yusef says he hates the cops because of "the way they make me feel when they looks at me. They got more power and pull me over 'cause I'm black. It's a mostly Hispanic neighborhood and the cops is mostly white and Hispanic. They don't bother the Hispanic kids." Yusef complains mostly about Latino officers, but what he doesn't want to admit is that they know he's a dealer and treat him accordingly. Still, the NYPD targets African Americans for stop-and-frisks far less often than their rates of criminality would indicate.[11]

Ironically, police success in eradicating major drug gangs made available the street corners that Yusef now shares profitably with friends. As is typical with new gangs, Yusef's crew is much smaller and exercises more caution than their predecessors. Yusef is reluctant to sell to people he doesn't know. He also has fewer layers of supervising personnel than he would in a bigger gang, but his long-term earnings potential is significantly lower. Corporate drug gangs operate like a pyramid scheme or a law firm, where those who live long enough eventually make it to the top and earn most of the money. Yusef's arrangement is more democratic—and safer, thanks to the NYPD.

Although violent crime has declined, Rice students belong to an extremely high-risk group. African Americans commit almost 70 percent of the city's violent crimes, although they account for only a quarter of the city's population.[12] Nationwide, eighteen- to twenty-four-year-old black males are eight times more likely than whites to be the victim or perpetrator in a homicide. Actually this ratio is significantly greater since Hispanics are usually counted as white in offender tallies, and they have the next highest rates to blacks.

Among African Americans, males living in high crime areas such as Harlem and the South Bronx are the most vulnerable, and gang members face extreme danger. Professor David Kennedy, director of the Center for Crime Prevention and Control at the John Jay College of Criminal Justice, says at least half the nation's 14,000 yearly murders are gang-related—not, as the government reports, less than 10 percent—and a disproportionate number of victims are young minority males.[13] Savelli believes that closer to 80 percent of homicides are gang-related. He points out that no accurate statistics regarding gang activity are available because many police agencies like the NYPD don't publish this data or report it accurately to the federal Department of Justice. "Most cities say publicly that gang activity is minimal," Savelli observes, "because it's bad for property values, business investment, and tourism."

According to an inside study of a large New York City gang, the annual death rate for foot soldiers was "more than 40 times the average for African-American males in the 16- to 25-year-old age group. On average, a drug seller could expect 0.59 wounds (virtually all from bullets) and 1.43 arrests each year. The most alarming statistic is that gang members who were active for the entire 4-year period had roughly a 25-percent chance of dying. Furthermore, there was an average of more than two nonfatal injuries (mostly gunshot injuries) per member and nearly six arrests for the 4-year period. By comparison, homicide victimization rates for black males aged 14 to 17 in the United States are roughly 1 in 1,000 per year, or about 100 times lower than observed in this sample."[14]

In reflective moments, Yusef talks about all the young men in his neighborhood who have been killed, severely injured, or put in jail. Sadly, for black youngsters in other big cities, survival prospects are much dimmer.

The homicide rates in Washington, D.C., and Detroit are five times higher. Chicago's is twice as high, Los Angeles 70 percent higher, and so on.[15]

For perpetrators, the downside of New York's effective policing is a higher risk of getting caught.[16] "There's a much better chance of a young black male being arrested now than ever, if they're involved in illegal activity," Savelli explains. He points out that in the late 1980s and early 1990s, when he was on the Drug Enforcement Administration (DEA) task force, there were only about three hundred police officers assigned to narcotics. Several years later, when Savelli founded NYPD's Citywide Anti-Gang Enforcement, drug enforcement had grown to about five thousand officers. More important than sheer numbers in the gang and narcotics divisions, the proactive nature of NYPD policing almost ensures arrest and successful prosecution for repeat offenders.

Despite the dangers, temptation remains strong, since "New York City is still the major drug market in the country. The U.S. accounts for only 5 percent of the world's population but consumes 55 percent of illicit narcotics," Savelli emphasizes. "It's tough for these kids with so much dealing going on where they hang out. Any kid who doesn't get involved is a tribute to his or her parents and school."

But the fact remains that most inner-city teenagers lack the positive influences of a strong father, or father figure, and a functioning school. Even with these in place, deliverance is not guaranteed. About 85 percent of gang members nationwide are black or Latino, and over 90 percent are male.[17] Yusef feels the pull in this direction as strongly as he does toward what Orlando represents. He sees the long-term advantages of heeding the principal's call, but so much of his identity, and those of his neighborhood friends, is invested in the gangsta persona.

That a principal participates so intimately in students' lives outside of school, sometimes to the point of intervention, is what attracted Geoffrey Canada to Rice and why he agreed to speak pro bono. He recommends the school to students in Harlem Children's Zone programs because Rice provides a balance of academics and personal involvement that enables them to cope with the street and meet graduation requirements.

Few educators realize how traumatized and re-traumatized inner-city students are by violence from very early ages, Canada says. It is vitally important to keep gang influences out of the classroom and provide a safe space where youngsters aren't looking over their shoulders in the hallway or worrying about getting jumped by classmates on the way home just because they do their homework. Canada concluded that nothing could be more insane than the oppressive anti-intellectualism of hip-hop culture, which glorifies criminality, setting up a youngster for a lifetime of victimizing and victimization.

Orlando ended the workshop by reinforcing Canada's essential points. There were few questions from teachers. Instead, a contemplative quiet followed their hushed attentiveness during Canada's talk.

"Now I understand why some students act so immaturely in class," Rene-Campbell remarked. "They weren't able to have a normal childhood and it gets worse, but they're safe here so it comes out."

———

For Rice Men, friendships with local dealers and gang members are as dangerous as they are commonplace. After the first day of school, senior Jose Ortega was hanging out on a street corner near his apartment in Washington Heights with several longtime friends, flip-flopping from Spanish to English about nothing in particular. One of his compadres suddenly yelled "Run!" and took off toward his apartment building. At first, Jose stood still, seeing no reason to flee. Nothing destroys a street reputation faster than showing fear. Then two other friends ran in different directions. Finally Jose heard the crack of gunshots and saw a young man pointing a pistol in his direction. Jose sprinted toward his own building while the assailant fired off several rounds at him, but missed.

"I ain't runnin'," one young man called out defiantly as the shooter drew near. Those were his last words. Seconds later he collapsed on the sidewalk and died in the gurgling of his own blood. Jose's friend refused to run away because he "owned" the corner. That convergence of crumbling concrete was his drug-dealing venue, and his presence there was his only claim to a livelihood. Still, it seems foolish that he stood his ground instead of beating a strategic retreat, though he might have reasoned that the odds of being hit by an untrained gunman on the run were low. Or perhaps it was merely a matter of the fatalism that characterizes many of the urban poor.

Jose had hung around with the murdered drug dealer several times a week since childhood but said he would get over the death quickly. "Hey, it could have been me," was Jose's only comment and was less a revelation of indifference to his friend than the emotional fatigue of a combat soldier. Cancer is slowly erasing his mother, and his father was recently diagnosed with a malignant brain tumor. Jose was hospitalized for stress recently and comes to school now with dark circles under his eyes. Widziewicz counsels Jose while Orlando offers encouragement, although neither has been able to establish intimacy with the young man. Jose says little, and his face looks increasingly like a resignation signature.

Few Rice students have not been touched by the untimely death of a close relative or friend, and most have seen both. That so few members of the underclass live long, healthy lives breeds a sense of metaphysical powerlessness that augments feelings of social, political, and economic helplessness. As Canada noted, the carnage in his generation doesn't occur only during the most vulnerable age range for gang involvement and violent death on the streets; every year he sees too many of his contemporaries die from hard living and the resulting health problems.

It's difficult to determine how many Rice Men belong to gangs. Some students say there are dozens of foot soldiers and several captains from the Bloods at Rice. Others discount these claims, saying that many of their classmates claim gang involvement to bolster their reputations. According to an internal NYPD intelligence report, there are 1,337 active gang members in the Manhattan North district. Most live near Rice, including 234 of the area's 585 Bloods and 42 of the 105 Crips. Only one Rice student is included on the NYPD's active gang list: Paris Lane started his sophomore year on probation and wears an electronic ankle bracelet to monitor his movements, ensuring that he leaves home only during school hours.

Orlando would not have admitted Paris, but Derrick Haynes, an assistant varsity basketball coach, got to know Paris at Spofford, a juvenile detention center in the Bronx, where he works as a corrections officer. Believing that Paris was salvageable and would sever his gang connections, he vouched for the young man. Given Haynes's enormously muscular physique and experience with delinquents, Orlando felt assured that Paris wouldn't cause problems.

Other Rice students are only peripherally involved with criminal street gangs. They might know or be related to members, and sometimes socialize as neutrals. Or they might belong to a street gang composed of teenagers who hang out and call themselves Bloods, or make up another name. But many criminal groups begin this way and drift into illicit activities as opportunities arise, or when they are challenged by another gang. A young minority male alone on the streets is defenseless, but seeking protection with a group of friends, regardless of their intentions, renders him vulnerable to street law. "An eye for an eye" draws many teenagers into vendettas with more violent groups. Rice students live on the very narrow border between two distinct and mutually exclusive worlds. Their ability to navigate both is a testament to their acumen and strength of spirit, but the risks are as numerous as they are ubiquitous.

Dealing drugs exerts an attraction as relentless as gravity; not succumbing takes courage. Onyxx Echeverria lives with his elderly, disabled mother, who's a retired cleaning woman, in a housing project on 125th Street near Columbia University. Onyxx is an amiable white Hispanic who this year was elected the first nonblack student council president since Rice became predominately an African American school. Onyxx's mother is very proud of her son. Long abandoned by Onyxx's father, she also lost her older son to the Latin Kings, the Hispanic counterpart of the Bloods, several years ago. He visits the family regularly, but his gang involvement is so deep he believes the only way out is horizontal.

When Onyxx was a freshman, his former public school peers—many novice gang members—started challenging him to fights as soon as they saw him wearing his Rice vest to school. Onyxx's two-hundred-pound frame helped him hold his own and earn respect. Now he still passes the same youngsters every day parked in the common areas of his housing project selling drugs. Onyxx holds a part-time job at the local pharmacy across the street and helps fill drug prescriptions. He contributes to household expenses and pays his family's portion of his Student Sponsor Partners voucher. It would be easy for Onyxx to supplement his income marketing contraband, and the drugstore would provide perfect cover. But he refuses, determined to make his ailing mother proud.

Recently one of Onyxx's classmates came to see Orlando after school.

"You know my dad's in jail in Florida for drugs," Rashidi Robinson began. "Two of my dad's friends came up to me yesterday and said they'll give me money if I do certain things, but for now they're just going to give me some money."

Orlando sat across from the youngster at the round table in the middle of his office and nodded. Rashidi is about average height with a muscular build. He looks slightly overweight because the pants he wears almost every day are several sizes too big and strapped to his body with a long belt. Rashidi pulled a fifty-dollar bill out of a deep pocket and waved it like a flag.

"But I've been thinkin' 'bout what you told us," he continued. "I should go hungry before I take drug money."

"Good," Orlando's voice resonated deeply, anchoring the young man.

"I got real upset with myself today in class," the senior confessed, his voice climbing into upper registers. "I was actually sitting there figurin' out how much I can make doin' this. Ain't that weird?"

"Not at all," Orlando answered. "Your mother really struggles to pay tuition." The youngster has several siblings. Fortunately he's an SSP student, but even paying the minimal contribution is a strain and tests his mother's emotional stability.

"I've decided to say no, because peoples like money," the senior said. "It's good business, but it's the wrong business."

Rashidi stood up slowly and muttered, "You know what I need now?"

"What?"

"A hug."

Orlando's success at Rice rests on his ability to keep street culture out of the school and create an attractive alternative. Urban Catholic schools stop gang activity and other street rivalries at the front door, as symbolized when Rice students take the do-rags off their heads as they step into the building. The ritual is almost sacramental. The young men instantly lose their street swagger and transform into students not much different than their peers at predominately white Catholic schools. Securing the school's psychological perimeters via discipline and structure allows Orlando to offer his boys an option that is both a proven, traditional path to manhood and one that nurtures the young men's African American or Hispanic identity without developing a false sense of self-esteem. Any doubts about the veracity of Orlando's empowerment ethos—albeit overblown at times—are answered by his presence, which incarnates his message. And he has a charismatic way of making up for harsh reprimands with kind words and patient listening.

Underclass and working class males have always had difficulty making the transition to manhood, and many rebel at school. They tend to skip class often, then drop out as soon as they reach legal age. Instead of submitting to the authority of teachers, mostly women, they define their masculinity on the streets. Gang membership, crime, and violence give them a means to acquire power, status, and a sense of identity. Once out of school, they often graduate from turf to more serious gangs.

Street gangs were composed mostly of ethnic whites until white flight broke up their "villages." Beginning in the 1970s, black and Hispanic gangs took over as their rivals withdrew. Interviews with gang members of all races over several decades reveal a common rejection of the link between schooling and success, and between personal responsibility and destiny regardless of race—which are exactly the links to hope that Orlando reestablishes.

Studies show that schools that do the best job reducing delinquency rates provide an intellectual balance that sets an academic tone—which Orlando accomplishes by inspiring his students to try to get on the honor roll and making it cool to be smart—and maintains a warm and restrictive environment where rules are clear, fair, and applied with care. Remarkably, other factors such as "the physical and administrative arrangements of the schools made no difference: Size, floor space per pupil, age of buildings, pupil-teacher ratios, the source of financial support, and the socioeconomic makeup of the student body were unimportant."[18]

"Gangs be sellin' guns and drugs all over," a ninth grader explains to Kim Davis the following Monday, November 15. "If you got the money, anybody can get a gun."

In the wake of Geoffrey Canada's workshop, Davis has been talking to his guidance classes about how to deal with violence in their neighborhoods. "Are you saying that the gun problem is surrounded by a drug issue?" Davis asks.

"You can't stop drugs or guns from being on the street," a classmate shrugs as if he were a homicide detective at his retirement party.

"I know this kid who was always bothering this guy, taking his money," a stocky freshman sitting next to Ephraim says. "The guy came with a gun, and the kid didn't even run. He just stood there and they argued, then he got shot in his head, way dead: payback."

The students know exactly how this scenario became fatal. As Davis explains, boys learn from older males about the verbal sparring that establishes the male pecking order in the African American community. He says it's difficult even for middle-class blacks from the suburbs to comprehend these rituals. At Rice, it's not unusual to see two black students accidentally bump into each other or have a small disagreement, and then trade angry words that soon become insults. Soon the two young men stand squarely, chest to chest, exchanging threats. The problem is neither can back down without losing face, so it becomes difficult to defuse the confrontation, even if one or both want to.

Teenage boys are notoriously lacking in conflict resolution skills, and in the 'hood, they often pay with their lives, Davis remarks. The ante can go up quickly if one youngster starts "playing the dozens." Often done amicably between friends or relatives, the "dozens" is a verbal joust with the other's mother as the target for hyperbolic and often sexually laden jibes. The game can quickly turn dangerous between strangers or even acquaintances. "What boy wouldn't die to protect his mama's honor?" Geoffrey Canada asked at the workshop. He said he worries about the boys in his program far more than the girls because these conflicts can explode so easily. No matter how hard a youngster works to get through school and avoid ghetto pitfalls, he can lose everything in a moment if his mother is insulted or his manhood challenged, Canada pointed out. Even if a confrontation doesn't lead to an immediate scrap, residual anger feeds the payback option.

As Widziewicz points out often, Rice students tend to have egos with far more bravado than do students at the white Catholic schools, but these egos are also more brittle and thus less adept at avoiding a fight.

"Now I want to work on some ideas about how to deescalate conflicts," Davis introduces the crucial practical part of his lesson. "When somebody says something, you feel like you've got to top them, and it gets to a point where everybody's afraid to back down, right?"

"Yeah," a chorus of grunts answers.

"When you're in that situation, you really don't think clearly. You just want to get a gun and shoot somebody," Davis continues. "But when someone's pushing your buttons, they're manipulating you. So you need to control your emotions, or the situation can get out of hand."

Davis cites Malcolm X's emotional speeches that produced few arrests afterward. "He knew how to get his point across and stand up for his pride and dignity without creating chaos and bringing about an outcome he didn't want," Davis explains. "I'm not saying you shouldn't defend yourselves when you need to, but you can save your dignity without losing control."

Ephraim ponders Davis's remark, knowing how easily he would be outmatched in a fight. A major reason he plays the fool is to avoid being taken seriously by his peers. The truth is all Rice students need to avoid confrontational situations. As strong and athletic as many are, they are no match for experienced street fighters and have so much to lose. Several say they own guns and claim to have "cracked niggers" with their fists when challenged. But as Linwood puts it, "none of us Rice dudes is serious." Even Yusef and Paris Lane are far from the hardened killers Linwood's father deals with.

Linwood walks freely around his housing project without fear because of his father's reputation. When a newly recruited dealer for the local gang insulted Linwood's sister recently, Linwood ran downstairs and confronted the young man in front of his boys. The youngster was about the same size as Linwood and didn't think of backing down. He assumed fellow gang members would back him up and so answered with attitude. Linwood punched him squarely in the face and beat him until he rolled up into a ball and cried. His friends stood by and watched, knowing that if the fight wasn't fair, Linwood's father would descend upon them with his associates like storm troopers.

To Yusef, Malcolm X's advice is both attractive and beside the point. Yusef doesn't lose control of his emotions under pressure, just as Malcolm X recommends, and he makes logical decisions—albeit from the mistaken premise that conflicts are best settled by avoiding discussion and striking first. It was precisely because Malcolm X talked too much that his enemies had him gunned down, Yusef concludes.

On the other hand, Yusef knows well that sooner or later, drug dealers end up dead or in jail. In classes and school hallways, Yusef still communicates warily in monosyllables, as if a classmate might pull a gun or lunge at him with a knife without warning, so he'd better not be distracted by grammar. Fresh in his memory is his cousin's stabbing by fellow Bloods at James Monroe High School for "stupidness: for selling drugs and other things on the wrong block. They stabbed him up good, in the face and in the chest and back. They was trying to kill him, but he's all right now. They not keeping the rule, acting like little punks."

As Yusef's seventeenth birthday approaches, he admits growing tired of these punks and yearns for a better future that an education and the conflict resolution skills Davis propounds would make possible. But on Colgate Avenue, there is no future tense—or more accurately, there's plenty of tense but very little future for most.

———

Yusef slips out of the gym's locker room on the sixth floor around 6 P.M. on Tuesday, November 23, without saying a word to his junior varsity teammates. He made the JV team and hopes to become a starter, but is having trouble adjusting to his more gregarious peers who are anything but on the court. Yusef learned the value of a tight unit on the street and hates how the better players think that passing the ball to a teammate amounts to a turnover.

A few minutes later, he mumbles Orlando's name as he stands in the principal's office doorway, then realizes that he put on his do-rag and baseball cap walking downstairs. Yusef swipes off his headgear as Orlando turns to ask him to wait while he finishes several e-mails. Fifteen minutes later, Yusef follows Orlando out Rice's front door, across Lenox Avenue, then down into the 125th Street subway stop. In twenty minutes, they're wading through waves of commuters on the 42nd Street subway platform.

Orlando started inviting Yusef to "hang out together" shortly after the morning wake-up call ritual began. Of course, Yusef dropped hints until he was asked. At least once a week after school or on weekends, they see a movie together or go to Times Square to visit a video arcade and go out for dinner. Tonight, they head first to Virgin, a three-story music store on Broadway at West 46th Street. Yusef marches directly to the rap section where he studies the new CDs on display. He idolizes Tupac and Biggie Smalls, two rap stars whose thug personas became death warrants, while his current favorites include Mace, Bennie Seagal, and DMZ. Yusef flips through the rows of CDs checking to see if any of these antiheroes released a new album this week. As usual, it was Orlando who suggested the visit to the record store, and as usual, he insists on buying Yusef the CD he finds most enchanting.

Next, student and principal go for dinner at the Olive Garden, a nearby franchise restaurant at 47th Street on the narrowing block between Seventh Avenue and Broadway near where these two major arteries crisscross. Orlando prefers to take his students to black-owned establishments, but he doesn't know of any in the area. Yusef remembers his first experience in an upscale restaurant at Sylvia's in Harlem, where he was overwhelmed by the lengthy menu. Finally, he ordered what looked familiar—pork chops with macaroni and cheese—since sitting at a linen-covered table with formal place settings was adventure enough. Tonight, he peruses a more exotic document for the first time: an Italian menu.

Last night, Orlando took several students who made the honor roll to dinner and was especially pleased that the group included Donald Shetland, the sophomore he found staring at the honor roll in the foyer at the end of September imagining his name there. Donald's behavior also improved to the point where Abbasse recommended him for student of the month and Orlando happily agreed—much to the delight of Donald's struggling mother.

Orlando plans to screen *The Nutty Professor* for another group of honor roll students later this week. This coming Sunday, several Rice Men who happen to be Catholic are invited to meet Orlando for Mass at his church. Afterward, he plans to take them out for video games and dinner. There are several students Orlando takes out alone, but Yusef is the only regular. Orlando socializes with students so frequently that last Wednesday, when the feast day for St. Gregory the Wonder-Worker, who is the patron saint of desperate situations, was mentioned during morning announcements, a junior asked if the principal was hosting "some kind of dinner tonight for everyone."

Yusef peers out the Olive Garden's front windows at the illuminated billboards framing Times Square with the advertising industry's version of paradise: dozens of unnaturally shapely women and a few sculpted men lounging comfortably in revealing underwear. Laid out on separate billboards are their trappings—a luxury car, chic leather briefcases, presumably to hold investment portfolios, and a designer raincoat—like accessories in a young girl's cutout book. Scores of neon lights glimmer, or perhaps wink seductively, while large video screens beam images of superficial success. Yusef has seldom been this far downtown and has never stopped to contemplate the mainstream's cauldron of desire. Light years from the 'hood, success suddenly seems a reachable aspiration with Orlando sitting across the table. Although the principal would rather that his boys strive for a more Afrocentric version of utopia, he's happy to see them connect with materialistic goals since at least they see themselves as worthy.

"We talked about the issues I was having," Yusef recalls later, "like how young black people is growing up looking for advice that my moms couldn't give me 'bout relationships with girls and the street and drugs and stuff like that." He confesses that since starting at Rice, females have become a problem. Just wearing a Rice sweater is lure enough. "They coming up to me on the subway; I don't even put no game on. It's like you got a million dollar contract. Just say my name when they ask and that's about it. They give me they phone number." Yusef has called several young women and decided to limit himself to two girlfriends—a compromise between the monogamy Orlando propounds and the street's polygamous bravado—so he'll have time for homework. Yusef realizes that doing well at school is the ticket to everywhere and more importantly, to pleasing Orlando.

In September, Orlando invested some hope in Yusef, but not much faith. With every outing since, Yusef has become more candid about his street life and more trusting that the principal won't reject him for his transgressions. Orlando finds this openness compelling, especially after his summer stint serving on the grand jury where Yusef could easily have been one of the young black offenders—or one of their victims. After every case was presented, Orlando did his duty but felt like Pontius Pilate forced to wash his hands and send another lost boy in a young man's body to perdition. Before him now is a black youth with a past, taking responsibility for his own agency; Orlando finds the prospect of Yusef's redemption electrifying.

In Widziewicz's assessment "Orlando is a missionary and I'm a monk. My focus is on deepening what's there, on developing a student's inner authority based on uncovering what will truly make him happy. I love the theological simplicity of nurturing these kids to the next stage. For me, it's an occupation; I can go home at night, unlike Orlando who's out to save souls and devotes himself totally, then plays the martyr if it doesn't work out."

As the pasta arrives, Yusef talks even more openly about the Bloods and drug dealing. He realizes he can't serve two masters but wants to postpone the choice, as in St. Augustine's youthful plea: "Give me chastity and continence, but not yet." To his credit, Yusef hangs out less with gang members and is looking for a straight part-time job. But he's lying to Orlando when he claims not to be dealing anymore. He still sells at the same corners, albeit less often, and worst of all, he can't resist dispensing "a little weed" to classmates at Rice. Yusef rationalizes the lie, saying that otherwise he wouldn't have any spending money since "they don't hire guys like me downtown." Like many of his peers, he hasn't actually applied for any "downtown" jobs.

Yusef knows Orlando is pointing him in the right direction. Every day, he sees the posters the principal mounted in the hallways of W. E. B. DuBois, Duke Ellington, Ben Carson, and others who embodied the best of African American culture and achievement and who show what it means to become an exemplary black male. But Yusef has also tasted forbidden fruits: rolls of cash in his pocket, easy women, and a reputation in the 'hood. He's seen the expensive cars on his block and mansions on TV.

Yusef's stairway to this heaven is contained in the clothbound notebook he always carries in his backpack, in which he prints lyrics like incantations that he prays will transform him from the forgotten frog at the edge of the urban swamp into the shining prince of hip-hop:

Got so much cake, you can call me a baker
My bank account look like I played center for the Lakers . . .
Girls try to warm me up 'cause I got a freezer on my neck
Want me to knock them up, so they can take half my check . . .
Chicks are like weed / their easy to bag . . .
I don't fuck no more, that's just a waste of time
I'm getting so much head now, I think I'm smarter than Einstein . . .

Some cats don't like me / They want to bust my brain
Other cats plotting/They want to bust my chain . . .
Nine got a sweet tooth and my finger's itching
Turn brains and dreads into red licorices . . .
Talk smack, hold this hollow nine
Pass your hood, have your block looking like Columbine . . .
20 years what I face / get caught for trafficking. . . .

"The gangster . . . appeals most to adolescents with their impatience and their feeling of being outsiders," wrote a movie critic in the late 1940s, "but more generally he appeals to that side of all of us which refuses to believe in the 'normal' possibilities of happiness and achievement; the gangster is the 'no' to the great American 'yes' which is stamped so big over our official culture. . . ."[19]

The difference today is the degree to which the "no" is promoted by media conglomerates and emulated especially in disadvantaged communities. The gangs depicted in *West Side Story* were alienated lower-class teenagers acting out their dilemmas on society's ignored margins. Eventually most became working stiffs and if they didn't make it to the middle class, their children did. For today's urban youngsters, the gangsta attitude has become the cultural norm, and those who uphold traditional routes to success are marginalized as sellouts to whitey, as inauthentic blacks.

Rap music originated in an impulse to bear witness to the disintegration of urban areas, as the crack wars precipitated a quantum leap in inner-city violence. But now rap glamorizes a misogynistic, homophobic, and murderous version of street culture that is mass-marketed in a vicious circularity. In order for the genre to maintain its authenticity—and so its appeal to white teenagers who buy most of the CDs—as Geoffrey Canada pointed out, minority teenagers have to keep shooting each other in the street, dealing drugs, going to jail, and so on. "The best brains in the country sit around board rooms and design ad campaigns to ensnare poor black and Latino kids," he said at the workshop. "They spend millions of dollars on research and advertising. Of course, they're going to succeed and our kids pay the price." It doesn't help that famous rappers claim gang connections. An unofficial NYPD report lists DMX, Lil' Kim, 50 Cent, and many others as affiliated with Bloods, while Ice T, Snoop Doggy Dog, and the Dogg Pound are noted as Crip affiliates.

Packing a weapon and selling drugs has become an axiomatic symbol of coming of age in the 'hood. After all, street culture depends on boys remaining trapped by their genes: proving their maleness by taking risks and displaying physical aggression. The majority of black and Hispanic young men are not dangerous criminals, but many adopt the pose under enormous pressure via the media—with urban public schools providing little counterbalance—which cripples their capacity to rise in socioeconomic terms and leads to criminality as a self-affirming gesture in this skewed version of manhood.

With Orlando, Yusef is starting to move beyond these postures but, for the moment, he is enjoying the thrill of balancing on the edge of a precipice.

Rice High School, at 124th Street
and Lenox Avenue.

Orlando Gober speaks at the orientation for
new students on September 8, 1999.

Principal Gober's lapel buttons.

Brother J. Matthew Walderman speaks at the orientation for new students.

Kate Hebinck mentors freshmen in her English class.

Orlando Gober gives out communion wafers to Rice students at annual Mass at All Saints Church, September 17, 1999.

Ricky Rodriguez (*center*) meets his sponsor, Robert Keith (*left*), from Student Sponsor Partners, for the first time.

Gregory Vazquez (*center, with glasses*) and fellow
Rice Men listen to Orlando Gober exhorting
them to make the honor roll.

Orlando and Yusef Abednego
(*arm around Orlando's shoulder*)
during lunch in the cafeteria.

Orlando Gober and Chris Abbasse confer about
student behavior after Kwanzaa lunch.

Andre Barrett (*no. 12 Raider's jersey*) scores in tournament win at Madison Square Garden.

Kawone Williams wears hip-hop outfit on
a dress-down day at Rice.

Teachers talk during intermission at African American Heritage Day program (*left to right, back row:* Olivene Browne, John Spinale, Brother Bill Sherlog, Ed Flood).

Al Widziewicz
counsels a senior on
college admission process.

Steve DiMattia
teaches Advanced
Placement English.

Tim Hearn reviews
class-performance grades.

Prince Youmans writes a paragraph
during English class.

Linwood Sessoms speaks at
graduation breakfast.

Seniors line up outside St. Patrick's Cathedral
prior to graduation ceremony.

Rice graduates celebrate inside St. Patrick's
Cathedral after receiving diplomas.

Chapter Fifteen

———

"I'M SETTING UP A MEETING with St. John's, Fordham, Manhattan, and Iona about sending student teachers to Rice and helping us recruit their graduates," Orlando informs Brother Walderman. Given Rice's fragile financial situation and, in Orlando's view, lack of a comprehensive strategy, negotiating with education schools at local Catholic colleges and universities is a practical way to offer a wider range of courses and improve teacher quality.

Brother Walderman nods his head as he drives the Brothers' new Saturn across the George Washington Bridge. It's 9:30 A.M. on Friday, December 3, and Rice's president and principal are traveling to Baltimore for the African American Catholic High School Consortium's annual conference. The Consortium was established in 1995 by the National Black Catholic Congress to ensure the survival of predominately black Catholic high schools. The Consortium consists of the senior administrators at twenty-eight secondary schools across the country with enrollments of 75 percent or more African American students.

Both Brother Walderman and Orlando seem nervous at the prospect of driving together for the next five hours and representing Rice as a team at the conference. They seldom attend functions or spend any time together to avoid clashes that are partly a function of their personalities, but mostly the result of radical differences in education philosophy.

Orlando has not forgotten Brother Walderman's perceived attempts to sabotage him during his early years at Rice. In 1995, their personal acrimony boiled over when Orlando announced he was taking a group of students to the Million Man March in Washington, D.C. Brother Walderman objected strongly, saying that Rice should not participate in an event organized and presided over by Louis Farrakhan, the outspoken leader of the Nation of Islam. Farrakhan's public comments, and those of his followers, are often overtly racist and anti-Semitic.

"If Colin Powell was in charge, I wouldn't mind," Brother Walderman told Orlando.

"It doesn't matter to me who minds," Orlando fired back, then stomped away from Brother's office, fuming. In Orlando's view, Colin Powell represents what white Americans think every black man should be. "I have nothing against Colin Powell," Orlando later explained, "but I don't like people telling me I should be like him rather than like Al Sharpton, or Jesse Jackson, or even Farrakhan."

Orlando defied Brother Walderman and took ten students to the march by train. In response, Brother Walderman docked him a day's pay as a statement of dissatisfaction. Orlando came back feeling so inspired he wrote an article for the school newspaper about what the event meant to him as an African American male. He also praised Farrakhan for his leadership abilities, which Brother Walderman saw as a legitimate reason to ban the article's publication. The two educators argued vehemently for days until Orlando, still defiant, mailed copies of the article directly to the parents, which enraged Brother Walderman to the point of threatening Orlando's job.

"Go ahead and fire me," Orlando yelled. "But then you explain it to the parents."

Brother Walderman dropped the issue, and neither has raised it since.

Orlando believed Brother Walderman's view was too narrow. "Farrakhan's presence was less important than the larger picture of what he was trying to accomplish." On the other hand, Brother Walderman was appealing to a universal morality that eschews traffic with any hate-monger. Certainly Orlando would have resigned in protest if Brother Walderman attended an event connected to a white supremacist. Yet what Brother Walderman failed to appreciate was the depth of Orlando's sense of identity, which transcended the circumstances of the march.

"Brother Walderman has no right to tell us what to do in our own community," Orlando fumed. "Whenever we talk about real self-determination, whites get scared and feel excluded."

Eventually Orlando's rage subsided and his relationship with Brother Walderman returned to the "marriage" that both continue to describe as difficult but working. According to the Christian Brothers in charge of the Eastern Province, it functions better than any of their other president-principal arrangements.

Typically Orlando says, "I'm very annoyed with Brother right now, but he really gives me carte blanche when it comes to my jurisdiction. He puts a word in here and there, but I really don't have to fight him any longer. My anger with him comes from wanting to do important things but then finding out we're dragging our feet."

Brother Walderman explains his perspective, saying that "when I was assistant principal, I would demand things we couldn't afford, but sitting here now as the president I see the reality of the problems, and we have to maintain a budget." According to the financial statement prepared by Rice's auditor, the school is a "going concern." As Brother Walderman puts it, "our financial status is extraordinarily tenuous." This year, Rice will run a $100,000 deficit, which is much less than previous years, thanks to increased enrollment. Relative to the school's $3 million budget, the deficit represents only a small percentage of operating costs but continues a long-standing habit of operating in the red.

Over the last decade, Rice built up a $1.2 million debt to the Christian Brothers' Eastern Province, which they forgave, but the order can't afford to do so again. There was an additional accumulated deficit that several generous alumni took care of. One city businessman, who graduated from Rice in 1951 and wishes to remain anonymous, has donated $1.5 million in the last five years alone. Joseph Murphy '52, the chairman of the Country Savings Bank, put up a total of $200,000 to outfit Rice with two computer labs and computers for all the offices. Most recently an alumnus wrote a $100,000 check to renovate and equip the sixth-floor workout room. Most of these donors, as Orlando points out often, are in or nearing their seventies and won't be able to continue their philanthropy indefinitely.

Unlike Jesuit schools, which have traditionally served children of more affluent families, urban parochial schools seldom build up endowments to take care of capital expenditures and see them through difficult times. Feeling Rice's vulnerability, Brother Walderman is disciplining expenditures so that "not a dollar more is spent than comes in." Recently he asked Orlando how many students the school could hold, which would tell him the maximum amount of money that could be garnered through tuition over the next several years. Orlando responded that Rice's resources could accommodate five hundred students plus an additional one hundred if the Brothers' residence on the third floor were turned into classrooms.

"We're sitting on a gold mine but have no strategic plan," Orlando sighed with exasperation after Brother Walderman left his office. "Harlem is going through an economic renaissance that's bringing in billions of dollars." On every block, workmen are cleaning out and rebuilding what are becoming prized residences for professionals who can no longer afford to buy units even on the Lower East Side, which are going for a million dollars or more. The same property in Harlem currently sells for half to a third that price. Both black and white families are moving in, and there are no viable high schools in the area to send their children to other than Rice and Frederick Douglass Academy.

"We'll be able to charge five thousand dollars or more for tuition," Orlando said with enthusiasm, "and we could double or triple the number of students if we could find a way to expand."

Orlando was horrified to find out recently that two double-wide, five-story brownstones adjacent to Rice on Lenox Avenue were offered to the Brothers at a bargain price, but no deal was concluded. For forty years, Cora Walker, the first black female to be admitted to the New York State Bar, operated her law firm there until she retired several months ago. Hoping the properties would continue to serve the community, Walker offered them to the archdiocese and then to Rice for a million dollars—well below market value.

The additional space would have allowed the school to accommodate enough students, especially given the increase in tuition that could be charged in the emerging market, to overcome its "going concern" status. Orlando angrily described the failure to secure the brownstones as a prime example of Brother Walderman's shortsightedness. He recognized that Brother does an excellent job raising enough funds to keep the school open, "but he's too caught up in trying to pay the bills every day to see the long-term opportunities and prepare a professional business plan." Brother mistook the price tag as an insurmountable expense, Orlando said, instead of an investment that the same alumni businessmen, who sink considerable sums into merely keeping Rice's doors open, would seize as a chance to make the school self-sufficient. Expanding next door would also allow Orlando to make Rice more competitive, by offering a greater range of courses.

"The time to grow is now," Orlando declared, "because real estate is going to be astronomical soon."

Sabotaging this vision, Orlando complains, is the common situation at Catholic schools where a member of a religious community is responsible for managing finances and raising money—two activities that he or she often is least prepared for by training and temperament. Nuns, brothers, and priests typically choose the religious life partly as a way of escaping material concerns. As well, "all educators are taught not to be concerned about money and doing so indicates they're in it for the wrong reasons," Davis remarked recently after observing the amateur approach to solvency at Rice. "In Catholic education especially, you don't discuss it because your mission to teach kids is from God."

While there is truth in this assessment, in the particular case of Cora Walker's brownstones, board member Stephen Fitzgerald '63 tried to negotiate the purchase several times. Unfortunately the deal was undermined by members of the Walker family, who wanted to sell at the highest price.

Within the current tradition, Orlando observes, seeking money is often approached as a form of "begging without any sense of how to use the funds to generate something that sustains itself. But at St. Mark's, we hired a prestigious fund-raising firm to set up our development and train us in how to approach donors." Orlando also learned that parents, even in poor neighborhoods, are capable of far more than what's usually demanded of them. At Rice, the parents generated about seventy-five dollars per family through raffles, bake sales, and other activities. In contrast, at St. Mark's, parents took the initiative, once they were fully informed about the school's finances, and raised three hundred dollars per family in a neighborhood that is significantly more impoverished than Harlem.

Orlando criticizes Brother Walderman for not attending the various parents' committee meetings and for treating them as "those poor minorities." Even parents with meager means can prove invaluable, Orlando attests. Many have contacts and other useful resources. Turning the parents into participants gives the school a virtual development staff of hundreds of members.

In fairness, the problem with Brother Walderman's fund-raising is that there aren't three of him. Brother has to raise over $700,000 a year in donations from a wide range of corporations and their foundations, including J. P. Morgan, the Pfizer Foundation, the New York Times Company Foundation, and Merrill Lynch Foundation. Each solicitation requires considerable attention on Brother's part to nurture relationships and complete application requirements. He also seeks support from family foundations, such as the Gilder Foundation, the Woolard/Friedman Endowment Fund, and the Brennan Family Foundation. Then there are sources under the archdiocese's umbrella, principally the Inner-City Scholarship Fund, all of which provide crucial assistance and demand his attention. Considering how many students have their tuitions paid through the Student Sponsor Partners, Brother liaises regularly and speaks on SSP's behalf at various functions.

Orlando is well aware of the extent of Brother Walderman's development efforts, but he practices a willful disregard, although not out of spite or lack of appreciation. For Orlando, an idea conceived is an idea born, full-fledged. It's not that Orlando believes his educational visions should be instantly fulfilled in narcissistic fashion, but that the means exist in God's eternal present. So if manna doesn't fall immediately from heaven, there must be something wrong with Brother's approach.

Brother's view is more pragmatic but certainly not lacking faith in things unseen, considering the amount he must materialize on a very tight schedule to avoid closing the school. To make ends meet, Brother will have to keep enrollment up over four hundred students and costs down at the same time. This means more arguments with Orlando, since he'll interpret the increase in students as a signal to press for more resources. But Brother has decided that he can't bear to continue fighting with Orlando and informed him recently that in June he is going to step down as president.

Today, Brother dresses casually in a white cotton turtleneck and navy blue khakis, and aside from the impatience he characteristically demonstrates while driving, chats amiably with Orlando, even about Rice business. Both men have relaxed visibly since beginning the drive and seem nostalgic—like two combatants who have grown to respect each other's strengths and regret the prospect that their battles are about to end.

Orlando has mixed feelings about Brother's decision. Although it seems that Orlando will be free to pursue his vision for Rice, he might be saddled with a less accommodating president. But negative thoughts don't stick long to his consciousness. Mostly Orlando has been considering who to hire as assistant principal, so he can devote more time to counseling students and to teaching.

In the evening, the Consortium holds a reception at the Holiday Inn near Baltimore's picturesque inner harbor. The next morning, Brother Walderman and Orlando sit at a large table in a board room at the inn waiting for the conference to begin. The first annual meeting in 1995 brought together representatives from almost all the black Catholic high schools across the country. Many presidents and principals remarked that they had seldom if ever had the opportunity to talk to administrators at similar institutions before. Most Consortium schools are located in urban centers around the country, with the biggest concentrations in Detroit, which has four, and New York City and New Orleans, each with three. However, since representatives must pay their own traveling and accommodation expenses, annual meetings have become local affairs. Principals and presidents from only four member high schools are attending this year.

"The problem with Catholic colleges is they don't support our high schools," Brother Walderman responded to Orlando when he talked yesterday about his plan to meet with administrators at Catholic education schools. "Catholic schools have always been adamantly independent. We're site-based institutions, which allow us to get things done, but we don't coordinate much with each other."

Of the more than 1,200 Catholic high schools nationwide, 230 have student bodies composed of a third or more minorities. Of these schools, 97 serve a substantial number of Hispanics, and 60 serve a majority of African Americans.[1] Although these schools seek to fulfill the Church's commitment to social justice, they seldom enjoy a nurturing relationship with a Catholic institution of higher learning.

In reality, the Catholic school system in America is less a system than a loose confederation of schools that were founded beginning in the mid-nineteenth century by various religious orders and dioceses to meet the urgent needs of immigrants. Cooperative relationships among schools and orders were a secondary concern at the time. Most institutes served children from impoverished or working-class families and had to stand on their own with few available resources. They tended to compete with each other for enrollment more than provide support. The same spirit carried over to the postsecondary level and was fueled partly by the long tradition of internecine rivalry among religious orders dating back centuries in Europe.

Unfortunately, contemporary Catholic schools continue this tradition despite the enormous changes in their circumstances that make working together advantageous, if not imperative. As Brother Walderman points out, a pipeline was never established between Rice and Iona College, the Christian Brothers' own postsecondary academy in nearby New Rochelle, where the Eastern Province is headquartered—which is absurd in retrospect.

John T. Butler, the president of Archbishop Carroll High School in Washington, D.C., and the Consortium's co-chair, introduces the first guest speaker, Paul Jeffries, the assistant director for career development at Xavier University in New Orleans. Jeffries speaks glowingly about Xavier's summer enrichment programs, hoping to encourage member high schools to send students.

Xavier was established as a high school in 1915 by St. Katherine Drexel, who founded the Sisters of the Blessed Sacrament to minister to black and Native Americans. As a university, Xavier focused on training students for careers in the sciences. Currently, Xavier ranks first in the nation in conferring undergraduate degrees in biology and doctor of pharmacy degrees to African Americans. The university is also first in placing black students in medical schools, making it, in common parlance, "Katherine Drexel's third miracle." To encourage interest, Xavier founded a Summer Science Academy for high school students with rigorous programs two to five weeks long in biology, chemistry, math, engineering, business, computer science, theology, and health sciences. Scholarships are available for needy students so parents and secondary schools need find funds only for transportation and housing.

"Could you guarantee slots for Consortium schools?" Butler asks. He would love to send aspiring students to Xavier's summer programs, then encourage them to apply to the university.

"I don't think we could guarantee any," Jeffries replies bluntly.

"But we are the black Catholic schools, and you are the black Catholic college," Butler pleads. "This would be the perfect way to partner for Catholic education."

"The director might be interested," Jeffries concedes and seems surprised that Butler pushed the point. Clearly it would not be making any difference to Jeffries's approach if he were speaking before a consortium of Baptist schools or to public school officials.

"Is Xavier's mission to work hand in hand with the Catholic high schools?" Orlando asks, feigning confusion, before adding pointedly: "What relation do these programs have to recruiting from and supporting black Catholic high schools?"

"The programs are designed to recruit interested students, but not specifically black Catholics," Jeffries replies dismissively, then changes the subject to announce that "Xavier made the hundred best buys in education," as if the college's good fortune makes up for neglecting its roots.

"But we're talking about a partnership to start grooming black Catholic students," Butler rejoins.

"I'll try to get admissions to reach out to Consortium schools," Jeffries promises, but his words echo off walls of indifference.

Orlando shakes his head in frustration. When he came to Rice from the Lutheran school system, he was shocked to discover that Catholic colleges and universities make no effort to recruit from Catholic high schools. Nor do they encourage their graduates to teach at Catholic schools.[2] That the only black Catholic university in the country is proving to be equally insensitive Orlando finds especially galling.

Lutheran colleges, in contrast, seek admissions from their high schools and tailor their education programs to train teachers for their own system. Orlando still flies to Fremont, Nebraska, every summer to give a weeklong workshop for graduating teachers at Midland Lutheran College. He tutors the virtually all-white audience on classroom management and lesson mastery, and talks at length about teaching inner-city African American boys. After the student teachers graduate, almost all will spend at least part of their careers at Lutheran schools, where they provide a consistent approach to academics and teach from the same religious point of view.

Catholic education schools, on the other hand, focus primarily on preparing students for higher-paying positions in the public system in order to stay competitive with secular institutions. There is seldom even a suggestion that graduates serve for a few years in the Catholic schools that gave many a quality education and facilitated their forefathers' rise from abject poverty. What has been forgotten is that this contradicts the basic historical tenet of Catholic education, that religion and education are inseparable. Catholic schools were founded expressly to provide a Catholic education for Catholic children. Catholic colleges were established to train young men and women for religious vocations—which meant preparing them to staff Catholic schools, parishes, and other institutions—or for religious avocation, which meant preparing them to become workers or professionals who would, as faithful Catholic parents, rear the next generation in the faith.

In this manner, Catholic schools powered the Church's growth from the humblest of origins to becoming the country's most populous and influential denomination. By the 1960s, when the country's first Catholic president was elected, Catholics ranked among the highest in per-capita income and education levels.[3]

Chapter Sixteen

—

AFTER THE XAVIER UNIVERSITY REPRESENTATIVE finishes his presentation, Butler passes out a summary sheet from *CHS 2000: A First Look,* a quantitative report on Catholic high schools. The data indicates that the majority of Catholic high schools are just beginning to confront their fiscal issues. Butler then initiates a discussion about financial solvency.

"Ninety percent of the schools now have a development office and 72 percent have started planned-gift programs, which suggests some maturity," Butler reads aloud. "Unfortunately we haven't started, but I've been nudging in that direction."

A few moments later, Butler adds that "over a third of Catholic high schools are mounting capital campaigns."

"St. Ignatius Prep in Chicago is probably the one with the $46 million endowment," Brother Walderman surmises. "It's over a hundred years old, and so many Who's Who went there."

"Gonzaga, on the outskirts of Washington, just completed a $22 million campaign," Butler relates. "It came in just like that," he adds with a finger snap.

As all here know, both St. Ignatius and Gonzaga are owned and run by the Jesuits, who have a long history of serving prosperous families and instilling a sense of obligation in their graduates to become benefactors.

Brother Walderman points out that Lasalle Academy, a 150-year-old Lasallian high school on Manhattan's Lower East Side, recently completed a campaign and raised $2.3 million from graduates, mostly of humble origin. None of the Consortium schools have large endowments, and many have none. Like Lasalle, they could aim at modest capital targets, but hesitate since they have no history of working with professional fund-raisers. Endowments are becoming increasingly important as costs rise.

In response, as Butler relates, "there's talk in the D.C. archdiocese about cost-based education, and we're moving in that direction. Officials are suggesting that schools pass along at least 80 percent of the true cost of schooling to the families, since the archdiocese can't increase its subsidies."

"Then what happens to the poor?" Sister John Francis Shilling, an Oblate Sister of Providence, asks with concern. For the last eight years, Sister John Francis has functioned as both the principal and president of St. Francis Academy in Baltimore. Brother Walderman remarked to Orlando that in comparison, Rice looks affluent. The academy was established in 1828 by Blessed Mother Elizabeth Lange to teach the children of slaves, which was illegal. Mother Lange founded the Oblate Sisters of Providence, who continued the tradition of serving mostly African American students from destitute families.

"The idea behind cost-based education is that if you keep tuition artificially low, you're not helping the poor who can't afford it now anyway," Brother Walderman responds sadly. "Instead, the way to subsidize the truly impoverished is to charge those who can afford it enough to cover costs, and then devote donations to the poor."

But at inner-city schools like Rice, this would mean raising tuition by 65 percent and then continuing to increase it by 10 percent per year. Few current families can afford this, so the school would have to attract more middle-class parents and perhaps move to a more affluent neighborhood. But as Brother Walderman always points out emphatically, the Christian Brothers were founded to teach poor boys. So Rice, more than any other Christian Brothers school, continues this prime directive.

"The Church's lingering presence as an educational haven for aspiring children in poor city neighborhoods," Charles R. Morris writes in *American Catholic,* "is still the crown jewel of Catholic social endeavor."[1]

I read Morris's book shortly before accompanying Orlando and Brother Walderman to Baltimore. As I listened to the Consortium educators talk about fiscal issues in confounded to somewhat defeated tones, the descriptive term "lingering" came to mind.

Rice has always been a haven for the poor, as have many other schools, so why is there a financial crisis now? Surely today's Catholics collectively have magnitudes more money than earlier generations, which could easily offset the impact of rising costs. Yet on average, 130 Catholic schools have closed every year since 1965, and that figure is accelerating. Worse, the closings have occurred mostly in urban centers with large concentrations of disadvantaged families that needed them most.

So how did urban Catholic education devolve into a "lingering presence," and what can be done to reverse this? To answer these questions, I decided to research how Catholic schools evolved and present a synopsis here. What I found was a most extraordinary story of social transformation—certainly one of the greatest in history. When Irish Catholics began arriving in large numbers in the 1840s, they were the poorest and among the most dysfunctional and despised people in the world. By virtue of the Church's institutional responses, primarily Catholic elementary and secondary schools, the Irish progressed from the nation's first underclass to the working class, and then to the middle and upper classes. Today, Irish and other Catholics are among the most successful groups in the country.

It should be noted that public schools, and other public and Protestant initiatives, made significant contributions. However, the focus in this and the next chapter will be on the Irish immigrant predicament and the Catholic response, both to understand schools like Rice and because Catholic schools have retained the essential elements of what worked, while public schools abandoned these methods for the most part—and suffered the consequences.

In order to appreciate the enormousness of this achievement, a detailed account of the conditions faced by educators and public officials in the mid-nineteenth century is given below. The account's sometimes graphic nature may serve to give the reader a visceral sense of the immensity of the obstacles schools faced then as well as demonstrate powerfully why there is no justification for failing or fiscally troubled schools today. Certainly conditions are different now, and the ethnic and racial makeup of urban centers has changed dramatically. But these do not excuse or explain the state of contemporary inner-city education.

New York City took in more immigrants than any other port of entry and became central to the development of the institutions and culture that succeeded with the Irish, and then formed the template for successive waves of impoverished immigrants, likewise facilitating their transition to the mainstream. The more specific focus here is the worst of the Irish Catholic slums—considered the most squalid in the world—known as the Five Points, which covered much of the area that now constitutes Chinatown.

In 1805, New York City had only 70,000 residents and like the rest of the country, few Catholics. Poor Irish began arriving in significant numbers in the 1820s. By 1840, the city's population had exploded to more than 300,000 people; almost a third were Catholic, with the majority being Irish. The first potato famine hit Ireland in 1842, precipitating a deluge of even more impoverished immigrants.

As millions starved in the Irish countryside, those lucky enough to gain passage across the Atlantic endured a perilous journey. Conditions on board what became known as "coffin ships" were horrendous. "In 1847, about 40,000 died making the voyage, a mortality rate much higher than that of slaves transported from Africa in British vessels of the same period."[2]

The Irish landed at port cities, principally New York, Philadelphia, and Boston, with no resources to go much further than they could walk. They sought out the cheapest housing and crowded into dozens of degenerating neighborhoods like Five Points, named after a five-cornered intersection behind City Hall, in Lower Manhattan. Most of the area's buildings were two or three stories high with adjoining stables and workshops that were constructed as an artisan's or a shopkeeper's residence and place of business. As the Irish flooded in, these small structures were subdivided into tiny apartments, including cave-like cellar hovels with no amenities for an entire family, plus boarders who helped pay exorbitant rents. Most buildings were in such disrepair they failed to keep out the wind, rain, and cold. In the summer, lacking proper ventilation, they turned into sweat boxes.

The Irish maintained their rural habit of living with livestock. Pigs—and their droppings—were everywhere. In addition, horses dumped close to a billion pounds of horse manure and twenty-two million gallons of urine a year onto city streets that were seldom cleaned.[3] Not surprisingly, cholera epidemics—known as the Irish Catholic disease[4]—were a regular occurrence, and illnesses like tuberculosis kept the death rates permanently high. Few Irish lived past forty, and their mortality rate was seven times higher than that of other New Yorkers.

But the Irish kept coming. Over 850,000 immigrated to the United States through the New York harbor between 1847 and 1851 alone.[5] Incredibly, life was much better in Five Points than back home. When Frederick Douglass visited Ireland in the 1840s, he was almost "ashamed to lift my voice against American slavery" since blacks in bondage often had significantly better living conditions.[6] Writing about Emancipation decades later, W. E. B. DuBois remarked that at least the freed slaves were "not as poor as the Irish peasants."[7]

The Irish came completely unprepared for urban life. The majority had grown up on small, crude farms, and many lacked the funds to venture inland for rural employment better suited to their skills. New York especially became the catchall for the most destitute of new arrivals, growing quickly into the most populous city in the Western hemisphere with the largest concentration of urban poor.

The Irish took the least desirable jobs as laborers, domestics, seamstresses, and so on—sometimes displacing African Americans, who are always hurt by mass immigration. The thrifty often opened saloons or groceries that functioned as unlicensed grogshops and popped up four to every intersection. Often proprietors spiked drinks. One saloon used a form of turpentine that gave a small amount of alcohol an economical kick, but also blinded hundreds of customers.[8] Insane asylums filled up with Irish men and women who had employed alcohol's cure for the effects of poverty and displacement. The number of drinking holes bore a strict correlation to the poverty of a block's residents, about a dozen per block in Five Points. Here the Irish socialized, partly because their apartments were so small and depressing, and partly because sobriety seemed a feeble antidote to the misery of their everyday lives.

The Irish arrived with a centuries-old history of severe alcoholism, and the drinking characteristically led to fighting. Irish neighborhoods all over the world developed reputations as violent areas inhabited by brutes reveling in their "laughing savagery."[9] Nativists warned that the Irish would never become acceptable Americans. They were depicted as "beaten men from beaten races, representing the worst failures in the struggle for existence."[10] In neighborhoods such as Five Points, the Irish seemed bent on proving their faults, giving native-born Americans and other immigrants plenty of reason to discriminate and move to other neighborhoods.

Low-income Protestant neighbors and working-class rivals despised the Irish, and many of America's elite leaders, businessmen, and intellectuals— including John Quincy Adams, Samuel Morse, P. T. Barnum, and John

Jay—lobbied for restrictions on Irish Catholic immigration and citizenship. Given their historically clannish propensity, it is no surprise that the social, economic, and political unit for the Irish became the neighborhood gang. They had to defend themselves against beatings and insults from nativist gangs, and find ways to survive in a very inhospitable city. The Irish gangs fought back and turned their thuggery into a profitable venture, offering printed menus listing prices for breaking bones on up to "doing the job"— which again, reinforced the prejudices against them.

Gangs became the socializing agency for most children in Irish slums. Youngsters were often beaten by drunken fathers and neglected by besotted mothers at home, so they grew up partly or wholly in the streets. An estimate in 1849 put the number of homeless children at forty thousand in a city with about half a million residents. By eight years of age, most children were expected to contribute financially to the family. Some were pulled out of day schools and consigned to work long hours in factories, or sent to beg in the streets. Sometimes, they supported a parent's alcoholism; more often, their pennies fended off homelessness and starvation.

Opportunities for income for the Irish were often illegal. In 1855, less than half were legitimately employed and virtually all in low-paying jobs.[11] Alternatively, gangs initiated youngsters into the fine arts of thievery, burglary, gambling, con games, and prostitution. Children roamed in bands throughout the city and formed junior versions of adult gangs. There were the Little Forty Thieves, and members hung out in dives that catered to youngsters under twelve, where the boys bought whiskey for the prepubescent girls.

Contemporary observers remarked about the viciousness of American (mostly Irish) youth. "The intensity of the American temperament is felt in every fiber of these children of poverty and vice. Their crimes have the unrestrained and sanguinary character of a race accustomed to overcome all obstacles. . . ."[12] Young boys learned to handle themselves in a fight, and if tough enough, they graduated to an adult gang in their teenage years. Few boys spent much time in school during the 1840s and 1850s.

Some crooks used their profits to start a business and became wealthy. Most spent their loot as quickly as possible on their own ruin. The city's criminals were malnourished, filthy Irish boys who had been abandoned by their whoring mothers—not the glamorous gangsters depicted in movies and played by grown-ups.

The Tammany Hall political machine oversaw both legal employment in city agencies and illegal jobs in the vice industry, with workers floating between the two overlapping worlds. It was no coincidence that the most no-torious dens of iniquity were located closest to police headquarters. Prosti-tution defined New York's social life, and bordellos could be found even in the best neighborhoods. A contemporary historian wrote that in Five Points, "nearly every house and cellar is a groggery below and a brothel above."[13]

In the 1840s, 60 percent of Irish immigrants were women, and many had been widowed or abandoned by their husbands. Often they ended up on the street with children to support. Within a decade, the number of whores, mostly Irish, increased fivefold to fifty thousand, serving at over a thousand brothels and at the concert halls, theaters, saloons, cigar stores, and restaurants that promoted their businesses with sex for hire.[14] Migra-tion from rural areas, especially New England, combined with immigration to produce a far larger pool of female wage workers than needed. Employ-ers obliged with wages so low a shop girl wasn't paid enough to live in a flophouse. There was often little choice but the skin trade to avoid home-lessness and starvation.

A Victorian double standard regarding male sexual behavior and grow-ing legions of young men from all classes freed of traditional supervision took full advantage of the plight of the female poor. Many of the twenty-four thousand women with manufacturing jobs in 1860, for example, also drifted in and out of commercialized sex to supplement incomes.[15]

Destitute little girls abandoned to the streets found it difficult to avoid becoming a "nymph of the pave." They formed their own sub-underclass. More often than boys, they worked long hours in sweatshops, for example making envelopes by the thousand for pennies. The temptation to avoid the drudgery of work was as strong as the work was unsteady. At mid-century, diarist George Templeton Strong wrote that "No one can walk the length of Broadway without meeting some hideous troop of ragged girls, from twelve years old down . . . with thief written in their cunning eyes and whore on their depraved faces."[16]

Hospital wards filled with women suffering the long-term effects of sex-ually transmitted diseases. Widespread among men was the belief that hav-ing sex with a virgin cured sexually transmitted diseases. The girls for sale became younger and younger, also because a premenstrual female didn't have to worry about pregnancy. It was not uncommon for a mother to pros-titute her own daughter, since whores looked at their station as a step above the factory slave's. But prostitutes were beaten and robbed by pimps, used by police, and quickly wore out their looks. Alcohol and drugs hastened the fading of beauty, and a young woman found herself at progressively cruder brothels, houses of assignation, or street corners.

Observers remarked that "Lower than to the Five Points it is not possible for human nature to sink."[17] The social pathologies of the Irish were seen simply as evidence of their genetic and cultural inferiority. By 1873, there were a million New Yorkers, half of whom were Catholic. Their situation seemed hopeless. Charles Loring Brace, a Protestant philanthropist, had founded the Children's Aid Society twenty years earlier to offer shelter to the thousands of Irish children who slept in doorways and coal bins. In his book, *The Dangerous Classes of New York and Twenty Years Work Among Them,* he warned that the mostly Catholic underclass might become permanent and wreak long-term havoc on the rest of society. An Oxford historian, on a lecture tour of America, recommended that "The best remedy for whatever is amiss [between the United States and Britain] would be if every Irishman should kill a Negro and be hanged for it."[18]

Demographics were becoming destiny in the mid-nineteenth century, an equation that many social scientists and educators take for granted with today's underclass. Since the assassination of Dr. Martin Luther King, Jr., in 1968, "the black middle class has tripled, as measured by the percentage of families earning $50,000 or more. At the same time—and this is the kicker—the percentage of black children who live at or below the poverty line is almost 35 percent, just about what it was on the day that Dr. King was killed."[19] The progress made by most African Americans in recent decades is astounding, but a huge gap exists between those who have entered the mainstream and those left behind.

As Brace predicted for the Irish, today's underclass threatens to become permanent, and certainly many of its children are wreaking havoc. Half the country's murders are committed by African Americans, mostly males fourteen to twenty-four years old. Of this demographic, which constitutes only 1.2 percent of the nation's population, perhaps half live in high-crime areas, and their children are the most likely to repeat destructive patterns. Most victims are African Americans, but black-on-white homicide is twelve times more likely than white-on-black.[20] With the rise of Latino gangs, urban Hispanic youth are catching up in the violent crime category.

In an admirable attempt to address the causes of urban poverty and dysfunction, William Julius Wilson, a leading sociologist at Harvard, argues that most of the financial and social problems that have developed in recent decades were caused by job loss, resulting from structural shifts in the economy and the erosion of the manufacturing sector.[21] Gone is the era when decent-paying, low-skill jobs in manufacturing and construction were plentiful enough that dropouts routinely climbed toward middle-class status or made it easier for their children to get there. In contrast, undereducated young men in disadvantaged neighborhoods see few alternatives and turn to drugs, gangs, and crime, and often abandon their families. Overcoming socioeconomic barriers then becomes more difficult for their children, reminiscent of the downward spiral of Irish immigrants during the mid-nineteenth century.

Obviously most Africans did not come to America willingly but were brought here as slaves centuries ago. There are important parallels, however, that make the transformation of the Irish relevant for today's underclass. During the Great Migration, 6.5 million blacks moved from their rural existence to urban centers in order to escape prejudice and poverty, as the Irish did previously and every other ethnic and racial group since. Beginning around 1910 through the early 1970s, waves of black migrants poured into northern cities, taking over many of the same neighborhoods where European immigrants had begun their transition to the mainstream.

Despite the persistence of racial animosity, African Americans saw the journey north as their "Flight Out of Egypt," as Chicago's most prominent black newspaper termed it.[22] Jobs were better in "North Mississippi" and blacks had more rights, the newspaper assured their readers down South. The civil rights movement brought legal equality, and the majority of African Americans have achieved middle-class status. But in recent decades, with the loss of decent-paying low- and medium-skilled jobs, education has become crucial to employment. Tragically, public education broke down in underclass and working-class areas when it was needed most, trapping their children in poverty and dysfunction.

According to Wilson, the only appropriate solution involves massive government intervention to provide jobs, improve child and health care, upgrade public schools, and transfer many inner-city residents to the suburbs. "The challenge of bringing inner-city disadvantaged children into the mainstream of American life," as Henry Louis Gates, Jr., chair of Harvard's African and African American Studies Department, emphasizes through one of the interviewees in his book *America Behind the Color Line*, "is without question the most pressing, most important social challenge in American life."[23]

Like Wilson, Gates supports vast experiments in social engineering. But before considering initiatives that don't have a prayer of working as long as inner-city youngsters continue to drop out or graduate with low academic skills, it would be instructive to see exactly how the Catholic hierarchy and educators dealt with a far more challenging situation a century and a half ago. The Irish and successive waves of immigrants joined the mainstream without massively expensive government interventions, which in any case enjoy little popular support today.

Chapter Seventeen

———

THOMAS JEFFERSON BEST ARTICULATED THE role of education in democracy when he wrote, "If a nation expects to be ignorant and free, in a state of civilization, it expects what never was and never will be."[1] By the turn of the nineteenth century, virtually everyone, other than slaves, was literate without spending years in the classroom. Most children, including the few Catholics in the country, learned to read at home and soon consumed difficult texts that today are reserved for the last years of secondary school or college. Early America is replete with stories of astonishing success in all fields by individuals such as Benjamin Franklin and George Washington, who were largely self-educated.

That a child would learn to read at home and progress quickly to the Bible was not remarkable at the time. But then came the Irish and waves of other immigrant groups who had had little access to books or schooling. Their poverty and lack of familiarity with city life created an unprecedented problem as social ties unraveled and temptations for dissolute behavior abounded. Since most had been farm workers in their homelands, they couldn't make an easy transition to the trades, which were being destroyed by industrialization anyway. With the rise of the factory economy, fewer families handed down skills from one generation to the next via apprenticeship. Parents worked long hours away from their children and often took piecemeal work home for badly needed pennies. The immigrant story is largely one of child neglect, along with the rise of institutions to deal with the partially to fully abandoned, both children and adults.

By the 1820s, the massive influx of destitute peasants was irrevocably under way. The port cities where they landed lacked services or any sense of a warm welcome, but their numbers fed the Democratic political machine, which guaranteed continued immigration. The notion of universal education took on urgency as business and political leaders saw the Americanization of new arrivals, and their integration into the factory economy, as vital to the nation's survival. Schooling was seen as too important to be left as an informal process and a privilege reserved for the middle and upper classes.

Denominational schools were established to educate the lower classes on a charitable basis with some public financing. Then in 1824, the Public School Society (PSS)—the precursor to the current system and run by the city's Protestant elite—convinced the state legislature that they could provide a program of education that would attract the unschooled children of New York City.[2] Funding to the few Catholic schools ended, while PSS schools agreed to become nondenominational, albeit generically Protestant and insistent on continuing the practice of reading from the King James Bible. Protestant churches never saw this as a move toward secularism. Rather, church and state worked together toward a common goal that was interchangeably American and Christian. Immigrants brought crime, poverty, and a papist threat to the new country, which PSS schools were instituted to combat.

For Catholics, education offered the opportunity for their children to better themselves and eventually join the mainstream. In the 1840s Archbishop John Joseph Hughes campaigned to regain public funding for Catholic schools. He became the prime mover in the Church's national effort to transform poor Catholics into decent, productive Americans without losing their religious identity. Public schooling presented a thorny dilemma, since significant anti-Catholic and anti-Irish prejudice was transmitted by the textbooks, and by the attitudes of Protestant teachers and administrators. Hughes was determined that his flock would not become second-class citizens here as they had been in Ireland. More importantly, the Catholic hierarchy feared that "if Catholic children fell into the clutches of the Protestant public schools, their allegiances, frames of reference, and the authority to which they turned for religious teachings might all be transformed. They would be absorbed into a Protestant American landscape, lost to the Church, and thus deprived of ultimate salvation."[3]

Hughes's bid for funding met extraordinary resistance from the Protestant establishment all the way to the state legislature where it was defeated. In a sense the Protestant elite also lost, since the Public School Society was replaced by a nonsectarian public system. While Bible reading and other overtly Protestant practices persisted into the twentieth century, they could not be applied universally, and their elimination became inevitable.

Hughes found the new approach as unattractive as the old. "Nonsectarianism, the Catholics warned, was dangerous to society, for it permits 'the will of the pupil to riot in the fierceness of unrestrained lusts.' While the intellect is trained, 'the heart and moral character are left to their natural depravity and wildness. This is not education; and, above all, this is not the education calculated to make good citizens.'"[4]

Hughes knew how easily the Irish fell prey to their own appetites. A Catholic education for Catholic children was seen as the only appropriate antidote. There were priests and bishops who believed the common schools would suffice, but Hughes and the majority of bishops insisted that Americanizing immigrant children was an important but secondary concern.

The Catholic hierarchy began building an entirely separate school system across the country. The rallying cry could have been "separate but equal"— in the true sense—and to this day, Catholic schools in Canada are called "separate schools." In literature, as in the mythology of many cultures, charting one's own or a people's path is always the way to maturity and authentic identity, which in the nineteenth century was largely defined by religion. "[Hughes] was unremitting in his efforts to create a parallel Catholic universe within which the faithful could live compatible American and Catholic lives, including hospitals, cemeteries, orphanages, houses of refuge, 'banking' institutions, and a full array of schools from infant schools to universities and seminaries."[5]

Part of the motivation was what would today be called social justice, but underlying these efforts a more important war for souls was being waged. "Catholic priests [were] troubled by the Protestant ethos of public institutions, including schools and orphanages, as well as hospitals. In private and public institutions operated by Protestants, priests were frequently denied access to Catholic patients. Protestant clergy . . . conducted Protestant services in juvenile wards to capture young minds and hearts. . . . As in the case of the parochial school, the Catholic hospital seemed to Church leaders an essential fortress against the assaults of proselytizing Protestants."[6]

Providing alternative Catholic schools and other institutions posed an immense problem since the Church was completely unprepared for mass immigration. In 1805, New York's first Catholic school opened at St. Peter's, the city's only parish. By 1839, tens of thousands of poor Catholics had already landed, and the potato famines in Ireland would soon unleash tidal waves of immigration. Yet there were only eight parishes in Manhattan, each with a school, serving a mere 3,000 Catholic youngsters in total. By 1858, parochial school enrollment grew to 13,000 students "with nearly 11,000 at the primary 'free school' level (6,100 girls and 4,800 boys). . . . The public schools, however, enrolled close to 158,000, a very large proportion of whom had to be Catholic."[7]

The Irish, however, shunned schooling and other civilizing influences. Frederick Douglass referred to Irish slum dwellers as "the filthy scum of white society."[8] If Hughes had heard the comment, he would have responded in his characteristic pugnacious style. But he would not have disagreed with the substance of Douglass's remark. Hughes blamed the plight of the Irish on the long history of English oppression that had reduced the Irish to material and spiritual poverty. Cut off from their cultural heritage, the Irish poor regressed into a primitive existence, dwelling in hovels that were little better than caves. But what held the new immigrants back more than the hostility of others was their own ignorance and self-destructive behavior, according to Hughes. Although the prejudices of nativists were far more formidable than those facing minorities today, the relative ease with which German Catholics ascended made it clear that the Irish were their own worst enemies.

When asked what he was going to do about the "Irish problem," Hughes answered: "We are going to teach them their religion." The majority of immigrants who fled Ireland came from the south and west, where peasants were among the poorest, the least anglicized, and least churched in the country. The English had imposed severe restrictions on the teaching and practice of Catholicism, and on the number of priests. Outlying areas seldom had any contact with the Church. Most Irish Catholics arrived in America with a hodgepodge of beliefs and religious practices that were more superstition than religion. They were Catholic in name only, more as a badge of honor against the hated English than as an identity they understood.

"Teach[ing] them their religion" had this obvious catechetical component but more importantly encompassed all aspects of education and character formation. "In our age the question of education is the question of the church," Hughes preached.[9] Education was inseparable from religion, and religion incorporated all the positive values and attitudes that would elevate a youngster both into the mainstream and into heaven. This view was so strong that Catholic parents were told to boycott public schools even if that meant leaving their children to roam the streets. In 1840, the Church's Fourth Provincial Council of Baltimore prioritized Catholic school expansion. By 1884, the Third Plenary Council of Baltimore required all parish priests to establish schools—on pain of excommunication.

As a result, the parish became the religious and social center of the Catholic community, turning squalid chaos into ordered neighborhood villages. In the classroom, from the pulpit, and through participation in the multitude of Catholic societies that evolved to meet the social needs of parishioners, Hughes and other bishops throughout the country orchestrated a radical shift in values through their priests, nuns, and brothers. They emphasized the sacrament of confession as a prime means of instilling a code of personal responsibility. Every Catholic adult was held to account on a weekly basis for his or her behavior. At Immaculate Conception parish on East 14th Street in 1867, for example, missionaries held a three-week religious revival where they heard 28,000 confessions, attracting penitents from all over the city.[10]

"The Catholic Church is a church of discipline," Hughes declared, not so much as a prescription for psychological repression but as a means of overcoming pathologies. Alcoholism was a major problem, and given how and where the Irish socialized, spirits were impossible to avoid. Hughes co-founded a Catholic abstinence society and imported a famous Irish crusader whose fiery sermons yielded 20,000 abstinence pledges in 1849. Stories survive of parish priests who met workers on their way home on Friday evenings to make sure their wives got the better part of the weekly pay before they went out drinking. The classroom and church-related societies created self-discipline and self-restraint in daily lives, backed up by the considerable influence of parish priests.

Given the high levels of prostitution exacerbated by low pay, an overabundance of Irish women, and the large number of abandoned wives and widows, counseling more prudent behavior seemed laughable. However, instead of retreating lest anyone be offended, as occurs today, priests and nuns preached a strict code; sex outside of marriage was deemed sinful without exception. And the preaching was fierce, as anyone who attended pre–Vatican II Catholic schools can attest. Self-restraint was ingrained in the Irish character to the point where, by century's end, Irish women were known for their modesty.

To rebuild families and improve the status of women, Hughes and the teaching orders put the Church's Marian Doctrine at center stage.

Irish women would hear from the priests and nuns that Mary was Queen of Peace, Queen of Prophets, and Queen of Heaven, and that women were important. The "ladies of New York," Hughes told them, were "the children, the daughters of Mary." The Marian teaching encouraged women to take responsibility for their own lives, to inspire their men and their children to good conduct, to keep their families together, and to become forces for upright behavior in their neighborhoods. The nuns, especially, encouraged women to become community leaders and play major roles in church fund-raising activities—radical notions for a male-dominated society where women didn't have the right to vote. In addition, Irish men and women saw nuns in major executive positions, managing hospitals, schools, orphanages, and church societies—sending another highly unusual message for the day. Irish women became important allies in Hughes's war for values; by the 1850's, they began to be major forces for moral rectitude, stability, and progress in the Irish neighborhoods of the city.[11]

In schools, boys learned to respect girls and girls learned to respect themselves. Rates of illegitimacy and sexually transmitted disease began to decline. Girls grew up to run church societies instead of brothels and embraced legitimate professions in an Irish community where the ethos of self-help was balanced by mutual aid. Social groups provided assistance for personal and family problems:

> Hughes encouraged the formation of the Irish Emigrant Society, out of which the Emigrant Industrial Savings Bank emerged. The society helped find people jobs in sail making, construction, carriage repair and maintenance, and grocery stores. The society expected those it sponsored to behave properly on the job and work conscientiously, so as to reflect credit upon their patron. Those who misbehaved incurred the wrath not only of their employers but of the Emigrant Society and the parish priest, both unembarrassed about using shame to encourage good behavior.[12]

The values that helped the Irish turn themselves around were taught in every venue at the Church's disposal. Parishes were established at a furious rate, with Hughes's administration (1842–64) founding sixty-one parishes in the archdiocese; John Cardinal McCloskey (1864–85) established eighty-eight parishes; and then Archbishop Michael Corrigan (1886–1902) created ninety-nine parishes. New York had been established as a diocese in 1808 and originally covered all of New York state and northern New Jersey. In

1850, the pope elevated the bishop of New York to archbishop, meaning he would preside over dioceses in the area. This created the Archdiocese of New York, which was reduced to a tenth its original size as dioceses such as Newark, New Jersey, were erected.[13]

Despite the pace with which parishes were founded, the archdiocese couldn't keep up with the demand. From 1820 to 1870, Manhattan's population exploded by 800 percent to the point where its thirty-eight churches averaged almost 12,000 parishioners. The schools could accommodate only a fraction of the borough's Catholic children. From 1840 into the 1870s, less than 10 percent of the city's children attended parochial schools even though half the population was Catholic. Nationwide there were about two hundred Catholic schools before the Civil War, and this number grew quickly to thirteen hundred by the mid 1870s.[14]

Parish schools became the most important arena for social engineering via education and moral training. While the vast majority of Catholic students flooded public schools—by 1869, they accounted for half the public enrollment and that percentage increased for decades—the influence of Catholic schools transcended their market share. They graduated many of the laywomen who went on to teach at public schools. By 1870, 20 percent of New York City's teachers were Irish women, and the proportion rose to the point where Orestes Brownson, perhaps the most influential American Catholic theologian of the day, questioned the purpose of building Catholic schools if children were going to be educated by Catholic teachers at public school. Catholic teachers taught in the city's predominately Catholic wards, turning public schools into de facto parochial institutions. "By 1930, half of all of Boston's school principals were Catholics, most of them from the Jesuits' Boston College. The head of teacher development for the public schools was the sister of the priest in charge of teacher training at the college."[15]

Meanwhile, according to New York City's Commission on Charity, in 1867 there were still "about 30,000 (some said 40,000) children between the ages of five and twelve who receive[d] no education, and whose days [were] passed in poverty and idleness. Utterly desolate and without parents and without the actual effective sympathy of those who could raise them above want, how [could] it be that as they [grew] up they should be other than dissolute and criminal?"[16] These abandoned youngsters resisted civilizing influences, to the consternation of missionaries, teachers, and foster parents—whenever such services were available—until a more concentrated version of the Catholic school ethos proved effective.

Dr. Levi Stillman Ives, a convert who was a former Episcopalian bishop, founded the Catholic Protectory in 1863, basing its program on religious training in a highly disciplined environment: "Every child committed to this institution will be thoroughly trained in the faith and morality of the Gospel as revealed and entrusted to the Catholic Church." Rather than being a mere platform for religious indoctrination, the Protectory's approach was founded on the experience of religious orders in Europe, notably the Lasallian Christian Brothers, and on the positive results that intensive religious instruction had had on the behavior of street kids in a Catholic school in Boston. Dr. Ives combined this with vocational training so that youngsters could support themselves in a trade—while some did make it to college—without resorting to crime. In order to eliminate poverty, the underclass first has to become a working class.

When the Protectory finally closed in 1938, over 100,000 mostly illegitimate children (two-thirds of whom were boys) had been raised from "indolence, stupidity and vice" by inculcating an active recognition of their "obligation to God, to their parents and to society" to become both "worthy citizens of our glorious Republic" and "fit candidates for the heavenly mansions above."[17] The Protectory's success rate—and that at similar institutions across the country—demonstrated the socially productive relationship that can exist between church and state. Wounded human beings in highly dysfunctional situations respond best to clear statements of right and wrong backed by God himself—as Orlando never tires of saying.

Children understand intuitively that without ultimate accountability, the big question isn't about morality but about getting caught. The social benefits of correct behavior make little sense to youngsters at self-centered stages of development when parents, if there are any, work long hours away from home and so cannot monitor them well. It is no coincidence that worldwide the institutions with the best success in socializing and educating the underclass employ an omniscient deity to keep tabs on the young.

Initiation into the divine gang via the sacraments included forgiveness for all past transgressions and celebration of the pact between sinner and God Almighty as both father and friend. Regardless of the arguments that could be mounted against the existence of God or the empirical validity of religion, faith is a powerful—and perhaps utterly essential—tool for those caught in cycles of degeneration and nihilism. Many in the upper classes have evolved toward a completely secular and agnostic, if not outright atheistic, belief system. The key word here is "evolved." Even the most ardent materialist would have to admit, based on the evidence—including the colossal social failures in godless communist systems—that those beneath them would be served best by following the same evolutionary path through the religious orientation of their ancestors.

The positive role of public schools and Protestant initiatives cannot be overestimated, notwithstanding Catholic objections about Protestant proselytizing. The Children's Aid Society, for example, rescued at least as many Catholic children from the streets as did the Protectory. There were orphanages, industrial schools, the Young Men's Christian Association, and many other institutions that helped the children of the poor. What's noteworthy is that the surviving evidence points to a high reclamation rate as abandoned and abused waifs were turned into productive earners by learning trades and at least rudimentary Christian values. Nor were ethics ignored at public schools. "The unrestrained passions of men are not only homicidal but suicidal," wrote Horace Mann, a leading exponent of the common school movement, "and community without a conscience would soon extinguish itself."[18] Moral training was an integral part of the elementary curriculum.

Of enormous significance to the growth of Catholic education was the ability of bishops and parish priests to recruit European religious orders to teach in the schools, until they could be replaced by native-born recruits. Not only were these minimally paid teachers needed for the diocese to afford running the schools, but the quality of their instruction determined the scholastic success of the school. Orders with long teaching histories, such as the Jesuits and Sisters of Charity, then the Ursulines and Lasallian Christian Brothers, were better trained both in academics and classroom management than their public school peers. Only 10 percent of public school teachers had earned teaching certification by 1868; a teacher-training college was established two years later in Manhattan. To be sure, many of the teaching sisters also were not well educated in the early decades of parochial education, but they did know how to keep order.

Not only were conditions outside the classroom difficult, but inside, overcrowding was an understatement in today's terms. In 1868, parochial schools averaged 111 students per class. Unable to keep up with the demand, parish priests simply packed as many bodies as possible into a room, or the church basement, increasing the average class size from 75 in the preceding decade. The city's public schools, in comparison, averaged 39 students per class. But at the poorer public schools where parents were mostly of foreign origin, classrooms often held between 60 and 100 children with the least experienced teachers assigned to the lower grades.

Accordingly most public teachers used the Lancasterian system—a British adaptation of a Hindu institution that was created to inculcate "a curriculum of self-abnegation and willing servility."[19] In general, nineteenth-century pedagogy was heavily invested in rote memorization and other forms of drilling, including calisthenics, plus reading and singing recitation.

Despite the inadequacies of public schooling, basic skills and discipline were transmitted adequately enough to alter the lives of countless poor children. "In 1835, in a ninth grade class of thirty-two boys, there were two future judges of the Supreme Court, at least one member of the Legislature, a City Register, several principals and assistants, and one Assistant City Superintendent of Schools, one clergyman, and three or four highly successful merchants. They were nearly all sons of men who earned their bread by daily toil."[20] Eventually, the city's public schools became fully professionalized and were the envy of the world.

It usually took three generations before education had a dramatic effect on social class. Poor children tended to be absent half the time during the few years they spent in both public and Catholic charity schools, and the curriculum was often limited. But the transition was made first to the working class, then aspiration and academic improvement facilitated the rise of later generations to the middle and upper classes.

Education was so important to the protection of the Faith that Rome exhorted American bishops not only to build schools but also to ensure they weren't inferior to the public schools. The curriculum at St. James parochial school, across Paradise Square from Five Points—where the sons of families a step or two up from destitution, such as Alfred E. Smith's in the 1870s, were schooled—included English grammar, approved classics, elocution, arithmetic, history, geography, and religion. St. James earned a reputation as academically demanding and very strict, and this Lasallian approach became the gold standard that was imitated at public schools.

Later in life Al Smith said, "I never read a book for entertainment in my life." After years of rote learning that included the drills and forced memorization that characterized nineteenth-century pedagogy, Smith developed a distaste for book learning. As a student, he performed in the parish's drama society and excelled at elocution. But after dropping out a month before graduating from the eighth grade, due to his father's death, the young man read voraciously, first newspapers, then bills before state legislature, when he was elected assemblyman in 1903.

Smith's career was distinguished by a remarkable capacity to comprehend complex legislative documents and recall their minutiae. "It was noticed . . . that his speech was not only fluent but rhetorically correct. . . . But he had been taught long ago at the St. James School to speak in complete sentences, and moreover he seemed to have an innate sense of the right word to use, especially when the wrong one might change the whole purport of a bill. . . ."[21] Smith's school and parish could well be considered the paradigm for the Catholic system of schooling that remained virtually unchanged until the post–Vatican II era. The formalistic character of those schools, epitomized by nuns teaching the catechism with rulers in hand, and American Catholicism in general "sprang from the Cullen/Hughes recipe for upgrading Irish peasants and immigrant hordes—go to Mass, receive the sacraments, send your children to Catholic schools, do as the nuns and priests say, give money, avoid drunkenness and impurity. . . . Educated Protestants scorned the American Church's lack of mysticism . . . but it created sober and, within limits, successful working men and women, reliable graduates of a petit-bourgeois boot camp, whose children had clean faces."[22] The building and maintaining of parish schools became almost a matter of dogma, with some priests denouncing from the pulpit parents who continued to send their children to public school.

In 1918, Smith was elected New York State's first Catholic governor and served four terms. In 1928, Smith became the Democratic nominee for president. He lost the federal election, with anti-Catholicism playing a decisive role. However, the fact that an Irish Catholic had progressed so far was astounding. Throughout the nineteenth century and into Smith's childhood, Irish Catholics were mercilessly depicted in Protestant publications as stupid, depraved, and simian-like.[23] The prejudices against the Irish made advancement difficult. "No Irish Need Apply" signs were commonplace, and employment ads stipulated "any color or country except Irish."[24] Education in both the formal and broad sense accounted for the dramatic shift in how the Irish were perceived. As well, Irish American professional and upper classes had a stake in the success of their less fortunate brethren:

After the exodus to America, well-off Irishmen who had achieved or been born to some measure of wealth and social standing sought to impose their social values on the Irish-immigrant masses as a means of ensuring their own influence and prestige in the new land. They often forged alliances with the Catholic Church in America. Both hoped to impose social control upon impoverished Irish Catholic immigrants by encouraging "industry, thrift, sobriety, self-control, and domestic purity," habits that would cement newcomers to the Church in America and shape citizens willing to be led by those who had already considered themselves to be their group's stewards.[25]

Parochial schools were the primary venue for transmitting the desired values, and affluent Catholics contributed generously, benefiting socially in the long run from the results. What began around 1606 with the establishment of the first Catholic school on the continent, in St. Augustine, Florida, became a vigorous, independent system mostly in urban immigrant centers around the country. By 1884, a complete system was envisioned that would school the faithful all the way through college. The percentage of New York City's children being educated at Catholic schools increased steadily to 18 percent by the beginning of the twentieth century.[26] Nationwide, 10.1 million Catholics sent 854,523 children to 3,811 parochial elementary schools, which was closer to half of all school-aged youngsters, since cities other than New York were not as overwhelmed with Catholic immigrants.[27]

Because of the financial burden the schools entailed, many parishes couldn't found them, at least not right away, and not all bishops supported this vast project. A school controversy erupted in the late 1890s pitting leading bishops against each other, and required papal intervention to resolve—in favor of a separate Catholic system.[28] But by the end of World War I, attitudes became universally positive, as the earning power of Catholics increased. The half-century of progress in Catholic schooling began in 1917 with 102 seminaries preparing 6,898 young men to become priests. There were a total of 1,537,644 students in 5,687 parish schools, with 216 academies for boys, and 676 academies for girls. Many of the academies operated as secondary schools, and some were really elementary schools with academic aspirations.

Even the Great Depression failed to dampen Catholic ambitions. "Most parish churches in New York City that did not have a school had plans to build one by . . . 1939."[29] By 1957, the Catholic population had grown to 35.5 million, and elementary education kept pace with 3,616,455 students in 9,274 schools. Secondary education grew dramatically with 722,763 students in parochial, diocesan, and private high schools. Catholic universities and colleges also proliferated at an astounding rate, with 259,277 young men and women in 259 institutions.[30]

Nationally Catholic education reached its zenith in 1965 with 5.6 million students in 13,292 schools (10,879 elementary and 2,413 high schools). This has been termed the Catholic triumphant era, which was initiated with the election of John F. Kennedy as the first Catholic president. But the more significant achievement belonged to ordinary Catholics. According to Father Andrew M. Greeley and his fellow researchers at the National Opinion Research Center,

> On almost all standard socioeconomic indices, Catholics were almost precisely at the national white median score by the 1960s, and substantially above average by the 1970s. Greeley, however, took the additional step of disaggregating the data by ethnic group. The vast majority of American Catholics were the descendants of four distinct waves of immigration—the Irish, peaking in the 1850s; the Germans, peaking in the 1880s; the Italians, peaking in the early 1900s; and the Poles and other Slavs peaking in the 1920s. When Greeley corrected for the recency of immigration and education of fathers, Catholics outperformed every ethnic group except Jews. In terms of education, income, and other standard measures, Irish Catholics ranked above every Protestant grouping, while all other Catholic groups were moving rapidly toward the Irish standard. . . .[31]

What if, from the civil rights movement era to today, African Americans had emulated the Catholic approach? As early as 1787, African Americans were building separate institutions insofar as they were permitted. The Free Society of Blacks established a welfare program at Mother Bethel's Church in Philadelphia where aid was given to the poor but refused to individuals whose conduct was deemed irresponsible or immoral. The African School was established in 1815 by a free black in his home in Brooklyn. Other private schools were established here and elsewhere (as early as 1798) until the public schools became more amenable. Still the tradition of historically black independent schools survived—giving birth to such prestigious universities as Morehouse and Fisk—with about four hundred schools today serving 52,000 African American students across the country. Most are primary-level institutions with a religious affiliation (forty out of seventy in New York City) and cluster in urban areas where public schools fail. Most of New York City's historically black independent schools were established in the 1970s and 1980s, as parents looked for alternatives that provided academic quality within Christian and Afrocentric values. Research on outcomes indicates that students in historically black independent schools score significantly better than their public school peers in the same school districts and higher than the national norm on standardized tests.[32]

Blacks have the capacity and means (given the tremendous wealth in the African American community as a whole today) to build whatever institutional nexus they need to deal with underclass problems, at the same time fostering their identity as uniquely African, American, and for the most part, Christian. No doubt if more than 3 percent of African American children attended historically black independent schools or other private and parochial schools in New York, for example, dropout rates would decline significantly, and gaps in income and academic achievement would close. But the will to create solutions independent of government disintegrated for the most part in the mid 1960s.

> Blacks in northern cities like Chicago . . . were far more demoralized and dysfunctional than southern blacks, [Martin Luther] King [Jr.] discovered. The moral influence of the black church was much weaker than in the South. Illegitimacy, welfare dependency, and criminality were more prevalent than in the South, with its much stronger bourgeois values. No longer, explains historian Christopher Lasch, did King address "a constituency that cared to hear about self-help, the dignity of labor, the importance of strong families." King's associate Hosea Williams put it bluntly: "We're used to working [in the South] with people who want to be freed."[33]

As a result, Dr. King began advocating government programs "to help the frustrated Negro male find his true masculinity by placing him on his own two economic feet. . . ."[34] Later he criticized the War on Poverty as "not even a good skirmish." The unforeseen consequence of this understandable approach at the time was that the success of its appeal for government intervention left the recipients at that intervention's mercy. Control over the future of the black underclass, and then the Hispanic, was ceded to functionaries, social workers, and public educators who have little to gain from the success of their programs. Instead, the greater the failure the greater the reward, as tax dollars feed the public sector's voracious appetite. The logic of bureaucratic solutions is that to solve even one social problem would ultimately require all the money in circulation. Accordingly, what's worth doing really is worth doing poorly.

In contrast, when African Americans take charge of their own destiny with a visionary approach, even within public education, and force the system to serve the students, success usually results. For example, Frederick Douglass Academy is a combined middle and high school in a neighborhood of low-rent apartment buildings and housing projects in upper Harlem. Residents can see Yankee Stadium across the East River, but only the local drug dealers can afford season tickets. True to the profile of most schools in similar areas, the academy's predecessor was a miserably performing middle school until it was closed in the late 1980s, reemerging several years later under the leadership of Lorraine Monroe, a former New York City deputy chancellor for instruction. Now 80 percent of the four hundred middle-schoolers score at the proficient level or above on statewide reading and math tests. The academy consistently earns a ranking among the city's top fifteen schools. Just as consistently, the entire senior class more than doubles the graduation rate for minorities at urban public high schools across the country, and virtually all these students are accepted into college, including highly competitive institutions such as Columbia University and Dartmouth College.

The secret of Frederick Douglass Academy's success pertains to Monroe's modeling the school on the traditional principles that guided Martin Luther King, Jr.'s education at Morehouse College in Atlanta, Georgia. It would be at least as correct to say she adopted the Catholic school model. The students wear uniforms and must agree to abide by the school's code of behavior and academic focus or face expulsion. There is no admissions test, so academy students display the full range of aptitudes. But once discipline and academic demands are established, students rise to meet expectations. Underpinning this is the ancient Catholic view that, as Brother Walderman often says, "we all have value and worth, because we're created in the image and likeness of God." Restated in purely humanistic terms, the concept of intrinsic worth and capacity carries the same formative power. Frederick Douglass Academy's current principal is determined to provide an education equal to the city's Upper East Side private schools to each of his students. "That's why we have nineteen [sports] teams, including fencing," says Dr. Gregory Hodge, who grew up poor in Harlem and took over the academy in 1995. The school also arranges "for trips to places like Rome, Japan, and Mali, as chances to learn." All the junior high students are required to study Japanese as an introduction to the larger world both culturally and with a view to future career opportunities.

"We've just got to bring back that old Southern feeling," Orlando laments often when he thinks of Mrs. DeVane and her fundamental view that the path to excellence is both narrow, strict, and traditional, "because that was the reason that we were all successful."

If Catholic schools—and public schools at the time—equipped the lowly Irish, what reason could the educators in charge of failing districts today give that carries any validity?

On Sunday afternoon, December 5, Brother Walderman and Orlando drive away from Baltimore and the African American Catholic High School Consortium's conference with a deepened sense of camaraderie with each other and their peers, although not with Xavier University's representative, who remained oblivious to the need to strengthen relationships with black Catholic high schools.

The Consortium educators exchanged anecdotes and discussed shared dilemmas with their colleagues, temporarily overcoming isolation. Brother Walderman seldom interacts with administrators at similar schools in New York, let alone in other cities. But to Orlando's disappointment, his peers lacked a sense of urgency about resolving fiscal and developmental issues. "They look at themselves as managing rather than creating something," Orlando reflects in his office a week later. "No wonder we're sliding backwards. We need to approach our schools like venture capitalists, not beggars. But at this point, we don't even have a plan to develop a plan."

The religious orders, parishes, and dioceses running Catholic schools are still trying to come to grips with massive changes in staffing, costs, and enrollment. From the 1940s through the early 1960s, the proportion of New York City's one million school-aged children attending parochial school rose to 36 percent.[35] New York City peaked at 488 Catholic schools with 360,200 students in 1967. This success, however, contributed to the current crisis. As Catholics became more affluent, they tended to move out of the parish-centered urban villages where most of their schools had been built.

Contemporaneously Vatican II's attempt to modernize the Church precipitated an identity crisis of seismic proportions. When asked why the Council was necessary, Pope John XXIII answered, "I want to throw open the windows of the Church so that we can see out and the people can see in." Vast numbers of nuns, brothers, and priests not only looked out the Church's windows, but left their vocations entirely. Since then, the Church has attracted few recruits.

In 1965, there were 180,000 religious sisters in the United States. Today there are about 68,000, and this number will decline rapidly in the next decade, since "there are more religious women over the age of 90 than there are under 50."[36] The Catholic school system "had literally been built on their backs through the services they contributed in the form of the very low salaries that they accepted."[37] For generations, nuns were frontline troops in the battle for academic achievement and moral character in struggling Catholic communities. Had Vatican II occurred a generation or two earlier, the underclass would still be largely composed of white Catholics.

The proportion of religious staff at Catholic schools has plummeted from 96 to 4 percent nationwide.[38] Currently the Christian Brothers do not have a single novice in training in North or South America. The catastrophic loss of the religious teaching orders necessitated the costly hiring of vast numbers of lay teachers. They must be paid many times more than the nuns, brothers, or priests they replace. As a result, school costs have spiraled, pushing tuition up at a faster rate than the growth of family income. As the number of Christian Brothers declined, Rice's tuition increased slowly from $200 per year in 1948, as was the norm, to $400 in 1963.[39] Then it rose steeply to $3,550 for the current year, about $800 less than the national average.[40]

In addition, after Vatican II many Catholic parents started balking at paying tuition that rose relentlessly from kindergarten through twelfth grade. Especially if they had several children, this provided motivation to move to the suburbs, where public schools were comparable academically and sometimes better—and tuition-free. Then the minority families moving into the urban areas abandoned by ethnic whites were not only poorer, but faced higher tuition with the hiring of lay teachers. As much as possible, dioceses and religious orders struggled to keep their schools open and affordable as part of the Church's commitment to social justice that Vatican II reinvigorated. In the case of African Americans, most were non-Catholic and initially less motivated to send their children to parochial school, since many urban public schools remained viable into the 1980s. The need for alternatives has increased since then, reflected in the growth of minority enrollment at Catholic schools to 7 percent for blacks and 11 percent for Latinos. As well, 13.8 percent of parochial students are non-Catholics.[41]

Even so, the financial pressures on Catholic schools caused enrollment to decline for twenty-six consecutive years, before finally stabilizing in the early 1990s. But this respite didn't last long. Although prelates such as New York's John Cardinal O'Connor were determined not to shut a single school, recent years have seen waves of closings, as dioceses can no longer support schools running deficits. Sadly the institutions most vulnerable to closing are the ones serving the most vulnerable populations. Almost

45 percent of all Catholic schools are still located in urban areas, demonstrating the moral strength of the Church's commitment—and its fragility.[42]

Since the 1960s, almost half of Catholic schools nationally and in New York have gone out of business. Most of the recent closings have been elementary schools, perhaps because the academic differences between the public and Catholic systems are more apparent in the later grades, attracting parents who are more desperate to find alternatives and so are more motivated to find a way to pay tuition. Meanwhile Catholic schools are opening in suburban and affluent areas where many Catholics have moved. The fact that Catholic parents prefer their own schools even where the public alternative is viable provides hope. But this doesn't help urban schools, and many like Rice might soon lose the battle with insolvency.

Currently there are 2,320,651 students in 7,498 Catholic schools nationwide. This breaks down to 1,682,412 students at 6,288 elementary schools and 638,239 students in 1,210 secondary schools.[43] The New York archdiocese and Brooklyn diocese together currently operate 348 elementary and 75 high schools with 164,000 students, and despite losing half their students in the last forty years, together they still would comprise the nation's eighth largest public school district.[44]

This massive loss in enrollment occurred while the number of Catholics in the country doubled. In addition, the Hispanic share of the Catholic population is now 33 percent, far greater than their 12.7 percent representation at Catholic schools.[45] If the Church were seeking to educate these congregants as adamantly as they did the Irish and other white ethnic groups, there would be an aggressive campaign under way to both subsidize tuition and build new schools, instead of continuous shrinkage to the point of maintaining only a "lingering presence," as Morris described, in urban education. Many of these missing Catholics are among the neediest, and they lack the skills and means to improve.

This is not meant to denigrate the enormous efforts being made to sustain inner-city schools. For example, the Archdiocese of New York provides forty million dollars a year to keep its inner-city schools—108 elementary and high schools, primarily in Manhattan and the Bronx, serving disadvantaged minorities—afloat with archdiocese money, private donations, and especially fund-raising by the Inner-City Scholarship Fund, the Endowment for Inner-City Education, and the Patrons Program. This works out to a subsidy of $950 for each elementary student and $2,250 for every secondary student of the 42,000 students at these schools.[46] Some programs pay a student's entire tuition, such as Student Sponsor Partners, while others provide funding directly to the school. The Patrons Program, for example, matches an individual or a group of highly successful New Yorkers to a particular school, which they adopt. The patrons form an advisory board and seek ways to raise money for the school.

Still, the schools are "hemorrhaging students, almost always because the families can't sustain tuition," says Susan George, the Inner-City Scholarship Fund's executive director. George points out that tuition for the elementary schools increases by 7 percent while the costs increase by 11 to 12 percent per year.[47] As quickly as new funding sources are found, the gap between tuition and cost increases like negative compound interest. As a result, fewer struggling families can afford to pay the mounting tuition despite all the efforts.

Orlando finds this predicament outrageous and blames it mostly on the Church hierarchy's lack of vision. Although Catholic education costs twenty-five times more than when religious orders staffed the schools, he argues that the Church hasn't done nearly enough in response, nor have they even tried to formulate a national plan adequate to the task. Instead, individual Catholic school districts are caught in a massive game of catch-up, albeit valiantly played, that's probably doomed in the long run, precisely because of the inexorable logarithm that George describes.

As Orlando points out, few of the country's sixty-four million Catholics are adequately engaged in the solution.[48] On average, the 21.66 million U.S. Catholic households give $305 a year to their parishes. If that was increased by only 25 percent—or $1.50 per week per household—the gap between tuition and cost at struggling urban schools would be covered, thereby solving the immediate crisis.[48]

Protestants give far more than Catholics—in fact, five times as much.[49] As Orlando often points out, the generosity of Catholics has withered in an inverse relationship to their prosperity, due less to stinginess than a lack of leadership. No doubt if Orlando represented the U.S. Conference of Catholic Bishops, he would challenge and inspire Catholics until they turned their pockets inside out.

Chapter Eighteen

ORLANDO SITS IN HIS OFFICE AT 6 P.M. on Tuesday, January 18, preparing his mid-year teacher evaluations, which he'll present to them one-on-one, focusing on how best to deal with ongoing problems. Orlando schedules Kate Hebinck's evaluation for two weeks from today. He's worried that she might leave Rice out of frustration at the disruptive behavior and inconsistent work ethic still characterizing her freshman classes. She hasn't told Orlando or any of the teachers about her tentative plans to go to France with her fiancé next year, but he intuits that she's leaning that way.

Orlando appreciates how much responsibility Hebinck takes for the fact that a third of her students are still failing as the third marking period ends. It is becoming mathematically difficult for many ninth graders to pass the year unless they engineer a quick turnaround. From his observations and Abbasse's, Orlando knows Hebinck is doing all she can, and replacing her with a comparable teacher would be very difficult. Her contribution to Rice's academic mission is crucial. Only insofar as the freshmen can be put on track to literacy will they succeed at Rice and go on to college.

At the start of the next day, Hebinck stands in front of the blackboard on which she has written five sentences illustrating a set of common homonyms she presented in the fall. She's reviewing grammar—again—that the H-period students persist in getting wrong because, instead of paying attention, they continue to engage in the undercurrent of laughing and talking that disrupts all but her honors class and is most pronounced with this group.

"No, no, that is not how you get my attention and you know it," Hebinck snaps at Ephraim after he loudly calls out an incorrect answer.

"Remember, P-A-S-S-E-D is an action word," Hebinck points back to the blackboard. "In this sentence, the action word is 'ran'; that's what the dog did. It ran P-A-S-T. The word 'past' is an adverb here and a homonym for 'passed.' Does anyone have a question?"

Blank stares answer. Hebinck bangs a piece of chalk on the blackboard's ledge in exasperation. Although she makes students take notes, most students don't pay attention as they write and certainly don't refer to the notes when doing homework or preparing for a test. They constantly repeat the same errors, as for example in Ephraim's confusion of *there* and *they're* on the weekend assignment: *It's to late to be acepted because they're al'ready to many applications.*

Ten minutes later, Hebinck ends the lesson out of futility. She hands back the latest drafts of a writing assignment, a single paragraph about high school that students have been revising for a week and a half. First there was an in-class brainstorming session and then Hebinck repeated each step in the composition process in meticulous detail.

Some students, such as the slightly built youngster sitting in front of Ricky Rodriguez, write competently. His paragraph begins: *In gym we play a lot of different sports to help us become better athletes.* But others like Ricky struggle. After several revisions—the first a confused amalgam of misspelled details—Ricky's paragraph approaches coherence:

> In school we have seven subjects. The one subject that I like most is gym. Gym is a place where I haves fun with my friends. In gym we play games such as, basketball, soccer, baseball. After we play the games, we must be able to put on our close on, so we can get to the next class. And the coach looks for ability of each one of the players. And in many ways it helps you with problem of life. Gym is a place to have fun with friends and interac with other people. And a class that anyone can get a 100.

The middle sentences of Prince's short paragraph after four drafts read: *There are only fifty-two or fifty-seven seniors. Most of then are basketball players. There are baseball players in the school to. Also there are some football players, but they are very fewe.*

"My image of Prince," Hebinck comments later, "is watching him put his head down in class and not even try to write. His body language says, 'Why bother doing this assignment? It makes no impact on my life.' For most, there's a wide road called the process of being educated, but Prince is in the ditch. We try to force him onto the road, but he doesn't want to be there, although he likes to talk to the people who are passing by."

Hebinck began the year planning for the freshmen to write several five-paragraph essays and read two or three novels. She wants to cover literary terms, analyze literary techniques in poetry and short stories, and also cover the more confusing elements of grammar like verb tense. Now she worries that she won't come close, especially with this class.

On Friday, Hebinck's face flushed crimson in anger as the usual suspects threw pens and paper balls, and giggled as she tried to teach. Instead of handing out detentions or reviewing rules and procedures again, which hasn't worked, she sought an intervention for the first time in her career.

Abbasse readily agreed to talk to her students, knowing that she must be nearing her breaking point to ask for his help. Twenty minutes into today's final period, he appears at Hebinck's door, as arranged, and she departs. He insisted that she not be present, so the students would talk freely.

"Why do I have to scream at you?" Abbasse yells at John Caballero almost immediately. John continued talking with a classmate as Abbasse entered the room. "Why did Miss Hebinck ask me to talk to you guys?"

"People are disobedient," John shrugs defiantly. This is John's second tour of the ninth grade, but his first at a Catholic school.

"Obviously people are disobedient," Abbasse snaps. "You think this is a big funny joke?"

"The expression on my face ain't saying it's a joke," John fires back.

"Oh, the laughter and that smile don't mean anything?" Abbasse demands angrily.

"I was thinking about something somebody told me earlier," John mumbles. "I'm just a student doing his work."

"Stop that fronting game, it doesn't work with me." Abbasse booms. "Mr. Caballero's attitude is a perfect example of the problem. But I don't want to suspend people because many of you won't make it until June."

Some faces feign the aggrieved look of the wrongly accused. Others nod slightly; they have complained about how the antics of a persistent few prevent all from learning. "I get angry for only one reason," Hebinck told her class recently, "and that's when there's an injustice. You're all here to learn and I'm here to teach, but some people have made that impossible and it's not fair." Hebinck knows well that disadvantaged students face serious obstacles that education helps overcome and "only fools would get in the way."

"I want to hear about the reasons for these difficulties, and I want you guys to be honest," Abbasse directs as he paces back and forth in front of the blackboard.

"Miss Hebinck speaks to us like we're kind of slow," one student complains.

"What happens when she tells you something?" Abbasse asks.

"We're not listening," another admits.

"Therefore she repeats it in a very direct manner to make sure everybody heard and understood," Abbasse pile-drives his words the same way Hebinck has to in relentlessly repeating her instructions.

"I had Miss Hebinck for summer school, and I guess I got a reputation," Nelson Castellano whines. "When I ask her a question, she's like, No, 'cause you were talking. She won't listen."

"You have to prove the reputation doesn't fit anymore," Abbasse responds. "Just because you behave for one day doesn't mean your reputation is over. In all honesty, Nelson, if you want to put this out in public, you're one of the first names mentioned to me when I got back here in September. Don't blame Miss Hebinck; everybody has talked to me about you and your sarcastic comments."

Nelson straightens slightly and mumbles to himself. Hebinck considers him a saboteur, even though he often offers perceptive insights into class readings. Unfortunately Nelson also takes nasty verbal jabs at his classmates, and he bogs lessons down in obvious questions. "He's in the habit of being spoon-fed," Hebinck commented after talking with his mother. "He's always catered to at home and doesn't seem to value the intellect he has."

"How are you going to change your reputation?" Abbasse presses.

"By being good."

"What does that mean?"

"Don't screw around and get detentions," Nelson sits up to say, then returns to his slouch.

"I'll be straight, Nelson. I've dealt with you before, and you've told me later that the truth wasn't like what you first said," Abbasse says with quiet intensity. "Correct?"

"Yes," he grimaces.

John Caballero raises his hand solemnly. "She has good days and bad days," he says as if he's evaluating Hebinck as the dean's colleague. "Sometimes you ask her to explain the homework and she'll tell somebody from the class to do it. That makes me feel small."

"Why?" Abbasse asks.

"I don't know."

"Did she go over the assignment before?"

"Yeah, but I didn't know it."

"So what's the problem with asking a classmate to help you?"

"But there was a handout I didn't get," John protests.

"So she should hold everybody up for you?" Abbasse asks incredulous.

"When Miss doesn't feel like helping, it makes you feel small," John pouts.

"Any excuse not to accept responsibility—it's become so ingrained," Abbasse declares, articulating the fundamental cultural problem that he and Orlando struggle constantly to address.

"Sometimes Miss Hebinck won't be in class yet, and she gives me a DT for being late," complains Desmond Frazier, a tall freshman with basketball potential and a pleasant but mischievous smile.

"You were late, right?" Abbasse recalls the incident.

"Yeah, but how could she say I was late?"

"Your point is you did it, got caught, but don't think it's fair because she wasn't in the room yet?" Abbasse shakes his head. Every day, students complain about being treated unfairly instead of accepting their agency. Prince often jumps up when Hebinck turns her back to write on the blackboard and dances to get his classmates laughing. When she yells at him to stop, he feels disrespected and pouts. Then he talks back, eliciting a stronger response that he counters, earning a detention. Yet Prince still sees himself as an innocent victim, who is neither deserving of a reprimand nor capable of altering his behavior. This existential impasse similarly paralyzes about a dozen freshmen, and their teachers are losing patience.

"Look, if you have a disagreement with the teacher about a detention, or if you think the teacher disrespected you, raise your hand and ask to talk after class, or you can see me," Abbasse explains, emphasizing that students always have a voice, as long as it is channeled properly.

Whenever a student has a conflict, Abbasse sits down with the young man and listens intently. Usually the teacher was right but neglected to let the student express his side, which created more conflict. Abbasse seldom cancels a detention, and students never complain—once they have been given what they crave: undivided attention.

"You need to learn how to 'diffuse' conflicts with teachers, not escalate them," Abbasse continues. On the street, students learn that backing down means you're "soft," which earns ridicule, a beating, or worse. " 'Diffuse' means to spread it out so it's not so big. Escalate means to make it worse."

This message is not new. Abbasse regularly sends students to his office to calm down for a period when they tell him about differences with a teacher that could become serious. Abbasse sends for the class work, then mediates after school. "In my first years of teaching," he explains later, "I assumed that kids understood simple things, like how to greet someone. But I've learned that we're not only teaching them algebra and biology, but also how to be adults. They don't learn healthy interactions on the streets or often, at home, so we can't expect them to handle arguments properly without coaching."

"What if we have a problem with you?" Ephraim challenges with a wink in his voice. "Who do we go to?"

"Mr. Gober is the final boss," Abbasse smiles. "It's up to Mr. Gober and me to discipline the teachers, and it's up to Mr. Gober to discipline me, if needed. Then it's up to your parents to discipline Mr. Gober. Remember, you're at the bottom of the totem pole, but that doesn't mean you don't have a say. There was an incident last year with a junior where I said something at his lunch table that embarrassed him without my realizing it. He brought his mother in; we talked it out and I apologized. I make mistakes and so do you. The question is whether you're learning from them."

"I can't adjust to these clothes," John Caballero suddenly announces, as if wrong turns are like left turns that eventually lead back to respect in the dean's eyes.

"Find somewhere else to go," Abbasse tosses back.

"This sweater makes me hot and itchy even on cold days."

"That's the rule of the building, and everybody's got rules. Two months ago, we asked a teacher to leave because he wasn't doing what we asked." Abbasse refers to Jonathan Mason's dismissal. Mason had paid lip service to Orlando's advice, but refused to apply it.

Eric Sealy, a pudgy youngster with a high-pitched voice, took a well-worn thumb out of his mouth to say, "I think she's a good teacher. She puts stuff on the board and explains it—but don't ask no questions."

Every year, Abbasse is amazed at the number of African American teenagers who suck their thumbs. An eleventh grader in his first year at Rice lays his head down on a cafeteria table every morning before school and sucks his thumb without the least sense of self-consciousness. Abbasse remembers a Rice senior on the steps of St. Patrick's Cathedral moments after graduation ceremonies several years ago with a large pacifier in his mouth—and many other Rice Men wore oversized pacifiers around their necks that year—holding his infant son in his arms, who was also sucking on a pacifier. Psychologists have noted that in recent decades thumb sucking has become more common among older children with increasing rates of family dysfunction. Remarkably students never make fun of thumb suckers, intuitively understanding the need for this comforting, albeit regressive, habit.

Eric refers to the moment halfway through class yesterday when Hebinck refused to answer questions.

"She told me about all the comments and smirks," Abbasse replies.

"Sometimes we talk and laugh for nothing," Eric confesses.

"Finally someone's being honest," Abbasse exclaims. "If something's really funny, have your quiet laugh. But don't gas it up, as you guys say."

"I got suspended for mad funny shit," Hanif Claxon, a dark-skinned youngster with becoming dimples, blurts out and his classmates explode with glee.

"I can see exactly what Miss Hebinck is talking about," Abbasse yells. "This stuff is so disruptive. You've just spent twenty minutes telling me what's wrong with Miss Hebinck, and then proved everything she told me. The problem is you guys are so busy with what's going on around you, you can't focus on what she's saying. Your job is to be quiet, listen, learn, and ask questions if they're needed."

Abbasse glares at each student one by one in a suddenly silent room, before asking about their responsibilities as students. They all chime in with the correct list of behaviors: "focus on our work," "stop excessive talk," "laugh with people, not at them," and so on.

"So I go back to the original question," Abbasse says with exasperation. "If you know what your responsibilities are, why do you continue to act immaturely?"

"It's a habit from my old school," Hanif admits.

"True," Abbasse nods. "But you're all responsible for yourselves, and you've been here long enough that there are no more excuses. I've been letting students get five or six detentions before being suspended, but from now on, I'm going by the handbook and it'll be four."

A grumble rolls around the room.

"It's not about detentions, fellas; it's about doing the right thing. We want to see everyone stay four years and go on to college," Abbasse says as an ambulance wails up Lenox Avenue toward Harlem General Hospital on the corner of 137th Street. The hospital has one of the best trauma units in the city, specializing in gunshot wounds. "But there needs to be an immediate change, or the next step is out."

To emphasize, Abbasse recounts how one classmate's mother begged the principal to let her son stay, but Orlando wouldn't reconsider. Both the principal and dean continue to struggle with how much attention to give disruptive students, versus nurturing the "good kids." They know they'll lose many problem students no matter what they do, while quieter young men, who also struggle with serious issues at home, are ignored and just as quietly leave or fail out. On the other hand, some of the current juniors and seniors made remarkable turnarounds after troublesome starts. But as Abbasse reiterates as the period ends, the freshmen have drained away his reservoir of patience for this school year.

Chapter Nineteen

MEMBERS OF THE JUNIOR VARSITY basketball team drop by Orlando's office after practice to chat a few minutes before going home on Monday evening, January 31. Missing among them is Yusef, who quit the team two weeks ago after a difficult month at Rice.

In the middle of December, Yusef stood in Orlando's doorway after class with his head hung low.

"Did you hear what happened?" he muttered.

"Yes," Orlando replied, pleased that Yusef owned up to his mistake at lunch.

"Are you upset with me?" Yusef buried his chin in his chest.

"Why would you think that?"

Yusef stood rigid for a moment, then exhaled, "Because you care about me."

"That's very difficult for you to say; you're not used to it," Orlando replied tenderly and felt sad that Yusef was unaccustomed to fatherly love until Rice.

Yusef flopped onto the couch, visibly lighter and looser. Then again with effort, he lifted the words "I disempowered myself today" out of his chest.

"Are you throwing my slogan back at me, or has it become part of your vocabulary?" Orlando hears students arguing in the hallway when they're unaware he's standing nearby. Often one will say, "You're starting to disempower me." The conflict dissipates, convincing Orlando that students are internalizing his message. But there are times students parrot his words in his presence to ingratiate themselves.

Yusef shook his head and then described how he almost got into a scuffle earlier. While standing in the lunch line, Yusef noticed that Mark Wilson was pointing his finger at him and talking to fellow juniors. Yusef immediately assumed Mark was saying something negative.

"Why are you talking about me?" Yusef jumped ahead to confront Mark.

The two boys traded jibes, then started pushing each other. Mark had the advantage of size, strength, and martial arts training. But Yusef was winding up inside to unleash his street acumen, which, as dojo fighters often discover, is more dangerous. Fortunately Brian Copeland, the Earth science teacher, was standing nearby and rushed over to separate the two before either landed a punch.

Abbasse soon arrived, sat Mark in the hallway, and sent Yusef to his office to calm down. Each earned a detention and a stern talk. Since the fight wasn't "full-fledged," neither student was suspended. Throwing punches warrants a three-day suspension provided no one was hurt, while a real fight mandates expulsion. At the beginning of the school year, Abbasse suspended several freshmen for minor skirmishes to send a message to the incoming class. He also suspended a student who was "hyping the situation on the sidelines." But Abbasse felt counseling would be more effective with Mark and Yusef.

"What were you trying to prove?" Orlando asked him after Yusef recounted the incident.

"Nothing," Yusef shrugged.

"Mark's a junior and you're a sophomore," Orlando pressed. "Are you trying to establish a reputation?"

"I don't go for that," Yusef scoffed.

Orlando nodded, realizing that Mark had more to prove in a confrontation since Yusef's street reputation was well established at Rice. Mark had never demonstrated he could fight outside a dojo, as far as most students knew. Last year, he successfully defended himself and Gregory Vazquez when they were confronted by several homeboys on the street after school. But few of their classmates heard of the incident. When Copeland intervened, Mark was struggling more than Yusef to restrain his emotions as they scuffled. Yusef was pushing back vigorously and knew he was supposed to walk away, but he hadn't lost control: "not sweatin' it," as he said afterward.

But a month later cracks in Yusef's cool became apparent. On Tuesday, January 11, the junior varsity basketball team played St. Raymond's High School at the Gauchos Gym, an athletic facility in the Bronx, south of Yankee Stadium, where Rice's freshman, junior varsity, and varsity teams play most of their home games, and where the varsity team practices.

John Shea, the head coach, and Abbasse (who manages to find time to serve as an assistant coach for the junior varsity team) put Yusef into the game several times as a second-string guard, only to bench him a minute later.

Near the end of the game, Yusef's frustration boils over. "This is Steve Burts's team," he exclaims loudly enough that both coaches and all the players can hear. As the team's star, Steve, a sophomore two years younger than Yusef, is being cultivated for the varsity team. He comes by his talent honestly since his father plays professional basketball in Europe. "Burts gets thirty-six minutes a game whatever happens."

As play continues on the court, Abbasse studiously ignores Yusef, but Shea turns his ear toward him.

Yusef notices and huffs, "Even if he makes mistakes, it's okay. But if I make one mistake, I get taken out."

Abbasse wants to tell Yusef that he was pulled for performing poorly, but decides "not to give his play for sympathy from his teammates any energy." In truth, Yusef made unforced turnovers and was often out of position.

In the dressing room after the game, Yusef dressed quickly and stood by the door when Abbasse gave a quick pep talk congratulating the players for their effort and the win.

"Shysty-ass coach," Yusef muttered loudly enough to be heard when Abbasse finished speaking. He glared at the dean, then stomped out of the room.

Abbasse caught up to Yusef before he left the building and told him to "cool off before you say something you regret." Yusef's "shysty-ass coach" remark struck Abbasse as one of the funniest expressions he'd ever heard. He decided to give the sophomore a pass and struggled to keep a straight face as he told Yusef "you have a bad attitude, and best go home and think about it." He urged Yusef to talk to Orlando about the incident the next day.

More damaging, since the beginning of December, Abbasse has suspected that Yusef sells drugs at Rice. The dean told Orlando, who talked sternly to Yusef but he denied the charge. Subsequently Yusef stopped pushing at the school and resolved to stop completely in his neighborhood too. Rumors that Yusef is a source for weed at Rice persisted, however, and this was enough to convince Abbasse of his guilt. The dean didn't consider whether those informing on Yusef resented that he'd become Orlando's favorite, despite his well-earned street reputation. More than a few classmates muttered, "What's the point of being good?" within earshot of Abbasse.

Then on Wednesday, February 3, a sophomore's baseball cap is reported missing, and several classmates tell Abbasse they saw Yusef take it. After school, the dean confronts Yusef, who admits that the cap is in his locker and describes how he found it on the floor in the morning.

"Why didn't you give it to a teacher?" Abbasse challenges.

"I was going to turn it in to the office after school," Yusef replies.

"That's very shaky."

"Then at lunch somebody said the hat belonged to Simeon," Yusef continues. "So I was looking for him."

"And?"

"I was told near the end of the period and didn't find him," Yusef counters. "I was on my way to get it now and turn it in."

"Whether or not you found it, and whether or not you were going to give it back, you put yourself in the position of looking guilty," Abbasse shakes his head. After seeing Yusef almost get into a fight with Mark Wilson and then blow up at the basketball game in January, Abbasse isn't inclined to believe him. "Besides, I've had several students tell me Yusef brags about belonging to a gang and about all the street fights he's won," Abbasse explains later. "It was just too many things."

Abbasse sends Yusef home on suspension until his fate is decided.

The next day, Yusef's mother is supposed to call or come to Rice for a meeting with the dean, but she doesn't make contact. Perhaps Yusef erased Abbasse's phone message, hoping Orlando would fix the problem.

Right after school, Abbasse recommends that Yusef be expelled, and Orlando puts off responding. He wants very much to give Yusef another chance. Whenever Yusef drops by, he lifts Orlando's spirits. For example, there was the afternoon in late November when "Yusef came to my office whining about a headache. He laid his head on my shoulder and I asked, 'What happened to the big-time gangster who would take a bullet and not flinch?'

" 'I don't feel well,' he whimpered like a little boy.

" 'Would you like to go home?' I asked.

" 'No, that's all right,' Yusef answered. 'I'd rather stay and finish a project I'm doing in the computer lab.' "

"I felt thrilled that this was the same young man who was on the street last year." Orlando reflected on the beginning of their relationship but can't determine exactly "what made us click. Maybe it was his sense of maturity.

He'd spent three years trying to get through the tenth grade, so he was consciously choosing to come here and turn his life around. He'd say I impressed him as a father figure, which was his way of articulating exactly what he needed in his life and he wasn't going to hide the fact from himself. Then he said:

" 'I'm a leader; I don't want to follow any of the cool kids at Rice.'

" 'That's funny,' I answered, 'because you got close to Mr. Gober, who taught you leadership.'

" 'Oh yeah,' he laughed. 'I'm like a leader-in-training.' "

"Yusef didn't see himself as dependent like some kids who come to me and want to be taken care of," Orlando reflects. "Part of the attraction was seeing the leadership strength in me that he sees in himself. I tend to draw students like Yusef or Prince who are needy but strong-willed and don't know how to exercise it positively. Students who are bright and quirky like Kawone Williams gravitate more to a Widziewicz type, or maybe to Abbasse."

Orlando considers a counseling program for Yusef, perhaps with Widziewicz, who has extensive professional training. "Yusef carries so much he wants to deal with, but can't verbalize yet."

But the present dilemma doesn't dissipate. Stealing has always been a zero-tolerance offense under Orlando. "I'm sure Yusef wants to be saved, and I'm sure everybody else wants to save him, but what valid excuse could I give for not expelling him?" Orlando exclaims in his office at 9 P.M. "The other students know the rules, so how can I give one person who's very close a pass? That sends the wrong kind of message. Credibility-wise, I can't allow him to stay. It's so sad when a kid does one dumb thing and there's no turning back."

Orlando will ask Abbasse to handle the expulsion tomorrow or Friday, since he can't come to grips emotionally with the loss. What neither considers sufficiently is whether Yusef is in fact guilty of stealing the baseball cap. He didn't argue vigorously in his own defense, which seemed to betray guilt but was more a statement of resignation. Yusef sees authority figures other than Orlando as prejudiced against him, so when Abbasse rejected his explanation, he shrugged indifferently. It's entirely possible that Yusef simply put off taking the cap to the office until after school.

Abbasse sticks with his gut feeling, and the flimsy evidence about this incident and the reported drug dealing. Meanwhile Orlando is too consumed with grief to be objective, so the deciding factor is perceptual. As Orlando eventually explains to Yusef, regardless of his innocence, his classmates will think that the principal made an exception if he's not put out, which can't be tolerated.

Orlando feels he is losing a son, which brings back memories of having to expel his favorite student at St. Mark's a decade ago. Three days before graduating, the young man brought a gun to school. "Putting him out was the hardest thing I've ever had to do, other than deal with Samantha Brown's death, until now."

Losing Yusef also fractures what remains of Orlando's desire to work as a full-time educator. "I always told myself that when I hit my thirtieth anniversary, I'd examine my commitment to teaching and probably do something else or become a part-time consultant." Orlando won't complete thirty years until the end of next year, but he suffers deeply from the accumulating stress of his career. "It's not easy being a person like me who's very upfront and outspoken, who can be very in your face and demanding. When you're in a public position, you become a lightning rod. But I've been dragging myself the last few weeks, upset with Brother Walderman for wanting to increase enrollment so much it will endanger the program; I'm upset with the freshman class for making us climb the walls; and I'm upset with some of the teachers. I question whether I still have the stamina, the vision, and the creativity to lead."

Several weeks ago, Orlando confessed his growing doubts to Gail Foster, the founder of the Toussaint Institute Fund, a not-for-profit organization in New York City that seeks placements in viable public and private schools for disadvantaged children. Currently Foster is consulting with Orlando once a week to write a charter school application. She hopes to finesse Orlando away from Rice to become the new school's principal.

"Orlando, people have bent you, but you have never been broken," she reminded him. Considering she's been a close friend for much of Orlando's career, the words were heartening. "The reason they can't break you is because you're doing what God wants you to do."

This spiritual underpinning, however, is exactly what Orlando feels slipping away. "I talk to myself all the time now about whether I'm fulfilling my own mandate as an African American man who happens to be a Christian educator, and what does that mean for the young men here." Orlando has gone as far as telling his brother Wylie that he might leave in June.

———

Over the next two weeks, Abbasse confers with Orlando about several students who stubbornly resist improving their behavior and are continuing to fail three or more subjects in the third marking period. He recommends they be asked to leave and Orlando agrees. At this point, they can transfer to a neighborhood public high school and still pass the year. If they stay at Rice, they will almost certainly fail out and then have to repeat the ninth grade in the public system, which increases the chances they will drop out.

Abbasse also works more intensely with persistent troublemakers who show improvement one day but then slide back the next. The dean wants them to achieve more consistency so they will make it to the next grade. On Wednesday, February 16, after a week without detentions, Prince was on his way to the washroom halfway through a period when he yelled "homo" from the hallway at a freshman in a different class. As punishment, Abbasse makes Prince carry boxes of donated books to the library at lunch today. Abbasse hopes to somehow break the spell that drives Prince to destroy his opportunity at Rice.

"The key with these kids is to ask students the day after an incident if they understand why they got into trouble," Abbasse explains. "Then hopefully I'll see them learning how to complain about a grade properly or listen patiently to the teacher's explanation for a detention without reacting negatively. As I talk to deans of discipline at other schools, I see that most aren't doing what we do."

Both Abbasse and Orlando speak privately to Prince several times a month. Concerning his behavioral problems, they methodically strip the youngster of his beloved excuses until he admits his agency. Unfortunately he tends to forget the lesson by the next morning. Now they believe that there is nothing they can do but wait until Prince decides to follow Rice's rules or breaks one too many.

Unfortunately Abbasse and Prince continue to trade jibes that the dean believes are humorously effective reminders to act properly. But Prince only appears to enjoy the exchanges, when in reality he takes offense and believes that "Abbasse is picking on me because he wants me to leave." Instead of having a thick, resilient skin, as it appears, Prince has no protective covering. All his nerve endings are exposed, and he acts like a clown to hide the truth.

Last week, Abbasse was about to put Ephraim "on contract," meaning that the freshman would sign a document spelling out his behavioral boundaries with the understanding that another serious violation would result in expulsion. He called Ephraim's stepfather, Marvin Smith, who told Abbasse that he didn't think Ephraim would survive on contract, since the combination of personal issues and neurological drugs undermine his emotional stability. Smith pointed out that his stepson's conduct and grades have improved, and he doesn't cough loudly in class anymore. Abbasse reconsidered, and the two men agreed to monitor Ephraim more closely and speak again soon.

Then today Ephraim walked into Bodie's classroom on his way to his global studies class to retrieve a pencil that a fellow student had borrowed earlier. Ephraim made no attempt to act unobtrusive, instead calling his classmate "ugly" in a loud voice. When Bodie told him to leave the room, Ephraim broke into a chorus of "Fuck that, fuck this school, and fuck. . . ." The more the teacher tried to assert her authority, the more defiant Ephraim became. Finally Bodie asked one of the janitors to get Abbasse. Later in the dean's office, Ephraim claimed that Bodie "yelled at me for no reason. I just went for my pencil and didn't do anything wrong."

After school, Abbasse again debates whether to put him on contract. His performance certainly warrants it, but Abbasse genuinely likes Ephraim and wants him to succeed. The dean decides on an in-school suspension and will confer with his stepfather.

In the weeks after Abbasse spoke to Hebinck's class, they both call the parents of at-risk freshmen. Nelson Castellano shows noticeable improvement soon after both the teacher and the dean speak with his mother. Abbasse recommends several books with viable strategies for a single parent raising a minority son in the inner city, which she reads. She then begins to set behavioral limits for her son at home.

"I gave Nelson a DT the other day for messing around that he probably didn't deserve," Abbasse recounts on Friday, February 25. "His immediate reaction was negative, but then he stopped himself and said, 'All right, Mr. Abbasse.' When I see a student taking responsibility, I know I can work longer with that young man." Also, Nelson's mother is responding to Abbasse's calls.

After several stern talks with John Caballero about the attitude he displayed in Hebinck's class, Abbasse reaches his mother.

"Mr. Abbasse, I don't know what you did, but he's scared of you now," she declares. "John gets his shirt and tie together at night now, and leaves early in the morning. He's determined not to offend you."

Abbasse hangs up pleased that he has finally gotten through. He can't predict what will work for a particular student, so he tries various approaches. He wasn't going to experiment for long with John since he saw little potential, but now he will invest much more effort in salvaging him.

During the first half of the school year, John's mother complained that Abbasse was targeting her son—as many freshman parents usually do. Perceptions began to change in January as parents saw their sons adjust to Rice's demands, and as they met parents of upperclassmen. Another mother vehemently protested her ninth grader's suspension, until she talked with a friend with a son in his final year. The friend reassured her that if Abbasse was disciplining her son, the boy did something wrong. The senior's mother praised Abbasse's approach and made a believer out of the freshman's mother, who apologized for her pugnacious attitude.

Unfortunately some phone messages were ignored by parents or perhaps erased by the students. Of the freshman parents Abbasse reached and invited in for a talk, only 20 percent showed up. In Abbasse's experience, most single mothers retreat quickly into denial when their sons get into trouble. They would rather avoid the truth than have to take charge at home.

On a day-to-day basis, it seems to Hebinck, and sometimes to Orlando and Abbasse, the battle to socialize and educate is being lost. But long-term, any Rice student who applies himself in a moderate way will have no trouble graduating on time. The question is which young men will choose to take advantage of what Rice offers.

Royce Pilgrim sits in his AP English class with a sullen expression on his face. He doesn't want to be at Rice, but his father insists he stay. As a result, he has carried on a controlled rebellion for four years. He has been suspended twice this year for insulting teachers and will spend the rest of the year on probation. In fact, he has been on probation every year and seems most comfortable there. He misbehaves just enough to keep himself on the edge of expulsion. So Abbasse has learned to oblige him and once on probation, Royce calms down. He will graduate and go to college, where his natural intelligence should eventually take the lead.

"In the ninth grade, we had mad fights, and kids brought guns to school and sold drugs," Royce recounts. "It started changing when Gober came. Many guys got kicked out who were mad cool with him, but he knew they wouldn't change so he did what he had to and Rice got better." Royce acknowledges begrudgingly that every year, his misbehavior becomes less egregious.

As a tree must be pruned to grow, so the principal and dean grapple with shaping Rice's student body. A significant proportion of freshmen will either fail out, leave, or be asked to leave. Four years from now, the current crop of freshmen will have lost at least a third of their classmates. But the senior class will include a significant number of those who were failing their subjects halfway through the ninth grade and constantly getting into trouble, but then made a turnaround because the pruning provided motivation.

Edmund Rice's adage—"Have courage; the good seed will grow up in the child's heart later on"—applies as much this year as in 1802, when he founded the Christian Brothers. For most students, it's not a matter of if but when, although this might have to occur elsewhere. Orlando and Brother Walderman will seek placement in a parochial school for virtually any expelled student who wants another chance.

Orlando has kept in touch with Yusef on a daily basis and started calling parochial high schools as soon as he was put out. Within two weeks, Orlando places Yusef at Our Saviour Lutheran High School in the Bronx. Like Rice, the school is 85 percent black, but much smaller with only 115 students. A big plus for Yusef is that he'll be a starter on the varsity basketball team.

This pleases Orlando so much his mood has brightened noticeably, and he's not talking to his brother about his thirty-year crisis or leaving Rice. He hopes to find a way to bring Yusef back next year, but hasn't thought of the right strategy yet.

Chapter Twenty

―――――

"HOW COULD THIS HAVE HAPPENED?" Orlando exclaims as he reads the morning newspaper in his office on Monday, February 28. This question has been roiling through his entire spirit since Friday when the verdict came down: not guilty. The four white police officers who fired forty-one shots at Amadou Diallo, the African immigrant who reached for his wallet in a darkened hallway a year ago—hitting him nineteen times—were cleared of all criminal charges.

Orlando throws his copy of the *Daily News* into the trash, disgusted that members of the multiracial jury in Albany, where the trial was moved to assure an objective result, said the evidence made it "very clear" that the officers were innocent of second-degree murder.[1]

The fact that the shooting occurred so close to Yusef's home adds to the principal's angst. In addition, Yusef is a known drug dealer the police target regularly for stop-and-frisks, whether or not he's retired from the trade, which puts him even more at risk of Diallo's fate.

Despite Orlando's fears, harm is far more likely to befall Yusef from rival dealers than from the NYPD. "Last year, New York's fatal police shooting rate was 0.48 fatal shootings per 1,000 cops, compared with Philadelphia's 0.72, Miami's 2.01. . . ."[2] But Diallo's death haunts the black community, in which many feel that any one of them could be killed without just cause at any moment by a white cop. Yet in Washington, D.C., for example, the predominately black police force fatally shoots mostly black suspects at more than six times the rate of the NYPD.

However, the overwhelming consensus among African Americans was expressed by protesters who said the verdict was a "flagrant miscarriage of justice."[3] Activists began protesting after the shooting last February. Al Sharpton and his followers staged demonstrations in front of police headquarters and many entered the building in order to be arrested for disorderly conduct. Black leaders and celebrities joined in daily acts of civil disobedience that earned them national media coverage for only a minor inconvenience, since they were usually released by the end of the day.

Orlando made one appearance at the police plaza to join the activists for several hours but was careful not to be arrested. He never returned, even though this is exactly the sort of civil rights strategy—albeit without any real danger, since police officers politely answered protesters' queries about how to get arrested and treated everyone with respect—that Orlando champions as the highest expression of African American racial consciousness. He remembers breathing the air of protest in his youth as the most exhilarating moments of his life. Orlando never tires of relating this to his students, especially during Black History Month, which he extends from the beginning of February through March.

Surprisingly, Orlando didn't encourage his students to participate, although at first it seemed he would. Shortly after the Diallo shooting, he sent a letter to Dr. Catherine Hickey, the archdiocese's secretary for education, calling for a Catholic response. Orlando termed the incident an indictment of the Catholic school system, since the four officers had Irish surnames. "The police and fire departments are filled with young Irish who are the products of our teaching," Orlando later paraphrased what he wrote. "What does that say about our schools when you have this type of widespread situation going on?"

The "widespread situation" referred to systemic police aggression against minorities that Sharpton and his followers claimed was at the root of the Diallo shooting. Critics charged that the city's remarkable drop in crime rates during the Giuliani administration was the result of a reign of police brutality that targeted minority neighborhoods. The facts prove otherwise. Relative to their crime rate, African Americans are not more likely to be arrested or subjected to a stop-and-frisk than other groups.[4] There have been rare incidents of police brutality, such as the torture of Abner Louima, a Haitian immigrant, by police officers at a Brooklyn stationhouse in August 1997, but certainly no campaign against minorities.

In the letter, Orlando charged that police officers were targeting Rice students. He told the *New York Times* that when he first came to Rice, reports of police stopping students were rare, but at least 10 percent of the student body was harassed last year.[5] Orlando detailed an incident in mid-March of last year when a police officer stopped Lorenzo Laboy—a senior who became valedictorian—and a classmate at the subway turnstile at 125th Street and St. Nicholas Avenue. They were questioned about their student subway cards. Lorenzo was on his way to an after-school job at Resurrection Church in Washington Heights, and both wore their Rice vests with the school name embroidered clearly in gold script. The cops demanded identification, asked a slew of probing questions, searched the students' book bags, then one of the policemen accused the duo of knitting the sweaters in order to pose as students and use the Metrocards.

Whether the patrolman was an outright racist or happened to have banged his head with mind-altering force seconds before encountering the two Rice students, Orlando saw proof of the insidious racial stereotypes and police-state tactics that led to the shooting. Certainly stop-and-frisk tactics have a negative impact on innocent young men, who both develop a suspicious relationship with law enforcement and, since they're forced to see themselves as suspects, become more inclined to act that way.

Dr. Hickey replied to Orlando's letter saying she wished he had informed her that this "harassment" (her quotation marks according to Orlando) was happening to Rice students.

"How idiotic to think this is only happening to our students," Orlando exclaimed as he read the superintendent's letter. "Minority students at other Catholic high schools must be experiencing the same levels of profiling." He interpreted Dr. Hickey's response as an attempt to dismiss him. Later he heard rumors that she didn't like the tone of his letter.

"But where's the Church's outrage?" Orlando asked Brother Tyrone Davis, who heads the archdiocese's Office of Black Ministry. Brother Davis is an African American Christian Brother who lives at Rice. He has been stopped by the police so many times walking around the neighborhood that now he makes sure he is wearing his clerical collar when he leaves the building.

"Don't bother writing Dr. Hickey again; she took the first as a personal attack," Brother Davis advised.

Orlando immediately wrote a second letter "making it clear that I don't care whether she likes my attitude. I told her she needs to respond as the superintendent of a school system that's serving more and more people of color. But she's out of tune with her students."

After receiving no answer, Orlando exclaimed, "She's not going to silence me." He planned to confront Dr. Hickey at a principals' meeting to say, "I want to know how you're utilizing your position to empower your students. That's what Jesus wants us to do. He'd be right down there at the protest, not sitting in some high glossy office with ten secretaries. I know this sounds radical, but that's what Jesus was, a revolutionary."

Orlando was also displeased with his pastor, Monsignor Wallace A. Harris, at St. Charles Borromeo. "The Sunday after the Diallo killing, he didn't even mention it. The next week, he told a story about a parishioner who was upset about Diallo but had recently related how happy she was to see a white face come through her front door when she called the police. Monsignor walks the middle Catholic line; it's very inappropriate for a black pastor at a black church in Harlem."

After resigning as principal of St. Mark's in 1992, Orlando drifted from the Lutheran church because he was "disgusted with school politics." For the next five years, he joined different congregations, usually with a Baptist orientation, but "I wasn't being fed spiritually." Then in 1997, Orlando was invited to Sunday Mass at St. Charles by Rice's principal, Brother Daniel Adams, whom he liked and admired. "I fell in love with the church's warmth and spirituality. I was moved by the incredible choir, the Afrocentric liturgy, and Monsignor Harris's homily that gave me food for thought. I felt at home after growing up in the Lutheran church's Missouri Synod; I'm conservative in theology as opposed to politics."

Orlando formally converted to Catholicism on Holy Saturday in 1998 at St. Charles. "It's a tithing church that's not poor. St. Charles breaks stereotypes and brings in five thousand dollars a week." It's also a church that attracts a few dozen whites to the Sunday morning Gospel Mass. As the Vicar of Harlem on a career path perhaps to become a bishop, Monsignor Harris sees no point in needlessly offending white Catholics and so followed the cardinal's balanced lead regarding Diallo.

Several weeks after the shooting, John Cardinal O'Connor addressed a contingent of officers and family members at the annual mass for the NYPD's Holy Name Society. The cardinal's remarks were intended for the entire department and as importantly, for the city's black leadership. Cardinal O'Connor put the Diallo shooting—regardless of culpability—into proper perspective:

> The majority of the between thirty and forty thousand police officers in the City of New York are people of tremendous integrity, of decency, of

honor. Some, certainly the minority, have made serious, grave mistakes that have been very damaging. . . . You all recognize this. You all feel very bad about it. You all want such tragedies avoided in the future. But we must start with the basic premise of widespread goodness within the New York City Police Department. Tremendous sacrifices are made. Many of you put your lives at risk every day.

Referring to the intense and rather nasty criticism of the mayor and the department, the cardinal cautioned, "if we begin with the premise that our Police Department is rotten to the core . . . filled with hatred toward those of another race, another religion, another color, whatever it might be, then it is utterly impossible for us to achieve peace with justice and reconciliation."

Throughout the trial, Orlando praised Cardinal O'Connor's approach, which included his meeting with Catholic school principals and students in April concerning police harassment. Orlando couldn't attend since he had scheduled his first annual Youth Conference that Saturday. He sent Mrs. Lewis, the ninth grade guidance counselor, and Lorenzo Laboy to represent the school. Brother Walderman and several other students joined them.

"Speaking for minority young men, we don't want to be the scapegoat for society's problems," Lorenzo told the cardinal. "We don't want to be looked upon as criminals because in the eyes of some authorities we fit the description. We want to be looked upon with respect."

Cardinal O'Connor nodded with empathy.

"Maybe there's hope," Lorenzo continued. "Hope for all people regardless of race, ethnicity, creed, state or life. Hope to create a society where all people are viewed as being created in the image of God."

Orlando reviewed Lorenzo's notes before the meeting and was satisfied that his message would be conveyed.

Meanwhile Orlando orchestrated the Youth Conference to train students how to deal with stop-and-frisks and other interactions with the police. He impressed upon the Rice Men and the young women—from St. Jean Baptiste High School, an all-girls institute with a mostly minority student body on the Upper East Side, on Orlando's invitation as a sister school—that their reactions could lead to an arrest or even to being shot down like Diallo. Several representatives from 100 Blacks in Law Enforcement Who Care conducted seminars on how to behave when stopped by the police and how to defuse confrontations on the street that can turn deadly.

Brian Copeland, the Earth science teacher, remarked that African Americans feel completely vulnerable in the aftermath of the Diallo shooting or any similar event. After a long history of police abuse, blacks believe that the forty-one shots could have easily—very easily—targeted any one of them or their children. The intensity of emotions evoked by the Diallo story reverberates with the sense of victimization and powerlessness that four hundred years of history have imprinted on the African American consciousness. The collective memory of every beating, rape, and lynching resurrects in the subconscious, and these ghosts are not easily put to rest.

During the next morning's announcements, Orlando unloads his rage about the Diallo verdict. "We pray for the young men of Rice High School and all our people caught in this cycle of violence. Emmett Till and Amadou Diallo were killed for the color of their skin." In 1955, fourteen-year-old Emmett was savagely murdered in Mississippi for whistling at a white woman. The racist perpetrators were acquitted in a verdict—similar to how the jury ignored the evidence in the O. J. Simpson trial—that mobilized support for the civil rights movement among blacks in the North. Orlando hopes the Diallo outcome will re-energize the current struggle. "We pray to find a way to express our frustration and anger in a way that promotes a just society."

Today is February 29, African American Heritage Day at Rice. In consultation with several black faculty members, including Olivene Browne, the eleventh- and twelfth-graders' math teacher, and Kim Davis, Orlando created a program celebrating "the long-term struggle of the people of African descent to find our true identity."

At 10:30 A.M., the sophomores and juniors replace the freshmen and seniors in the cafeteria for the program's second performance. Jordan Jones, a sophomore, delivers a shortened version of Jesse Jackson's famous speech to the 1984 Democratic National Convention. Jordan recently recited the speech at a forensics competition at Xavier High School, placing first in the declamation category. He shows as much promise as Mark Wilson, who placed fourth in the state finals last year with the same speech. This was a remarkable achievement according to Steve DiMattia, the forensics coach, since the competition included Iona Preparatory and Regis high schools, ranked among the nation's best.

Like Mark, Jordan works obsessively on his delivery and on getting high grades in all subjects. Also like Mark, Jordan uses these activities to keep his mind off family problems, and he stays at Rice as late as possible every night. But while Mark avoids conflicts with his grandmother at home, Jordan doesn't have a home to go to.

As a freshman, Jordan lived with his father, mother, and sister in a brownstone the family owned nearby. "I had the corner bedroom on the top floor. I can still close my eyes and walk through the entire house," Jordan recalls as stoically as possible. "We had four floors and a basement, two kitchens and four bathrooms."

Jordan's father has a master's degree in mathematics and was working on Wall Street. Unfortunately he became a heavy cocaine user and got his wife into the habit. Eventually he lost his job, went bankrupt, and couldn't prevent the house from being repossessed last February. To her credit, Jordan's mother stopped using drugs and secured a secretarial position while she divorced her husband. She took Jordan and his sister to stay at the apartment of a relative, who soon ran out of hospitality.

Staying with friends only delayed the inevitable: by June, Jordan and his family were living in a homeless shelter. "It was a horrible place," Jordan recalls in monotones. "One woman wanted to fight my mother because she was sitting in a seat the woman had the day before. I almost had to hit a Dominican woman because she called my mother 'a fucking nigger.'"

As Jordan recites the speech, his voice sounds with melodious clarity despite the cafeteria's shabby acoustics. His face radiates enthusiasm, and he captures everyone's attention with his sincere, magnetic intensity. "Our time has come. Our time has come. Suffering breeds character. Character breeds faith," Jordan intones the climactic ending of Jackson's inspiring vision. "Our faith, hope, and dreams will prevail. Our time has come. Weeping has endured for nights, but now joy cometh in the morning. Our time has come. . . . We must leave racial battleground and come to economic common ground and moral higher ground. America, our time has come. . . ."

Applause ricochets off the mural behind Jordan that depicts the African American gladiators of the civil rights movement. But what Jordan really feels is an overwhelming numbness. No joy has graced his mornings since his family life disintegrated. Throughout the summer, Jordan and his mother and sister progressed from overnight housing to stays of various lengths at different facilities to their current one-bedroom apartment on the other side of Queens. They're awaiting a two-bedroom apartment closer to Rice. "The worst thing is the humiliation," Jordan confesses. "I see friends walking down the street in Harlem, and they talk about going home and I say, 'Oh yeah, I'm going to my house too,' so they won't know."

Jordan has confided only briefly in Kim Davis, the juniors' guidance counselor, whose middle-class upbringing and upwardly mobile demeanor appeal to him. Otherwise Jordan smiles broadly and acts carefree.

Fortunately, Jordan has an SSP scholarship that enables him to continue at Rice. Also on the positive side, Jordan's father went to a rehab clinic and was recently released. "I'm going to chill with him after school," Jordan said this morning. "We had a good relationship and I love him. He had a problem but he's getting better. My dad's going to be the manager of a store soon." The last sentence hung awkwardly, almost buoyed by hope.

Orlando stands at the back of the room wearing a pumpkin-hued suit and black shirt with an orange tie. He joins the students' loud applause and beams with pride for Jordan's talent. Jordan also sings and dances well enough to perform on Broadway someday—but not before graduating college. Jordan is determined not to be poor. Although Orlando doesn't know the sophomore's full story and doesn't have a close relationship—which Jordan would consider a betrayal of his father—he supports the sophomore's desire to achieve material success. As much as he wants his boys to reincarnate the idealism that inspired his own life, he understands that coming up from poverty, most students ache first for security and possessions.

Orlando is pleased that the second rendition of the Heritage Day program is going better than the first, when the choir hit some strange harmonies singing "Amazing Grace," the classic hymn to African American woes, written by a former slave trader. Perhaps the ubiquity of the song in black culture points to the ultimate reconciliation of the races.

Mark Wilson serves as the event's master of ceremonies and introduces Olivene Brown, who reads Maya Angelou's "Still I Rise." Mark then delivers Dr. King's "I Have a Dream" speech in his rich baritone. At the end, "Free at last! Free at last! Thank God Almighty, we are free at last!" resounds through the cafeteria and earns a standing ovation.

Orlando strides to the podium to end Heritage Day with his thoughts about the long struggle for equality, which he also delivered at the earlier performance. Seeing the juniors in the audience reminds him of the Diallo verdict, since he has had several discussions with them—or monologues, to be more precise—in English class. Swiftly overcome by righteous indignation, Orlando can't help but say, "Many of you think our quest for justice is ancient history; the Dream speech was over thirty-five years ago. But do not be mistaken, you still live in a racist society." His voice isn't loud but its intensity sharpens with each word. "The reason I speak against the

N-word and other negative language is because when you use it you internalize the disgusting macho of racists."

Orlando pauses a beat, then resumes with increasing volume: "THEY are very happy when you stand on street corners doing nothing. THEY like it when you yell, 'Yo, nigger,' because THEY don't have to put you down any longer—you're doing a better job of it yourselves. THEY'RE happy to see you degrading yourself." These words march out as if wearing black berets and as if the consonants were black-gloved fists thrust into the air.

Although students use the N-word often off campus, its usage has been eliminated inside the school building. Degrading language has become the spice Rice students throw into conversation to remind each other they're black—or perhaps more accurately, not white and so entitled to use the word that defines the entire history of slavery and oppression. Slowly they are seeing that the same word confines and defiles.

"We live in a society that we can overcome only if we smash the oppressor's stereotypes and educate ourselves," Orlando shifts into his preacher's cadence, "if we stand up and defend each other." He describes how truly empowered brothers, such as Martin Luther King, Jr., and Malcolm X, scared "them" to the point where "they had to put a bullet in his head." Orlando slides smoothly to the singular for "bullet in his head," since Malcolm wasn't assassinated by "them," but by black rivals. "Dr. King wasn't a punk; he wasn't soft," Orlando continues. "He pushed his people to great heights with marches, sit-ins, and boycotts. So we call upon you sleeping giants to awaken from the racism that victimizes you every single day of your lives."

Orlando pauses to examine his boys, who sit in complete silence with eyes riveted on what has become a rant. But Orlando is so passionate in his convictions and so electrifying in his delivery that he captivates their imaginations entirely.

"The question is, what are YOU going to do about it now?" Orlando asks with x-ray eyes. "What are you going to do? If nothing happens, then every young brother who looks like you might go for his wallet one day and be murdered. Some of you can express what you're feeling in art or writing, and others in public demonstrations. But there has to be a continual obsession with the fact that we do not have justice in this society."

Orlando's voice echoes off the cafeteria walls—and off the confusion the juniors feel about where Orlando's leading them. Yesterday in his English classes and privately in his office, he intimated strongly that Rice students should rise up en masse and march downtown in protest. By day's end, Onyxx Echeverria, the student council president, proposed doing just that, with the enthusiastic backing of fellow students. Orlando immediately crushed the idea without explanation. Today he's challenging the students again, but to do what?

"I want you to like yourselves and be proud," Orlando resumes gently before unleashing his fury, "so society won't think they have the right to take a plunger and violate a man the way they did in a police station—not in the 1950s or the 1960s, but two years ago. And this didn't happen in the Deep South, but in liberal New York." Orlando refers to the Louima incident. "I want you to believe in and defend yourselves, so society won't think they have the right to shoot you forty-one times and get away with it."

Orlando's emotional charge reverberates through the rows of students. Everyone seems to be holding the same breath that he just exhaled.

"People think I'm arrogant," Orlando almost whispers, "because they don't like to see an African American man stand up and be bold. I know the game. I hear it at principals' conferences in this great Catholic system we're part of." Orlando's indignation rings out, then he adds, "Don't be fooled; I'm not fooled," as if talking to himself. Although Orlando's ego has no difficulty inflating, his public stance—right or wrong—is usually closer to President Harry S. Truman's "I don't give them Hell. I just tell the truth about them and they think it's Hell."

"I remember a fifteen-year-old who was angry at the death of Dr. King and heard his mother weeping in her kitchen in St. Albans, Queens," Orlando recalls and the students visibly relax; they know he won't challenge them to march downtown now, since his autobiography is taking over. "That young man decided to pick up the cause—sometimes good, sometimes not good—of the Black Panther Party." As Orlando explained recently to the juniors in English class, the King assassination galvanized his radical propensities. Otherwise he would never have ventured far from the conservative bounds of his Lutheran upbringing and Mrs. DeVane's mentoring.

"I don't care what anyone says, the Black Panthers were rich with brilliant young brothers and sisters who this young man learned from and who established his racial pride," Orlando slips back in time with the transfixed look of a mystic beholding a divine apparition, albeit speaking in the royal third person. "They taught him about his responsibility to the race and inspired him to dedicate himself as a teacher to uplifting his people. Today he stands before you proud to be a Panther and proud to lead the best school in New York City."

The students break into thunderous applause, genuinely moved by their principal's zeal.

"As long as I stay in this wonderful profession, I will always fight for the survival of my people," Orlando announces the resolution to his thirty-year crisis, although none of the students other than Yusef were aware of it. "There is no other reason for me to live than to serve humankind."

The students file out of the cafeteria and back to their classrooms. They joke quietly and warmly with each other, evidently having absorbed the sense of personal and racial worth that Orlando's speech and the event were choreographed to transmit.

Back in his office, Orlando admits that he posed, "What are you going to do about it now?" as a call to action but then reconsidered. He is still furious with Dr. Hickey for what he perceives as the superintendent's refusal to take him seriously regarding Diallo. To defy her, he would love to head a protest march, but he knows it would probably cost him his job. Given the equivocal nature of the Christian Brothers' support, he doubts they would stand behind him if Dr. Hickey took offense. She hasn't indicated opposition to such a demonstration, and otherwise Orlando respects her leadership. So the call to action became rhetorical, and instead he segued to his favorite topic: his Black Panther past and how radicalism continues to inspire his role as principal.

Orlando justifies his penchant for hijacking school events and class time to further his political agenda by saying that education and politics are inseparable and therefore, it is his duty to proselytize. Teaching academics and preparing Rice Men for college is vitally important, but to what end, he asks, beyond socioeconomic progress for the relatively few young men he influences? The answer, Orlando says, is that he is preparing them for leadership positions in the black community in accordance with his ideals.

Given the Christian Brothers' history, Orlando says he has considerable latitude to include social and political dimensions of the African American experience. The Brothers are still proud of their participation in the fight against the British for Irish independence—including running guns for nationalist rebels, according to several brothers at Rice. It would not, however, help fund-raising efforts if Orlando advertised this involvement in retaliation for being told to limit his radical outpourings.

Orlando believes it is vital for him to model what it is to be an authentic— ergo, politicized—black male, which connects his students to the long tradition of African American civil rights heroes. This is especially important now that the media steeps youngsters in the macho narcissism and vapid emptiness of rappers and other celebrities, including many sports stars.

Orlando also considers his political rants as inoculations against the hostility and racism that he believes lurks just beneath the surface in the greater society, which his boys will start encountering at the college level. Consequently his "obsession" with racial injustice becomes a pedagogical imperative.

As usual, Orlando didn't prepare his remarks to the students beforehand. He felt moved by the Spirit as he stepped to the podium and opened his mouth, trusting that "God would speak through me."

I tease him about God's familiarity with Black Panther philosophy, and how he never contradicts Orlando's take on any issue. Orlando laughs as if I've caught him red-handed, and I hold my breath fearing I've crossed a line whites aren't supposed to traverse.

"I feel a presence inspiring my words," he replies with sincere humility.

I recall Al Widziewicz's concern after Orlando's speech that "religion isn't serving him well in that he presents himself as a Black Panther messiah." Widziewicz worries about his "megalomania tendencies."

But Orlando turns his ideological faucets on and off at will, and he is becoming better at doing so every year at Rice. If he loses control, it is usually momentary or if sustained, part of a plan, for example when he railed at the ninth graders after a pair of sneakers were stolen. Perhaps his excesses need to be seen relative to the dimensions of the task he attempts. Recently Orlando told two varsity basketball players who struggle with grades that "I never asked you guys whether or not you see Mr. Gober as a father, but I'm telling you I've claimed you as sons. Whether or not you claim me isn't the issue. I want to see you move from point A to point B academically and as young men, and I feel you can do it with my guidance."

In an op-ed piece yesterday about the Diallo verdict, Orlando Patterson, a Harvard sociology professor and 1991 recipient of the National Book Award for nonfiction, wrote that "Crime prevention measures that are proved to work well—from programs aimed at youths at risk to therapy and rehabilitation for offenders both in prison and after release—are all in some way paternalistic."[6] Certainly the most important crime prevention program—or the most deficient, if lacking in fatherly guidance—is schooling. In Patterson's analysis, the lack of paternalism in social institutions is the root cause of incidents such as the Diallo shooting, since the view that the state has no "right to tell a citizen what is in his or her best interest" leads to the surrender of "our liberty to the increasingly powerful police operations, like the street crimes unit in New York. . . ."

This paradox is the exact opposite of what antipaternalists envision, but boys do not become responsible men without father figures, both human and divine, modeling male identity. The lack of paternalism leads to high crime and recidivism rates, necessitating a police/prison state as the logical antidote.

The expansive father role that Orlando takes on has poignant relevance for the rest of society. "In my own judgment, the American Black community has been an early warning system," wrote Paul C. Vitz, a New York University psychology professor, articulating exactly what both Orlando and Geoffrey Canada pointed out at the November workshop. "African Americans were the first to feel the scourge of drugs, but a decade or so later whites caught up; the same is true with regard to family breakdown and illegitimacy. The African American illegitimacy rate is leveling off at a high level, and the white rate is just beginning to accelerate. Sociologists are predicting that the result will be the development of a white underclass in American society. This underclass will also be a 'fatherless society.' "[7]

Chapter Twenty-one

————

SINCE MID-FEBRUARY, ORLANDO'S MOST ACTIVE and interesting political forums have been held in his English classes. For Black History Month through March, Orlando is conducting seminars on the civil rights movement, instead of preparing his juniors for the English Regents exam. He considers the history of race in America to be far more important than graduation requirements or the SAT. As much as he desires the prestige that higher scores would bring him and the school, Orlando chooses to take considerable class time away from vocabulary building, reading comprehension, and so on.

Today is Wednesday, March 1, and Orlando has invited Father Sam Taylor and Ed Flood, a global studies teacher, to talk to the juniors about Rice High School during the civil rights movement. The fifth-period class begins with Orlando passing around the 1963 Rice yearbook with Father Taylor's graduation picture and a photo of Flood in his first year as a teacher.

"In our day, we couldn't walk down 124th Street because the neighborhood wasn't African American," Father Taylor recalls. He grew up on West 118th Street at 8th Avenue and attended St. Thomas elementary school, which has since closed. Although much of Harlem was African American, the ten-block radius around Rice remained predominately Irish until the mid-1960s.

"Were there any incidents? Did you feel intimidated?" Orlando asks.

"No one ever said anything, but they gave you a look like 'what are you doing in my neighborhood?'" Father Taylor answers in his Southern-inflected Harlem accent. "I remember the principal, Brother Synan, saying our problems around here had to stop. So he gathered all the white brothers and the whole school that was mostly white and we marched down the street to let people know we were together."

"Father was a minority in a school and neighborhood of majority whites within a larger community that was majority black," Orlando turns to his students. "Do you get that?"

"Did you experience any racial bias from your teachers?" J.V. Agay asks Father Taylor.

"Not at all," Father Taylor replies.

Orlando frowns, unable to hide his disbelief that at the same time as African Americans were refused service at lunch counters and stores right on 125th Street, this attitude wasn't shared by some faculty members and students. Longtime residents have told Orlando that "the Christian Brothers wouldn't let us colored kids from the neighborhood use the gym or the swimming pool in the summer."

"The first time I experienced racism was in college," Father Taylor continues. "A professor called Harlem a ghetto and I thought it had to do with Jewish people and Hitler."

"What about from white students?" Will Adams picks up on the principal's displeasure. For the last few months, Will has flirted with expulsion for too many detentions, mostly for disrespecting teachers other than Orlando. Will acts out for attention since he lives alone with his grandmother. He also emulates Chris Hernandez, one of the most popular juniors who unfortunately is also one of the worst behaved. Recently, through Orlando's presentations, Will has been discovering a new identity—that of the proud, racially conscious black male—and now he's trying to impress the principal with it.

"No," Father Taylor answers. "There were about 150 black students who hung out together, but we all got along with everybody and went to the Rice dances together."

"I want Mr. Flood to give us his experiences," Orlando shifts the focus away from Father Taylor's disappointing testimony.

"In my first year, this place was packed wall-to-wall with students, over forty-five to a class, and tuition was thirty dollars a month, which was a high percentage of family income," Flood begins. "The push on academics was extreme. I had all freshman classes, and by the beginning of the second semester, I knew I had a lot of failures. I spoke to the principal, who said that was expected."

Academic standards were far more rigorous then, partly because educators were not yet inclined to lower standards to increase graduation rates and partly because it was much more difficult to get into college. Many didn't make it to senior year, and only half the graduates proceeded to post-secondary schooling. The rest went directly into the workforce.

"What about the changing face of the school?" Orlando asks. "What year did it swing to a majority African American?"

"By '73, the school had a third of each—black, white and Hispanic—and that lasted a decade," Flood recalls. "There was also a big drop in students as new Catholic high schools opened in Brooklyn and Queens and the population of Harlem declined." Black and white flight, looted and burned-out businesses, then drugs and crime put the area on the typical downward urban spiral. "Around 1980, most students were black."

"How was the increase in minorities looked upon by the administration?" Orlando presses.

"It wasn't about race, but religion," Flood replies firmly, knowing exactly what Orlando's probing for. "The culture was still very Catholic with confirmation classes for converts and the rosary. But they were losing brothers and took us lay teachers into lengthy discussions about admitting non-Catholics."

In Orlando's view, this was code for race. The Christian Brothers were really deciding whether to let the school go black, he believes. With the neighborhood changing, Rice had no choice but to shut down or become African American, which would have displeased those who believed the sole mission of Catholic schools is to teach Catholic—and mostly white—children. However accurate Orlando's assessment, the original mission of the Christian Brothers to teach the children of the poor prevailed, and the school remained open.

"What was the situation in Harlem in 1968 after King's assassination?" Orlando directs the discussion toward the watershed event he covered last week in class.

"I was in a restaurant nearby with a biology teacher who was African American when it came on the news," Flood recalls. "Everything stopped. I was driving him home when the riots and fires began. We just kept going because he was concerned about me, and we ended up in Westchester where we waited until things quieted down. Some parents had put their life savings into a business here that was destroyed. Afterwards it was like a roller coaster. You could go to a restaurant and be welcomed one year, but the next time encounter hostility, depending on what was going on."

"Over the years, have you ever aspired to work anywhere else and make more money?" Seve Sprouil asks, curious about this white-haired teacher with piercing blue eyes he's seen every day for the last three years at Rice. Those eyes, basketball coach Mo Hicks remembers as a student, "could stop you with one look." Flood was the dean of students then and kept order without ever raising his voice. He is still soft spoken, but his attitude has mellowed, although he still has the ability to walk into a classroom and take command with the power of his presence.

"The brothers take vows of poverty, chastity, and obedience," Flood replies, then pauses to grin slightly. "I'm married with seven children."

The juniors laugh as they give up a round of applause.

"Once I wanted to move sixty miles away and buy a house, but every time I was ready to leave I'd get another job I wanted here," Flood explains. "Fortunately my wife is a great financial manager." In order to make ends meet, Flood worked several nights a week and summers teaching at various public schools where he could have taken a full-time position. Flood admits that he stayed at Rice because he loved the students and the school. As a result, Flood's wife forbade any of their children from teaching in a Catholic school "because you won't make any money like your father," even though he was the assistant principal for nineteen years until 1996. Flood then took over the business office and hoped to become the principal. But Orlando was chosen instead, and Flood went back into the classroom. He holds no grudge against Orlando for winning the position and recognizes that on balance, Orlando is good for the school.

"So you weren't conscious of race here during the civil rights years?" Orlando refocuses the conversation.

"My parents trained us to see people as they are, not as they appeared," Flood replies.

This simple statement earns a respectful silence around the room. After learning about slavery and racial abuse in this and other classes, hearing about the tradition of decency among whites is as reassuring as they believe it is rare. Last week, one classmate blurted in a painful voice: "Why do white people hate us?" Another was genuinely surprised to hear that people other than blacks were ever enslaved. Still another student expressed indignation over the adjective in "Black Plague," saying that this is an example of whites giving the word *black* a negative connotation.

Orlando has too much respect for Flood to suspect any prejudice. As he says also about Abbasse, whatever biases he came with were shed long ago.

"Father Taylor," Orlando brings him back into the discussion, "would you say black students were conscious of race and that's why you were very close?"

"Yeah, we were conscious of race. Once I heard a white guy use the N-word on the street and we jumped on him," the priest nods. "But we didn't read the papers much, so we really didn't know what was going on in the movement."

Orlando's jaw drops slightly and his lips move without forming words. For the last three weeks, he has been screening the video of *Eyes on the Prize,* a PBS series chronicling the civil rights struggle, in both his English classes. One of Orlando's most consistent points is how much the entire movement depended on the involvement of high school and college students. His objective is to awaken his boys from their political lethargy. To hear that apathy was commonplace at Rice then, especially from a black male and priest who's very close with the students, undermines Orlando's fervor.

"Over the years," Flood picks up on Orlando's dismay and offers a change of subject, "I've asked parents who work in public schools and send their sons here, especially if they're not doing well, why? 'He could fail for free in public school,' I'd say. But often academics and safety weren't the main reasons. One father told me, 'I'm not sending him to get away from something, but to go for something.' And that something was the values he honored at church."

Orlando thanks the guests as class ends. As much as he likes and respects Father Taylor, he's annoyed at what he considers the priest's Uncle Tom side. During the forum, Flood described seeing Malcolm X giving speeches near the corner of 125th and Lenox Avenue beside Sterling Optical, perhaps a hundred yards from Rice. Orlando finds it incomprehensible to think Father Taylor and his friends paid little attention. To Orlando's chagrin, Father Taylor also serves in the National Guard as a chaplain and talks to students about joining the military.

Later, Father Taylor recalls what Rice was like when most of the teachers were Christian Brothers. "They were strict but fair," he recounts. "They taught us to be more disciplined, straightlaced, and responsible. They were also very personal and would stay after school to work with students or counsel them on personal problems. The brothers were very good teachers— much better than most now—who always reached out to students. It was very rare for anyone to talk back; the brothers put the fear of God in the young men. If they were still here, Rice would be much more disciplined and achieve more."

Father Taylor mentions several teachers on par with the brothers, but educators everywhere pale in comparison for the most part. He considers the loss of the religious teaching orders a national tragedy.

———

At four o'clock the next afternoon, Yusef appears at Orlando's office door wearing gray slacks and a red blazer bearing the crest of Our Saviour Lutheran High School.

"I had a strong feeling I'd see you today," Orlando declares.

Yusef mumbles something about missing Orlando since the weekend as he installs himself on the couch. Everett Wynn, a freshman who has improved his academic standing from five to only two failures in the last marking period and might pass the year, knocks on the open door. He asks about Mass on Sunday, and Orlando reassures him they can go together. Everett's family belongs to St. Charles, and he's been hinting for several weeks that he'd like to attend with the principal. Once Orlando heard that Everett's brother was back in jail, he made a point of inviting the freshman.

Everett stands awkwardly in the doorway for a few moments before leaving. Certainly the darts flying from Yusef's eyes are making him uncomfortable.

"Aren't you supposed to be going out on Sunday?" Yusef feigns concern for the principal.

"That's in the afternoon."

"I'd like to go to church with you sometime," Yusef muses.

"Really?" Orlando eyes roll slightly.

"Oh yes, but you've never asked."

"Because you never would have thought about going if you didn't hear Everett ask," Orlando shoots back. "You shouldn't go to church because you think I'm doing something with someone else."

"I really want to go," Yusef heaves almost inaudibly. It's still difficult for him to admit what he wants, although it's not religion.

Orlando remarks about how "territorial" he's becoming, which isn't unusual for those who get close to Orlando, then fear losing him.

Yusef heads upstairs to the gym to visit some of his former teammates. He returns a half hour later to his place on the couch and waits for Orlando to finish his work. At 6:00 P.M., without speaking about evening plans, Yusef accompanies Orlando up Lenox Avenue to the new Bayou Creole Restaurant just north of 125th Street.

After ordering dinner, Yusef catches Orlando up on how well he's doing academically at Our Saviour. Suddenly he announces that he's getting a tattoo on his shoulder "to cover the burns I got when I joined the gang."

"Why would you do that?"

"A couple of months ago, you gave me an ultimatum," Yusef looks away and speaks hesitantly. "You said either I get out of the gang, or I can't hang with you."

"I've been wondering," Orlando smiles broadly, giving Yusef the encouragement he needs to extract the words that express his vulnerability.

"I want to hang with you," Yusef labors to vocalize each syllable, "so I'm getting the burns covered."

As Yusef collapses back into his seat, a wave of relief washes through Orlando. Recently he heard from several students that they'd seen Yusef back on his corner in the neighborhood, which roused Orlando's fears that he'll read about Yusef being shot by rivals or the cops. Orlando knows that getting rid of the tattoo is mostly Yusef's way of shoring up his position. Not being at Rice every day has made him anxious that another student might become the chosen son. But Orlando eagerly accepts the transparency of Yusef's motives if it keeps him safe and in contact.

Orlando's smile withers as he addresses what's been distressing him. "I can't allow you back into Rice next year," he sighs, "because we have such a strong relationship and everyone knows it."

"That's cool," Yusef nods as nonchalantly as possible.

They have talked about the possibility of Yusef's return to Rice several times, but "perhaps it's best he stays at Our Saviour," Orlando reflects later, "since he's making more of an effort to pass his classes and go straight."

By the next day, Orlando confesses he will try to bring Yusef back next year because he misses Yusef like a parent who wants his son back. But first he will have to prepare his teachers to support the move and hope that none object. His mood brightens when he considers that Tim Hearn, the teacher most likely to take issue, might not be returning in the fall—if he can help orchestrate his departure.

Chapter Twenty-two

ORLANDO WALKS INTO HIS E-PERIOD English class seven minutes late on Friday, March 10. He spots Gregory Vazquez, a white Hispanic, at his desk in the aisle beside the window retrieving a clipboard from a neighbor. Orlando's eyes flash a question mark.

"Before you came in, I was passing around a petition trying to get an abandoned building turned into a youth center in my neighborhood," Greg explains, grateful to have a neighborhood. He was born in Puerto Rico, where he was not only beaten by his father but had to witness the man abusing his mother. Finally when Greg was eight years old, his mother took him and his sister to New York where the family lived in a cramped apartment with a relative for a year, but then survived for three months in homeless shelters.

Greg felt deeply frustrated that he couldn't protect his mother from violence or the family from destitution. As the boy became a man, his determination to succeed and his hunger for affirmation and social roots grew voraciously. Greg maintains an A average and plays on Rice's baseball, junior varsity basketball, forensics, chess, and bowling teams. He also sings in the Men of Rice Choir and is an active member of the National Honor Society. He's even preparing to run for next year's student council.

In recent years, Greg has enjoyed a stable household in a two-bedroom Bronx apartment that he shares with his sister, a cousin, his mother, and her partner—another woman. Greg struggled with feelings of shame and guilt for the first two years. "A lesbian relationship went against everything I'd been taught by the Church, my Latino culture, my schools, and friends. But slowly I realized my mother was happy, and my sister and I were being cared for by two loving people." Still, the family situation remains a secret at Rice, and Greg hasn't told anyone, including Orlando.

"Civic responsibility in action; I bless everyone who does that," Orlando replies as if he were making an announcement.

For Greg, this is just the beginning. He intends to go to Harvard to major in biology and become a doctor, and of course help to save the world. "Witnessing my mother's suffering has made me more compassionate," Greg reflects. "I empathize easily with other people's burdens and try to help people." Not surprisingly, Greg hopes to win the National Catholic Education Association's Elizabeth Ann Seton Award, given to four high school students nationwide for academic achievement and community service.

Greg takes Orlando's rare compliment with a bashful smile, but focuses more on the papers in the principal's hand. Orlando walks around the room handing back the corrected projects that students have been working on for the last month, and which constitute the year's major assignment. As Orlando screened *Eyes on the Prize,* he coached the juniors on composing an essay where they chose a person or organization involved in the civil rights movement and wrote about the struggle from that person's or group's point of view.

Greg can't wait to see whether he got the highest grade in the class. He believes he outdid Mark Wilson, his close friend and forensics partner. In truth, Mark has more literary and certainly more performing talent. In Brother Sherlog's humanities class last week, students were instructed to look out the window at Lenox Avenue, then describe what they observed. Several minutes later, students responded predictably with "People working on a construction project making Harlem better," "a pretty woman crossing the street," and "Crips comin' by."

"What's the worst thing you saw?" asked Brother Sherlog.

"The vulgar hieroglyphics of destitution on the tenement walls," responded Mark Wilson, paraphrasing a line from Jesse Jackson's 1984 speech to the Democratic National Convention, then stared straight ahead at the blackboard. His classmates roared, and Brother Sherlog couldn't help but smile in admiration at Mark's deadpan delivery.

Greg enjoys his friend's wit, but tries to work harder and outdo him. J.V. Agay, however, seems to be an invincible rival for both Greg and Mark. In class last December, Greg corrected the essay J.V. wrote about Frederick Douglass's *My Bondage, My Freedom* according to the school's writing rubric. Orlando was delighted by Greg's enthusiasm as he applied the rubric's five-part format both fairly and meticulously to his classmate's paper, finding only two minor errors and giving J.V. a 96.

Recognizing how far most Rice students need to progress to do well on the English Regents, SAT, and AP English and history exams, Kate Hebinck and Steve DiMattia formulated a schematic approach to composition by late September, based on the state standards for grading the English Regents exam, which these two teachers correct at Rice. When they talked to Orlando about the resulting rubric, he was so excited that he asked them to teach it not only to him and Mark Blanchard, the sophomores' English teacher, but to the global studies, religion, and history teachers. Orlando saw immediately that teaching students to compose every written assignment the same way would sharpen their skills. Further, as Ed Flood remarked during the faculty meeting when DiMattia introduced the writing rubric, students often don't transfer what they learn in English to other classes.

After establishing routines and procedures in September, teachers explained how assignments will be graded according to the rubric's five categories: meaning, development, organization, language use, and convention (grammar, spelling, and punctuation). The rubric was also applied to example paragraphs in class to teach students how to write accordingly. Composition skills didn't improve dramatically, but most teachers have seen progress.

Still, DiMattia continues to worry about the juniors who will be taking the Regents after the year with Orlando. Although the principal has relied heavily on the rubric, he's also spent considerable time screening and analyzing movies like *Soul Food*. Students won't be able to reference these in their Regents essays as literary works nor does watching them improve writing skills. As well, Orlando allowed his students to perform skits, create videos, or make oral presentations in lieu of some written assignments. While these projects displayed remarkable creativity—for example, three juniors shot a video entitled *Toys in the 'Hood,* in which they articulated inner-city problems using toys for the characters and setting—the exercise did nothing to advance their literary skills or broaden their knowledge of literature.

However, J.V.'s work bodes well, as does that of Greg, Mark, and several other students. J.V. wrote the assignment in the first person, as a fictional black teenager in contemporary Harlem who happened to be given a worn diary by a vagrant just before the man collapsed and died. The diary begins with the vagrant as a young man reflecting on Rosa Park's defiant refusal to give up her seat on a bus in 1955. Then each major event in the civil rights movement is chronicled from this point of view. For example:

May 2, 1963

I arrived here in Birmingham, Alabama yesterday to visit some relatives, when I found myself mixed up in a protest march to integrate public facilities. At the time, I really wish I wasn't there because the racist governor George Wallace and his henchmen including that bastard Bull Connor unleashed a busload of hurt on us. They stopped at nothing to have our peaceful marches come to an end. I still have the scars on my leg where the police dogs bit me, and I'll never forget the paralyzing pain of the fire hose. Part of me is glad that I had the opportunity to make a difference, that and the fact that I had the chance to join the Southern Christian Leadership Conference. . . .

If there's one thing I'll always remember, it's when some of the people who marched were attacked in their hotel rooms, even after the whole event was over. Once again, the scoundrel Wallace ordered the National Guard to converge on the Gaston Motel. Before the Guard's arrival, I made my first encounter with the Ku Klux Klan. I can't believe how crazy these people were, I mean they firebombed the hotel, and when people were scattering for shelter, the National Guard attacked them under orders of Colonel Widziewicz Lingo. . . .

"A creative and outstanding paper!" Orlando wrote on the last page of J.V.'s essay and gave him a perfect score in all the rubric's categories: "I am honored to be your teacher and principal." Orlando was also honored by the essay. In the diary's last entry, the narrator relates as his own experience what Orlando had told the class about himself in the wake of Dr. King's assassination:

April 4, 1968

I've been presented with many opportunities to express my anger and promote black pride like my fellow Panthers do, but part of me knows that hurting a white man like he has hurt my people will only turn me into a monster. I must say the monster in me almost came out when word of the beloved Dr. King's death sounded through the streets. . . . I could feel the blood rushing through my veins and all I could think of was hurting someone. Some Panthers came to my house to convince me to join them in some riots, but I was so numb I couldn't think straight. Thank God I collapsed . . . for who knows what I would have done had I not fainted.

Dr. King's murder galvanized Orlando's sense of outrage and pushed him toward militant politics. Black Panthers often stood outside Andrew Jackson High School passing out flyers, since the principal considered them too radical to hold student meetings inside. Orlando joined the Panthers as a tenth grader, just after the assassination, then circumvented the school's administration by founding the Third World Peoples' Club, which under Orlando's direction espoused an ideology almost identical to that of the Panthers. He recruited two hundred members, including students who belonged to the Black Panthers, the Young Lords—the Latino version of the Panthers—and some leftist whites. With fellow student Panthers, Orlando organized discussion groups, teach-ins, and rallies about European colonialism, the slave trade, and the emerging revolutionary focus of the civil rights movement. In addition, Orlando attended official Black Panther meetings in members' living rooms or at local churches with liberal pastors.

Although Orlando's politics were becoming increasingly radical, he remained the president of the very respectable and conservative Future Teachers Club. Orlando never lost faith in nonviolence as a means to attaining equality, as Dr. King espoused, but he also preached the Black Panthers' version of revolutionary socialism (an intellectual potpourri of Marxism, Maoism, and race-based social entitlements).

Orlando sought to resolve the inconsistencies between King's and the Panthers' approaches by believing that education and community activism are the keys to social advancement, thereby obviating the need for violence. After *Eyes on the Prize* showed Black Panthers marching with ferocious determination and armed with automatic weapons, Orlando offered counterbalancing accounts of the volunteer work he did in health care clinics and soup kitchens sponsored by the Panthers.

"Did the Black Panthers hate on people?" Da'mar McBean asks after looking over Orlando's remarks on his project. The principal gave him an 80, which Da'mar considers high enough, and urged the junior to add his own opinion to short accounts of the contributions that Rosa Parks, Ella Baker, Emmett Till, and Medgar Evers made to the struggle. Clearly Da'mar paraphrased, if not directly plagiarized, published material or Internet sources without adding any perspective. Curiously, Da'mar ended his project with the comment, *I did the report like this because I wanted you to see other people that really didn't stand out in the Civil Rights Movement.* Given the emphasis Orlando has been placing on Dr. King, the Panthers, and Malcolm X, Da'mar's explanation was understandable.

As in religion class, the students retain little knowledge from one year to the next about the civil rights movement. Since kindergarten, they've heard about Rosa Parks and others during Black History Month. But since they are not required to commit anything to memory, the facts wash over their minds leaving scant traces. The progressive pedagogical approach to progressive politics, as to everything else, leads to progressive amnesia. In contrast, Orlando hopes his rhetoric and passion will brand the juniors' consciousness. Just as does Brother Walderman, Orlando takes solace in Edmund Rice's saying about "the good seed" eventually flourishing in "the child's heart," but Orlando hopes to fertilize that seed with his own radical DNA.

For the students, today's discussion is driven by their fascination with armed Black Power rebels, which has the added benefit of getting Orlando talking about something other than the short story they were assigned to read and the literary themes they are supposed to be reviewing. Trying to return to Regents prep, Orlando quizzed them yesterday on vocabulary and lectured on the notion that every work of literature revolves around the concept of struggle, which gives them a thematic key for every Regents essay. Characters find themselves in conflict with nature, each other, and themselves, he reiterated. The point seems obvious, but it takes repetition to get students to see commonalities. That every story involves relationships and the dynamics of opposition came as a revelation to many juniors, who struggle to comprehend paragraphs.

"The original Panther Party never preached hatred," Orlando booms as he takes Da'mar's bait. "The white media portrayed us that way, but it wasn't true."

"Was there some kind of initiation, Mr. Gober?" Da'mar asks.

"Like going out and shooting people?" Orlando parries, and then responds, "No, nothing like that."

"Then how did you join?" Jermaine Anderson asks, incredulous. Neither he nor his classmates can conceive that the Black Panthers had assault rifles but didn't use them, and didn't have initiation rites like the gangs in their neighborhoods.

"You'd attend a meeting and hear what the brother Panther had to say," Orlando explains. "Then they'd ask if you were down with the fact that African Americans must do for themselves."

"It was all about words?" Da'mar asks in shock, recalling the Panthers in full battle fatigues in *Eyes on the Prize*.

"No. The Panthers armed themselves, but only for protection," Orlando sits down on the edge of his desk as his eyes begin to glow. "The cops were trying to murder them and destroy our entire nation."

"So the Panthers weren't thugs?" Sheldon Slade-Jones asks with surprise and hope.

"No, they were black nationalists, and that's what I am first," Orlando intones, thrilled to have drawn Sheldon into the discussion. The junior's home life hasn't improved, and he still hangs out late now on cold nights to avoid his mother and stepfather. But he's passing his classes and will soon have only one year left before he can go away to college. "Blacks have an absolute right to control their own destiny, choose their political, social, financial, and educational future. It's the Kwanzaa principle of self . . ."

". . . determination," the juniors chime in chorus. Orlando makes sure they know these principles by heart—perhaps the only required memorization in their K–12 experience—but this is the first time they've heard him relate his political philosophy to Kwanzaa tenets so directly. Of course no group in a democratic society can have absolute control over its future without impinging upon the rights of others, but Orlando states his case in extreme terms because he believes blacks have become far too timid.

"I read about some Panthers surrendering to the cops naked," Aston Lindhart wakes up to offer a rare comment.

Orlando explains that disrobing before surrendering was a survival technique because "the cops always believe you're carrying, which gives them the right, they think, to shoot you." Orlando adds solemnly that "many Black Panthers were murdered by the police."

In April 1968, Bobby Hutton, one of the original six Panthers, was shot to death by the Oakland police probably in retaliation for the wounding of several cops. As other Panthers met violent ends, the mainstream media uncritically accepted the view that they were brave revolutionaries who had become victims of a government conspiracy. Certainly there were racist elements in law enforcement across the country with its history of brutality against African Americans, but later analyses showed that far fewer Panthers were killed by the police than claimed, and only two of these could make any claim to police culpability.[1]

If the police were under instruction to eliminate Black Panthers, there was no need, since prominent Panthers were adept at self-destruction. They were killed by family members, fellow Panthers, a rival black power group, or unwittingly by police in the commission of a crime. Since the 1970s, many Black

Panther leaders have been thoroughly discredited for becoming murderous thugs operating under the guise of social reform. When, for example, a bookkeeper spoke out about Panthers embezzling funds, she was tortured and killed without mercy.

Still, a romantic view persists of the Panthers as heroic black patriots, which in Orlando's case constitutes a cherished article of faith that is fundamental to his self-image and self-understanding.[2] No doubt the Black Panthers began with promise. Despite embracing a worldview based on forms of Marxism that murdered more people in the twentieth century than all the religious wars in recorded history—after all, the Panthers were caught up in the radicalism du jour—they instituted laudable initiatives, such as the Free Breakfast for Children Program and antidrug campaigns.[3] Their outrage at racial injustice and desire for profound social change were understandable, but like many crusaders throughout history, they granted themselves a plenary indulgence for all crimes committed in the name of their revolutionary god.

What was lost in the Panthers' moral disintegration, and in the wider failure of the ideology of riot—the view that black rioting is a justified response to white racism—which allied white liberals with thugs parading as activists and community leaders, was the legitimate case for blacks defending themselves.[4] Over a century and a half ago, Archbishop John J. Hughes took just such a stand in a most convincing manner. Riotous clashes were common between nativists and Irish Catholics in New York beginning in the 1830s and 1840s, and Catholic institutions were sometimes targeted. For example, arsonists destroyed St. Mary's church and school near the West Side docks in New York, and a mob set fire to a convent near Boston in 1834.

Similar to African Americans nationwide today, the Irish were outnumbered ten to one and perplexed by what to do about the attacks. Consider the following account of how this dilemma was resolved, from a book with an enthusiastic foreword by Terence Cardinal Cooke:

> Understandably, the Catholics were divided about the best way to meet the problem. Some, like Bishop Francis P. Kendrick of Philadelphia, thought the best way was to endure it patiently, make no response, and offer no defense or resistance. Others, like Bishop Hughes, urged militant vigilance. The Catholics should demand protection from the public authorities and be prepared to meet force with force if the authorities failed to protect them or sided with their enemies. Experience showed the latter course to be correct. In April and May 1844, Philadelphia was swept by riots in which two Catholic churches were burned and looted, several people were killed, and many Catholic homes were destroyed. . . .

Things were different in New York, thanks mainly to Bishop Hughes, who blamed the Catholics of Philadelphia for not defending their churches, and warned Mayor James Harper bluntly that if a single Catholic church were burned in New York the city would become a second Moscow. When urged by some worried public officials to "restrain the Irish," he said, "I have not the power, you must take care that they are not provoked." He exhorted the Catholics to stand up for their rights calmly, and to be sure not to strike the first blow.[5]

Archbishop Hughes could have expressed his position succinctly as "Extremism in the defense of liberty is no vice. Moderation in the pursuit of justice is no virtue." This well-known quote was delivered by Malcolm X during a debate at Oxford University's student union in December 1964, footage of which the Rice students saw in *Eyes on the Prize*.[6] Of course, Malcolm X was quoting from Barry Goldwater's acceptance speech for the Republican presidential nomination earlier that year. Goldwater was as deeply disappointed with moderates in the midst of the Cold War as Malcolm X was with meek black leaders—and neither were advocating terrorist or criminal extremes.

Through the 1950s and 1960s, Malcolm X had opposed nonviolence and quoted the infamous battle cry from the Chinese Boxer Rebellion: "Kill the foreign white devils!" Then in the spring of 1964, he visited Mecca and witnessed people of diverse backgrounds mixing freely and interacting in harmony. At Oxford, he demonstrated this shift in perspective, saying: "I don't care what color you are as long as you want to change the miserable conditions that exist on this earth." He advocated the use of force in self-defense, emphatically rejecting "cold-blooded murder"—no differently than Archbishop Hughes. In fact, Martin Luther King, Jr., expressed the same point of view: "There comes a time when the cup of endurance runs over, and men are no longer willing to be plunged into an abyss of injustice when they experience the blackness of corroding despair."

What if the Black Panthers had tempered their extremism by maintaining a calm defensive posture, careful not to strike the first blow? The Panthers were never nearly as important as their fame suggests, but they could have protected the lives and property of people in their community, as did the Irish, and earned respect by combining strength with restraint. Like Hughes, Panther and other leaders could have promoted the same highly successful form of ethnic separatism that ultimately facilitated incorporation into the mainstream without the loss of identity, religion, or culture.

Despite the Panthers' failings, Orlando always paints them in celestial colors—especially the two most prominent founders, Huey Newton and Bobby Seale—as "the best and brightest of our generation." When a junior asked if Orlando had ever met them, he replied that he saw Newton and Seale speak at a Panther gathering in New York. Orlando was enthralled with their charisma and described Newton as "the smartest person I ever met, next to Dr. King." Orlando views any suggestion that Panther leaders were less than martyrs as utter blasphemy, and part of the vast white—both left- and right-wing—conspiracy that the media promulgates.

Widziewicz says Orlando is "stuck in adolescence, constantly reliving the radical 1960s." But this is exactly what Orlando intends as a source of constant rejuvenation for himself and his mission, to pass on the same role models that inspired the direction of his life. Orlando can't help but polish their tarnished images.

"This is heavy stuff," junior Allan Sanders said just after the last episode of *Eyes on the Prize,* echoing his classmates' feeling throughout the series, not merely about their principal's depth of conviction, but about watching their forebears stand up to police dogs and police batons, and ultimately win the battle for freedom.

Radical views, however, don't seem to be taking root. Rice students look at American capitalism as less an exploitive system than a cornucopia of opportunities—if they stay in school. There are injustices, and no doubt racism still exists, but such obstacles are not limiting—as Orlando repeats convincingly. Like the Irish underclass at the beginning of the Catholic education system, Rice students aren't looking to change the world, but to find their place in it.

Orlando ends the period with a kicker designed to bring his lessons home. He laments Bobby Hutton's death again to emphasize that Hutton was only fifteen years old when he co-founded the Black Panthers—"even younger than all of you."

After a ponderous pause, Orlando launches into an angry tirade connecting Hutton's shooting to the killings of Emmett Till and other well-known heroes of the civil rights movement.

"Do you see how history repeats itself today?" Orlando asks. "The blatant racism that murdered these brothers did the same thing last year to Amadou Diallo." Orlando leverages his weight from the edge of the desk where he was sitting, then walks purposefully across the front of the room to the blackboard. "Things are the same now as they were back then," he booms.

"No, they're not," Aston protests. His father, an African immigrant, is a doctor who ran a medical clinic downtown and provided the family with an affluent lifestyle, including frequent dinner parties with the city's social elite, until an inappropriate love affair lost him his job and broke up his marriage. As a result, Aston and his mother, a Jamaican with a Portuguese father, were forced to move into a small uptown apartment in Harlem where she struggles to pay the bills.

The young man's almost catatonic personality is his way of numbing himself, partly from the lack of academic challenge, but mostly from the anger and bitterness roiling beneath the surface. Aston scoffs at the suggestion that his troubles can be reduced to race. His fall from grace has given him an unblinking view of life at the bottom. He agrees with Orlando's prescription for transcending his current limitations, as he expressed recently in an essay for his humanities class:

> In the neighborhood in which I live, there are people who spend their time on the streets playing music, drinking alcohol and doing drugs. Meanwhile . . . their children are right by their sides. I refuse to become part of this stereotype, and instead use my time productively and educate myself, because education is the key to change and success.

Orlando ignores Aston's comment, perhaps because he doesn't want to deal with him, or maybe because the chatter around the room has grown too loud. Orlando is tolerant of students talking and joking around when class discussions involve his favorite topics.

"Black nationalists be against white people?" Da'mar yells from his desk in the middle of the room.

"No," Orlando answers. "We believe in our own nation, our own people. We are pro-black but not anti-white, and that's what the original Panthers stood for. I very rarely eat at a restaurant that isn't black-owned. But if I were against whites, I wouldn't be friends with half the staff at Rice."

After a reflective pause, Orlando adds, "Look, it's not up to whites to solve our problems. I don't care if they help or not, as long as they don't get in the way. That's why I don't believe in reparations; it won't solve anything. We already have enough resources to transform our communities."

"But we have so much against us," Shayne Howze protests. He's been quiet in English class since Orlando publicly humiliated him for daring to chew gum at the African American Heritage Day celebration.

"True, but God calls us to faithfulness, not fairness," Orlando counters. "As a community, we tend to focus too much on the issue of justice, while the essence of Christianity is faith in the overcoming, not in the obstacles. The real point of a Christian school is to teach you the power of faith."

Orlando continues emphatically that until "we form our own institutions and our own schools, we'll never be equal."

Essentially Archbishop Hughes and the Catholic hierarchy had the same insights. Despite poverty and prejudice, they became agents of their destiny and built a vast nexus of institutions and organizations from virtually nothing—but faith.

Orlando believes that it's time for the Christian Brothers to give Rice over to African American ownership. As do many black educators, he believes that integrating schools in the wake of *Brown v. Board of Education,* the 1954 Supreme Court decision that struck down the doctrine of "separate but equal," was a mistake. There's nothing about sitting next to a white student, Orlando often says, that makes black students learn better. In fact, integration has had the opposite effect; now African American youngsters often do even worse than classmates who are recent immigrants with first languages other than English.

Orlando is looking for ways to purchase the school via investors in the black community. He wants to turn Rice into a high-powered, Afrocentric academy, hopefully within the Catholic system. But Orlando's sense of race and radicalism would trump most restrictions that the archdiocese might lay down. So he would make Rice independent if necessary.

After the period ends, Orlando follows his students into the hallway. He stops behind Will Adams and Davon Elmore, who are joking with each other and using the N-word.

"You think that's funny?" Orlando thunders. "We have no racial pride . . ." he chokes with anger. "We have nothing."

Orlando storms off to his office discouraged that after putting so much time and energy into raising his students' consciousness, they slip back so easily into using the worst of racial stereotypes on themselves. To succeed, Orlando's consistent message is that they have to educate and comport themselves as gentlemen.

In the 1960s, during the sit-ins aimed at desegregating lunch counters and stores, students were often dispatched with instructions to wear their best clothes and act politely. This created a telling contrast to those who harassed them, as described by James J. Kilpatrick, a segregationist and the editor of the *Richmond News Leader*:

> Here were the colored students, in coats, white shirts, ties, and one of them was reading Goethe and one was taking notes from a biology text. [The students often brought schoolbooks with them to sit-ins so they could study.] And here, on the sidewalk outside was a gang of white boys come to heckle, a ragtail rabble, slack-jawed, black-jacketed, grinning fit to kill, and some of them, God save the mark, were waving the proud and honored flag of the Southern States in the last war fought by gentlemen. Eheu! It gives one pause.[7]

Ultimately the rednecks lost the battle to keep the South segregated and poise won. In the 1967 classic, *Guess Who's Coming to Dinner,* Sidney Poitier plays Dr. John Prentice, who simply cannot be denied what racists for centuries considered the ultimate concession: marrying a white woman who is from an affluent, influential family to boot.

Reflecting later, Orlando says, "I try not to be angry at students like Will and Davon, but I want them to be clear about the fact that the movement isn't just something in the history books, but continues to be relevant to what's happening in their lives right now."

Orlando's politics, despite sounding extreme, lead neither to the ideology of victimization nor riot. Instead, Orlando's underlying conservative religious and educational values keep him focused on quintessentially middle- to upper middle-class American ideals. "We are owed the right to sit at the lunch counter," Orlando repeats the early civil rights era proverb, "but not for someone else to pay for the meal."

Gregory Vazquez's mother teaches him the same lesson. She says we aren't owed anything because of our hardship; we have to work for what we want. Otherwise, as Archbishop Hughes told Irish congregants, we become our own worst enemies, regardless of the barriers we face.

As Spencer Longmore, one of Orlando's favorite juniors, puts it: "There's a lot of laziness in my neighborhood and people wanting to get money without working." Spencer belongs to a fractured family; he and a younger brother live with their grandmother in the South Bronx near Yankee Stadium, while another brother stays with the father, and the youngest boy lives with the mother.

"Without Mr. Gober and Abbasse yelling at me to work hard, I'd probably take the easy way out and get distracted by girls, cars, and the drug game," Spencer confesses. "My older brother went to Taft High School and never graduated. Lots of minority kids don't get to meet successful black men like the principal or the black engineer who runs the 59th Street Con Edison station, so they emulate hip-hop artists and celebrities instead and think, 'Why bother going to school?'"

Still, as much as Orlando is a positive role model for his students, his lack of social poise and of financial acumen make it unlikely that he'll ever raise the funds to own and operate a school or to take over Rice. Brother Walderman keeps him away from fundraising efforts, fearing that his personality, usually engaging and charming, will turn abrasive if he feels slighted. Convincing donors to make large contributions requires a protracted courtship in which diplomacy, tact, and public relations efforts are essential; there's no room for error. Grasping organizational finances, which Orlando steadfastly refuses to do, is also vital to running an educational institution. Although he was able to increase parents' contributions and their role in development at his former school, Orlando's single-minded pursuit of his dreams ran St. Mark's into considerable debt, which, Brother eventually discovered, was partly the reason he left the school for Rice.

Chapter Twenty-three

AS WELL AS SITTING REGULARLY in the ninth- and eleventh-graders' English classes—and visiting every course taught at Rice at least once and most several times—I frequently attend Steve DiMattia's Advanced Placement (AP) English class and Tim Hearn's AP chemistry class. I want to get a sense of the academic progress of Rice students over four years and see how prepared they are for postsecondary courses.

The class discussions that transpired in DiMattia's class as he covered Ralph Ellison's *Invisible Man* in the fall resonated with Orlando's screening of *Eyes on the Prize* in the winter, for the juniors. To a remarkable extent, synchronistic answers emerged to the overwhelming question that Orlando poses in his talks both in class and to the entire school: how to be an empowered black male in America.

In many ways, *Invisible Man* anticipated the civil rights movement and articulated what it needed to accomplish, and consequently has remained on the humanities curricula nationwide for decades. DiMattia covered the first half of the novel in lectures, and then assigned each of the remaining chapters to pairs of students to present in class.

"Why do you think the thirteenth chapter is the best in the book?" Kawone Williams asks at the beginning of his presentation on November 4. Kawone leans his wiry frame over his desktop toward the center of the discussion circle. As usual at the beginning of class, DiMattia exhorted the thirteen seniors to move their desks into formation, saying "I like it round and I like it tight"—at which they always jokingly groan.

DiMattia sits on the corner of his desk as Kawone and his partner, Ruben Barrero, take over. DiMattia is about six feet tall with a broad back and slight bulge at the midsection. Although not much overweight, with his closely cropped beard and round face, DiMattia has an early Burl Ives look. DiMattia is only twenty-eight years old, but his relentlessly receding hairline makes him appear more mature, even though his milky complexion betrays few wrinkles.

"Because it's got black food," Erin Gray answers softly. Unlike most of his schoolmates with missing fathers, Erin possesses an inner calm due, he says, to his father never having been a factor in his life. Erin knows nothing about the man and has never asked his mother for his name. As a result, he seems to have avoided the father wound that consumes so much of Orlando's counseling. "Chitlins 'n yams, and all that," Erin adds with a smile.

"Somethin' like that," Kawone laughs, surprising his classmates since he rarely relinquishes his acerbic persona.

"It's the turning point of the novel," Ruben Barrero interjects anxiously to make a contribution before Kawone takes charge of the presentation. Ruben's taciturn nature is the proverbial bright candle hidden under a bushel.

"The narrator gets a sense of himself," Aaron Ashe suggests. Although Aaron is very light-skinned and has aquiline features to the point where he could pass as white, he's one of the few students at Rice with a defined sense of racial identity. Aaron's father is a state trooper who wears dreads and is built like a heavyweight boxer or "Bob Marley on steroids," as DiMattia describes him. He graduated from Marist College and plans to retire in a few years so he can teach at Rice. Ashe steeped his sons in both African American and mainstream traditions. Aaron achieved the highest SAT score this year at 1170, while his brother Abrahim, a junior, had one of the highest PSAT scores. Aaron has applied to the United States Military Academy at West Point, as well as Howard and Emory universities.

"Exactly," Kawone exclaims. "The narrator has finally become what he's supposed to be: a powerful black man." Kawone speaks the last words with uncharacteristic reverence, before adding: "He's been a suck all through the book 'til now."

"Gotcha, Kawone," DiMattia says to himself, pleased that the assignment is drawing the enigmatic senior, one of his most gifted students, into literature's intellectual journey and the subject of race. At the end of last year, Kawone's English teacher told him that Kawone loved *The Great Gatsby*, but refused to read Frederick Douglass's autobiography.

"All our lives, we're told to get over race," he told the teacher. "Then y'all want us to read books about these things, and you still want us to move past it. There's no point."

This year, DiMattia interspersed analysis of poetry and short stories with the ongoing study of *Invisible Man*. Kawone was fully engaged in the discussion of Seamus Heaney's *Blackberry-Picking*, for example. His essay was mediocre, but an improvement over declining to hand in assignments about works related to the civil rights struggle.

In the first discussion about *Invisible Man*, Kawone contributed little because he was refusing to read the book. Then Kawone start warming up after a class discussion about the veracity of a shocking tale of incest in the second chapter. A sharecropper named Jim Trueblood lives in a shack in what's known in the novel as the "black belt," near a college for more-privileged Negro students in the Deep South. Trueblood claims that both his wife and daughter are pregnant with his children. He says he had a dream several months before and then woke up to the reality of having sex with his daughter who, for lack of beds in the family's tiny cabin, was forced to sleep with her parents. Fellow blacks at the college were horrified and tried to have him run out of the county. But local whites took pity on the man, and gave him money and more work than he ever had before.

DiMattia suggested that Trueblood made up the story as a way of "putting one over on whitey." The character is clearly an opportunist, DiMattia said, who might be spinning the tale as a way of "subverting" the white establishment. A lively discussion followed in which Kawone became angry with the teacher's hypothesis. When the bell rang, Kawone walked out of the room arguing with classmate Phil Tobias, who agreed with DiMattia that Trueblood was motivated solely for his own gain.

"Why would someone make up a story that set back race relations?" Kawone asked incredulously. His disgust was clearly expressed in the next essay assignment:

Trueblood belongs with animals. Grandpa Bledsoe and the Vet are intelligent black men. Each of them got to the point they are by some realistic manner. It took hard work and determination. . . . The Vet has degrees and is an achomplished doctor. how can you not respect that? Trueblood degraded his race even more just trying to get ahead. By stating that he had sex with his daughter it make white peoples points so more concrete. That blacks are animals with no morals and that they belong in cages. The man (if you can call him that) has no respect for his race or himself.

DiMattia couldn't give Kawone a high grade because the essay was too disorganized, and contained too many spelling, stylistic, and grammatical errors. But the teacher was pleased to see Kawone finally write with passion. Afterward DiMattia questioned Kawone about his attitudes toward race.

"The whole issue is stupid," he replied. "In Harlem, people are always blaming their failures on their skin color, but that can't be true all the time. They're just dumbing it down. I despise racism, and that's why I won't read books with racial overtones. We'd all be better off if we didn't have to say, 'You're white' and 'I'm black.' "

As much as DiMattia agrees with a race-neutral outlook, he knows Kawone can't ignore race entirely when he goes to college. He can get away with it in Harlem, but next year Kawone will attend Iona College, which reflects the demographics of the larger society. Iona's student body is 13 percent African American, 14 percent Hispanic, and over 60 percent white. DiMattia hopes to instill the capacity to work hard regardless of how students feel about the subject matter.

At least, Kawone is displaying enthusiasm as he continues with his *Invisible Man* presentation. He hands out photocopies of several quotes that he and Ruben selected for discussion.

Erin volunteers to read the first:

I passed on to a window decorated with switches of wiry false hair, ointments guaranteed to produce the miracle of whitening black skin. "You too can be truly beautiful," a sign proclaimed. "Win greater happiness with whiter complexion. Be outstanding in your social set."[1]

"Again the author uses the color white to convey a message," Kawone says. "Anyone have an idea what that message is?"

"That white's better," Erin answers.

"What Ralph Ellison is doing here is using something we all use," Kawone's eyes sparkle mischievously. "See this right here," he reaches into his book bag and pulls out a six-inch white tube with "Skin Lightener" imprinted in large red letters. "Now I use this every morning so, without knowing it, I'm trying to be a lighter complexion fellow. It never clicked in my head that I'm trying to be a white person. Understand what I'm sayin'?"

"I understand," several classmates chortle with embarrassment.

"He's pointing out that black people aren't happy with their dark skin," Kawone exclaims.

"Anybody see *Soul Food*?" DiMattia asks to affirmative nods. "There's a brilliant scene where the wives are hanging out together, and they're talking about how their husbands have this thing for lighter colored women: the lighter the woman the more attention the woman receives."

"And it's true today," Kawone chimes in. "If you see a black-skinned woman, most men don't want to talk with her—black men." Most Rice students openly prefer light-complexioned girls, and the darker boys are more likely to suffer rejection from girls, regardless of how handsome they are. Some of the young women admit that their parents have told them, "There'll be no more black babies in this family. You can marry either a light-skinned black or a white guy."

"When I read this passage," Kawone continues, "I looked in my drawer and said, 'Yes, I have that, and it's not helping the cause.'"

DiMattia raises an eyebrow as Kawone admits for the first time that he has a connection to "the cause."

"What are you going to do with that tube?" Erin asks.

"I'm going to keep it. I paid good money," Kawone quips, and his classmates guffaw.

DiMattia laughs heartily with the students, hoping they'll retain the day's insights regarding acceptance of self and race, and the deeper lesson that the novel seeks to explore. On the most apparent level, *Invisible Man's* first-person narrative is a literary incarnation of the African American dilemma:

> I am an invisible man. No, I am not a spook like those who haunted Edgar Allan Poe; nor am I one of your Hollywood-movie ectoplasms. I am a man of substance, of flesh and bone, fiber and liquids—and I might even be said to possess a mind. I am invisible, understand, simply because people refuse to see me.[2]

Beginning with the Middle Passage, the metaphor of the invisible black male succinctly expresses how dramatically African males and their descendents have had to conceal their sexuality behind submissive personas, on pain of being flogged, castrated, or lynched. Accordingly, one of the first statements seeking to ameliorate this obliteration of black masculinity came in the 1780s, when the British Society for the Abolition of Slavery on its official seal placed a banner over a kneeling slave that read, "Am I not a man and a brother?"

By the mid-twentieth century, this passive plea for recognition of the black man's full humanity, enduring despite slavery and Jim Crow laws, was on the verge of finally transforming—and being allowed to evolve—into active assertion via protests and social action.

> During the Montgomery bus boycott of 1955–56 . . . [a] union man and president of the Montgomery chapter of the NAACP, [E. D.] Nixon met with Montgomery's black ministers and chastised them for not publicly supporting the boycott begun by courageous women from their community. "We are acting like little boys," Nixon told the ministers. . . . "We'd better decide if we're going to be fearless men or scared boys." Martin Luther King Jr. responded to Nixon's call to action, becoming the leader of the Montgomery Improvement Association and one of the most eloquent spokesmen of the civil rights movement.[3]

This theme of asserting African American manhood defined much of the civil rights movement, articulated for example in the slogan painted on signs during the 1968 Memphis sanitation workers' strike: "I AM A MAN."

At Rice thirty years later, Orlando's attitude blares, I AM THE MAN, both to demonstrate to his boys how to become mature, empowered adults, and as his way of precluding any attempts, perceived or real, to treat him as "uppity." Like the lowly garbage men, Orlando is still haunted by what Ralph Ellison articulated in 1952 as the dilemma of the "invisible man" whose possession of a mind—of full humanity—is permanently in question because of his race.

This is expressed in the poster that Orlando mounted on the wall beside his office that reads, I CAN, I WILL, I MUST! Underneath the lettering is a large drawing of the principal preaching from the cafeteria podium. The purpose is to inspire students to achieve academic and all forms of excellence by following Orlando's example—that he can, he will, and he must—which he is driven constantly to demonstrate.

For Orlando, to be is to be seen, otherwise personal and racial oblivion would swallow him whole. This dilemma is shared by African American males and to a significant extent accounts for their bravado.

The deeper level at which *Invisible Man* operates seeks to overcome this existential and historical quandary by appealing to the universal. Ellison said in an interview that "the hero's invisibility is not a matter of being seen but a refusal to run the risk of his own humanity, which involves guilt. This is not an attack upon white society! It is what the hero refuses to do in each section which leads to further action. He must assert and achieve his own humanity; he cannot run with the pack and do this—this is the reason for all the reversals."⁴

Consequently, Ellison would rephrase Kawone's understanding that the narrator was becoming a powerful black man to say he became a powerful man who happens to be black. As a writer, Ellison put himself in the company of the best in the Western tradition. He didn't want to confine himself to an intellectual and artistic ghetto as a "black writer," any more than he wanted his fellow African American readers to limit themselves culturally and socially. As Ellison wrote at the height of the civil rights movement about his youth in Macon County, Alabama,

> I read Marx, Freud, T. S. Eliot, Pound. . . . Books which seldom, if ever, mentioned Negroes were to release me from whatever "segregated" idea I might have had of human possibilities. I was freed not by propagandists . . . but by composers, novelists, and poets who spoke to me of more interesting and freer ways of life. . . . Indeed, I understand a bit more about myself as a Negro because literature has taught me something of my identity as a Western man, as a political being.⁵

Ellison would applaud Kawone's interest in works beyond his culture. Although Kawone hasn't developed Ellison's taste for classical music yet, he no longer listens to rap. "It's the same clichés again and again," Kawone says. Instead, he prefers classic rock stars and enjoyed reading Franz Kafka's *Metamorphosis*. He also displayed considerable interest in class discussions of *King Lear,* which was reflected in his essay:

> It's almost puzzling to a point, how these characters that seem to be the victims are so easily duped. . . . In a very important scene we find Edmund and Edgar speaking about Gloucester's foul mood. Edmund says that it is because of something that Edgar has done. Edgar (the fool) believes him. Then Edmund says he hears troops coming and they're looking for Edgar, he then tells Edgar to leave this place post hast. . . . Then Gloucester arrives with a few servants, he finds Edmund bleeding from his arm or shoulder, somewhere in that vicinity. Edmund then claims that Edgar has gone mad with hate and deceit and attacked him. We all know that nothing is further from the truth. Edmunds wound was self-inflicted All in an effort to reaffirm Gloucester's growing dislike for his son Edgar. . . . Now his plotting

takes an even more insidious path. He and a few other characters come to the conclusion that they are better off with Edmund as Duke of Gloucester. They then conspire to remove Gloucester's eyes and do other atrocities to him. Edmund then becomes Duke or Earl of Gloucester. He then runs into the worst type of problems—women problems. Two women, sisters are fighting over him and in the middle of a war with France. . . .

DiMattia awarded a perfect grade, an obvious inflation, but he was very pleased to see Kawone put so much thought into a three-page, typed assignment submitted on time. Although the AP exam will be graded according to national standards, DiMattia can't evaluate his students solely by these standards. He believes strongly in rewarding progress according to each student's starting point.

As DiMattia pointed out several times during class discussions, Ellison's view that the fates of whites and blacks in America are inextricably linked, and that race should neither be ignored nor allowed to be a limit, provides the best framework for dealing with this fundamental American problem. That such wisdom is preserved in literary form, and the classics of Western and other civilizations are the heritage of every child, have meaning only insofar as educational institutions nurture students' ability to read comprehensively and think coherently. This is especially urgent for the children of those who suffer most from the consequences of discrimination. Then, as Orlando so passionately propounds, schools function as vehicles of liberation.

———

Liberation, however, usually comes with a steep price for inner-city minority parents who have to make enormous sacrifices to send their children to private or parochial schools, since there's rarely a viable public school alternative. Tragically, most disadvantaged families can't afford tuition and as a result, pay the highest possible price: lost opportunity.

"My best investment is your education," Kawone's mother, Stovette Williams, tells him often. After emigrating from Antigua, Stovette and her husband Rupert insisted that both Kawone and his older brother Kwame attend All Saints elementary school, despite the cost and the fact that the family is Episcopalian.

"My mom works at a fashion distributing company in New Jersey, but I never asked what she does there," Kawone says, admitting it would be too painful to know since her low pay indicates a career beneath her capabilities. "If she didn't put us through Catholic school, she'd have a house now, which is what she really wants."

Kawone's father is a construction worker, and "he lets me know every time I talk with him how hard he's working for the money to take care of us and send us to school." Usually Mr. Williams sits on the couch in the living room at night and makes a point of showing his son his latest collection of cuts and bruises from the job.

"Yes, I understand," Kawone replies. "You're working hard for the money so I can go to Rice." The son seems to handle these constant reminders well, but his parents' plight disturbs him greatly. "My dad is very intelligent and my mom has a heart of gold; they both could be doing other things. I feel the pressure, and I'll go to college because I want to buy some land in Antigua and set my parents up to live worry-free."

After his older brother, a '96 Rice graduate, dropped out of college last year and took a job as a furniture delivery laborer, the pressure on Kawone escalated. His mother keeps a gallery of photos of her two boys going through school on a side table in the living room. The shrine won't be complete until Kawone's college graduation picture is mounted on the wall above.

Kawone inherited the sour side of his personality from his father, who's "a little hard to deal with. He loves us just as much as my mother, but it's hard for him to be like, 'I love you, son.'" Instead the father's affection is expressed through arguments with his sons, mostly about politics. Kwame has no stomach for the incessant disputes, but Kawone finds the debates stimulating. "We discuss back and forth all day, and then he'll start arguing again the next day. We can't find common ground and joke around that we can't really hold a conversation. We both feel awkward, but I talk to my dad about everything."

Another debate continues in Kawone's psyche. Paradoxically he makes little effort to do more than pass his classes at Rice, which means his admission into Iona is largely because of Widziewicz's recommendation. But the senior will have trouble securing enough financial aid to spare his parents four more years of significant expense. Kawone is already resigned to living at home and commuting to Iona to save money, but tuition is over $15,000 and will increase.

Sadly, it would have taken minimal effort for Kawone to get over 1000 on the SAT and make the honor roll. But he can't escape the lethargy that high school inspires because of what he calls its "deadening conformity. You do what everyone else does or else. You wear the clothes they wear and listen to the same music." Slowly he's been breaking away, but he's still afraid "to run the risk of his own humanity," as Ellison characterizes his narrator's problem of coming of age. On one hand, Kawone admits to being overly concerned about what classmates think of him, and so holds himself back from excelling. On the other hand, Kawone has no interest in hanging around with the basketball players and others who are considered cool. He happily eats lunch and socializes with an assortment of misfits.

Widziewicz has gotten to know Kawone since he works as the guidance counselor's office assistant several hours a week for a small stipend. "I can't wait to go to college," he told Widziewicz, "and start exploring the things I really like. I gotta get away from guys always asking dumb questions like 'How long does this essay have to be?' I'm like, 'As long as it takes, you fool.' "

In AP English, Kawone sits across the aisle from Linwood, who struggles especially with poetry and Shakespeare. Linwood has difficulty comprehending the written word beyond the literal. As he scratched his shaven head and struggled with metaphors like "the burnt-out ends of smoky days" in T. S. Eliot's *Preludes*, Kawone hurled barbs like "you idiot" almost every time Linwood offered a comment, which usually lacked literary insight.

The best illustration of Linwood's difficulty occurred in the tenth grade when Mark Blanchard, the English teacher, was in the middle of reading Edgar Allan Poe's *The Raven* aloud.

"It's a bird? A bird's talking to this guy?" Linwood exclaimed, utterly incredulous. "Mr. B., what would you do if a bird ever talked to you? I'd be buggin' outta there."

Linwood takes Kawone's jibes good-naturedly. He's the first to acknowledge his deficiencies. But as he predicted at the beginning of the year, he outsmarted Kawone vis-à-vis college. Linwood kept himself on the honor roll, won several small scholarships, and has been accepted into Hofstra University's engineering program on full scholarship for five years. Recognizing that students like Linwood need to catch up to those who aren't getting in via racial preferences, the university pays for an extra year to afford the opportunity to repeat courses if necessary.

After graduating, Linwood plans to apply to the FBI to become a special agent tracking down white-collar criminals. He has no desire to enforce the law in inner-city neighborhoods where he knows the dangers well—dangers so real that it is no wonder the metaphorical seems foreign.

Still, Kawone's future looks bright. He'll spend the next four years commuting by train from an apartment on West 129th Street. He'll walk past the same drug dealers, gang members, and others who hang out on stoops and street corners. Many of these young men he knew as a child. They played with Kawone or his older brother and went to public school. None graduated high school and some have become memories. It's also true that since he lives in a two-parent, functional household, Kawone has little desire to leave.

After Kawone and Ruben's presentation, DiMattia ends the period as the bell rings with his customary: "We are . . ."

"Rice," the students respond loudly in chorus then head downstairs for lunch.

DiMattia pays regular homage to the Rice Man identity. At Iona Preparatory High School, the Christian Brothers secondary school near Iona College, DiMattia remembers daily seeing the sign over the main office that read, "There's something about being an Iona Man. If you are one, know one or have been one, you know what we mean." The Iona Man identity helped create a strong school culture focused on academic achievement and character development. DiMattia hopes his students buy into the lifelong value of education as the core of being a Rice Man.

As Henry Louis Gates, Jr., wrote: "When I was growing up in the fifties, becoming a successful doctor, lawyer, or businessman was about the blackest thing you could be."[6] Looking at the issue from an economic perspective, Gates asks, "So how do we get more black people into the middle class?" "Step by step," answers Franklin Raines (whom Gates interviews in his book), the first African American to become the CEO of a Fortune 500 company—a powerful man who happens to be black. Raines overcame poverty to graduate from Harvard's law and business schools. "There's no shortcut. To begin with, we've got to get folks the preparation that's needed. More people have got to finish high school. . . ."[7]

While Orlando has no trouble demonstrating the powerful black man persona, he resists seeing himself as a powerful man who happens to be black. He cleaves to black nationalism as originally espoused by the Panthers, although Newton and Seale eventually came to view this as a form of black racism, and aligned themselves with international socialism. Orlando ignores this evolution in their thinking, since he believes his students are so far removed from a proper sense of self and racial worth that they benefit most from a philosophy dedicated exclusively to them, espoused by heroes they can identify with.

In the outside world and at college, whites will focus on the African Americans they find acceptable such as Colin Powell, Orlando points out. But at this point in his students' development, Orlando stresses the need for militant partisans as role models to inspire his boys' will to stand up for and believe in themselves.

Historically, militancy as espoused by Malcolm X and the Panthers was a response to the humiliation and consequent loss of self-esteem that most African Americans endured in the wake of the civil rights movement. Although gaining legal equality was a magnificent achievement, most of those who benefited were what DuBois termed the "talented tenth." Aside from the various forms of prejudice that remained, the majority of blacks lacked the education and social skills to compete effectively. The coping strategy that evolved was the view that American society is irremediably racist, thereby justifying the revolutionary pose as both a rejection of mainstream values and ideological redemption.

The problem is that this further alienated the underclass from its aspirations as the poor fell into a ghettoized version of black separatism. Orlando's nationalism, in contrast, rejects this downward spiral. While he enjoys the trappings of radicalism and institutes an Afrocentric focus, he vigorously promotes the solution that the Frederick Douglass Academy defines as its mission: replicating the academic education that was the key to success for Martin Luther King, Jr., along with instilling the values implicit in his religious training. The transition from humiliation to worth takes a traditional route through the classroom, the family, and the church. This involves militancy but without violence, allowing Orlando to simultaneously emulate the Panthers and King. In terms of visibility, Orlando demands to be seen as both fully human and black.

Chapter Twenty-four

———

YUSEF TRAILS BEHIND ORLANDO AS they make their way through the crowd. It's 4:00 P.M. on Sunday, March 19, and the Fordham University gym is filling to capacity for the championship game between the Rice Raiders and St. Raymond's Ravens. The match decides the city Catholic high school trophy and the right to play in the state high school tournament. Last year, with a physically tougher team, Rice won both titles. This year, finesse will have to prevail.

Two weeks ago, Rice ended the regular season losing to St. Raymond's by five points. St. Raymond's has a taller team and a superb junior in Julius Hodge, who can take any Rice player one-on-one. Tonight the Raiders, led by Andre Barrett—who's only five feet, eight inches tall but one of the country's premier high school point guards—will have to play their best game of the year. With Kyle Cuffe, who's been recruited by St. John's University, at center and Andre Sweet, bound for Duke next year, at power forward, the Rice team has an even chance.

Yusef keeps his eyes downcast as he follows the principal because he doesn't know how to handle the attention that the two hundred Rice students in attendance and a large contingent of parents show Orlando. But he enjoys being seen with Rice's luminary and keeps as physically close as possible to ward off rivals. At least fifty "Yo, Gobe's" are hurled their way before the father figure and his virtual son find seats about ten rows above the Rice bench. Orlando gave the entire school the day off tomorrow as a way of celebrating the team's recent success and encouraging attendance.

St. Raymond's Ravens take an early lead, but the first quarter ends in a 10–10 tie. The game's pattern emerges with the Raiders outplaying their opponents, except for Julius Hodge, who blows by Rice players for lay-ups and hits outside shots. The Raiders play strong defense, and Barrett makes remarkable steals, then dribbles through the Ravens players with deft speed.

The second quarter begins with a roar as Paris Lane leads Rice's unofficial cheerleading team. With three sophomore classmates, Paris wears a long white Rice basketball T-shirt and a white bandana around his head.

"Rice Raiders, let's go. We got the weapons: left hand, right hand," Paris heads his quartet in the aisle at the east end of the gym. He mimes jump shots with his left hand, then his right. "We got the weapons, let's go."

Even from Orlando's seat on the other side of the gym, Paris's eyes glow with vitality. He wears blue contact lenses "to charm the ladies," as he readily admits. But more striking is his inner fire, which shines through every gesture. Paris has a truly charismatic personality and bursts with performance talent both on and off the court. Slightly taller than Andre, Paris is also an expert dribbler but possesses no sense of team play. Whenever he got the ball on the junior varsity team, he charged in a frenzy down the court and took a shot without looking for teammates. Rather than learning to co-operate, Paris abruptly quit to form an ad hoc cheering corps. He attends most varsity and junior varsity games to make his contribution in the way that best suits his personality, since he's in charge.

Rice jumps out to an 18–12 lead in the second quarter as Orlando watches quietly sitting beside Yusef. The two exchange comments, initiated mostly by Yusef as he explains St. Raymond's strengths and weaknesses. Orlando understands the rules, but has never taken an interest in the subtleties of basketball strategy or technique. With Yusef as teacher, Orlando displays a genuine interest.

"Ooohhhh," the crowd gasps as Barrett makes a crossover dribble that leaves a St. Raymond's defender at the top of the key guarding his shadow. When Barrett hits a moving shot over the opponent's center, his first basket of the game, a broad smile breaks across Orlando's face.

Andre Barrett makes the principal especially proud this year, maintaining his mid-90s average in all subjects and attracting interest from Stanford University, among dozens of other schools with competitive Division I programs. Barrett, a McDonald's All-American, is finishing at Rice as the first player with over 1,000 points and 1,000 assists. He has averaged almost 19 points, 12 assists, and 3.5 steals per game this year.

Barrett has chosen Seton Hall University for his college career, since he feels comfortable in a Catholic institution and likes the coach, who's an African American and former point guard. Tommy Amaker convinced Barrett that with the other recruits, the team will have a legitimate shot at the NCAA's Final Four.

Orlando campaigned for Seton Hall to give Barrett an academic scholarship instead of an athletic one. "If he was someone *else* with the same grades, they would give him an academic scholarship," the principal told the freshman classes in Hebinck's room, as part of his talk to begin the third marking period. Again he explained the grading system in detail, exhorting failing students to understand and correct their deficiencies. "See, you think racism is dead, but it's staring you right in the face every day."

The truth is that Barrett didn't score high enough on the SAT to warrant an academic scholarship. Orlando maintains he should have gotten the scholarship anyway, claiming that the SAT is culturally biased against African Americans. But that controversy has died out. Caribbean-educated teachers at Rice, such as Olivene Browne, contend that standardized tests are biased only against students who don't prepare for them. Barrett could have scored in the top percentiles, but as an athlete, he had no need to put in the extra work.

Underlying Orlando's complaint is the broad claim that black students are programmed to go for athletic instead of academic scholarships. "People"—meaning mostly white coaches, principals, and scouts—"push you that way, smiling and patting you on the back, but think about it," he challenged the ninth graders. "We've internalized it so much that many young brothers go to school with a basketball but no books." That's not allowed at Rice, as the freshmen learned in September, and Orlando wants them, and their future children and grandchildren, to understand why.

On the bench sits all seven feet, two inches of Shagari Alleyne, who wasn't allowed to join the team until the end of the regular season when he finally passed all his subjects. At the first parent-teacher meetings in November, Shagari's mother was so disappointed in her son's grades she made him bend down so she could slap him across the face in the hallway. Shagari then stayed after school most nights for private tutoring from Shayne Howze, the varsity team's manager. Had Shagari been training with the team all season, he might have raised his skill levels to the point where the coach, Mo Hicks, could put him into the championship game against St. Raymond's, which would have been beneficial against the otherwise taller team. Regardless of the effect on the varsity team's chances of winning another championship, Orlando held firm, and no one even dared suggest an exception for Shagari.

"African Americans believe their own hype that they're better ball players," Orlando thundered at the freshmen during the height of the basketball season. "But anything you do more—guess what?—you'll get good at. We have nothing in our genes that makes us better basketball players. That's a lie, a big fat lie. It's because you're out there on the courts from the time you're five years old. If you steal more, you'll be better at stealing. And if you study more, you'll get better at academics. It's very simple."

On Orlando's insistence, Barrett negotiated a deferred academic scholarship with Seton Hall. The university agreed to pay for the graduate program of his choice at the school if he stays for four years and plays basketball. With Barrett currently being considered for valedictorian, Orlando touts him as a role model for the freshmen, who are still having trouble accepting that studying is cool. "Results and responsibility, not excuses," Orlando punctuated his talk in an almost identical phrase to one of Brother Walderman's favorite admonitions. The principal pointed out that no matter how late Barrett got home at night after practice or a game, he always finished his homework and made it back to school from Queens on time.

Yusef comments on Barrett's deftness quarterbacking the Raiders, and also why he's missing shots. Barrett sprained his left wrist during the last playoff game, and although it's not his shooting hand, the injury seems to be throwing off his timing. Yusef has no trouble showing appreciation for Barrett's performance since he doesn't pose a threat. The point guard comes from a middle-class family with two parents who attend every game and so he has no need to become close to Orlando.

In their green and gold uniforms, Rice players charge down the court to take up their half-court offensive positions against the Ravens, wearing white outfits with red trim.

Seconds later, the first half ends with the Raiders leading 29–22 and a jocular mood being shared by their fans.

———

During halftime, Mrs. Pat Dyer comes over to thank the principal for the positive effect he is having on her son, Steve Jr., which is sweetened by the fact that Steve plays on the freshman basketball team and shows promise of making varsity, validating Orlando's priorities.

In a rapid burst of narrative, Mrs. Dyer recapitulates the evening she and her family met her son's sponsor at the Student Sponsor Partners annual dinner at Rice. It was October 7 and at six o'clock, Brother Walderman gave a brief talk in the library—which Orlando didn't attend, since it was Brother's affair—thanking the new sponsors, who typically pay half the student's tuition and agree to act as mentors and role models. The sponsor program raises funds through donations to cover the other half, except for a nominal amount paid by the students' families.

With his innate sense of the dramatic, Brother Walderman brought forward one student at a time for a formal introduction to his sponsor. The student then led the sponsor to the cafeteria to meet his family and share dinner at their table.

When Rich McDermott, an investment banker, sat with Steve's family, he was overwhelmed by the Dyers' gratitude and positive feedback about his investment.

"I remember coming here for parent orientation at the beginning of the year," Mrs. Dyer related. "Mr. Gober said, 'I'm telling you now, mothers: Don't come to me with no stories about your *little darlings*. If your *little darlings* didn't do anything wrong, they wouldn't be sitting in my office.' "

McDermott nodded his head knowingly. Although this was his first visit to Rice, he'd heard about Orlando from his wife, Martha, who until recently worked as a school coordinator at SSP.

"Us mothers were chuckling," Mrs. Dyer continued. "What Mr. Gober said was so important: 'There are so many people on the streets outside here whose mothers spoiled them, and now they are not responsible men.' We all said, 'Amen.' "

Beside Mrs. Dyer was her husband, Steve Sr., and sitting across the table beside Rich was their daughter, Angela, an eighth grader at I.S. 227 Louis Armstrong Middle School, one of the city's better junior highs. Steve Jr. occupied the head of the table and remained silent, obviously accustomed to letting his mother speak for the family.

"I had to catch myself since I was swelling up hearing him speak," Steve Sr., a powerfully built truck driver, spoke for the first time since shaking McDermott's hand. "That's how I grew up; you had chores in your house."

"I work at a public elementary school," Mrs. Dyer, an assistant teacher at P.S. 223 in Queens, said with dismay. She was also enrolled in an education degree program at York College, a City University of New York campus in

Queens. "There are good teachers there, but we can't get books, and there's no discipline. The kids can't read when they leave, so how do you expect them to pass the Regents? There's no way I was going to send him to a public high school, and I didn't know what to do."

"Getting accepted into the SSP program is a miracle," Rich answered. "There are over five thousand applications for 425 freshman slots every year." In Steve's case, however, there might have been divine intervention of a sort. It's possible Wylie Gober told Brother Walderman about the youngster's athletic potential. Not only does Brother Walderman speak effectively and with passion at SSP events, but he has a history of accepting the highest percentage of students with the least likelihood of graduating. It's reasonable to assume that SSP listens to his suggestions, and he might have dropped Steve's name.

Mrs. Dyer hopes her daughter will be accepted into SSP next year. "I don't want my children around those other kids. High school is a crucial part of their lives, and if Stephen or Angela get on the wrong track, they could be lost."

"That's true," her husband added with a worried look.

"We've been blessed," Mrs. Dyer looked at Rich and said. "Thank you from my heart; you have lifted such a burden."

"We're lucky enough to be able to participate," McDermott answered softly. "We'd feel uncomfortable not sharing."

Student Sponsor Partners was founded in 1986 by Peter Flanigan, an investment banker (and Martha McDermott's uncle), to combat the alarming dropout rate at the city's public high schools. For decades, the business community complained about the declining skill levels of graduates from the city's public schools. Even more urgent now is the growing number who don't even make it through the system. Flanigan's program matches this desperate need with available seats at area parochial high schools. Flanigan firmly believes in what over three hundred years of Catholic schooling devoted to the poor proves: that a no-frills curriculum devoted to academic basics and an insistence on discipline overcomes demographic, cultural, and economic obstacles.

SSP grew quickly from its initial cohort of forty-five students to almost 1,300 girls and boys at present, including 410 freshmen, attending twenty high schools throughout the city and in Westchester County, just north of the Bronx. All the secondary schools are Catholic, except Martin Luther High School, a Lutheran academy in Queens.[1] Eighty percent of SSP students graduate on time—SSP doesn't pay for a fifth year—and over 90 percent of these go on to college. Including this year's contingent, 3,500 young men and women have been given the opportunity to attend a parochial high school, which otherwise their families couldn't afford.

What makes SSP's success remarkable is that unlike like many scholarship programs, the program doesn't target gifted minority students. Rather, SSP selects those at risk of not graduating if they continue at zoned public high schools with abysmal graduation rates. Tens of thousands of eighth graders fit into this category every year, so SSP doesn't need to advertise, but instead reaches out through a network of public school teachers and administrators to seek recommendations for a limited number of youngsters.

Shayne Howze and Jermaine Anderson attended the same public junior high school in the Bronx. One day early in the eighth grade, their teacher pulled them both aside to suggest the SSP program and warned them strongly against continuing in the public system. She did not inform the other students, in effect screening them out as, in her judgment, less dedicated although certainly no less deserving. Otherwise SSP would be overwhelmed with applications.

In selecting candidates, SSP administrators balance academic, financial, and social need with a judgment about the student's likelihood to persist. Almost all SSP freshmen enter high school with reading and math skills as much as three years below grade level, and then they have to catch up just as do the majority of Rice Men. SSP youngsters come from financially disadvantaged families, averaging $9,000 per capita annual income, and over half of them receive public assistance. Three-quarters of SSP students come from single-parent households.

Part of the program's success is due to its mentoring dimension. Many sponsors such as Robert Keith, a stockbroker at Morgan Stanley, become involved precisely because of the opportunity to directly affect a young person's life. "I got tired of writing checks for causes," he says at a table on the other side of the cafeteria, where he is becoming acquainted with Ricky Rodriguez, his student, "and not seeing anything get any better."

Since many sponsors have demanding jobs and their own families, the extent of relationships with students varies greatly. McDermott intends to meet with Steve occasionally, but his wife is pregnant with their second child, which will greatly restrict his social activities. Linwood met often with his sponsor, Christopher Hunt, the author of *Waiting for Fidel*, a critically acclaimed travelogue, until he moved to Los Angeles. Now they maintain an e-mail and telephone connection.

SSP was the nation's first urban voucher program, whether privately or publicly funded. The voucher concept was first initiated through "tuitioning" laws in Vermont (1869) and Maine (1873) that still allow and pay for 738 small towns to send their K–12 pupils to public or private schools, excluding religious institutions, in adjoining districts.[2] However, it was SSP's success with inner-city minority students that inspired a tremendous growth in vouchers and other choice initiatives that continues today.

Seven states (Arizona, Florida, Maine, Ohio, Utah, Vermont, and Wisconsin) and the District of Columbia have instituted publicly funded voucher programs that pay for students to attend private elementary or secondary schools, mostly Catholic. In addition, tax credit and deduction programs have been initiated in seven states (Arizona, Florida, Illinois, Iowa, Minnesota, Pennsylvania, and Rhode Island), and those in Iowa, Pennsylvania, and Rhode Island provide significant amounts toward private school tuition.[3] In total, 150,000 students across the country participate in publicly funded programs that provide either full tuition or a significant portion of their tuition.[4]

Privately funded voucher programs have also proliferated, although most don't involve SSP's mentoring dimension. About sixty thousand students from low-income families participate in 115 programs in one hundred communities and urban centers in thirty-nine states.[5] Many are small local initiatives, with the largest, the Children's Scholarship Fund (CSF), providing twenty-five thousand scholarships a year to elementary students in thirty-eight mostly urban areas. When CSF started in 1998—with funds donated by Teddy Forstmann and John Walton, now totaling in the hundreds of millions—the response was overwhelming, as 1.25 million applications were submitted from twenty thousand communities across the country, even though the program wasn't advertised. To avoid processing millions of applications a year from families seeking alternatives to public education, which would absorb most of the fund's resources, CSF now distributes vouchers on a first come, first served basis. There are no academic requirements and students receive between 25 and 75 percent of tuition, depending on income and family circumstances.

In New York City, over 166,000 families applied for the 1,995 slots in CSF's first year. Currently 2,500 CSF scholarships a year are awarded. Since voucher programs typically follow SSP's example of targeting the children of the poor, they imitate the original mission of Catholic teaching orders, and fittingly send the vast majority of their students to parochial schools.[6]

Vouchers also help many Catholic schools with predominately minority populations stay open. Almost 20 percent of Rice students have their tuitions paid via SSP, average for schools in the program. Rice would not be able to stay open long without SSP, especially with rising tuition.

As do three-quarters of African Americans and most Hispanics, Orlando supports vouchers as a way of providing viable schools for at least some disadvantaged children stuck in failing public schools.[7] But he warns against reliance on them. Just as did Archbishop Hughes, Orlando believes institutions can and should be built via grassroots efforts, independent of government or corporate support. There is no reason, Orlando often says with a mixture of exasperation and hope, why African Americans can't build and run their own school system, as ethnic white Catholics did with far fewer resources.

As the halftime intermission ends, Orlando smiles broadly at Mrs. Dyer as she marvels at the transformation in her son's attitude. "Steve has matured so much since coming here. The clock rings at 5:30 and he says 'I'm up!' He's so excited when he puts on the uniform and becomes a Rice Man. In public junior high school, he had no spark."

Orlando thanks her for her comments and is just as happy to see her leave. His patience for other adults talking at length, even in praise, is limited.

━━━

The second half begins with St. Raymond's playing tighter defense inside, allowing Rice to take outside shots, which exposes the Raiders' weakness. The Rice players burst with athletic talent enabling them to "play above the rim," as their coach characterizes their style. But they haven't put nearly enough time into practicing jump or foul shots. The Ravens possess about the same physical prowess, but since they're taller, they grab most rebounds and score more put-backs.

Throughout the game, Hicks has been pacing back and forth in front of the Rice bench yelling and signaling instructions, mostly to Barrett. Hicks's three assistant coaches counsel players on the bench. When Andre Sweet is called for his fourth foul, assistant coach Derrick Haynes jumps up and stomps toward the referee, who fortunately has his back turned. Haynes has thick shoulders almost twice as wide as the referee's and moves with surprising agility. His intimidating physical presence protects a gentle and caring spirit, momentarily obscured by rage.

Last week, Haynes came to Rice after school to pull Paris Lane aside. "I've been hearing things," he told the sophomore in the foyer.

"Ain't nothin'," Paris's smooth but slightly raspy voice answered.

"We need to talk about this," Haynes pulled on Paris's red shirt. "You've been running with this color again." Haynes referred to the Bloods, the gang Paris was dealing for when he was convicted.

"We just chillin'."

"A slip for you is more than somebody else's," Haynes warned. "I'm afraid you're going to end up back on the street doing the same things."

Paris promised to be careful and stay clean, but Haynes couldn't read his heart. As usual, Paris was very self-assured and convincing, which gave Haynes pause. The more carefree and reassuring Paris acts, the more trouble he's in, Haynes knows from the Bridges Juvenile Center, known as "Spofford" since it is located on Spofford Avenue in the Bronx.

The Ravens edge closer, even though their improved strategy only equalizes the level of play—except in one category. Julius Hodge is hitting almost all his foul shots, while Rice players are making about half of theirs. With less than a minute to play, St. Raymond's takes a 57–56 lead on a turnover.

Then with fifteen seconds left in the game, Andre Barrett has a chance to bring the Raiders within a point but misses a foul shot. After a flurry of desperate shots and fouls from several Rice players, St. Raymond's wins the championship 61–56.

For the Raiders, to have led for most of the game, then lose at the end, seems impossible and proves devastating. The players pull their jerseys over their heads in shame or wander around the court stunned. Brother Walderman runs onto the court to wrap his arms around Kyle Cuffe's waist and offers consolation. The coaching staff and the parents rush onto the hardwood and try to pull their players out of their emotions and back to the understanding that it was just a game.

Rice's basketball success earns a considerable amount of press coverage, attracting many young men to the school who might otherwise go to a larger and better-equipped school. Every year, there are a few students who move to New York from as far away as Mississippi to live with a relative and play at Rice. Many freshmen choose Rice hoping to play for the Raiders someday. But as Hicks tells players and parents, what matters is getting through high school and using sports performance to secure an athletic scholarship— and then graduate. Almost all Rice students who go on to play college basketball stay four years and graduate. Felipe Lopez could have entered the NBA draft early, but stayed at St. John's University and graduated with better than a 3.0 GPA. Chudney Grey, another Rice graduate, currently plays for St. John's and has the highest GPA (close to 4.0) on the varsity team.

Catholic school graduates are recruited more heavily than those from public school, Hicks attests. "They know that a kid coming out of Catholic school is better prepared academically and has a better work ethic, with a sense of respect." The coach points to his own experience after graduating from Rice and going to Loyola University on a basketball scholarship. His teammates from public school, he says, were not nearly as well prepared for college work.

"A lot of students come here for the big team," Hicks reflects, "but they're stunned to find that basketball is really downplayed at Rice. Then they see the small, dingy gym on the sixth floor. Our reputation gets a lot of students, but they see it's more about education and about growing mentally and spiritually. There's no pressure on us to win here; it's not our focus. If we lost every game, but the kids were growing spiritually, the administration would still be happy. With Mr. Gober taking over as principal, it has become increasingly clear that Rice puts academics before sports."

Orlando leaves Fordham's gym quietly with Yusef, taking cover in the departing crowd. The principal doesn't have much of a personal relationship with the athletes since they have the coach and his assistants for father figures. The players' grief will have more than enough attendees, and Orlando has to get back to his office to mark student projects. Besides, the starters are moving on to NCAA Division I programs next year.

Five minutes later, Orlando and Yusef exit the gym, and the principal hails a cab. Yusef takes a bus home, then visits Rice a few days later since he has heard that Paris is doing drugs and getting involved with his old gang again. Yusef can't wait to tell Orlando.

"You're not going to help Paris the way you help me, are you?" Yusef asks as he tugs nonchalantly on a loose thread on the sleeve of his blazer.

"Would you want me to?" Orlando replies with surprise.

"No," Yusef shrugs. "You can see him if you want to every now and then, but not the way you see me."

"You don't have the right to tell me that," Orlando retorts angrily at Yusef's presumption but understands the source.

"Oh no, it's just that, you know, you don't have enough time," Yusef tries to recover. "You're tired, so you can't take anybody else."

Orlando can't argue with the "tired" observation, but unfortunately doesn't stop to contemplate its accuracy. "It's not your job to take care of me," he says crossly.

"I got you," Yusef catches the warning.

Orlando reassures Yusef that their relationship will grow, even if he becomes personally involved with one or several other students. What he doesn't tell Yusef is that he has no plans to cultivate a relationship with Paris, whom he considers "too smooth to trust." Unlike Yusef, who also possesses serious street credentials, Paris never shows vulnerability, perhaps because he has spent time in jail where he witnessed the consequences of weaknesses. In contrast, Yusef's defenses look more formidable than they are. He is hesitant to let people in, instead of determined to keep them out.

Chapter Twenty-five

———

J.V. AGAY SITS IN TIM HEARN'S AP chemistry class trying to maintain his poker face. It's Thursday, April 13, the day after J.V. learned that Hearn is leaving Rice in June. J.V. hasn't shown the pain he's been feeling for months about his father's life-threatening heart ailment. Maintaining a 97.8 average has kept his mind occupied, and Hearn's class provides the intellectual challenge he hungers for.

"He's the only teacher who really understands me," J.V. lamented after class yesterday. His normally intense eyes looked blank and his shoulders drooped like an abandoned child's.

Hearn made a point of telling his classes that his departure has nothing to do with them. "It's a professional move," he repeated to reassure his students, since most have been forsaken by older males. He added with emphasis, "Don't let anyone make you think otherwise."

Last Friday, Hearn sauntered into Orlando's office for his yearly evaluation, holding a copy of Orlando's assessment, which he had retrieved from his mailbox, between the thumb and index finger of his left hand as if it were a dead fish.

"You look nonplussed at the review," Orlando remarked as Hearn sat across from the principal at the round table. The science teacher's body sank into an uncharacteristic slouch, and his eyes looked around the room at everything but Orlando.

"That's true," Hearn shrugged as he dropped the assessment onto the table.

"Do you want to comment on that?" Orlando pressed.

"The evaluation was tepid," Hearn scoffed. He wanted to point out, with a chorus of obscenities, that Orlando hadn't observed even one class all year, yet gave him three instead of his usual four or five out of five in several categories. "I've done a damn good job and deserve a much higher rating."

Orlando responded defensively, criticizing Hearn for refusing to do projects and take his classes to the science labs downstairs for experiments.

Hearn made no effort to refute the charges because they were factually true, but he considered them irrelevant. Aside from exceptional youngsters, most Rice students are not easy to teach science to. Most arrive ill-prepared for chemistry and physics, and few display sufficient motivation to catch up. For all the school achieves, Hearn spends significant class time reviewing—and then re-reviewing—basic arithmetic and reading comprehension, so that students can decode chemistry and physics problems. Covering even a substantial proportion of the state curriculum becomes so difficult that projects are a luxury his students can't afford.

Besides, Hearn points out he doesn't have the time to mentor students properly for serious projects, which aren't mere busywork. Already he teaches two Regents chemistry and two physics classes, AP chemistry, a Regents biology review for students who failed previously, plus the Extended School Period, all of which he prepares for with meticulous care. He also has lunch duty, covers for absent teachers since he's at school every day, and takes care of all the school's science equipment.

Not being recognized for his contributions began almost immediately after being hired in July 1995. Hearn's assigned classroom had nothing but an old blackboard and a dozen desks. He spent the month renovating and rewiring the room, and he built his desk and a large demonstration table with shelves. All materials were purchased at Hearn's expense, and he outfitted the room with periodic tables, maps, clocks, and other teaching aids. Hearn started at Rice earning $32,000 a year, which rose to $40,000 this year, out of which he's spent almost $20,000 after taxes on equipping Rice for science education.

Hearn also rescued Rice's entire inventory of science equipment, which a demolition team was throwing out as they were gutting the basement to install new labs in August 1995. No one had thought to store the equipment elsewhere. Hearn put thousands of dollars' worth of apparatus in the empty swimming pool, then cleaned layers of soot off each piece. That no one thanked him was not a consideration at the time, but the lack of recognition eventually corroded his commitment to the school.

To some extent, science simply hasn't been a priority for administrators. "Never once in my five years here did Mr. Gober come downstairs to sit in on a lab." In truth, Hearn is proud of his students' comportment during the half-dozen times a year they perform an experiment. "Everyone goggled and aproned-up with no problem and handled the Bunsen burners without incident," he said. But Hearn chooses to spend time on basic skills rather than perform as many lab procedures as Orlando would like. Given the resources Rice has and the academic level of incoming freshmen, the school arguably does as well as can be expected at improving math and verbal skills. But the students are not at the point where Hearn can direct them to research-oriented endeavors and still cover the curriculum.

Realizing there was enough interest to form a serious science club, Hearn wrote a successful grant application last year and received $15,000 in total from the Toshiba America Foundation, the William E. Simon Fund, and IBM to create the Harlem Atmospheric Weather Observatory at Rice. Hearn spent eight weeks last summer working full-time without pay building the weather station. He installed instruments on the roof to measure wind direction and speed, humidity, temperature, and rainfall. He fed cables to his "command center," a small room he completely renovated across from his classroom and outfitted with a data-collecting station and a computer. Student volunteers take readings several times a day now and broadcast a weather report to the school with the morning announcements. Under Hearn's direction, they post information about storm fronts on maps in the hallway and his classroom, and they have submitted their data to the National Oceanographic and Atmospheric Administration.

The observatory was officially christened on December 7 when WABC-TV's Lee Goldberg broadcast the morning local weather report from it. At the opening ceremony afterward, C. Virginia Fields, Manhattan borough president, and representatives from the mayor's and governor's offices offered congratulatory remarks, both for the observatory's scientific contribution to Harlem and in honor of Rice's official acceptance as a Vanguard school, which Orlando announced publicly for the first time. Woody Dorsey, the African American manager of the 59th Street Con Edison station, was thanked for his contributions, as were representatives from National Action Council for Minorities in Engineering and Brooklyn Polytech.

Completely ignored in all the acknowledgements was Hearn. As several students remarked with resentment, Orlando "took all the glory." Hearn never complained but felt slighted.

As Hearn listened to Orlando at the evaluation meeting, he reflected on his career at Rice and considered the principal's complaints ridiculous to the point of insulting.

"Considering all the problems we have to deal with as teachers, I know I've performed exceptionally well," Hearn let his feelings show. "And this piece of paper"—he picked it back up with obvious disdain—"is of no consequence to me."

Anger flushed in Orlando's face. His nostrils flared as he took several quick breaths, then closed his notebook, signaling the end of the discussion.

"Are you returning to Rice next year?" Orlando asked suddenly.

Hearn hesitated. After being overlooked at the observatory opening, he interviewed at Frederick Douglass Academy, where several teachers disaffected with Orlando's leadership have migrated. At thirty-seven years of age, it seemed the right time for Hearn to switch to the public system for better salary and benefits. Hearn hadn't made a final decision and didn't want to resign yet, since he'd invested so much of himself in the school. But he realized Orlando was using the poor evaluation to push him out the door.

"Early in my career, Mr. Gober would shout me out at faculty meetings for teaching practices I devised," Hearn later recalls as he tries to analyze why Orlando wants him to leave. Hearn had developed a classroom management system the students named "Power Points" that has produced excellent results. Several teachers have adapted it to their teaching styles, and Orlando borrowed liberally from Hearn's innovations since becoming principal without recognizing the source. It made no sense that the principal was targeting him at this point.

After completing a master's of both arts and science in science education at Columbia University's Teachers College, Hearn began his career at an all-girls Catholic high school near his apartment on the Upper East Side. Although not Catholic, Hearn chose to teach at St. Jean Baptiste for three years out of frustration with the bureaucratic labyrinth imposed upon the public system's hiring and licensing processes.

Hearn then worked for a private tutoring company until he began at Rice in the summer of 1995. The transition to teaching mostly black and Latino boys from disadvantaged neighborhoods was challenging. As a former National Science Foundation graduate fellow with three published papers,

Hearn knew he had much to offer. In 1989, he walked away from a Ph.D. program at Cornell University and a career in lab research to go to Teachers College because "I realized I wanted to deal with people instead and felt more attracted to teens than college students. They're a tough crowd but not jaded, and I believed I could get them fired up about science. They're trying to figure out what type of a person they want to be, so I try to present myself as a model."

But he didn't know how to deal with "violence in the broad sense that characterizes inner-city culture." While Rice students are often loud and aggressive, "they're very upfront and honest, which is touching. But they also have a lot of inner turmoil, born of the prevalence of crime on the streets, that teachers have to deal with." Students sabotaged Hearn's lessons so severely during his first year he questioned whether he belonged there.

Throughout the following summer, Hearn contemplated solutions to his discipline problems but recalled nothing practical from his education classes at Columbia. Then he remembered a text, Randall Sprick's *Discipline in the Secondary Classroom*, which he had ordered several years earlier but never read.[1] The book, one of the first in the growing field of research Sprick refers to as "positive behavior support," articulates what struck Hearn immediately as a workable approach. Instead of getting caught in heated exchanges with students, he focused on observable behavior.

"Most students misbehave because they've never been taught how to act in the first place," Hearn reflected after seeing the new method work, "so they get into subjective disagreements with teachers about what it means to 'do your work,' arguing that slouching or staring out the window doesn't matter. But no one can dispute whether they're holding a pen. They might be thinking about sex through the whole period for all I know, but if I can get them to act attentive, chances are they're learning, and at least they're not bothering other students."

Hearn was the first teacher at Rice to begin the school year teaching classroom procedures instead of subject content—which Orlando eventually drafted as school policy but gave all the credit to Harry Wong. Hearn's approach is much stricter, beginning exactly one minute before the first period of the first day. Hearn positions himself just outside his classroom's doorway to check each student for dress code violations before allowing him inside. Chatter stops abruptly as students meet his penetrating blue eyes. Hearn often blushes, appearing angry at the sight of them, partly because he has very fair skin and white blond hair. He turns crimson literally in a heartbeat, although he's really fighting his natural shyness.

The seniors taking physics or AP chemistry act more relaxed but still fulfill Hearn's expectations, which all have grown to appreciate since they make passing much easier. These expectations are expressed in two fundamental modes of behavior: "working independently" (during lectures, demonstrations, and tests) and "working co-operatively" (during class discussions, group work, and lab experiments). As soon as the students sit down for their first class of the year, they are directed to copy from the blackboard detailed articulations of these modes:

While working independently, students are expected to:
(1) work quietly;
(2) be sitting in assigned seats;
(3) ask relevant questions after raising their hands and waiting to be recognized;
(4) show academic posture.

While working co-operatively, students are expected to:
(1) be sitting in assigned seats;
(2) talk quietly to colleagues seated next to them or to others in the work group;
(3) take turns talking about the subject at hand;
(4) show academic posture.

Hearn walked up and down his room's precisely ordered aisles, on Tuesday, September 14, coaching the juniors in the Regents chemistry class on note-taking. Other than the scratching of ballpoint pens on notebook paper, only the creak of Hearn's leather shoes on the tile floor could be heard. At first glance, he looks like a geek with a pen protector in his shirt pocket and a stopwatch hanging from a cord around his neck. There's a pedometer on his belt, which helped him determine that, on average, a teacher walks five miles a day. But these details are less quirks than aspects of the teaching persona Hearn has created to pique his students' curiosity.

For the next few days, Hearn explained his system and gave written quizzes, which constituted the grades for the week. On that Friday, he did a final review and then asked for a volunteer to again demonstrate correct academic sitting posture, "learning's observable starting point."

Spencer Longmore raised his hand, waited for a nod from Hearn, then picked up his notebook binder and sauntered over to the empty desk positioned at the front of the class facing the students. Both tall and muscular, Spencer took a sitting position with manly grace.

"Let's get some constructive criticism of Mr. Longmore's idea of academic posture," Hearn initiated the discussion the students have already had twice this week.

"His posture's okay, but his back is not pressed against the seat," Allan Sanders assessed. "And even though he's ready to work with his binder open, he's not bent over and waiting."

"He's not exhibiting extreme thirst but he is ready to go," Hearn replied as he paced to the front of the room then slid behind the demonstration table with its eight-foot-long, black slate top.

"Is his derriere placed appropriately with respect to the rest of his body?" Hearn asked, overenunciating the French term to the point of comedy. "We need an expert on derrieres."

Donel Nanton rises from his seat. A few inches shorter than Spencer and equally muscular, Donel flashes to the front of the room in a brightly colored shirt to inspect Spencer from various angles.

"His derriere is firmly on the back of his chair," Donel observed.

"Spencer Longmore's back, neck, shoulders, head, and derriere are basically vertical and that's appropriate for academic posture. It's also appropriate for job interviews and other applications in the real world," Hearn emphasized. "Now let's get even more specific about the signals Mr. Longmore is sending."

Spencer appreciates everything he's learning at Rice that prepares him for college and a career. "Minority kids fail because they're lazy and want to get money without working," Spencer later voiced his observations from growing up in the Bronx where few of his junior high school friends remain on track to graduate. "Even smart kids get lost without someone pushing them like Mr. Gober and Mr. Hearn. African American youth see rap artists and celebrities on TV and think becoming a star is the only way to success. They can't get there so they give up and turn to drugs, the fast way. They don't get to meet engineers from Con Ed and executives who are black and quietly make six figures, like we do at Rice."

"Spencer's feet are at a forty-five-degree angle," Alphonso Thompson offered.

"Like a duck?" Hearn quipped and got a few laughs.

"No, like a marine," Alphonso fired back. He's a handsome youth, about six feet tall, slim and light-skinned.

In early August, a Navy seaman waited outside Rice for Alphonso as summer school ended. The seaman, recently back in Harlem on leave, was stockier and several years older than Alphonso. He challenged Alphonso to a fight as soon as the junior opened the front door to go home. Alphonso swung wildly at the sailor, even though he had never met the man before and would almost certainly lose the match. Fortunately a classmate had walked out the door an instant before to find himself between the two combatants. He pulled Alphonso back into the school, calmed him down, and then went back out to discover that the seaman was acting on behalf of a cowardly friend who had been offended when Alphonso unknowingly "hit on" his girlfriend.

Alphonso's father, one of two single fathers at Rice, sent him to a military-style boot camp that teaches young men to control their tempers, for the rest of the summer.

"What else?" Hearn stood erect in dress shirt and tie, as if he were trying to look taller than his six feet. Were it not for the dry sense of humor that students catch onto as the year progresses, his bearing would seem irremediably military.

"All four legs of the desk are on the ground," Alphonso added, again almost barking back his response as if he were going to punctuate it with "Sir!"

"Good point. These single-piece desks have to last another twenty-five years or more. So leaning back is very hard on them," Hearn said with a slight snicker. The wooden desks bear gouges etched with ballpoint pens and protractors since the beginning of the civil rights movement.

Hearn adjusted his aviator-style glasses and surveyed the back of the room, then shouted, "Mr. Lindhart, are you awake?"

"Yes," Aston answered in a hollow voice.

"The signals you're sending with your body position make me think not so," Hearn remarked.

Aston sat up straighter but in slow motion.

"When I'm speaking, where should your eyes be?" Hearn asked, looking back at Alphonso.

"Looking at you," he replied.

"Exactly. Your eyes should be on the speaker. I might be checking your eyes especially during a demonstration. If you're not looking at me, a little voice in my head says 'I wonder if you're listening.' You might be, but not looking sends a signal," Hearn explained. "Also, if my superior officer, Mr. Orlando Gober, walks by this classroom and sees Mr. Lindhart with his eyes closed, that would send a signal to Mr. Gober about what goes on in this class. Now, maybe we're having a great discussion, but need I say more? We all draw conclusions, right or wrong, based on what we see."

Hearn is adamant about every detail of his expectations during the entire length of each period, all year. Surprisingly, not only do the students comply but they do so willingly.

The carrot and stick come in the form of the clipboard with his weekly record sheets that Hearn always carries. Hearn uses the sheets to calculate the 20-percent class participation portion of student grades. Unlike most teachers, Hearn doesn't base the performance mark on an overall impression or on notes taken haphazardly after class. Instead, he has devised a grading system that allows him to keep track of each student's compliance with his "working independently" or "working co-operatively" guidelines as he teaches.

Earlier in the week, Hearn handed out mock versions of his record sheet. Down the left side was a list of the students' names, while across the page were two columns for each school day, one shaded for demerits marked with abbreviations in Hearn's neat script and the other, without shading, chronicling positive behavior with another set of obscure letterings.

Hearn translated the abbreviations, explaining that each student is given an automatic 80-percent performance grade at the beginning of every class, which can be raised or lowered depending on how the student behaves. Showing his clipboard to the class as if it were the Holy Grail, Hearn noted that an A in the shaded area, for example, indicates a 10-percent reduction for lack of attention, as when a youngster stares out the window; a P, for posture, in the same column might record a student slouching. In the positive column, the letter Q chronicles questions asked or answered, just as a C, for proper conduct, indicates that a student read a passage aloud to the class, for example. Hearn has become so adept with his abbreviation matrix that he's able to keep a detailed account of each student's overt behavior in real time. Students can regain points lost as the period progresses, which encourages them to act positively even after mistakes have been made.

Basing classroom management on observable behavior appealed to Hearn as a scientist and helps him teach the scientific method since the students become accurate observers of their own behavior. Hearn keeps his weekly record sheets on file and students often review them to see how they ended up with a certain grade. "My system never forgets," Hearn points out, "and as long as I set myself up as a fair and consistent dictator to judge whether an action is rude or disrespectful, students rarely challenge my assessment."

Hearn admitted that his system demands time and energy. A daily grade has to be determined and calculated into weekly tallies. He began the practice of educating Rice students on how their grades are determined, extending his behavioral breakdown to academic categories—again without a word of acknowledgement from Orlando when it was made school policy. Worse, Orlando criticized Hearn for not posting his grades on the outside of his classroom every Friday. Hearn had already established a habit of reviewing grades with individual students at his desk. Had Orlando recognized Hearn's innovation, Hearn says he would have accommodated the principal's demand.

The Power Points system allows academically challenged students to earn close to a perfect 20 percent, so they need only 50 more points to pass. The same is true for all classes at Rice, but Hearn's approach gives the student the tools to determine their classroom performance grade with precision.

"The system works best for the worst-behaved students because it teaches them exactly what to do on a moment-to-moment basis and rewards them for it," Hearn observed. "The role-playing we do, like how to sit, get out notebooks, and hold a pen properly help make my expectations part of muscle memory." Amazingly, students who slouch their way through every other period sit erect and ready in Hearn's class.

The better students have as much motivation to comply since they would have great difficulty making the honor roll with a low class participation grade. "The bottom line is, my system allows me to teach," Hearn explained, pointing out that once it's in place, he can devote the entire period to content.

As a result, Hearn's students testify that since they are forced to pay attention and act like they are learning, they can't avoid absorbing knowledge regardless of how inspired they feel.

Watching student behavior in classrooms throughout Rice reveals that some teachers, such as Orlando and Olivene Browne, achieve order by virtue of the strength of their personalities. Most teachers, however, have neither the charisma nor the experience with inner-city students to teach effectively. Orlando instituted standardized rules and procedures to address this problem, and in significant measure, he learned the value of a systemic approach by observing the level of quiet focus Hearn achieves.

But rules and procedures haven't eliminated the low-level chaos that corrodes the learning process in many other classrooms. Consequently, several teachers who recognize Hearn's mastery have asked to sit in on his class. Afterward, Hearn explains his methodology, pointing out that the extreme level of detail he uses suits his personality and subject but isn't necessary. Steve DiMattia experienced difficulty during his first year, then adapted Hearn's system to his more relaxed approach. DiMattia grades classroom performance on far fewer behavioral categories and gives students additional leeway because class discussions are more integral to English than science classes. Brother Bill Sherlog, the juniors' religion, humanities, and U.S. history teacher, fashioned a simplified version, adding his eccentric sense of humor. Brother Sherlog classifies students into three behavioral categories—the quintessential student, the sponge, and the dissident—and grades accordingly.

Even Abbasse, a charismatic and physically intimidating figure, had his problems with defiant students when he was a teacher. "So I went to Hearn's system, and it worked well," he recalled. "I always tell teachers with classroom management problems to see Hearn. It's a great system for a novice, a timid veteran, or anyone in trouble."

Part of the underlying problem pertains to the lack of adequate training new teachers receive at education schools. "They read all this theory crap," Abbasse said, "but don't learn anything about the nuts and bolts of getting students to perform academically when they don't want to." Hearn couldn't recall one useful idea from his two master's degrees from Teachers College.

In practice, most teachers seek a successful balance of teacher- and child-centered pedagogies. "To say there's one model is ridiculous," Abbasse asserted. "Great teaching is like being a great thief. You take whatever works from whoever's doing it and mold it around your personality and your kids."

For Hearn, who had taken much from others too, the question was whether, regarding his relationship with Orlando, there would be honor among pedagogical thieves. Hearn looked at the ceiling, hesitating to answer Orlando's question about whether he would return next year. "I can't grow here as a teacher anymore," he thought. "As much as I love Rice and the students, I feel really tired."

"No," Hearn exhaled with relief. "I'm looking elsewhere."

"I'm sorry to hear that," Orlando replied but without much sincerity. Several weeks before the observatory ceremony in December, Orlando began predicting in private that Hearn would leave. But this "prediction" might well have been a self-fulfilling prophecy. "My gut belief is that white

Americans have a very difficult time with black Americans in positions of power," Orlando commented, "because all of us grow up with power in white hands. So when they have to 'bend' to a black person's point of view or telling them what to do—they'd be the first to deny it—I think it bothers white men far more than it does white women. There's something in each one of them—whether it's Mark Blanchard or Hearn or the Christian Brothers—that says when it gets to the point where I can't take him, meaning me, telling me to do certain things, then I'll go. I predicted when I became principal there would be a continual erosion of the white faculty because I'm the principal."

It never occurred to Orlando that his personality might be alienating his staff more than his skin color. When Orlando began at Rice, "a crew of young male white teachers were running the place," DiMattia recalled. "They were all really great teachers, but Orlando saw them as a cabal and set out to destroy them." Certainly some had no respect for Orlando and were trying to get rid of him. But Orlando's abrasiveness and racial attitudes contributed to the tension, as much as their aggressiveness.

While Orlando interprets opposition as racially motivated, teachers sometimes object when his leadership becomes "Soviet-style," as DiMattia describes it. "It was Mr. Gober's hubris to have evaluated Hearn not according to his value to the school, but whether he was conforming to his dictates. Hearn became a counterrevolutionary in Mr. Gober's eyes and had to be eliminated."

Hearn remains confounded that Orlando sees anything racial in their relationship. During Hearn's first year, there was a student who would call out racial epitaphs as Hearn taught. He'd shout "white" or "cornball" or worse and get his classmates laughing.

"Tyrone, maybe you're not behaving properly because something is clouding your vision," Orlando, then the dean of students, addressed the student in his office in a meeting with Hearn. "But if you think Mr. Hearn is a racist, does it make sense that he's married to a black woman?" Hearn's wife, Velva, grew up in Antigua and married Hearn eleven years ago.

"Nah," Tyrone shrugged.

"And does it make sense that Mr. Hearn chooses to come to Harlem to teach black teenagers if he's a racist?"

"Not really," Tyrone admitted.

The next day, Orlando made a point of visiting Hearn's classroom to address all the students. "Gentlemen, I used to think that a white man couldn't be a role model for young black men," he began with Hearn sitting to the side, "but recently because of Mr. Hearn, I've begun to rethink that."

"I hung on every word," Hearn recalled. "After that Mr. Gober wasn't a close associate, but just before he became principal we had a long talk in the teacher's lounge. For two hours, he complained about all the things he wanted to do at Rice but couldn't because the Christian Brothers tied his hands. He said he was feeling depressed and thinking of leaving." Hearn counseled Orlando to stay, saying he belonged at Rice and pointed out how much the students looked up to him.

"During my ten minutes of the conversation, I told him that teaching at Rice was a personal journey," Hearn remembers. "Before coming to Rice, I would cross 96th Street on the East Side and look north, then ask myself: 'What's life like up there? There's got to be something good going on in Harlem; people live there. What are they like?' All my friends said don't go up there but I said, 'Why not?'"

"How do you like teaching here?" Orlando asked.

"Where I grew up in Harrisburg, there were no blacks," Hearn answered. "The only memory I have is that they would sit behind me at the Hershey Bears hockey games and kick me in the head. I was afraid of blacks, but now they're just kids and I'm thrilled when I get them excited about science."

Orlando listened quietly, then ended the conversation politely. Hearn left feeling they had had a good talk and were growing closer. Instead Orlando acted with more reserve than before, and they never talked again in depth. In the opinion of Velva, Hearn's wife, Orlando is driven by jealousy. Right after the long talk, Orlando began politicking for the principal's position. "The problem is he wants to be master teacher, father, mentor, confidante, and friend to his students," she said. "It's not bad that he wants to be everything, but that makes it very difficult for him to work with others." As Orlando's influence grew at Rice, so did Hearn's. He became the de facto head of the science department even as Orlando wiped out department head positions in order to consolidate power. The respect Hearn earned from students grew as his classroom management system allowed him to reveal the depth of his knowledge of chemistry and physics. He wowed students with exploding hydrogen balloons and inspired them to learn.

In terms of outcome, Hearn's accomplishments don't seem overly impressive. "Every year out of about eighty chemistry students, fifteen to twenty would sit for the Regents exam," Hearn relates. "One year, I had eleven out of fifteen pass, while another year only one. Other years, eight out of fifteen would make it." When students showed an interest, Hearn was effective. Two years ago, Hearn had typically been able to cover only 30 percent of the Regents curriculum in senior physics. Two weeks before the exam in June, two seniors—one African American and the other Hispanic—took on the challenge of trying the exam. Hearn supplied review books and tutored the students after school. Both not only passed, but scored 77 and 78, respectively, which were respectable scores considering that 85 is designated as passing with distinction.

The chemistry and physics Regents exams aren't required for graduation by the state, but most Rice students, Hearn firmly believes, are capable of passing. "Unfortunately, the minority mentality gets in the way: 'I don't have to do anything; I'm black or Hispanic so I'm entitled. I don't have to work like an idiot. All I have to do is show up,' " Hearn says later, albeit reluctantly, then points out that his wife is far more critical. "With most students, there's no sense they really have to learn the material. Instead they care only about getting the diploma."

Evidence that many minority students don't work as hard as their white and Asian peers—because they don't have to, and few teenagers can be motivated otherwise—is found every year in the SAT results. African American students from families earning more than $100,000 a year score lower than white students from families making under $10,000.[2] This demographic includes what is impolitely referred to as "redneck trailer trash," and it would surely gall civil rights leaders to admit that these youngsters outperform their far more privileged children.

Out of necessity, Hearn gears his classes down and grades exams accordingly. He is able to get almost all his students to Rice's passing level by year's end, which is an accomplishment anyone would applaud after observing classes early in the year in which students still struggle with fractions and decimal points.

The Harlem Observatory gave students a science focal point under Hearn's direction, which precipitated a growing faction of the best students establishing a close relationship with, in Orlando's eyes, a rival. In addition, Orlando described Hearn as having an "extremely anal" personality, meaning he wouldn't approve the principal's plan to bring Yusef back next year.

After Hearn left his office, Orlando planned to recruit a black, or if necessary, Hispanic replacement. But there are few science teachers of any race available with credentials comparable to Hearn's. It was wishful thinking on Orlando's part to believe he could also find someone with refined classroom management skills honed specifically for inner-city students.

The next Tuesday morning, April 11, Hearn discovered that Orlando had e-mailed the faculty with a list of teachers who would not be returning to Rice next year, which included Hearn. Word of his departure soon spread through the student body.

"There he goes again," Velva commented that evening. "Mr. Gober wants to be the bearer of the news, the one who knows everything, and he wants to demonstrate that to everyone."

Hearn didn't want to tell his students for another month, but yesterday he was forced to address his departure. Today he looks down at J.V. and feels sorry for the young man. J.V., Greg, and Mark are the only juniors in the AP chemistry class, and Hearn was looking forward to teaching them again next year.

In addition to the juniors, only three of the class's fifteen seniors possess adequate math skills to pass the AP exam. Orlando forced the other seniors into the class as part of his stereotype-breaking agenda. But he hadn't convinced any of them to try, any more than he had consulted Hearn on the wisdom of placing them there. Orlando had simply imposed his vision on students such as Linwood without considering that as minorities, they knew they didn't need the AP credit to get into a mid-level college and get funded. This was another example, as both Hearn and DiMattia observed, of Orlando having a worthwhile idea, but his unwillingness to build consensus resulted in poor follow-through.

Even though Orlando had the school pay for the textbooks and the test at a cost of more than two hundred dollars per student, a predictable dance ensued. Only a few students regularly complete their homework, thwarting Hearn's ability to cover more than a third of the curriculum, which means the class has less content to study for Rice tests and exams. The midterm was necessarily light in scope, as the final will be, rewarding their sabotage. Worse, the handful of students who worked hard were held back and now have no chance of passing the AP exam. "J.V. might get a 2 out of 5, but no one else will get more than the lowest possible score," Hearn said with disgust. "Most won't even bother taking it. Hell, most won't bother to get a calculator out of their book bag to do a problem in class without my prompting. Meanwhile, J.V. and a few others are doing the calculations as I write out the problem."

J.V. was looking forward to trying the AP physics course next year and asking Hearn for private tutoring to prepare properly for the AP exam. Now he'll have to deal with a new first-year teacher, who almost certainly won't have Hearn's expertise. J.V. could have taken a scholarship to any other

Catholic high school with a much better academic record, but chose Rice because he feels uncomfortable around more affluent peers. Now he's beginning to regret that decision.

Hearn expects Orlando to initiate a second discussion to work out their differences and persuade him to stay at Rice. But days pass without a word from the principal.

Chapter Twenty-six

LAST FALL, STEVE DIMATTIA LEARNED how to deal with Orlando's demand for projects in a way that reduced their burden and could have saved Tim Hearn his job. At a curriculum meeting, Orlando chided DiMattia for not submitting his grades for the first report card two days in advance of the date marked on the school calendar. DiMattia replied that the grades were due on the calendar date, since there was no indication otherwise. Orlando insisted that two days before was school policy, which was news to DiMattia.

"The only reason you're saying that is because you're late and making up an excuse," Orlando boomed.

DiMattia argued vehemently and "we screamed at each other for five minutes. That was on a Friday, then I realized over the weekend that sometimes in Mr. Gober's world, two plus two equals five. The only solution was to play along or quit."

Afterward, DiMattia approached Orlando's insistence on projects with the "play-along" attitude. He simply designated certain essays as projects so he could provide a mark in that category. Orlando never questioned him nor had any interest in determining the truth. He knew DiMattia was a good teacher, so the only issue was whether he would comply with his orders, or at least appear to do so.

The other lesson DiMattia learned was that arguing honestly with Orlando carries no long-term consequences. On the following Monday, Orlando acted as if he and DiMattia had never exchanged a harsh word. What Orlando cannot and will not tolerate is being dismissed. "If I make him feel that I'm listening and he's in charge, he's okay," DiMattia attested. "Every boss expects his employees to carry out directives and express objections in a respectful manner at the appropriate time."

When Hearn's attitude toward Orlando's evaluation was dismissive, the principal felt invisible. Since Hearn is white, Orlando's emotional response was charged with anger rather than the sadness he might feel when dismissed by members of his own race. Had Hearn chosen to listen to Orlando's reasoning and then argued his case, regardless how forcefully, at least he would have been treating the principal as a man "possess[ing] a mind." The focus of the encounter would have shifted to proving whose mind was thinking more clearly. Orlando's racial agenda, vis-à-vis white teachers, has as much to do with this sensitivity as with his desire to preside over a predominately black faculty.

"Orlando can be quite reasonable when dealt with directly," DiMattia concluded. "Later at a faculty meeting, he was directing us all to do something. I made a suggestion; he thought about it a moment, then said, 'That's better,' and we went that way. He just has to be approached the right way."

———

Aside from intrafaculty disputes, preparing inner-city students for college takes its toll on teachers. "Every year, every teacher at Rice has to battle against the deeply ingrained distrust students here have of serious scholarship," DiMattia observes after classes on Friday, May 5. "If something looks hard, they assume it's beyond their abilities and feign disinterest. Even the brightest students like Kawone limit their intellectual development by shying away from challenges." A larger issue that underlies this distrust "is the fact Rice Men simply do not read. Every teacher complains that getting them to cover even the bare minimum of material is 'like pulling teeth.'"

Reading problems begin early in the life of most disadvantaged children. They start school with much smaller vocabularies than the children of professional parents, which correlates highly with significant differences in I.Q. Professional children average 117, compared to 79 for welfare children.[1] In addition, affluent parents display more sensitive and encouraging attitudes. They also involve their children in more complex discussions that stimulate intellectual development.

Nor does home life foster catching up. There are few, if any, books available in Rice students' apartments. The culture of reading is so foreign, Linwood says that it would not be cool to even talk about a book, let alone read anything beyond what's required for school. Even this is done sporadically. Linwood often questions the better students in the cafeteria before class to pick up a few details, so he can make a point in the class discussion.

Instead of reading, DiMattia notes, students ingest a steady diet of rap music and most carry notebooks with reams of lyrics. "There's nothing like rap in literature. It's an odd combination of killer, criminal, and powerless victim, and functions as the ultimate ploy: how better to keep a people down than turn them into pointless thugs?"

"Great books counter rap's corrosive influence," DiMattia argues. He also encourages reading as a habit so his students will have a chance to catch up to their peers at college. Other than a core group of six students in AP English—Aaron Ashe, Antuan Barnett, Isaiah Gonzales, Phil Tobias, Erin Davis, and Hayward Washington—and several in the general class, the response has not been encouraging. In December, Steve DiMattia threw all the assignments from his regular senior English class into the garbage. The essays were poorly composed and riddled with grammatical errors. "Their passivity is amazing," he remarked. "They act in class as if they have no intelligence and the teacher owns it all, so they have to rent his brain for the period. But then they can't take it home to do the assignment."

Instead, the passivity turns aggressive in the form of outbursts or destructive acts, such as pasting large orange and black posters all over his classroom, as one or several seniors in his regular English class did last month. The posters advertised the release of a rap album, which the student knew DiMattia despised, and they were coated with an adhesive that destroyed the expensive world map he had purchased for the classroom.

Most discouraging for DiMattia was the indifference afterward. No one ever came forward to claim responsibility and offer amends. The seniors didn't take up a collection to pay for the ruined map, nor did they apologize as a group for the lapse in judgment.

Such instances of ingratitude, along with constant resistance to learning among students, the school's lack of resources, and the heavy workload create for teachers what DiMattia calls the "Boxer Syndrome."

"Boxer is the giant horse in *Animal Farm* that works himself to death," DiMattia explains. "He paws the ground and says, 'I will work harder,' every time the pigs threaten to tear down the barn. Catholic educators are so dedicated to the cause that they tend to act like Boxer."

The teaching load at Catholic schools is often overwhelming. Every day, DiMattia has two general senior English classes, an AP English class, two junior SAT classes, a remedial reading class, plus Extended School Period. There's also lunch duty and forensics after school. In addition to class preparation at night and on the weekends, teachers spend an enormous amount of time grading assignments. Other than class participation, the grading categories Orlando insists upon—homework, quizzes, tests, essays, projects, and midterm and final exams—require correcting often on a weekly basis for six marking periods. For DiMattia, this adds up to a seventy-hour work week, in addition to maintaining a healthy relationship with his pregnant wife.

"I'm burnt out at the end of the year," DiMattia says as he looks forward to completing his fourth year at Rice. "But this time around, I'm so tired of being tired."

On Monday, May 15, DiMattia goes to pick up copies of one handout for the regular English classes and another for the SAT classes, but finds out that the copy machine is broken again.

"I'm killing myself to teach these kids," DiMattia declares as he walks away, "but the bosses don't care enough to do their job." He also recalls how often the school bus broke down, creating problems getting his debate team to and from competitions. Finally a donation paid for a new one, but from a resources point of view, it always seems to DiMattia that something is missing or broken, which adds unnecessarily to the frustrations of teaching. In fairness, the copy machine malfunctioned so often it was replaced, but the second machine performed so poorly that Brother Walderman christened it, "Never from the mind of Minolta."

At the same time, DiMattia realizes that "it will never matter how good I get at what I do at Rice; I'm going to get the same three-percent raise as the worst teacher in the building." Consequently DiMattia feels his motivation draining away. "There's no institutional way to recognize outstanding teaching. Maybe someday an enlightened administrator will advocate a merit-based system, but the mediocre teachers—and that's most of them—would scream and yell that what they do can't be measured, which is bullshit, or there's not enough of it to measure."

DiMattia contemplates his experience at Rice. On the one hand, he enjoys the "act of teaching" and believes he has much to give his students. He has an undergraduate degree in political science from Holy Cross and is currently completing a master's degree in history at Fordham University— both Jesuit institutions. In fact, he's a product of the entire range of Catholic schooling. DiMattia was educated by Dominican Sisters at the elementary level, then the Christian Brothers in high school. After graduating from Holy Cross in 1993, DiMattia taught a social justice class and worked as a grant writer at a Lasallian middle school in Manhattan for a year. For the next two years, DiMattia ran the development program at a Marionist high school in Hollywood, Florida.

DiMattia learned his teaching skills on the job. After absorbing what Hearn, Abbasse, and Dino Murphy offered—he still uses Dino's curriculum and notes for his English classes—DiMattia became competent at managing a classroom and bringing Rice's reluctant students into the world of literature, which he has enjoyed as a voracious reader since childhood.

DiMattia started the year with hope, especially for the AP class. "The AP exam focuses on purposeful language and why it's chosen to achieve an effect," DiMattia explained in September. "You need to focus on why the writer put the words on the page." Throughout the year, he could count on his core group to do the readings, initiate intelligent discussions, and write reasonably well-constructed essays. Other students such as Andre Barrett did the work but almost never spoke in class. But Linwood and several others clearly lacked the skills to be there.

On a major assignment about Kafka's *Metamorphosis,* a typical paragraph in Linwood's essay read:

> We all know that the 'Metamorphosis' mean's change. In the Metamorphosis Gregory had a physical change, emotionally change and mentally change. Before the change he would bring in money for the house and he was paying his fathers debt off. But now after his change they felt they no longer needed Gregory because he could do nothing for them. Gregory had Isolated himself from the rest of the family, he would lock all doors in his room so no-one could get in also at work he had been Isolated. Then after the change Gregory's father made him stay in his room all the times, which isolated him from everyone else. One last important thing would be Gregory's relationship with his sister, how it had faded out or away. Gregory's family became very annoy with Gregory they got tired of Gregory which Gregory notice's. Is this why Gregory went to a state of no return.

DiMattia didn't know where to stop laughing and start crying. But he gave the senior an 84 for handing in three typed pages with opening, closing, and main body paragraphs. As with AP chemistry, only a few students will take the AP exam, and none have a chance of passing since DiMattia has had to pace the curriculum so that students like Linwood could keep up. If he'd been able to do the class with only his core group, perhaps Aaron and one or two others would pass, DiMattia says.

But as DiMattia realizes, the success of Rice's high-end students is not the school's main goal. "Aside from my criticisms, the students here, compared to their peers at public school, pick up a resiliency that enables them to get to a functional level. They graduate and go on to college or jobs."

Since coming to Rice, DiMattia has wanted to have an impact on the school beyond his classroom. Last month, Abbasse told Orlando that he intends to return to public school next year and is considering several offers, including a teaching position at Frederick Douglass Academy. DiMattia submitted his name as the replacement, thinking he would make a competent dean of students and get involved in school policy decisions. The change, he hoped, would alleviate the weariness that's penetrating to the marrow in his teaching bones. But two weeks later, he withdrew from consideration and began looking for a public relations position in the financial industry. DiMattia realized that he wouldn't be able to work closely with Orlando. Not only is his top-down style frustrating for someone with initiative and a different perspective, but Orlando's temperamental disposition makes a daily working relationship difficult.

The Boxer Syndrome continues to take its toll. Mark Blanchard, the sophomores' English teacher, recently gave notice. Because of the salary limitations and stress of teaching, he's leaving to attend law school. Without any experience, Blanchard took over from a predecessor who became so frustrated trying to establish order in his classroom that he quit without notice in February last year. With Orlando's mentoring, Blanchard eventually earned the students' respect. But the daily battle to conduct meaningful discussions and get students to listen quietly seven periods a day has become a grind that twenty-seven-year-old Blanchard cannot bear to contemplate for the next three to four decades. For many young teachers, teaching at a Catholic school is like a two- to three-year stint with the Peace Corps. It fulfills the need to give back to society and help uplift those less fortunate. But the desire to continue on this difficult path wanes, and the most talented find much better career opportunities elsewhere.

Blanchard remarked that if he stayed at Rice he would "retire a millionaire: with a million aspirins, that is."

If DiMattia decides to leave Rice along with Hebinck, Blanchard, and Hearn, both the English and science departments will be decimated. In addition, Abbasse's potential departure poses a problem since the only current faculty member capable of taking over the critical position of dean of students is Kim Davis, who has no ambitions in that direction. Hiring an outside dean would likely fail, at least in the beginning, because he or she would have to get to know the students and learn to work with Orlando at the same time. The school year would likely become a lengthy training session at the students' expense.

The Boxer Syndrome is also affecting the principal. "Every year, my brother complains about being tired at the end of the year," Wylie Gober observes, "but this year it's worse than ever." Shortly after Samantha Brown died of the asthma attack in 1985, Orlando became a Type I diabetic and requires daily injections. Wylie worries that Orlando isn't taking care of himself, as he takes care of every student and detail at Rice, and remarks that his brother's mood swings are occurring more frequently.

Wylie hasn't voiced his concerns. "Orlando comes across as unapproachable, even for me, and I'm his brother," Wylie confesses. "People feel afraid to talk to him professionally or personally. He's more like our mom, and I'm like my dad, who's easier going. Orlando puts himself under tremendous pressure to get what he wants done as principal. He sets difficult, self-sacrificing tasks and works harder than anybody. Then he wants to be recognized and expects others to buckle under his vision. He grew up ten years before me when the black race was fighting to be recognized. But lately he's been saying, 'I'm tired of fighting battles.' "

Chapter Twenty-seven

————

AT THE BEGINNING OF MAY, Orlando complained about severe lung congestion as he has several times this year. He was also experiencing stomach upset and gas to the point where he ordered an herbal remedy to clean out his digestive system. His parents use it regularly and find that it boosts their energy levels. But when the remedy arrived, Orlando deferred taking it until the summer since he felt too fatigued to endure the purging. Instead, he started a regimen of vitamins and herbal teas, but he's still dragging.

On Tuesday, May 16, Orlando gets fired up at the awards assembly to honor the end of the fourth marking period. He sermonizes about the recent Million Mom March in Washington, D.C., on Mother's Day, when hundreds of thousands of demonstrators called for stricter gun laws. "Every year, five thousand young people are killed by handguns," Orlando's voice rises to a thundering climax, demanding in effect that the Second Amendment be repealed. Of course this has nothing to do with presenting academic and behavioral awards, but the exercise revives Orlando's radical spirit and seems to heal his ailing body.

Chatter at the back of the room inspires a quick transition to a lecture on "verbal violence" and "the harm we do to ourselves as a people." Orlando hits his preacher's cadence and beams with righteous energy.

Reinvigorated, Orlando turns back to giving out the awards. With both pleasure and surprise, he presents Kawone Williams with the "Student of the Month" certificate. For the first time in Kawone's high school career, he bounds to the podium for a behavior commendation and makes no attempt to mask his excitement. The inscrutable senior shakes the principal's hand vigorously and exclaims, "Damn." Orlando suppresses a laugh as Kawone walks away with the award honoring his shift in attitude—a minor miracle. As the year ends, Kawone almost acts friendly toward Linwood.

Next, a thin sophomore with a milky white complexion shakes hands with the principal, but looks shyly away as he accepts his behavior honor roll certificate. Orlando is pleased to the point where tears almost flow. Since coming to Rice in the fall, Mario Durando has never been a problem student, but he earned detentions regularly because of his friendship with another sophomore who acts out in class. Normally the youngsters would be separated and transferred to different classes. But Mario desperately needs his friend's support, so Orlando tolerated minor breaches of the conduct code as he nudged the boys gently toward compliance.

Eighteen months ago, shortly after New Year's Day, Mario's father accosted him, his mother, older brother, and a cousin at gunpoint. Four months earlier, Mario's mother had thrown the man out of their apartment in Washington Heights because of his long history of verbal and physical abuse, and pathological fits of jealousy. For several years, he insisted that she work at the family bodega, but then flew into rages, accusing her of taking drugs and cheating on him. Finally, she had enough. During a period of estrangement that followed, the father's behavior improved to the point where it seemed the couple could reconcile.

However, in early January 1998 he arrived at the family's apartment to return the CDs and stereo speakers that he'd borrowed from Mario for a Christmas party. When Mrs. Durando returned from work, her husband pulled out a gun and threatened to kill her. He demanded that everyone get down on their knees.

"I'm sick of you," she yelled defiantly and refused to obey. She stepped forward and challenged him to pull the trigger or get out.

Mr. Durando shot his wife to death in front of Mario, his brother, and his cousin, and then turned the handgun on himself.

After the funerals and a custody battle between the two sides of the family, Mario moved in with an aunt and her three daughters, including his cousin Elizabeth DeLeon, who worked in the Manhattan district attorney's office. She recommended that Mario transfer to a Catholic school. DeLeon believed the young man needed a warmer environment than the large neighborhood high school that he attended. She also worried that the guilt, depression, and sheer horror of witnessing his parents' murder-suicide would render Mario susceptible to drugs, gangs, and poor academic performance. Mario had no trouble qualifying academically for Rice. Naturally Brother Walderman was moved by the boy's story and the stoic determination he detected underneath Mario's emotional fragility. Brother arranged for a benefactor to pay Mario's tuition.

Making the behavior honor roll pleases Elizabeth DeLeon, who sits at the back of the cafeteria, more than Mario's high grades. At home, he retreats inward, or wanders off in the neighborhood and loses track of time. She worries these patterns indicate that Mario loses touch with reality. For DeLeon, the behavior citation shows that Mario is responding more to others and healing from the tragedy.

Orlando has little direct involvement with Mario, since the youngster never confides in him or in any other teacher or administrator. But the school's environment is clearly having a positive effect. Later in his office, Orlando talks at length about how he nurtures an environment conducive to overcoming such traumas. Unbeknownst to everyone else, Orlando's health is deteriorating, and he reaches for affirmations like lifejackets. For the next ten days, graduation preparations command Orlando's attention, allowing him to ignore how he feels. Insomnia plagues him, but instead of considering the cause, he focuses on the students. As soon as they arrive in the morning, Orlando's energies revive.

Then on Friday, May 26, the graduation breakfast for parents provides Orlando with a positive charge; he floats on a comforting emotional cloud for several more weeks and feels physically healed.

By 10:00 A.M. that morning, the parents, siblings, and other family members of seniors have gathered in the cafeteria and sit in groups with their imminent graduates. Orlando sits at the head table with Brother Walderman, Father Sam Taylor, and two ministers, including Elder Percy Hicks, the pastor of Linwood's church. The senior invited him, recognizing the preacher's invaluable guidance during his turbulent adolescent years.

As scrambled eggs and bacon are being served, Orlando sounds the day's theme: "These are the three most important words in the African American community: OUR YOUNG MEN." The audience applauds, and Orlando talks for several minutes about the value of Rice's graduates to the African American community. Then each senior comes to the podium beside the head table to pay homage to the person who has contributed most to his finishing high school on time.

"I thank God, without whom nothing is possible," Darren Elmore begins by acknowledging the divine, as does virtually every classmate. After the tragic loss of his two older brothers, he might have the least reason for gratitude. But Darren's voice quivers with emotion as tears of joy flow down his cheeks.

Darren's mother, a handsome and remarkably poised woman, walks gracefully to her son from the table where she sat with both her remaining sons and takes the young man's arm to steady his underlying grief—and hers. They lost Darren's father to mental illness, and his mother's second husband received a lengthy prison sentence several years ago. The family struggles constantly with poverty. Had Brother Walderman not matched Darren and his younger brother Devon with benefactors, neither would be able to attend Rice and finish high school.

Darren stills his trembling hands, then picks a red rose from the bouquet in front of the podium. He presents it to his mother, honoring her support during the last four years.

Most seniors give a rose to their mother, while some present it to a grandmother or sister. "This rose is for my grandma Rose," says one senior, "who helped me through my mother's death."

"I want to thank all the women in my family," Shawn Patterson intones eloquently despite his issues with the written word. Shawn wears an Oxford button-down shirt and dark chinos, looking like the Morehouse man he might become. "I want to take apart this rose and give petals to everyone who's been special in my life; my mother, my girlfriend, and my daughter, who inspires me."

On the way back to his seat, Shawn drops a petal into Orlando's hand that seems to burn a hole in his palm. Virtually every student, and many of the parents, make a point of expressing heartfelt thanks to the principal.

"I like to be lazy at times, but Mr. Gober pushed me to achieve," Andre Barrett confesses. "I wanted to just sit back and let senior year come to me, but he kept telling me to pick it up since academics is more important than basketball." Top universities all over the country had been trying to recruit Andre beginning in his sophomore year. Once he decided to accept Seton Hall's offer early this school year, he was content to do the minimum and stay on second honors. He didn't even have to fill out the college application forms or write an admissions essay. But Orlando warned that he wouldn't let him play basketball if he failed to make first honors.

Orlando's determination not to coddle his star athletes played out dramatically over the last week and a half. On the afternoon of Wednesday, May 17, the last day of school for the seniors, Orlando called Linwood, Kyle Cuffe, and several classmates to his office after hearing that the seniors had been "wilding out" in the fifth floor bookstore, throwing T-shirts and books at each other.

"You niggas is all scared. I hate being around scared niggas," Linwood scoffed as they waited outside the principal's office in the foyer. "You got all this education and don't know nothing; they not going to suspend you. We got finals starting tomorrow, and no matter what they're going to give you the diploma."

All five seniors calmed down, but Kyle continued to fret, since in addition to horsing around, he had hurled the F-word at Ish Rivera, the Spanish teacher, who investigated the ruckus in the bookstore.

Linwood pounced on Kyle's apprehension, saying that a basketball player getting into college, as Kyle did to St. John's, doesn't qualify as a legitimate admission.

Kyle ignored the ribbing. He knew he was in real trouble, while the others would get nothing more than a tongue lashing.

At the end of the day, Kyle was back in the lobby almost in tears. Orlando banned him from graduation exercises, since he didn't take responsibility for his actions, while the others did. Kyle will receive his diploma but won't walk down the aisle at St. Patrick's with his classmates.

"I'm going to tell my mommy," Kyle declared.

"I'll never forget that," Abbasse said later.

Kyle was upset at the thought of disappointing his father, who suffers from seizures. Not being able to see his son march up the aisle at St. Patrick's will upset him greatly.

"He cursed at Mr. Rivera loudly in front of other students," Abbasse recalled, "which made it impossible for us to reverse the decision."

For the following week, Kyle lobbied his teachers to speak on his behalf to the principal.

"In four years, I've never done anything wrong," he pleaded.

Brother DePiro agreed that he had a good point. DiMattia also expressed sympathy, but said, "I'm not going to get between you and Mr. Gober." He understood that Kyle's banishment is a matter of principle for Orlando that no amount of persuasion would temper.

"If I give in, he'll never learn the lesson," Orlando explains later. "Kyle has a bad attitude sometimes. When they lost against St. Ray's in the final, he wouldn't shake the winners' hands. Anyway, Kyle's not really losing anything, and he's still heading off to the big time. But I'm fed up with how spoiled these ballplayers can get. As soon as he got his scholarship to St. John's and the season was over, Kyle didn't bother working hard and slipped off the honor roll. Meanwhile, other guys are busting their butts so they get into college and get tuition assistance. Any double standard with athletes destroys a school's integrity. Other students who have to struggle get very bitter about special treatment, and it undermines their desire to achieve."

At the graduation breakfast, Rice's other basketball star, Andre Sweet, gives Orlando an educator's greatest reward: a spontaneous display of insight and maturity. Andre talks about how Rice, under Orlando's leadership, "pushed me in academics, basketball, and life. You helped me accept my role as a role model for my little brother and sister. I see now it's not really about me at all, but about them."

Again and again, seniors thank their principal for getting them to stop hanging out in the streets or playing video games, and do their homework instead. "His Black Panther spirit rubbed off on all of us," Ruben Barrero began, "and taught us the determination to keep going when we didn't want to do our work."

As the graduating class and parents echo deep appreciation, Orlando fights back tears. "I was overwhelmed with reassurances that I'm making a difference," he says afterward. "Hayward got up to say 'I love you' in public and confessed he used to see declarations like that as a sign of weakness. For his first two years here, he saw me as 'soft,' as the kids say. But it's amazing to see him make that transformation."

Orlando finds the breakfast as draining as it is exhilarating. "I started shaking because I wanted to burst out crying, or get up and leave. They pulled their stupid antics through the years, and I think what I'm doing isn't registering with these guys. But one after another came over and blew me away."

"Mr. Gober is the first black male to act as my father figure," says Rashidi Robinson from the podium. Rashidi is strikingly handsome in a new cobalt blue shirt and sleek navy khakis. Both he and Linwood Sessoms express true delight and bewilderment with "I never thought I'd be here today" and "Wow, I'm going to college now."

"Society says it can't be done," says Sheila Sessoms, Linwood's mother, punctuating the ceremony. "A shout-out for Mr. Gober, the first African American Catholic principal in New York City."

"I'm truly speechless," Orlando stutters blissfully.

By 6:50 P.M. that Friday evening, all the seniors and the faculty gather on the uptown side of St. Patrick's Cathedral. Teachers and administrators wear black graduation gowns, while the students don green gowns with yellow lapels, reflecting Rice's colors. To add Afrocentric flair, Orlando had stoles made from kinte cloth for each student. The stoles are narrow like a priest's and drape over each young man's shoulders, reaching to his waist.

On Orlando's cue, the students form two lines behind him, and the teachers assemble likewise behind the seniors. Orlando leads the procession around the cathedral's corner, then through the massive bronze doors at St. Patrick's front entrance. Beaming with the full range of fatherly emotions, Orlando enters the sacred cavern and walks up the center aisle with the graduating class in tow. Their joy is as palpable as the delight emanating from several hundred faces watching their sons, grandsons, and brothers.

To add to the intellectual dimensions of the event, Linwood dons a pair of drugstore glasses with wire-rimmed frames to impress the attractive young ladies in the audience. As usual, Linwood's mother pays no attention to her son's antics. She holds her hands to her chest and smiles, thoroughly entranced by the miracle of matriculation. Linwood's father stands near her in a pew on the north side of the transept in an expertly tailored navy blue suit. He wears his hair in six-inch dreads, and his eyes relinquish their "brooding stare," as Linwood describes his father's penetrating gaze that's "always checking out your heart." Linwood's father simply cannot speak throughout the entire event. Although both he and his wife graduated high school on time—unlike most parents here—the example he set afterward didn't helped his son's chances. He is caught in conflicting emotions of regret and pride, and seized by a profound sense of estrangement created by his long absences. Finally he is present at a most significant milestone in his son's life, but as an observer. Linwood resists sharing the event with him.

All around the cathedral, cameras flash and video cameras record the long-awaited walk that eighty-one freshmen began, but only forty-five seniors—minus Kyle Cuffe but including several students who came to Rice as sophomores—are finishing. The setting sun illuminates the magnificent rose window over the cathedral's main entrance behind the spectators. Soft light bathes the new graduates in an other-worldly glow as they approach the altar.

The seniors walk between rows of massive white marble columns that seem to lift toward the vaulted ceiling, rather than anchor the structure in bedrock, just as the shared aspirations of the graduates and their teachers and parents arch skyward.

The organist plays Sir Edward Elgar's "Pomp and Circumstance" as the graduates glide up the marble aisle. Indeed, the cathedral—dedicated 121 years ago, and still the continent's most impressive Gothic structure—is almost as much a work of air as stone. Over eight thousand organ pipes, some larger than a car, surround the congregation—not only in the choir loft behind, but in rooms around the altar and also above along both sides of the nave. The marble and granite forming St. Patrick's four-hundred-foot-long Latin cross design resonate like a sounding board, encapsulating everyone as if in a stone flute. All hearts beat to the music's pulse, heightening the sense of transcendent accomplishment.

As the seniors are seated in the first rows of pews, the faculty continues into the sanctuary where they sit alongside the altar. Meanwhile, Orlando proceeds to the lectern to the right of the altar. He looks down at the seniors and beams ecstatically at their achievement and the validation it brings him and the school. He can't help but think of those who didn't make it, especially if they should have. But the sheer joy of seeing those who kept faith, including Linwood and a dozen others he thought would not survive four years at Rice, overcomes his sense of loss.

Orlando congratulates the seniors on generating a total of $3.5 million in scholarships (this includes all the scholarships offered to Rice seniors, and most were accepted by at least five schools) and on posting a 99-percent college acceptance rate, with one senior enlisting in the Navy. He plans to speak at length, albeit extemporaneously, but the moment's emotions overwhelm him with fatherly joy and his preacher persona steps aside. Instead of forcing a speech, Orlando reads the main points from Mary McLeod Bethune's "Last Will and Testament," which was her farewell address to African American youth: "I leave you love; I leave you hope; I leave you the challenge of developing confidence in one another; I leave you a thirst for education; I leave you a respect for the use of power; I leave you faith; I leave you racial dignity; I leave you a desire to live harmoniously with your fellow man; I leave you, finally, a responsibility for your young people."[1]

Orlando then introduces Aaron Ashe, the valedictorian, who delivers the ceremony's most impressive remarks, capturing the Rice Man story so poignantly:

We struggled to get here and the struggle almost defeated us. I remember waking on many mornings exhausted by homework, hounded by deadlines, weary of essays, projects and class times, feeling alone and unappreciated, knowing I wanted to be free to make my own choices. But I arose and continued the struggle. I tucked in my shirt, put on my sweater and met the deadlines. Now I understand that because of this, I am ready to be free, and capable of making my own choices. We must struggle before we can be free.

Frederick Douglass understood this. He said: "If there is no struggle, there can be no progress." His work as an orator and abolitionist made the Civil War about emancipation; he knew that for Africans to enjoy full citizenship in this nation they must take arms and join in the struggle themselves. By the war's end, every black veteran could return to his family and say proudly, "We are free because we earned our freedom, and our freedom cannot be denied."

We too have earned our freedom, although it is a freedom of a different sort. We have the freedom to pursue opportunities; we have the freedom and the power to choose one path from another; to paint our own picture and not to have it painted for us. We can stand here tonight and say we are free because we earned it. . . . I remember many times when friends of mine were expelled and there was nothing I could do. They chose to end their struggle too soon. We must honor their choices as we learn from them. Because we persevered, we now understand that the struggle was worth it, that it made us men, and that it is what prepared us for the struggles to come.

That the war for emancipation from urban slavery is being fought in the classroom via academic and character formation is a profound insight Aaron expresses with mastery. He maintained a 95-percent average over four years, earning an appointment at West Point and an academic scholarship at Howard University, which he accepted. Aaron also talked about the volume of work. Since grades were required in five categories for all subjects on a weekly basis, with report cards issued six times a year, Rice students endure the student version of DiMattia's Boxer Syndrome. For students like Aaron, many of the assignments were sheer busywork. But for others, repetition broke down their resistance to the learning process and carried them through to graduation.

Both Abbasse and Widziewicz see Rice's success as somewhat deceptive. About ten seniors still read and write at the seventh to ninth grade levels, and yet all have been accepted into four-year college programs with grant and scholarship money. Others, such as Joe Carrington, lack the motivation to carry them through another four years, because as Widziewicz puts it, "all the mommies go home now: Mr. Gober-mommy, Mr. Widziewicz-mommy. At college they're going to have to do it for themselves. I tell the seniors I don't want to see you next year on 125th Street with that embarrassed smile saying, 'I didn't go to school because I didn't buy that chemistry book since it cost too much.' "

"More beneficial for some of these young men would be vocational or technical training," Widziewicz says and tries to communicate to students when appropriate. But as Abbasse says, "with the African American community especially, when you suggest to parents that their son should become a carpenter or a computer technician, they protest: 'What do you mean he can't be a doctor or a lawyer?' College is a status thing and if you mention anything else it's like, 'because I'm black?' "

Part of the problem is that there's literally a college for anyone with a high school diploma. One senior took the placement test for SUNY Purchase and his reading comprehension was assessed at the seventh grade level. Purchase turned him down but SUNY Old Westbury accepted him. He might be able to get his academic skills up to high school proficiency there over the next four years. Sadly, the only profession with standards low enough for such graduates is teaching.

Two-thirds of the graduating class has a legitimate shot at making it through a respectable college program. Linwood is determined to get his engineering degree, and he begins with a full load of remedial courses this summer at Hofstra.

Aaron ends his speech thanking his mother and father—significantly, almost all the seniors who did well academically or athletically had two parents actively involved in their lives.

Orlando then calls Brother Walderman to the lectern and announces that Rice's president would be leaving at the end of June after nine years during which he demonstrated "his absolute commitment to the young men he cared so deeply about. We might not always have agreed on day-to-day specifics, but we never wavered in our agreement that these young men came first and foremost in every decision we made."

The two men shake hands and hug warmly. For all of Orlando's critiques, he respects Brother's devotion to his boys and likes the man more than he admits. He also feels badly about how Brother Walderman's career is ending. Keeping Rice from bankruptcy and raising funds to assist the majority of students with tuition could be classified as a minor miracle. In fact, most of the seniors thanked Brother at the breakfast not only for welcoming them every morning, which provided enormous emotional stability in retrospect, but mostly for his financial help. In most cases, the scholarship,

SSP voucher, grant, or benefactor's support made the difference in their ability to attend the school.

Unfortunately Brother Walderman had to rely too much on a small group of generous alumni to perform his magic, Orlando relates later. The most philanthropic angel had been covering budget shortfalls with gifts of $100,000 a year or more. As lean as Brother's budgets were, he wasn't able to completely rectify income and expenses. Finally the alumnus said he wasn't going to provide any more funds to fill fiscal gaps.

Brother was criticized by the board of directors, Orlando said, until he spoke on Brother's behalf, pointing out that every year they approved the budget, sharing responsibility for the school's tenuous situation. Brother Walderman appreciated the support, saying later it was about time considering how often he had defended Orlando. Afterward, a Christian Brothers superior called Orlando asking for suggestions, which he understood as a way of pushing Brother Walderman out and offering the president's job to him. Orlando turned down the proposal, saying what Rice really needed was a professional fund-raiser and that Brother's tenure was not the issue.

"I've offered them so many suggestions about the programs I ran successfully at St. Mark's and never heard a word back," Orlando scoffed afterward. "We have to get away from the idea that we're owed anything. I'm very much against discrimination and I appreciate what the alumni do, but nobody's obliged to give us anything. Instead, we owe it to ourselves to do the things that build our dignity and solidify cogent plans for the future. Then we should look for assistance with matching grants and the like that augment what the families are generating."

Next year, Brother Walderman will take the Christian Brothers' version of a sabbatical and visit their schools in several countries. The departure has a bittersweet taste since Brother feels he has given all he could to the school and he's burning out. The reassignment has put him noticeably at ease over the last two weeks.

"Four years ago, I was the first person to speak to you when you entered Rice High School," Brother Walderman begins softly over the cathedral's hush. "Tonight, I am the last person to talk to you as you leave. The circle is complete."

Garbed in their graduation gowns, the seniors certainly heeded what Brother said four years ago: "You want to walk down that aisle at St. Patrick's as a senior and receive your diploma. This is your ticket to the next stop on the education train."

Brother takes a deep breath and launches into a long speech delivered almost at the speed of an auctioneer. He exhorts the first graduating class of the new century to take on the problems of the world—from atrocities, oppression, poverty, and war—and make a difference. For four years, Rice prepared them for this task, Brother emphasizes, by giving them an "education for L.I.F.E." He expounds on each letter in the acronym as Love, Involvement, Fortitude, and Enthusiasm.

To illustrate these qualities, Brother Walderman recites a well-known Teddy Roosevelt quote:

The credit belongs to the man who is actually in the arena, whose face is marred by sweat and blood; who strives valiantly; who errs, and comes short again and again because there is no effort without error and shortcoming; but who does actually strive to do the deeds; who knows the great enthusiasms, the great devotions; who spends himself in a worthy cause; who at best knows in the end the triumph of high achievement, and who at worst, if he fails, at least fails while daring greatly, so that his place shall never be with those cold and timid souls who know neither victory nor defeat.[2]

The "worthy cause," Brother reminds the graduates, should embrace the teachings of Jesus, just as the school included the Eucharist at last night's graduation Mass. Incorporating social justice and a relationship with God into their lives, Brother concludes, "will prepare you for the only admissions test that really counts—getting into heaven."

The Roosevelt quote provides eloquent perspective on the often flawed efforts of Brother, Orlando, Abbasse, and the teachers. These should be judged from the inner city's education battlefield, not from comfortable sidelines many socioeconomic rungs away.

Brother Walderman steps aside to allow Orlando to present the graduating class to the audience; they respond with a standing ovation. Orlando leads the procession of graduates back down the aisle to give back the sons, whose lives in great measure he took over four years ago, turning their boys into men. Families reunite on the front steps, their voices charged with excitement and a sense of accomplishment, as if St. Patrick's is exhaling them in a joyful parting song.

Linwood crowds around Orlando with several classmates as they pose for photographs.

"Oh my God, I feel four hundred pounds lighter," Orlando exclaims. A score of grateful goodbye hugs later, he slips away to meet the faculty for dinner at a nearby restaurant. Two years from now, he hopes to present Yusef with a Rice diploma, which he feels would provide a poetic end to his career as principal.

Meanwhile, Linwood finds his family and begrudgingly expresses that he's pleased to see his father. "He hasn't been around for two or three months, probably got locked up," Linwood said earlier. "I told my moms I didn't want him coming to my graduation. He crossed me before." But seeing him stand beside the family tall, handsome, and silent, Linwood's heart softens. "If he'd just stop thinking he's John Gotti," Linwood laments with a smile.

Joining the Sessomses is Linwood's SSP sponsor, Chris Hunt, who flew from Los Angeles with his fiancée to attend the ceremony. Linwood has talked often enough with Chris since freshman year that friendly conversation comes naturally. Linwood kids Hunt by questioning his beautiful girlfriend's choice of a future husband.

Linwood's father leaves ten minutes later to drive his father, who spent most of the ceremony in the car since his health is failing, home. Mrs. Sessoms returns to the Bronx with Linwood's older sister Ebony, who came home early from SUNY Albany because she's pregnant.

"Ebony just told my moms, so the abortion shit is dead," Linwood relates later. "She scared to tell my dad since he might kill her boyfriend. But my mom's the general; her mouth runs the family." As a result, Linwood feels little apprehension about his sister's future. His father will bend to his wife's will, and Ebony will finish her schooling since her mother's threat to kill her if she doesn't generates more fear in the long run than her father's anticipated anger.

Linwood walks across Fifth Avenue with Hunt and his fiancée. A clear twilight in translucent indigos brushes by St. Patrick's twin spires, then arches over a secular cathedral on the opposite side of the street. The Rockefeller Center's stone façade, lit by floodlights from below, soars above the seat of the archdiocese. But St. Patrick's still dominates the landscape, perhaps because Charles R. Morris's description of the cathedral as a "leaping prayer" in *American Catholic* still holds true.

Linwood turns up West 50th Street with Hunt and his future bride in tow, looking for a restaurant for dinner.

"We are stepping across the threshold as men, not only of Rice," Antuan Barnett, the salutatorian, said in his speech, "but of the world."

Chapter Twenty-eight

"THANKS TO MR. ABBASSE FOR KEEPING me here when he should have let me go," was a common refrain at the graduation breakfast. It was also an understatement. As Abbasse recalls, students like Linwood would tell teachers to "fuck off" and would even challenge him into their junior years. Half the seniors say they don't know why they were allowed to stay at Rice while many other students were expelled, seemingly for less. What they didn't understand is the deeply subjective side of Rice's strict behavioral demands. Together, Orlando and Abbasse made judgments about the long-term prognosis for troublemakers based on the degree of family support and sincerity of the student's efforts.

Inescapably their judgment involved how much they believed in a student. Once Orlando heard peers such as Yusef rat out Paris Lane, the principal's natural distrust of charismatic rivals took root. Prince and several other students fell under Paris's spell after the Christmas break, and both Orlando and Abbasse considered him a bad influence by then. After school, these students followed Paris to his neighborhood, around 116th Street and Frederick Douglass Avenue. It's not Harlem's worst area, and Paris's foster mother operates a well-organized, loving household. But Paris associates with local drug dealers and gang members, and he's never short of expensive clothes or cash. For Orlando, it was obvious that he was "back in the game," and there was no need for proof. There was nothing Paris was caught doing that warranted Orlando telling him not to return, so close to the last day of school, but Orlando isn't going to chance that Paris would endanger or corrupt any more of his boys. Who would better know the power of a pied piper than Orlando?

Paris possesses the most magnetic personality at Rice. In mid-February, Orlando presided over Rice's freestyle rap contest where Paris took command of the crowded gym and orchestrated a crescendo of approving responses as he fired off rhyming chants in a breathless barrage, "Sittin' down with my chick's moms / I'll be flippin' if she inflicts harms. . . ."

Paris began his triumphant last round in a confessional mode against Aaron Ashe, who had bested his opponents until this showdown. "No thanks to fools, the more shanks they use," Paris shot off. "I make gangsta moves smooth as Langston Hughes. . . ."

When he finished, students on all grade levels cheered wildly, pronouncing Paris the victor.

It was not, however, a triumph that Orlando appreciated. He feared Paris's lyrics were more descriptive than metaphorical. The same could be said for Yusef's, but he was staying clear of drugs and gangs, at least as far as Orlando could tell. As well, Orlando harbors no fears about Yusef's influence over other students, since he's a loner.

In May, Abbasse saw Paris exchanging something small with a classmate for a ten-dollar bill. The dean ordered both students to empty their pockets, but no drugs were found, although Paris had two hundred dollars in ten-dollar bills in his possession. Several other students attested that Paris was selling drugs at Rice. To make sure, Abbasse walked over to Paris's neighborhood after school, where residents confirmed that Paris was dealing and they even pointed out the exact street corner. Since Abbasse had already spoken to Paris several times about rumors he was selling contraband, he recommended strongly to Orlando that Paris be dismissed; the principal agreed.

Jahman McKenzie was also asked to leave. By the end of March, Jahman had earned dozens of detentions for talking back to teachers or making negative comments to students. Otherwise he was well behaved and kept himself on the honor roll with ease. No doubt he would qualify for highly selective Ivy League colleges as a senior. But both Orlando and Abbasse lost patience both with his attitude and the ineptitude of his parents to effect any improvement.

On parents' night in March, Abbasse had another in a series of long conversations with Jahman's father about his son's behavior, this time with Jahman present. Mr. McKenzie agreed with Abbasse's views on the importance of polity in the classroom.

"Do you know what these dreads mean?" Mr. McKenzie asked Abbasse, as he held out long strands of his hair. "These dreads mean academics and discipline; them mean we're strong like Haile Selassie, Malcolm X, and Bob Marley."

Abbasse quoted Marley's most famous song lyric in response: "Emancipate yourselves from mental slavery. None but ourselves can free our minds."

McKenzie sang the rest of the song, then told his son to listen intently to Abbasse and do what he says. "Mr. Abbasse's got dreads too, although they're a little different from ours." Abbasse had his hair down that evening.

Afterward, Abbasse expected to finally see an improvement in Jahman's attitude, but the freshman wasn't able or willing to curb his habit of throwing verbal darts whenever challenged. His classmates knew that any jibe would get him to respond with enough emotion to disrupt the classroom. By year's end, Abbasse concluded that his parents supported the idea of discipline but must in fact be spoiling him at home. He'd also come to dislike Jahman's arrogance and recommended that the young man not return in the fall. The principal concurred, even though he lamented losing such a bright student.

Expelling these and several other students represents a significant shift in administrative policy at Rice. Sitting at the graduation breakfast, Abbasse truly appreciated the dramatic change he'd helped engineer with students such as Linwood and Rashidi. "This year, they'd say something wrong, then look up to see me and apologize. The parameters Orlando and I established have been in place long enough that they understand their limits. Even when they got a detention, they'd say 'I know, I shouldn't have said or done that.'"

But continuing to midwife the same transformative process with the current underclassmen is taking its toll. When Abbasse turned forty-two in April, "one student came up to me at lunch and said, 'You don't look so good, Mr. Abbasse; you need to go to the gym.' Another told me I look like a pear." Shortly afterward, one of the cafeteria cooks told Abbasse that he looked good—for a forty-eight-year-old. The dean couldn't counter that he felt younger.

Nurturing hope against hope, Orlando and especially Abbasse spent considerable hours every week monitoring, disciplining, and counseling half a dozen students who in retrospect were clearly hopeless. One freshman continued his deliberately disruptive behavior almost into May because the administration felt sorry for his situation. The freshman's mother was terminally ill and his older siblings were "bums," as Orlando put it. The young man had few positive influences at home, but he happened to draw a very dedicated SSP sponsor. The man's advocacy motivated the SSP coordinators, the young man's social worker, and both Orlando and Abbasse to undertake a joint effort to reach the youngster.

Instead of responding in kind, the ninth grader sought every opportunity to challenge authority, including ducking out of a detention in full sight of Abbasse, then lying to his mother when the dean called her about the incident.

"He argues back, instigates, refuses responsibility, and he's a saboteur," Kate Hebinck assessed in mid-April. "When he's in class, things always go wrong. Today, another student asked where literary symbols come from and he said 'from your head.' Everybody thought that was so funny because of the sexual connotation. 'Head' is a word you can't say in class. So the student who asked the question was embarrassed and saved face by saying something back. Then the two of them went back and forth and ruined the class."

The troublesome student received few detentions until December, then became rebellious for reasons he never articulated since he resisted counseling. No matter how many times he met with Mrs. Lewis, Orlando, or Abbasse, he never let go of the smugly defiant persona that his mother encouraged by denying that her son was misbehaving, even after he admitted to stealing a test from a teacher's desk. By the end of April, he was put out of Rice, and social services put him into a group home.

Afterward, Abbasse regretted that he hadn't expelled the boy much sooner, judging that he would have had a much easier time finding a public school more amenable to his temperament. Most significantly, both Orlando and Abbasse again felt that dealing with him and other similar students caused them to neglect quiet classmates who were failing out and would have responded readily to their attention.

By far the student with the most detentions and suspensions by New Year's was Ephraim Yisreal. Many of his antics were outrageous, but always with such a humorous edge Abbasse couldn't stay angry at him. In February, he brought a harmonica to school, disrupted several lessons, and then sang a song in the new Spanish teacher's class about hair on her chest. The truth is she tended to wear low-cut tops that exposed what the freshmen thought only occurred on male bodies. Ephraim was given a suspension and warned that next time he'd be put on contract.

But soon afterward, he brought in an old camera he'd rigged to give the user a shock. With great enthusiasm, Ephraim walked around the cafeteria at lunch offering classmates the supposed chance to take photos of their friends. As usual, Abbasse had to squelch the urge to roar with laughter in order to discipline him. For Ephraim, the prospect of another detention or a day on suspension in Abbasse's office was almost a treat. He protested the punishment but admitted he enjoyed the time with Abbasse, who always kidded him. Often Ephraim looked forward to the end of the day when he knew Abbasse would give him attention and make him laugh.

At the end of March, Ephraim was caught putting liquid laxative into the jug of punch served to students at lunch. Fortunately only two students had to rush to the restroom since Prince heard about the plot and warned classmates. Finally, after four suspensions and over seventy-five detentions, Abbasse put Ephraim on contract on April 13 with his stepfather agreeing that there was nothing else either he or the dean could do. Two days later, Abbasse made Ephraim come in to school for Saturday detention with several others on contract to make them write letters about their ongoing battle with Rice's rules. Ephraim wrote:

> It's very hard being on contract. I thought it was going to be a walk in the park. It's not, you have to be on your Ps and Qs. . . . It's easy for me to do the right thing. But temptation. I can avoid temptation by staying away from bad influences like when someone challenges me to do something I know will get me into trouble. I can say no. I can not talk back to teachers and not try to make the class laugh. But temptation.

The letter showed Abbasse that Ephraim understood exactly what his problems were and how to deal with them. Of course, his methods were eccentric. In the first week of May, Brother Walderman found him sitting on the bench in the fifth-floor hallway during a morning class with his book bag open, and books and notebooks lying all over the bench and the floor nearby. As Brother approached from the stairwell on his way to Abbasse's office, Ephraim was busy cleaning his sneakers with white shoe polish. When Brother asked what he was doing, he looked up with a puzzled expression. Ephraim had seen Brother Walderman most mornings welcoming students, but after arriving late to the student orientation in September, he never learned the man's name or position.

In disjointed spurts, Ephraim explained he had a strong feeling he was going to get into trouble in his next class, so he decided "to chill out for a while." Brother grilled him about where he was supposed to be this period. Ephraim's answers made no sense to Rice's president, who didn't know Ephraim had permission from Abbasse to take time-outs. Nor did Brother realize that for Ephraim to sit on the bench until he felt self-composed represented a major step forward in the young man's struggle to take responsibility for his actions.

"I'm getting too old for this," Brother finally said and walked away.

Ephraim finished polishing his shoes, went to class, and got through the month without a behavioral blemish, thereby avoiding expulsion. He even earned the right to attend the final Rice Jam on May 13.

On June 9, the last day of classes, Orlando notes Ephraim's steady improvement and agrees that he should return especially since Abbasse recently decided to spend another year at Rice. Abbasse still plans to transition back to public education but has put it off another year, in large measure because he felt guilty about the number of freshmen who had been expelled or who were being told not to return. Abbasse is happily giving up his position as dean to take over the tenth grade math classes next fall where he'll continue working with this year's freshmen. Abbasse also wants to help train the new dean to ensure that the work he has done at Rice over the last decade isn't lost.

Most of Ephraim's teachers are pleased to see the young man continue. Aside from his eccentricities, he's a comedic joy in class. For example, when John Shea was covering Exodus in religion class, he asked what each student would do if he were Moses coming down from the mountain with the Ten Commandments in hand and saw his people regressing to idol worship.

"I'd tell them: 'Yo, shut up. This is God's joint," Ephraim replied.

In March, Shea read the story of Samson slaying a thousand Philistines with the jawbone of an ass. Ephraim recapitulated the biblical encounter writing that Samson's weapon of choice was a "butt-bone."

While the flipside of Orlando's sometimes vociferous scolding is his hugging-father persona, Abbasse acts like the doting uncle whenever he doesn't feel the need to be strict. Student who don't hug or dote back and get into trouble often run the risk of alienating the principal or dean.

Ricky Rodriguez was seldom personable with adults, but he expressed his appreciation for Abbasse's constant attention, which the dean found both charming and affirming.

"All the niggas do is act like fools," Ricky exclaimed at the end of May, articulating the unvarnished truth in his view. At lunch, he sat alone at the first table by the cafeteria's back door, as he had since October, observing his classmates at what Abbasse termed the "knucklehead table."

After the first marking period, Abbasse put the most troublesome students together so he could keep them from getting detentions for silly behavior from other teachers on cafeteria duty. Mostly he wanted to gather them together for informal group counseling in which he joked about their behavioral and academic problems as daily reminders. The table included the usual suspects: Prince, Nelson Castellano, Jahman, Dwayne Aiken, and six or seven others at various times. Of course, they threw food at each other and tried to get away with childish antics whenever Abbasse turned his back.

Ricky was included in this group, but only for a few days. Clearly his issues had nothing in common with these students, so Abbasse let him sit alone. Then "instead of letting me eat, Abbasse talked to me every day about controlling my temper," Ricky looked back over the year in June. "Kids was always picking on me trying to get me angry." Separating him from peers helped avoid confrontations.

In the spring, Ricky caught a classmate stealing money from his book bag. His first instinct was to take a swing, but Abbasse's ingrained warnings about consequences overpowered his desire for revenge. "Funny thing is as soon as everyone saw I wasn't going to hit him, they stopped bugging me. I learned a big lesson and earned respect at the same time."

For the first two marking periods, Ricky failed two subjects and was weak in several others. Then he started doing all of his homework every night— a seemingly obvious strategy that had never occurred to him until he heard it from teachers and administrators daily for months. Work that seemed difficult before soon became "mad easy" and Ricky's average shot up to 87.

But many of the "knuckleheads" and other failing freshmen resisted this simple prescription to the point where Abbasse, working with Hebinck, instituted a homework clinic in December. This allowed several students, including Prince and Nelson, to get their grades up to passing or close enough that they were both on track to return in the fall.

A big surprise is Nelson Castellano's change in attitude and work ethic. An uncle established a close relationship beginning in the Christmas break that transformed Nelson's outlook. Suddenly he displayed a strong faith in God and in the possibility that he had a better life planned for the two-time freshman. Nelson ends the school year with a smile, as he passed all his subjects, and plans to come back to Rice—and eventually go to college.

More surprising is Prince's finale. After steady improvement, he hung out more with Paris as the weather warmed and reverted to posting 10 out of

100 on homework English assignments. His complete essay for one assignment read: *This Ecclesiastes by King James Version is about time and a time to do something or lose something.*

"I really feel sorry for Prince," Orlando said. "He's such a good kid trying to get over the loss of parents. I tell him over and over all year, 'I love you and I want you to succeed. But you have to do your part.' But he refuses."

"I bent the rules because his grandmother had no control over him. He was basically on his own," Abbasse said about the large number of detentions teachers gave Prince that didn't result in him suspending the freshman. The dean kept prodding Prince and by the first week of June, there was enough improvement that it seemed Prince might fail one or two subjects but be able to return.

Then Prince received a detention for a minor infraction. Abbasse expected to see the young man's mischievous face at the end of the day in the cafeteria and intended to ask how he would get through the summer without their comedic repartee. Instead, Abbasse saw Prince slip out the front door on his way to meet Paris. Abbasse ran after and caught Prince at the corner of 125th and Lenox. Considering all the leeway Abbasse had given and how often he'd defended Prince's tenure with teachers lobbying for his dismissal, the dean took the escape as a personal insult. More importantly, Prince's disobedience was a public event that would result in his expulsion unless it was resolved immediately.

Abbasse told Prince to return to school and serve his detention. Prince shrugged his shoulders and walked away, saying he didn't feel like it today. Abbasse watched in shock as Prince rounded the corner with Paris to head west on 125th Street, the city's thoroughfare named after Dr. Martin Luther King, Jr., who would have boxed the young man's ears.

Abbasse trudged to Orlando's office feeling betrayed, and the principal was heartbroken. They had to put Prince out, and to send a strong message to other students, they wouldn't let him take his final exams on site. "No matter how much we did for him, he still had a very difficult time trusting adults," Orlando reflected. "He tested us all year as his way of saying, 'If they really love me, they're going to stick by me.' But there are limits."

"Often I warned Prince he was going to end up back at public school," Abbasse related. "He'd say, 'I don't care. I survived it before and I can survive it again.'"

"If only a male like me could have taken him into their home and worked with him. He needs twenty-four-hour parameters and support," Orlando lamented. "Then I'm sure he would have made it."

What makes one student take responsibility, while another makes a career out of avoiding it, involves the mystery of personal choice. Ricky Rodriguez faced the same family problems and neighborhood influences as his peers. He attended a low-performing public school and entered Rice with sixth-grade skills, poor study habits, and little sense of academic accountability. Throughout his freshman year, former friends and classmates on his block saw Ricky going to school in his Rice sweater vest.

"What you be doing in that school?" they sneered. "Why not cut class and hang with us?"

"Because I'm good at school and you ain't," he shot back.

Next came insults and threats, "but they never got a gun to back it up," Ricky says as the year ends. He recounts how he resisted the pull to make the easy and culturally approved choice to fail, which was especially strong in the fall. But the desire to please his mother and the confidence he could do so grew the longer he survived at Rice.

Another temptation manifested via the Rice vest, which Ricky found acted as a female magnet. Ricky's girlfriend, a junior at another Catholic high school in the Bronx, often competed with his homework for attention. She even tried to get pregnant, Ricky says, so they would have to get married. But Ricky understood "the point of Catholic school" in his conversation with Abbasse after the fight with Durrell. He resolved to submit to its discipline and avoid temptations. Still, without Abbasse's constant prodding, Ricky might have slid back into old patterns.

Unfortunately many of Ricky's classmates mistook the dean's prodding for the actual transformation he was pushing them to make. To be pointed at a destination is not the same as arriving there, or at least heading in that direction, as some students realized too late.

Another component in Orlando's decision to tighten behavioral standards next year is his desire to hang onto good teachers. He felt fortunate to have Hebinck at Rice for the last two years, but her competence has been undermined by childish student behavior.

"What's been missing in Mr. Gober's empowerment message is restraint," Hebinck commented with tired eyes in mid-May. "Too many students feel entitled to challenge authority other than his. With the white teachers especially, they seem to feel it's permissible to be rude on principle. A reverse discrimination is being fostered that spoils the classroom."

Hebinck finally told him about her plans to go to France. Then last week, Orlando promised her less tolerance of student misbehavior to entice her to reconsider returning in the fall. In response, Hebinck decides to return to Rice on the condition that she teach sophomore English. With more support from Orlando, she is confident she will be able to build on this year's accomplishments, even though there were fewer than hoped for.

The same third of her students repeatedly failed every marking period, although a few averaged 70 by June. Several others were close enough to get a boost from the principal. Of 121 freshmen who finished the year, 25 percent failed English. Hebinck says that if she were to write a book, she'd entitle it *The Not-Victim Book*. "The students in trouble wouldn't even copy down assignments," Hebinck recalls. "If I told them to take out their pens, the response, even if unstated, was, 'You want me to be responsible? What next?'"

In total, twelve freshmen failed more than two classes, and another seven were asked to leave for behavioral reasons. Three other freshmen say they will transfer to public school to avoid Rice's demands. There were far fewer multiple failures than after the first marking period, an improvement that should be credited partly to Hebinck's drilling of basic skills that helped her students perform better in all their classes.

Covering adverbs and other grammatical building blocks, and then teaching literary terms, style, and structure in short stories, poetry, and novels proved so much of a challenge that Hebinck had to "dumb down" her approach. But in retrospect, she laid a more solid foundation than was often apparent during the daily battle. Also Hebinck earned considerable respect in the students' eyes despite their behavior. At the end of February, two freshmen got into a scuffle in the seventh floor hallway and allowed her to get between them to break it up. "If a weaker teacher, especially a woman, had tried that," Abbasse said, "they would have pushed her aside and kept on fighting. Students show respect in weird ways like that. It helped that she makes the effort to go to their awards ceremonies and basketball games. Establishing a relationship outside the classroom aids enormously with classroom management."

The school year ends with Orlando enthused about next year's prospects. Not only are Hebinck and Abbasse returning, but it seems he'll be able to get rid of several teachers he considers incompetent. He fires Rene Bodie, the ninth-grade math teacher, pointing out that during her five years at Rice, she never once made a suggestion or asked a question related to the educational advancement of the students. Orlando might also be able to get rid of Lou DiMello, the gym teacher, who has been building a basketball camp business that might soon employ him full-time. Orlando also terminates the math teacher who replaced Jonathan Mason, who was also hired primarily because of his skin color. In fact, the replacement wasn't a math teacher, nor had he studied it at college. However, Orlando doesn't plan to change his recruitment preferences since his ideology fuels the hope that he'll attract a more competent and less diverse staff.

Fortunately such stalwart teachers as Brother Sherlog, John Shea, and Olivene Browne are returning in the fall. Bother DePiro is transferring to Archbishop Curley Notre Dame, a predominately Haitian and Latino high school, in Miami, Florida. He'll be missed as a competent math and religion teacher. He could have stayed at Rice but is choosing to continue his mission of teaching disadvantaged minorities at a school with a more supportive principal. While heartily agreeing that religion should be taught at Rice, Orlando sees it as the Brothers' purview rather than making it cool to be smart in religion class too, and the students consider religion a throwaway subject partly because he doesn't push to increase its academic demands. Although the administration can't afford to make religion a barrier to graduation, either Orlando or teachers adopting his approach could nurture a culture in which learning about Catholicism and world religions would be valued and rewarded more highly.

Ed Flood will be returning for his thirty-eighth year. It's entirely possible Rice's walls would fall down if he didn't. Although he is naturally taciturn, his carefully timed words of advice help new teachers adjust to Rice's teaching rigors. With a look or his mere presence, Flood transmits the essence of Rice's history and traditions, instantly stilling students who otherwise might act out and risk their seat at the school. The value of his constant influence on generations of Rice students is difficult to appreciate fully. Many current Rice Men talk about older brothers, cousins, uncles, or fathers who were taught by Flood, and the same is true among many of the alumni who return to support the school.

Chapter Twenty-nine

——

CLASSES END ON FRIDAY, JUNE 9, and two weeks later, Orlando feels that he's recovering from exhaustion. "Teaching the two English classes all year was very draining," Orlando says as he sits in his office. Memories of the various symptoms he has suffered all year slip away. Instead he voices concern for Abbasse's health, noting the dean's habit of going for a drink after work has been aggravating his stomach problems. During the day Abbasse still seems to live on Mountain Dew and he seldom eats.

Orlando enjoys a burst of energy after lunch as he plans next year's course offerings. "I love teaching, but it's very strange that I think I'm better at administering. I'm more relaxed and comfortable in the principal's role."

But Orlando can't get away from liking the experience of being in the classroom with students more than running the school. He decides to take over AP English next year since it will require only one small class a day. "It'll be easy," Orlando says, "since I can send them to the computer room often to do independent projects."

Orlando slots Steve DiMattia to take over the juniors' English courses, a demanding proposition with over one hundred students to prepare for next June's Regents exam. Not only does DiMattia have no desire to take on the eleventh-grade load, he has less motivation to give up the AP class, which was his most enjoyable period. He also feels far more qualified than Orlando, even though none of DiMattia's students passed the exam.

In New York State, 24 percent of African American students who took the AP English literature test scored high enough to earn college credit, compared to 68 percent of white students. Clearly there were public schools that did better than Rice in this regard. Rice's strength, however, lies more in getting their students through high school than in getting them to excel. DiMattia believes that both are possible, but it will take several years to build the entire English program, and especially the AP course—which he has been looking forward to doing—to the point where students can pass the AP exam.

Earlier this morning Orlando interviewed an African science teacher to replace Hearn. "He knows his stuff but I have the same feeling I did about Jonathan Mason," Orlando comments afterward, "that he won't be able to handle the kids."

"Education is not a unique experience," Kim Davis comments on Orlando's hiring policies later, far from the principal's ears. "You don't teach a particular group one way and another group another. It might seem better to take teachers who have something in common like being black or from New York. But many who do well here, like Hebinck and Shea, aren't from that mold, while many who are do poorly."

Orlando decides to hire the African, then brushes away his worries despite the fact that the new teacher will have more than double the number of juniors to deal with as Hearn, who floundered in his first year.

At 4:30 P.M., Orlando fields a call from Yusef, who has been working full-time at a local restaurant. He has been too busy to see the principal, but he calls regularly like a dutiful son. Yusef successfully completed the year at Our Saviour, to Orlando's delight. Perhaps he can bring Yusef back in September, but he's less needy now with his renewed vigor and with Yusef doing well at the Lutheran school. Playing varsity basketball has made Yusef feel more significant than he ever would at Rice.

Instead of taking time off to rest or go on a vacation, Orlando decides to teach the U.S. history and English Regents classes through July for those who failed the exams in June. Despite DiMattia's concerns, all the juniors passed the English Regents except for one, who will retake it in August. After screening *Eyes on the Prize* and spending much of February and March discussing the civil rights movement, Orlando focused on Regents prep exercises for the rest of the year. DiMattia graded the English Regents and said he was impressed with the quality of the student essays. He praised Orlando for relentlessly drumming vocabulary, literary elements, and composition skills into the juniors during the last months of the school year. In turn, Orlando complimented DiMattia and Hebinck for their roles in creating the writing rubric that proved pedagogically valuable.

Throughout July, Orlando teaches prep classes for both the English and U.S. history Regents since only four juniors failed U.S. history. By the end of the month, the classrooms become very uncomfortable because of the heat. Orlando complains to Wylie that he's very tired and suffering from severe indigestion.

On August 5, Orlando attends the evening reception for the parents of next year's new students, but according to his brother Wylie, "isn't himself at all." The next day, Wylie convinces Orlando to book a doctor's appointment for the following Wednesday, August 9. During the examination, Orlando refuses to take off his shoes to let the doctor inspect his feet, assuring him there is no problem in his extremities. Foot exams are a common procedure with diabetics, who often suffer injuries or develop sores without noticing due to loss of peripheral sensation. Regrettably, Wylie thought Orlando was merely being his normally obstinate self.

The doctor diagnoses Orlando with severe dehydration. After the appointment, Orlando insists on returning home by himself since the doctor's office is in Harlem close to his apartment. An hour later, he calls Wylie from a pay phone and leaves a message asking for bottled water and fresh fruit. He says he's too weak to shop for himself and had to stop several times on the way home. When Wylie got the message, he wasn't able to return the call, since his brother's phone was disconnected. In July, Orlando discovered that someone had stolen his phone card's access numbers and run up $747 in long distance charges. Orlando called the phone company but was treated rudely. He went immediately into protest mode and angrily refused to pay the bill, only to lose his service.

The day after the doctor's appointment, Thursday, August 10, Wylie arrives at Orlando's apartment building to drop off the water and fruit. Since Wylie is double-parked, Orlando comes downstairs to the lobby. He looks fatigued but manages to carry three heavy shopping bags to the elevator. Wylie notices Orlando is sweating profusely, and his shirt is soiled as if he'd thrown up on himself.

"He was losing sense of how he looked to others," Wylie recalls later. "He would never leave his apartment wearing socks and no shoes."

The next morning, Wylie returns to bring Orlando his paycheck and several documents from Rice to review. "He was sitting in his La-Z-Boy in his boxers," Wylie says. "There was a bad smell and I knew he was sick. Obviously he'd been throwing up because his blood sugar was getting so high his body was rejecting food. At some point, he must have stopped taking insulin. He was still coherent, but going in and out."

Orlando reassures Wylie he is all right and doesn't need anything more. Having been trained to render unquestioning obedience to his older sibling and principal, Wylie takes him at his word and leaves. Later that day, Wylie gets a call from the doctor saying Orlando's test results show that his blood sugar level is dangerously high at five times normal. The doctor tells Wylie to take his brother to the hospital immediately.

However, Wylie waits four days until the following Tuesday morning, August 15. He can't explain this delay, other than that he felt paralyzed with fear and couldn't summon the nerve to bring Orlando—his domineering father figure, mentor, and principal—the bad news.

At 11 A.M., Wylie knocks on Orlando's apartment door for twenty minutes before rousing his older brother.

"Wait a moment, I'm coming," a weak voice finally responds. Fifteen minutes later, the front door opens, and Orlando wobbles in the entrance way as an overpoweringly rancid odor tears at Wylie's nose. Orlando is still wearing the same boxers and T-shirt Wylie saw him in the previous Friday. His clothes have been soiled several times over now. Wylie determines that Orlando spent the entire weekend alone in his La-Z-Boy recliner in the living room and has become delirious.

Orlando leans on file cabinets just inside the front door with obvious difficulty in remaining erect. Wylie helps him back to his chair, then spends the next hour feeding him by hand. Orlando's sugar levels are still lethally high, and he can't keep any food down. Far more disturbing, Orlando's lower right leg has blackened, which Wylie recognizes as a sign that gangrene has set in.

"I'm going to call an ambulance and take you to Harlem General," Wylie finally finds the courage to say.

Orlando stirs from his delusional fever long enough to blurt out, "No, no, no. I'm okay. No ambulance."

Incredibly Wylie chooses to respect his older brother's wish despite the obvious emergency. He goes out to get Orlando some cash from a nearby ATM, then returns to feed him again, but two hours later, Orlando still can't get hold anything down.

Too intimidated to take charge, even in the face of an obvious health crisis, Wylie decides to return home to Brooklyn. Orlando has dominated his brother's decision-making so much since childhood that Wylie can't function without his approval. Al Widziewicz describes their relationship in Jungian terms, as having become each other's shadow. While Orlando took on the persona of *puer eternis*, "the eternal and omnipotent young male," Widziewicz explains, Wylie became utterly powerless and dependent. Wylie felt unable to leave Orlando's bright light and stand on his own. It is telling that it was Orlando instead of their parents who escorted Wylie to his freshmen student orientation in 1978. The shadow side for Orlando is now cast, in that the force of his personality cripples Wylie, endangering his own health.

Fortunately on his way back to Brooklyn, Wylie stops at Rice to seek advice from Brother Sherlog, who tells him to get Orlando to the hospital right away. Wylie agrees but then drives out to Brooklyn to get his brother Dennis, since he knows that Orlando won't agree to ambulance transport. Wylie plans to carry Orlando to his car with Dennis's help and then take him to the hospital.

By the time Wylie locates Dennis and gets him back to Orlando's apartment, eight more hours have passed and it's 11 P.M. This time Orlando makes no response to their loud knocking at his front door. Dennis and Wylie go back downstairs to get the custodian to open the apartment.

Once inside, they discover that Orlando has lost consciousness and is in critical condition. Wylie calls the city's Emergency Medical Service, which arrives quickly and puts Orlando on insulin in the apartment.

At the emergency room, the admitting doctor is amazed that Orlando survived the weekend with blood sugar levels over 600. "This man should not still be alive," the physician exclaims.

The next morning, a biopsy is performed on Orlando's right leg showing that the gangrene is spreading. Wylie has to sign permission papers to have Orlando's leg amputated above the knee or soon he will die. Although necessary at this point, giving assent proved very difficult for Wylie.

"One minute my strong brother was walking around telling people what to do," he says later. "Then he's in a coma dying, and I have to make decisions about his life."

Father Taylor administers last rites on Wednesday mid-morning, then he and Brothers Walderman, Sherlog, and DePiro pray at Orlando's bedside in shifts until he's taken to the operating room at 1:00 A.M. on Thursday. The surgeon gives Orlando a fifty-fifty chance of surviving for more than a few hours after the surgery, predicting that the infection had spread to his internal organs.

The bedside prayer vigil resumes after the operation as Orlando remains in a coma, hanging between life and death. To everyone's relief, that afternoon Orlando regains consciousness.

By the following Wednesday, August 23, Orlando progresses to the point where students and parents are allowed to visit. The sheer number of people making their way to his room has the staff of Harlem General wondering if Orlando might be a celebrity. For the principal, the outpouring of love and concern buoys his floundering spirit. Even students who failed out or were asked to leave, such as Prince, make the pilgrimage.

"It figures Gober would go to Harlem General," Linwood remarks half in sarcasm and half in a good-humored attempt to lighten the ponderous walk across Lenox Avenue at 135th Street to the hospital.

When Linwood enters the principal's private room, Orlando's eyes brighten noticeably but the oxygen mask prevents him from speaking. Linwood grasps the principal's hand and talks loudly about how he is ready for college.

Orlando struggles to sit up straight and fumbles to unlatch the oxygen mask. "Hallelujah," he finally stutters. "Let the bells ring out, Linwood says he's ready."

Linwood listens intently, struggling to decipher the principal's slurred speech. Orlando reaches awkwardly for a large plastic cup with a straw to discover it's empty. Linwood grabs the cup and almost runs out of the room to the nursing station to ask for more ice water.

Orlando has had an unquenchable thirst since regaining consciousness. When Linwood returns, he labors to convey how pleased he is that the young man immediately offered to refill his water cup.

To hide how much it disturbs him to see Orlando in such a broken state, Linwood launches into declarations of how he's going to "kick butt" at Hofstra in the fall. He has reason to be optimistic after just finishing the six-week remedial program on campus for incoming freshmen in need of an academic upgrade. Linwood says he applied the lessons he had learned at Rice diligently and so earned top grades.

Then he describes returning home earlier this week to see young men his own age hanging outside his project, talking as usual about "dazing somebody's dome to get respect."

"They're such idiots," Linwood shakes his head.

He mentions going to several parties in the last few days but feeling strangely out of place. "Can't wait to get back to Hofstra," Linwood says.

Five minutes later, Linwood storms out of Harlem General into the twilight. "How could Gober have disempowered himself like that?" Anger, disillusionment, and fear sweep back and forth across his face. "He's such a hypocrite. This shit didn't happen overnight; he must have known. How could he have allowed this to happen? He almost died."

After Linwood's departure, Orlando becomes groggy again. Despite appearing lucid during short conversations with visitors, he has limited awareness of his condition. His temperature is still high, and he is being given pain medication to such a degree that he doesn't yet know that he has lost his leg. Wylie quakes at the prospect of telling his big brother and has the surgeon handle the task two days later.

"How could you let this happen to me?" Orlando yells at Wylie the next afternoon. For several days, he blames various family members for what he describes as a betrayal.

Not until the following week, when Orlando is transferred to St. Luke's hospital on Amsterdam Avenue and 113th Street—where he believes he'll get better medical treatment as he recovers—does he express gratitude for Wylie getting him to the hospital in time to save his life and then making the difficult decision about his leg.

"He's a proud man and it was very hard for him to say thanks," Wylie says later. "The burden of guilt lifted from my shoulders. But why does he put the people he loves in such a tough position?"

Before leaving that evening, Wylie asks Orlando the overwhelming question: "How could you let this happen? You tell the students to be responsible and choose manhood but then allow this. Why couldn't you take care of yourself as well as a teenager?"

"I know," Orlando replies solemnly, without lashing out angrily, as Wylie expects. "I must have been in denial. I was feverish, but I thought I had the flu. It never occurred to me that these were symptoms of my sugar level spiking over 600."

"When did you start feeling sick?"

"Around the beginning of May," Orlando admits and shakes his head at the obvious absurdity.

"He does everything for the right reasons: to serve God and fight for our race," Wylie says. "But there's a selfish side to it. Look at how he didn't take care of himself and what it cost everyone. Instead of balancing out his life— taking vacations and developing friendships—he remains a loner so he can devote himself to work. Then he gets upset when the sacrifices don't get recognized. I hope he's learning to let go of the martyr role."

"If losing your leg and almost your life to diabetes doesn't make you wake up and examine yourself, will anything?" Al Widziewicz exclaims after visiting Orlando. He hopes the principal will finally "develop an observing ego, so he can reflect on himself, not just practically and physically, but also psychologically and spiritually. He created a caricature of himself or a mask, as we all do, to become successful, but he never takes it off, probably because then he'd have to look at himself and deal with the fact that he hasn't developed any healthy adult relationships."

Last year when Widziewicz began at Rice, "I asked him several times if he was taking care of himself, since as a therapist my observation was that he didn't. On a good day, he brushed me off, and on a bad day he reacted as if I was a racist, a condescending white guy know-it-all. So I backed off."

Physically, Orlando is beginning to heal, and his doctors announce that surprisingly he didn't suffer permanent liver and kidney damage. Emotionally, Orlando is comforted by the daily parade of students and parents from morning through the evening. He had no idea he was loved and appreciated so much, despite his disappointing and bewildering them with his illness. The response from the parents of seniors at graduation was overwhelming but understandable, since their sons were graduating and off to college. But freshmen and sophomore parents, many with sons experiencing behavioral and academic problems, stand by his bedside daily, offering prayers on his behalf. When Orlando began as principal, he had serious doubts about how far his boys and their mothers would go in the direction he wanted to take them. Lying in bed utterly helpless and vulnerable, Orlando feels more validated than at any point in his life.

Yusef visits but not often. The students who were closest to Orlando find it the most difficult to see him now so undone. Yusef phones every day and to please Orlando, pledges to stay out of trouble at Our Saviour and then graduate without losing any more time. This literally brings tears to Orlando's eyes, which Yusef can't help but hear as his former principal sobs, and he decides to fulfill the promise no matter how difficult that might be.

Rice teachers come to the hospital to discuss plans for the upcoming year and make Orlando feel that he's still in charge. The Christian Brothers have decided to pay Orlando's full salary for the coming year and hope he'll be able to return. Brother Walderman will stay on as president instead of taking his sabbatical, and Ish Rivera, who has taught Spanish for the last seventeen years at Rice, will handle administrative details in the newly created vice-principal position.

The results from the math Regents provide a challenge for the coming year. After 76 of the 108 sophomores failed the exam in June, Brother assured the parents of new students that Rice's math department would be "reinvented," and there would be significant improvement this year. Two of last year's teachers were fired, and Abbasse will prepare the sophomores for the Regents at the end of next year. However, the former dean of students might regret accepting the math challenge, since 69 of the 71 sophomores who retook the math Regents this summer failed again, some with single-digit grades.

Just before Labor Day weekend, Steve DiMattia arrives at St. Luke's to tell Orlando in person that he's resigning. "It is time for me to do something else," DiMattia says as he describes his new position as an account executive for an investor relations firm in midtown Manhattan. He makes no mention of his disappointment at losing the AP class and being assigned to the juniors. He took this as an insult and decided to endure no more of Rice's shortcomings. Still, DiMattia has a profound respect for Orlando and sees him as a flawed literary character who is as fascinating and inspiring as he is frustrating to deal with sometimes.

Orlando expresses his disappointment at DiMattia's departure and offers his blessing. The principal makes a point of telling DiMattia that Shayne Howze was the first student to visit him in the hospital, since the young man disrespected DiMattia often as a freshman.

"Sometimes even the ones with worst attitude come around," Orlando offers as tribute to their efforts over the last four years together.

After DiMattia departs, Orlando begins to mentally reconfigure the English department.

More than ever he wants to teach again and has no doubt he'll make it back to Rice. Orlando envisions walking into the school on his own without a wheelchair or a walker. He prays hourly that God will heal the open wound on his stump, cleanse him of all infection, and rehabilitate him quickly so that he can be fitted for an artificial leg by year's end.

———

Sorrow ripped through me as I stood at the foot of Orlando's bed in Harlem General's intensive care unit the day after the amputation. He hadn't fully regained consciousness and was still at risk of losing his life. Like everyone at Rice, I was in shock at seeing this dynamic educator reduced to the pathos of tubes and electrodes in the middle of an open ward, surrounded by a dozen other patients slipping through monitors into eternity. Would he join them? I gasped at the thought of the loss to Rice and the young men whose lives he touched so profoundly.

Orlando has faults, but the positives he brings to a school with so many at-risk students are incalculably more important. Although I agreed with Al Widziewicz's assessment, like him I was filled with sadness far more than any sense of judgment for Orlando's self-neglect.

I was also angry, but more at myself than him. Late last fall, Orlando was planning a celebration in North Carolina for his parents' fiftieth wedding anniversary. He told me that his mother suffered from diabetes, as did other members of his family. Reluctantly he admitted that he had the disease but insisted it was under control. I told him to let me know if any of his relatives suffered foot problems, since in researching an article about another disease, I discovered that a local hospital had developed a protocol, with a small number of other facilities across the country, for treating foot sores that decreased the amputation rate by 85 percent.[1]

I feared that Orlando's mother might be a prime candidate for foot problems. It never occurred to me that Orlando would develop foot wounds, nor did I detect any clues. He didn't limp and never mentioned open sores. Part of the problem is that diabetes patients lose sensation in their extremities. At the hospital, the clinic's chief physician told me about one patient, a construction worker, who happened to shoot a nail into his foot with a nail gun, but didn't realize it until he tried to take his boots off that evening.

Still, I felt responsible for not sensing that Orlando was in trouble. We spent several hours a day together, but he framed his struggles in emotional and ideological terms, which I took at face value. I knew he often wasn't eating properly, but his blood sugar levels seemed to affect his moods rather than indicate a health crisis. In hindsight, I should have pressed Orlando more about his condition since it was my job to observe, including what people hide.

Just after Labor Day, Orlando's hope of making a comeback at Rice suffers a setback. When he was first rushed to the emergency room, his other foot had open wounds too, but the surgeon decided that he might be able save it. However, the sores haven't healed much despite massive antibiotics. On September 7, Orlando's doctor informs him that gangrene is setting in and the foot should be removed, or again his life will be endangered.

Orlando refuses to comply, protesting angrily that he'll never be able to return to Rice if he loses both legs. The chances that he'd ever be able to dispense with a wheelchair would be minimal. Given Orlando's age and lack of natural athleticism, it's going to take months of exercise before he'll be able to walk unassisted with one artificial leg—and he might not ever master this beyond short distances.

"But Mr. Gober, the back of your heel is open," the doctor pleads. "You can put your finger right through it."

Orlando sends the surgeon away, declaring that his foot will heal. He anoints the foot with the holy oil that his aunt Lila Brown brought back from Israel in the summer. When Orlando was unconscious after the operation—in fact, in a coma—and his survival still uncertain, she anointed his forehead with the balm. Orlando awoke the next afternoon and began to recover.

Now he prays that the oil will close his wounds, since he sees no point in surviving if he can't work with his boys.

Several minutes later, Orlando proclaims—his voice still hoarse and unsteady—that "this experience has changed me. God always has to put me flat on my back before I'll listen, when it's about me."

Al Widziewicz worries that Orlando's turning inward is hampered by this religiosity. "He tends to get pious and say that 'God is going to heal me,' which is only part of the human equation." Widziewicz doesn't deny the power of faith, and Orlando could use some divine intervention. Diabetic patients who have suffered a lower-extremity amputation run a significantly higher risk of losing the other foot and of dying than nondiabetic patients.[2] "He still needs a mirror," Widziewicz insists.

But Orlando's capacity for self-reflection is bound by impatience at his own problems. Soon he concentrates on what's going to happen at Rice in his absence. Will the shift in school culture persist? Will boys study as hard and keep themselves on the honor roll? Will the racial consciousness he worked so hard to instill dissipate? Will his boys receive constant reassurance that they are loved, valued, and worthy? Then there's the father-wound problem and the counseling program he and others under his direction have instituted to address this gaping wound. Will the guidance department carry his torch or light their own and stray?

"I asked Steve DiMattia to do forensics as a major way of breaking stereotypes," Orlando reflects. "As a school, we've done so much in the past two years. Who would have thought these boys would like to play chess, join an investment club, or sing in the choir? I encountered so much opposition, not just because of the money, but due to the perception that basketball is all 'these boys' want. I had to prove them wrong. Now the brothers and all the teachers support these activities, but for how long?"

There's a plaque in Atlanta, Georgia, honoring Dr. Martin Luther King, Jr., with a quote from Genesis:

And they said one to another, behold, this dreamer cometh. Come now therefore, and let us slay him . . . and we shall see what will become of his dreams.[3]

No one would say that we have completely realized King's dream. But it endures as a national imperative that re-ignites whenever a charismatic leader, despite personal frailties, steps forward. More importantly, the means to realizing this dream has been institutionalized to a great extent at urban Catholic schools across the country. Disadvantaged minorities are equipped for equal opportunity by graduating from high school and earning college admission, or entry into the workforce or the military. By virtue of this education, their futures will be determined by the content of their characters far more than the color of their skins. That's not to say they won't encounter any prejudice, but this cuts both ways since many programs favor blacks and Hispanics who qualify by virtue of a sound education.

But in danger of being slain at Rice are the innovations that Orlando brought to the school if he can't return and, nationally, the entire nexus of institutions within which Catholic educators operate. Although practices that prove successful tend to receive tenure at Catholic schools regardless of changes in personnel, what Orlando had instituted, as well as his charisma, would be difficult to duplicate. He planned to train a successor before leaving Rice, and had hired Kim Davis with that long-term strategy in mind. There won't be major changes at Rice next year, but afterward Brother Walderman and Abbasse will leave. Will those who remain honor Orlando's legacy if he can't come back?

What Orlando accomplished at Rice constitutes an important contribution to the Catholic model's success with African American and Hispanic boys. But this continuing development and refinement is threatened by the ongoing financial crisis that puts the very existence of urban Catholic schools in question tragically at a time in our history when they constitute an invaluable component of the public mandate of providing a quality education to all our children.

The plight of inner-city Catholic schools presents a challenge both to the general public, since maintaining these schools is vital to the common good, and to Catholics, whose forebears built the institutions that facilitated their transition to the middle and upper classes. In the end, it is a moral question. Do disadvantaged children trapped in chronically failing public schools deserve to receive the education that the affluent demand for their children? And do they deserve it now? To counter that by saying we need to improve public education is both painfully obvious and beside the point. If that ever occurs, it won't manifest until the Catholic model is adopted in some form, regardless of how much money is spent. In the meantime, urban Catholic schools offer hope.

Epilogue

———

AT THE END OF OCTOBER 2000, Orlando is discharged from the hospital and returns to his apartment to continue recovering. A home-care attendant cooks for him, runs errands, and takes him to doctors' appointments. Happily the wounds on Orlando's remaining foot are beginning to close, to the amazement of his doctor—but not Aunt Lila.

In mid-November, Orlando meets with Rice's board of directors in midtown Manhattan. He's still feverish from his infections, and his stump is healing more slowly than expected. Orlando admits that he might never recover to the point where he can work full-time again. Board members suggest that he consider retiring, which Orlando takes as genuine concern for his health.

In the elevator after the meeting, Orlando hears a voice clearly say, "Do your job."

Orlando turns to Paris, his attendant, and asks, "What did you say?"

"I didn't say anything," Paris replies.

"But there's only you and me on this elevator, and I heard . . . ," Orlando begins angrily, but then is seized with the belief that the voice was God's. Later Orlando says, "He was telling me not to worry about my health, because he'll take care of that. He was saying to do my job and I'd be all right."

Orlando chooses to heed the voice and focus on rehabilitation. "I really had nothing to fear, so why not trust that I'd be able to return to Rice. I'd been in the death zone, so what else was there to fear? When God calls me back, I'm ready to go. Until then, I'll continue to do his work."

Throughout the school year, Orlando is consulted occasionally about administrative decisions, but otherwise he recovers steadily at home.

Meanwhile discipline problems increase. Brother Walderman is consumed with fund-raising, and Abbasse finds himself overwhelmed teaching math to the tenth graders. Ish Rivera became the new vice-principal, and Wylie Gober and Olivene Brown share the role of dean of students. All three are hard-working and caring, but inexperienced and lacking forceful personalities. In addition, they fail to consult with Abbasse, who could mentor them on how to establish order and deal effectively with difficult students. It should be kept in mind that even at its worst, Rice would be considered a behavioral showpiece as an urban public school.

"You and Mr. Gober could see when I was down or in trouble in the morning," Jose Mateo told Abbasse in late November. "You would talk to me and motivate me, but now the new deans wait until we get into trouble, then punish us."

One change Brother Walderman made was to demand behavior at the Rice Jams that reflects the school's Catholic values. After the first one in October, he remarked that he didn't have to explain to the young men what he meant by appropriate behavior. They knew and acted accordingly without incident.

Academically, Rice suffers from Orlando's racial hiring policies. The African immigrant he recruited to replace Tim Hearn lasted only a few months. He couldn't handle the students and quit without giving notice or covering much of the curriculum. A competent replacement couldn't be found, so all the junior and senior science classes are completing the year via online tutorials. Abbasse supervises some of these sessions and admits that very little is being accomplished.

For even the most experienced instructors, teaching students with low skills is difficult. Abbasse struggles to prepare the sophomores for the Regents math exam. Most students still have difficulty with basic computations, and math isn't Abbasse's specialty. Only 25 percent of the sophomores pass the June exam. Even so, Abbasse is pleased the results aren't worse than for previous classes. He was able to eliminate their propensity for distracting chatter and believes a significant proportion will pass in August.

The Christian Brothers' tradition of order and the memory of Orlando's scorching reprimands prevent serious discipline problems from developing. By spring, Orlando's wounds had finally healed, and he made a dramatic return at the graduation ceremonies in May 2001. After being wheeled to the front of St. Patrick's Cathedral, Orlando struggled to stand erect on his artificial leg to salute the graduates. These were the young men he taught the history of the civil rights struggle in their junior-year English classes.

However, only thirty-two of fifty-nine youngsters, or 54 percent of those who started together at Rice, were present. One student owed too much in back tuition to participate in the ceremony. Several students failed out of the lower grades, and about fifteen were put out by Orlando, mostly in his first year as principal when he established the emphasis on academics. Several others were asked to leave by the end of their junior year for behavioral and academic reasons, and about seven chose not to come back since Orlando's return was doubtful. Then Da'mar McBean was expelled for getting into a minor fight in the fall of his senior year. Abbasse said that this was an overreaction on the new administration's part, and there were several similarly unnecessary losses to other grades during the year.

Happily, attrition rates have improved for the current sophomores and juniors, who will lose about 25 percent of their classmates by graduation. Orlando's gamble is beginning to pay off, but he feels a deep and enduring sadness for those he lost among the 2000 and 2001 graduating classes since he was closest to these young men.

In September 2001, Orlando resumes his duties as full-time principal, but with limited capabilities. Getting around the building proves difficult, and taking the elevator to and from all seven floors consumes so much time that his classroom visits become less frequent. Orlando cannot reestablish himself as father figure and promoter of the academic focus he envisions for Rice with the same dynamism for the juniors and seniors whom he knew as ninth and tenth graders. His health remains problematic as he struggles to keep his diabetes under control. Orlando has lost considerable weight, and looks both fragile and considerably older. What Rice's juniors and seniors behold is a broken man with his humanity on full display—not the imposing leader they once held in awe.

Worse, the freshmen and sophomores, who had never met Orlando, have no memory of him as a formidable presence. He can neither live up to the mythical status they have heard about, nor do they have to deal with Abbasse as his enforcer. Abbasse chooses to stay another year, determined to improve math results, but he exerts little influence beyond the classroom since he teaches seven out of eight periods a day.

Nor is Orlando able to reassert the same Charlemagne persona, as Brother Maistre describes his top-down administrative approach. The other administrators and the teachers function well for the most part, but some of the cohesion that Orlando had established weakens. Lost is the overt push for standard procedures, weekly grade postings, and the use of the same writing rubric by all the English, history, and social studies teachers. Still, overall Rice students perform and behave better than the year before.

In June 2001, Brother Walderman leaves for his sabbatical, during which he travels to Christian Brothers schools around the world, paid for by a member of the board as a parting gift. A new president is appointed who, according to Orlando and other staff members, acts as if he's determined to put the school out of business. Although a Christian Brother, the man shows little interest in the students and their problems. Over the 2001–02 and 2002–03 academic years, he demonstrates implacable indifference to Orlando's educational vision and makes no effort to raise supporting funds. As a result, Orlando slides into an almost permanent state of rage, but without the strength to fight back effectively.

"Brother Walderman was really an angel," Orlando declares in his office in May 2003. "The truth is, I always respected him. I pushed him hard to get the most for Rice, and I blew up when I thought he could have done more. But I never doubted his sincerity."

In Steve DiMattia's view, Orlando put Brother Walderman in a very difficult position, demanding far more than he could possibly deliver. Brother Walderman tolerated Orlando's prodding and eventually they formed a working partnership, albeit one that Brother found draining to the point where he left with no intention of returning.

During the 2002–03 school year, Orlando has a more positive impact as most of the teachers are willing to follow his directives, even though he's not able to check up on them effectively. Yet by May, it becomes obvious that coming back to Rice was primarily an act of enormous will, a personal triumph, and the result of Orlando's fervent belief that it was God's will. The problem is that on the one hand, he can't return to the Orlando he was, and the continuing attempt wears on his physical and emotional well-being. On the other hand, Orlando refuses to accept his diminished capacity and move on, by either finding new ways to administer or acknowledging that he should shift careers.

After final exams in June 2003, Orlando and Rice part company. It's an anti-climactic end to a career of complete devotion to urban parochial education. Kim Davis observes that in many ways, Orlando is as much a Christian Brother as any member of the community. His commitment— or vow of obedience—to Edmund Rice's mandate of educating the children of the poor is absolute. Although his earnings far exceeded the poverty line, he spent much of his disposable income taking his boys out for dinner, arranging events for students on the academic and behavioral honor rolls, paying tuition for students with no other recourse, and giving out cash for countless lunches.

Rice's board of directors lets Orlando go for his own benefit and the school's, as he had begun to lose touch with reality in the spring. He talked at faculty meetings about being healthier than ever, but as Brother Sherlog observed, in reality his diabetes was worsening again, as the accumulating stress of working with a recalcitrant president agitated his condition. "You could see the euphoria and then the crash according to Mr. Gober's blood sugar levels."

"The last two years were difficult for Mr. Gober, but the school still ran pretty well," Brother Sherlog says after Orlando's departure. "He wasn't happy about not being as involved with the students or able to control the teachers so tightly, but most of what he'd put in place persisted as long as he was in the building."

Unfortunately, this changes significantly over the next few years. Olivene Browne takes over as the interim principal for the 2003–04 school year, partly so the board can conduct a search for a permanent replacement and partly, she says, to pacify the significant number of parents who threaten to take their sons out of Rice in response to Orlando's dismissal.

Although some faculty and board members suggest Kim Davis as principal, they regrettably decided to pursue Franklin N. Caesar, who holds a doctorate in education and is the headmaster at Loyola High School on the Upper East Side. Although one could walk from Loyola to Rice in about half an hour, the institutions couldn't be farther apart demographically. Loyola is a Jesuit high school in an exclusive area, rivaling the best private academies in the country—and charges $22,000 a year in tuition.[1]

Caesar demands such a high salary that a board member pays him an additional $30,000 out of his own pocket.

What soon becomes apparent after Caesar takes over in September 2004 from Browne, whose tenure was adequate, is that although African American, he lacks the most important qualification for his job: expertise about how to educate inner-city minority students. Worse, Caesar interviewed as part of a team, with an experienced vice-principal and dean of students he promised to bring with him to Rice. When his team decided to take other positions, he neglected to inform the board, instead arriving in late August with a different duo who proved woefully ineffectual. The new vice-principal is a recent college graduate whose attitude toward Rice students Brother Maistre likens to that of "a bleeding heart white liberal coming to Harlem to save those poor little black kids, instead of trying to help fellow African Americans. Caesar is exactly the same."

Most appalling is the new dean of students, whose only experience with urban youth consists of a management position at the Gap. He leaves Rice a few months later. Caesar then hires an unemployed teacher with severe mental problems. The entire administrative team fails to establish order from the first day of school and increasingly, chaos rules. Behavioral standards disintegrate to the point where the Student Sponsor Partners program pulls out of Rice, the fiscal equivalent of a death sentence. The school cannot survive long after losing the 20 percent of students whose tuition is always paid in full. The 2005 freshman class threatens to be one of the smallest ever, and perhaps Rice's last.

Meanwhile Orlando is hired to teach an education leadership course at Mercy College in the Bronx. He also runs the teaching fellows program for older students seeking a second career as a teacher. At the same time, he resumes his rehabilitation regime and finally learns to walk on his artificial leg.

By the summer of 2005, Orlando longs to be involved with K–12 students again. He takes a position at an elementary charter school in the Bronx mentoring teachers-in-training on classroom management. "I'm finally getting a fantastic salary," Orlando says. "I feel great and have time for a social life. Yusef graduated from Saviour and came by for Father's Day. He's working, living with his girlfriend, and they have a new baby—almost makes me a grandfather."

However, Orlando soon grows exasperated with the charter school's younger and less experienced administrators. He sees their ideas about how to teach African American and Hispanic children as hopelessly naïve. The school's arts focus attracted Orlando, but behavior standards are too lax, and academics aren't emphasized enough to prepare students adequately for high school. As well, anathema to Orlando's approach is allowing students to call their teachers by their first names. And the protocol for administrative decisions involves sitting down with the entire team to talk about their feelings, which annoys Orlando terribly.

Orlando searches for a better situation and receives several offers, including the job of turning around a floundering charter school in Brooklyn. He also considers becoming the director of curriculum at Promise Academy I and II, a consortium of K–12 charter schools being launched in Harlem by Geoffrey Canada's Harlem Children's Zone.

On Labor Day afternoon, Orlando meets with longtime friend and advisor Gail Foster in Jackie Robinson Park outside his apartment building. He talks about eating well, finally taking time to relax, and no longer needing insulin. Orlando also speaks at length about his spiritual journey since losing his leg and then his position at Rice. Rather than falling into depression, Orlando maintains that "I was never bitter, but searched instead for what God wanted me to do next."

Turning around the school in Brooklyn appeals to Orlando's strength, but Foster counsels against the competency of the people in charge. Orlando responds that this is what he's been dealing with his entire career. As the twentieth anniversary of Samantha Brown's death approaches, Orlando is sensing a release from the burden that her loss placed on him: complete devotion regardless of personal cost. In truth, this was part of his persona anyway, but the enormous guilt Orlando experienced pushed him to extremes.

Orlando decides to accept the position at Promise Academy, which pays well for limited duties and low stress. Promise Academy I opened in September 2004 and soon ran smoothly. Promise Academy II is to open next week, and preparations are on track. As director, Orlando will be able to mold the curriculum around his dual principles of academic excellence and Afrocentric focus. He'll have contact with the students, but without the awesome burden of fulfilling the father role for hundreds of needy youngsters.

When Foster leaves for home, Orlando is at peace with the realization that Promise Academy resonates most with his current needs and aspirations, and he looks forward to the final interview with Canada, scheduled for tomorrow morning. Finally Orlando is accepting a full-time position that will allow him to leave around 4 P.M. without feeling exhausted and with the time to develop personal relationships.

The interview, however, never takes place because Orlando doesn't show up. His brother Wylie calls on Tuesday evening to see how it went, but there's no answer, and the same on Wednesday. By Thursday, Wylie fears something is wrong and calls the police, who enter Orlando's apartment to find that Orlando passed away in his sleep early on Tuesday, September 6.

An autopsy is never performed, so the exact cause of death remains uncertain. There is no wake and the funeral isn't held until Monday, September 19, because Orlando's father lost an older brother the day after he learned about his son's death. Willie Gober went to his brother's funeral in Ohio, before driving to New York to bury Orlando. About four hundred former students attend the service at Orlando's parish church, St. Charles Borromeo, in Harlem. Many others can't go because they are starting the academic year at colleges out of town.

Several Rice Men called out Goberisms, such as "Empower yourself and each other," during the liturgy. "Mr. Gober inspired me to achieve more than I ever thought I could," Victor Ramirez stood up to say when Monsignor Harris asked for testimonials. Victor graduated in 1998 and then went to Fordham University where he earned a bachelor's degree in communications. He now works for a sports marketing firm.

Gail Foster, the last person to see Orlando alive—and the woman he admitted privately that he always wanted to marry—delivered the eulogy. "Orlando's stand on academic excellence took on the drama of a Hollywood movie when he refused to let Shagari, who'd become a highly recruited starter, participate in the state basketball finals, because he failed to meet the grade academically," Foster recounted, concerning Orlando's last year as principal. "The team went upstate to play, and Mr. Gober stayed behind in his office waiting for the phone call about the final score. If they lost, he knew he would be out of a job." Since Brother Walderman was no longer at Rice, and Orlando made no attempt to conceal his disgust for the new president, this wasn't an exaggeration. The Rice Raiders won the state championship anyway, leaving Orlando both validated and bitter.

Holding back tears after the service, Ikay Henry remarks that " 'conform or leave' was the greatest thing I ever heard. Gober laid down the rules of school and life, and he didn't sugarcoat it. You can't mess around and you need the best education." Ikay graduated from Hampton University with a bachelor's degree in business management and was hired as project coordinator in New York City's Department of Small Business Services. "I had a really bad temper and wouldn't have made it through without him straightening me out."

Orlando's boys offer condolences to his father and his brothers Wylie, Dennis, and Alphonso. Rice Men mill around the church steps both before and after the funeral, uncertain of what to say or do, still stunned by the suddenness of Orlando's passing. "Mr. G. was like Superman to all of us; no matter what happened, he always bounced back," says Mark Johnson '02. "He was the most giving and strongest-willed person I ever met. I can't believe he's gone." Mark listened to Orlando's exhortations when just getting his high school diploma seemed impossible and discovered that he had substantial academic talent. Mark is now starting his senior year at Columbia University on scholarship.

Also at Columbia, majoring in pre-medicine and Latin studies, is Greg Vazquez, who says goodbye to the "dad of the school who oversaw us all, and I sure needed it when we were homeless. There's a big dent in my heart."

"OG challenged every young man according to his ability and pushed me way beyond where I thought I could go," says Jordan Jones, a senior at the University of Michigan majoring in engineering. He also plans to pursue a master's degree there. Jordan recalls how Orlando counseled him tenderly when his family was forced to live in homeless shelters. Instead of letting these personal problems become excuses, the principal demanded even higher performance, so he could get into an elite college on scholarship.

"We consider ourselves Rice brothers because of Gober," says Kawone Williams in a soft but raw voice. "We built camaraderie and didn't leave high school hating each other." Considering Kawone's acerbic tendencies, this is a tribute to the sense of community Orlando built among the students. Kawone graduated from Iona College and works as a teacher's assistant at a charter school in Harlem. He seems the most unlikely Rice Man to follow Orlando's career path, but Kawone discovered a passion for helping neighborhood youngsters succeed. In fact, other faculty members often call on him to deal with students acting out in the classroom. As Kawone perceives in retrospect, he absorbed the essentials of counseling during his four years with Orlando and Abbasse.

"Mr. Gober got rid of the N-word, and he always said that 'we are male by birth, but men by choice,'" Calvet Liburd chokes on his grief as he watches Orlando's casket being loaded into the hearse. "I remember this quote every day." Calvet is majoring in sports psychology at Morgan State University in Baltimore.

Yusef shuffles out of St. Charles and avoids eye contact as he heads dejectedly toward the subway. Orlando remained integral to his life as both father figure and best friend. Daily contact fostered Yusef's sense of personal responsibility, and he pulled completely away from drug dealing. But he sees Orlando's death as a cosmic betrayal and is too emotionally devastated to express his sorrow yet. Perhaps he'll turn to old friends from his neighborhood for succor; his memories of Orlando might rescue him from this or his grief might push him back to his life on the street.

"I took Gober's loss very personally," Linwood says, standing beside his mother on the church's steps. When Ikay called to tell him about their principal's passing, he was sitting at his desk at a midtown Manhattan branch of Bank of America. Linwood graduated from Hofstra University with a bachelor's in computer information systems and is just completing the bank's management training program. "Gober didn't get sick until after we graduated," Linwood remarks. "Everything happens for a reason, and God had him there specifically to get us through high school, because without him many of us wouldn't have made it."

Wearing a charcoal-gray pinstriped suit, starched white shirt, and purple tie, Linwood puts his arm around his mother's shoulders as they walk away from St. Charles. Later, Linwood says, "Gober saw something in me that others at Rice didn't, because he saw through the bravado of our culture: the bad boy persona. Gober knew that if you can switch the energy of a troublemaker from negative to positive, that a young man can become a leader."

Brother Walderman attends the funeral service with Brother Sherlog. Shocked and saddened, afterward he says that "Orlando was a man of immense pride in his race, his leadership abilities, and his talent for rallying students as a man of vision and inexhaustible energy. Orlando gave our young men a sense of real optimism that they could do it. In his own inimitable way, he was like a master painter. There are principles and lessons there for all of us. Like most extraordinary individuals, Orlando struggled to understand why everyone wasn't the same way. The gifted don't see the world as we do. But his single-minded strength gave the students faith that a better life loomed on the horizon. It was a fitting irony that he died on the first day of school, although decades too soon."

———

I visited Orlando a few weeks before he died when his physical and emotional well-being seemed better than at any time since losing his leg. As I wrote the book, we talked often by phone. I questioned him about the scenes and characters in the text, and his thoughts and motivations at the time, and I saw him at least once a year on trips back to New York City. After leaving Rice, Orlando finally gave his personal issues priority and was finally healthy enough to start working full-time again.

On a hot evening in late July 2005, I met Orlando at his apartment after he had worked a full day at the Bronx charter school, and had climbed in and out of cars, loading and unloading his wheelchair, twice. I assumed he was tired and suggested we order Chinese take-out, but he insisted on going out for dinner. Orlando showed no signs of fatigue, instead talking enthusiastically for several hours over ribs and chicken at Dallas BBQ restaurant at 166th and Broadway—less than a block from the Audubon Ballroom where Malcolm X was murdered. In May, the site had opened as a memorial and education center dedicated to Malcolm X, in collaboration with Columbia University.

Reflecting on his legacy at Rice, Orlando was very proud that he had eliminated the N-word on campus. More significantly, he pointed to turning Rice's culture into one that valued academics over sports, and to his success counseling fatherless young men through the difficult transition to manhood. He was also pleased that he had instituted celebrations of African American and Hispanic heritages.

He had said this countless times before, but now he spoke almost understatedly. Gone was the volcanic and perhaps desperate passion to justify himself, and I realized he made no reference to race or radical politics even when we discussed current events. For the most part, Orlando had become what in fact he was: a middle-class, socially conservative Democrat. Certainly he had faced racism in his personal life and career, but his nemesis turned out to be diabetes and his failure to take responsibility for this condition and to establish personal relationships.

Now Orlando mused about what to do with the money he was making. Politically he had taken to defending Hillary Clinton in online chat rooms and writing letters to newspaper and magazine editors. One appeared in the August 1, 2005 issue of *The Nation,* praising a recent article in the magazine about her.

Orlando mentioned the possibility of the new position at Geoffrey Canada's Promise Academy. After he assured me that proper diet and rest had stabilized his blood sugar levels for over a year, I believed that he was starting a positive stage as fit as a diabetic can be. Had Orlando died even a year before, I wouldn't have been surprised, but his sudden passing in September was as shocking as it was excruciating. He had become a friend, even though as a writer I kept enough distance to maintain objectivity.

And he was still a puzzle: why the recent fascination with Hillary Clinton? Orlando was staying up at night to hunt down stories about her on the Internet, and for example, responded angrily to one in *The Sierra Times,* an online right-wing publication, in January. Perhaps Orlando still needed a political crusade and was planning to volunteer for Clinton's eventual run for the White House. Orlando often lauded Bill Clinton's presidency and was thrilled when the former president rented an office in Harlem.

It struck me that Orlando was as interested as ever in leadership and looking for his place on a larger stage. He was well respected in Harlem and would have made an effective contribution to an election campaign, since he'd regained much of his vigor. To some extent I'm speculating, just as I guess about his cause of death. Diabetics have an increased risk for heart disease, stroke, and other fatal ailments. Whatever the physical mechanism, I think of his premature departure as tragic in that much was lost to the black community, to education, and to American society—and Orlando had much to live for. He was enjoying his life and gave many indications that finally he was happy.

A plethora of social, historical, and cultural forces played out in Orlando's career and persona. He was a unique combination of conservative and radical elements, and he inherited the dynamism of black preachers and civil rights heroes fighting for equality and freedom, in this case in the classroom. At the same time, Orlando sought to reconcile the faithful to God, despite longstanding injustices. In sum, he was as charismatic as he was enigmatic.

It could be said that Orlando never met a contradiction he didn't like. He spouted Black Panther rhetoric one moment and then launched into a personal empowerment message that would warm the hearts of right-wingers. But Orlando never worried about philosophical conundrums. What he said to his students and the teachers didn't have to make perfect sense; it just had to inspire the right result at that moment. Orlando was a performance artist on society's most important stage, where the nation's socioeconomic, political, cultural, and moral problems are ultimately solved—or not. The school room constitutes the most significant intervention into a child's life and so, the best opportunity for individual and group betterment.

"I leave Rice in God's hands," were Orlando's last words to me about the school.

For several years, Rice seemed to be slipping through God's fingers. But with Brother Walderman's return in September 2005, Orlando's prayer is finally answered.

After Brother's sabbatical ended in 2002, he was appointed the founding director of the Edmund Rice Institute at the Christian Brothers' headquarters in New Rochelle. The institute was created primarily to train the lay administrators and teachers in the order's educational traditions and spiritual heritage.

"The Christian Brothers are devoted to bringing the good news of Christ to the poor in a decidedly practical way," says Al Widziewicz, who left Rice in 2003 to work part-time at the institute, coordinating retreats and workshops. "They don't intellectualize their approach like the Jesuits or spiritualize it like the Franciscans. Their motto is simply *facere et docere:* do and teach. The classic Christian Brother serves the disadvantaged by teaching six classes of physics and coaching three sports, but eschews any sense of mysticism. It was all about making the underclass into a working class, and the Brothers are so egalitarian that they have become almost embarrassed that many of their schools now serve more affluent students."

But with only 259 Christian Brothers remaining in the United States and Canada, and none in formation, they will soon become memories. Within a decade or two, their schools will be influenced by their legacy only if there's an institutional means to transmit Edmund Rice's charisma. Currently, there are eighteen Christian Brothers high schools, two elementary schools, and one middle school in the United States. In addition, some Christian Brothers teach or administer at other Catholic schools across the country. Worldwide there are 2,500 Christian Brothers in Ireland, England, Australia, New Guinea, India, and Africa, as well as in the Americas. There are also missions in Liberia and the Sudan.[2]

Only three North American schools—Rice, All Hallows, and Archbishop Curley Notre Dame—still educate a predominately disadvantaged population, and Rice is the only one serving a mostly African American population. So the crisis under Franklin Caesar's leadership not only threatened Rice's existence, but the stake the Christian Brothers have in their original mission. With a projected enrollment of significantly less than three hundred students for the 2005–06 school year, after climbing to four hundred under Orlando, bankruptcy seemed almost inevitable. The Christian Brothers convened a council to resolve the crisis. As much as they wanted to preserve the school, there was only one viable solution: a take-charge leader.

At age fifty-nine, Brother Walderman considered his work at the Edmund Rice Institute a fitting culmination of more than forty years as an educator. But he made the difficult decision to return to Rice—difficult because much of what he'd accomplished had been lost. Yet the school was still too precious to abandon. As Brother Maistre remarked, "Not only does our school serve the most marginalized group in the country, but the majority of leaders in the African American community have come from small parochial schools like Rice."

Brother Walderman begins by recruiting an effective administrative team. He convinces Brother Christopher D. Hall, the dean of students at Archbishop Curley–Notre Dame High School in Miami, to take the vice-principal's position. Then Brother Walderman promotes Anthony Ashe, Aaron's and Abrahim's father, who taught at Rice for the previous three years, to dean of students.

Both Ashe and Brother Hall have extensive experience working with minority teens and bring instant credibility to current students who aren't familiar with Brother Walderman. Brother Hall spent the last twenty years as a teacher and administrator at Christian Brothers schools throughout the country. As well, he grew up in the Bronx and graduated from All Hallows High School, and like Ashe, who was raised in Harlem, he experienced similar difficulties to those facing Rice Men, since both are African American.

Ashe offers invaluable insight into the temptations and dangers that today's inner-city youth constantly encounter. Formerly a state trooper, Ashe was assigned to the Drug Enforcement Administration detachment for thirteen years.

Over the summer, Brother Walderman meets with parents to listen to their concerns. He also arranges a conference with the students on academic probation, "because I wanted to know what the kids who were getting into trouble were like. The good ones you always have on your side."

"It's terrible here," declares junior Carlos Rousseau.

"Why is that?" Brother asks.

"No one here makes us do anything, so we do whatever we want."

"I see," Brother nods his head. "Do you want to know something?"

"What?"

"That just ended."

And so it does. Brother Walderman forcefully reestablishes Rice's countercultural ethos. Soon behavioral standards return to what they were when Abbasse was dean of students and Orlando inspired, reprimanded, and counseled students toward accountability. Interestingly, Brother's approach shows sign of having absorbed many of Orlando's innovations and insights, but his dreams for the school are more in keeping with his capacity to fulfill them. Like Orlando, Brother brings a strong presence and certain leadership. Behind closed doors, he deals sympathetically with students' personal problems. Obviously Brother isn't African American, but he grew up in a working class family in the Bronx, and his long experience at Rice has given him insight into the added burden of being both black and poor.

Rice's enrollment bottoms out at 255 students in September 2006, but recruiting improves as parents learn of Brother Walderman's return, and he convinces Student Sponsor Partners to begin sending students again. The 2008 freshman class will have 125 students, meaning that within three years, enrollment will top four hundred. This doesn't solve the school's financial problems, since the per-student cost is approaching $9,000 but tuition nears $6,000. So the increase in enrollment actually translates into Brother needing to raise over $400,000 more per year to cover the $3,000 per-student gap. With a recent endowment only large enough to cover yearly capital costs, Rice's future is questionable, unless as Brother points out, the school charges full cost and becomes a more elite institution.

The other possible long-term solution would involve finding an alternative site for the school—in Harlem, since the commitment is to stay there—and creating a much larger school. The current building is aging rapidly, and the footprint isn't sufficient for anything but vertical expansion, which would work for a new condominium complex, but not a school. Board members are actively looking for a new location and could sell the Rice property for a considerable sum. But the new real estate would have to be acquired at below-market price to make the project viable and keep tuition low.

The graduating classes of 2006 and 2007 suffer a 25-percent attrition rate from freshman year, but this is due partly to the previous administration's mismanagement, and to Brother Walderman's having to expel several students who wouldn't accept his standards when he first returned and needed to make a statement. In addition, Brother can't always find a benefactor to cover tuition when a parent loses a job or a family breaks up. So while it's true that students who stay four years graduate on time, it's not true that the 98.6 percent graduation rate claimed by the New York Archdiocese holds true at every high school.

As pointed out in chapter 8, it seems that most of the students who leave early eventually graduate from the public system. Interviews with teachers, guidance counselors, and principals at Rice and other urban Catholic high schools strongly suggest that most students who spend two years or more at a Catholic high school persist through matriculation.

Ephraim Yisreal, for example, transferred to an arts-oriented public high school for his junior year to pursue an acting career. He graduated, but lost contact with his former classmates at Rice.

Paris Lane and Prince Youmans don't fare well. Both go to Thurgood Marshall Academy for Learning and Social Change in Harlem after leaving

Rice. Paris has difficulty finding time to study for the Regents exams, since it interferes with his drug dealing. He drops out of Thurgood and then another public high school. But as Martha Williams, his foster mother, recalls, Paris was haunted by his promise to her that "I'm going to make you proud." After viewing Mel Gibson's *The Passion of the Christ,* he returns home to tell Williams, "I'm making a change."

In January 2004, Paris enrolls in an adult program that grants a high school diploma and an associate's degree. He also finds a manager to help him launch his rap career. But then on March 16, Paris shoots himself to death in the lobby of a Bronx housing project building, moments after his girlfriend ends their relationship. The suicide is recorded by a police surveillance camera, and a digital copy is posted on an Internet Web site devoted to violence and pornography. Police investigators never determine who uploaded the tape, although it could have been someone in or connected to the NYPD. This racist and sadistic act compounds the tragedy and sparks protests.

No one understands Paris's precipitous action. After losing both parents to AIDS and his siblings to various family placements, he had found a new family with Williams. But Paris kept everyone at an emotional distance and resisted bonding with a father figure. Ultimately, he couldn't bridge the chasm between the reality of his life and what he longed for, as revealed in his rap name: Paradise.

Diplomas don't shield anyone from violent death on the street. Karl Mann graduated from Rice in 2002, despite living in a group home and commuting from Staten Island. Given his intensity and quick temper, persisting for four years at Rice was a tribute to his character. But he was stabbed to death soon after matriculating for talking to a young woman who, unbeknownst to Karl, had a vicious thug for a boyfriend.

Karl's graduating class suffered the usual 25-percent attrition rate, but assuming Brother Walderman will stay for several more years, the resulting stability will likely improve the retention rate significantly.

Prince Youmans drops out of Thurgood Marshall before graduating. His grandmother says Paris's influence eroded Prince's resolve, as it had at Rice. This was an exaggeration, but Paris's example and popularity was a negative influence. Prince now works sporadically at odd jobs, his grandmother reports, emphasizing that he stays out of trouble. In fact, pursuing his dream of a rap career is now a full-time occupation.

Even if every student who left Rice was counted as a dropout, whether or not he eventually graduated elsewhere, the school should still be regarded as a pedagogical miracle. The city's public schools graduate less than 40 percent of all students, and the proportion of African American and Hispanic males finishing on time is significantly less. If the public school chancellor improved graduation rates to better than 50 percent—let alone 70 to 80 percent—he or she would be hailed a genius and educators across the country would seek his advice. The long-standing fact that Catholic educators do significantly better with the most difficult demographic earns indifference at best from most politicians and public educators. One wonders whether they have a real interest in educating the disadvantaged. Brother Walderman should be offered a six-figure compensation to serve as a consultant for the public system.

Instead he rebuilds Rice and prays for fiscal manna. The academic tone Orlando set has become part of Rice's culture despite the intervening turmoil. The average SAT scores rose steadily to 860 on the math and verbal sections. As well, the percentage of students passing the math and Earth science Regents exams increased from abysmal rates to over 80 percent. Every year now, several graduates go to Ivy League and other highly selective colleges. More importantly, Rice Men are doing well there. Over 10 percent of the '02 class went to top institutions, such as Yale and Columbia, and have graduated or will do so soon. Some years have seen two or more graduates go on to Cornell alone. Adam Tavares '02 graduated from New York University and then was accepted into a Ph.D. program in psychology at Pepperdine University.

Many other students are admitted to excellent second-tier institutions. Ricky Rodriguez, for example, graduated from Clarkson University in 2007.

But perhaps the most important story is told by graduates such as Aris Martin, who became a construction worker instead of going to college. Although virtually every Rice graduate gets into a postsecondary institution and most go, about half graduate. A quarter drop out before the end of the first year, unable to make the difficult transition to a much larger institution where there's no Orlando, Abbasse, or Brother Walderman to provide daily direction. The other quarter make it through a year or more, but then usually experience financial distress. Most dropouts continue accumulating college credits, at least at community colleges, and virtually all become productive members of society who maintain integral roles in their children's lives, whether or not they marry or live with the mothers.

There are spectacular stories of students enduring homelessness while at Rice and then graduating from Columbia or the University of Michigan. There are also student athletes such as Andre Barrett, who piloted the Seton Hall Pirates into the NCAA tournament, graduated, and has been playing in the NBA since. Antuan Barnett, the salutatorian, graduated from Fairfield College, tried out for the Pittsburgh Pirates as a right fielder and played in the minor leagues, before taking a lucrative position with an investment firm on Wall Street.

But more significant than the exceptional profiles of achievement is the repetition of young men of moderate talents progressing from the underclass to the working class—and most will eventually earn entrée to the middle class. Ray Jones dropped out of college but was hired as a teacher's assistant at a primary school. His hyperactive and childlike personality helps him relate to young children. Ray is earning college credit in the evenings and is determined to earn a degree. Another Rice graduate who left college early now works as a clerk in city government. Perhaps he will never own a beach house in the Hamptons, but his view of Long Island Sound won't be from Riker's Island prison.

There were a few Rice students who did become prison inmates. The year after Orlando left, a junior on the honor roll moved to a new neighborhood in the Bronx, where he joined the Crips and was incarcerated on a murder charge. That year, another student was put in jail on a gun possession charge. In 2005, David Ifill '03 was expelled from Hampton University for his alleged role in the stabbing death of a classmate during a bar fight. David was charged with assault and battery, but the charges were dismissed after it was established that the incident began when several young men jumped him. David was expelled from Hampton right after the event, but instead of seeking reinstatement when his name was cleared, he enlisted in the Navy.

Still on the edge is Yusef, who works nights restocking shelves, first in a grocery store, then at a pharmacy. He has perennial plans to take classes at Bronx Community College but fails to register. Although Yusef doesn't live with his girlfriend any longer, he sees his son James often and supports him. So far, whenever his job's physical demands tempt him to sell drugs again, the memory of Orlando and the values he instilled deliver Yusef from temptation. Hopefully, Yusef will return to school and qualify himself for the business career he craves. He continues to dream of becoming a rap star and fills notebooks with lyrics. Several Rice graduates have set up recording studios and established their own hip-hop labels. Yusef maintains contact and has recorded several demo CDs there. Hope might not burn brightly for Yusef anymore, but it glows strongly enough that he perseveres.

Had there never been a Rice High School, Yusef acknowledges that he would probably be in jail or worse. For Rice to continue for the Yusefs of the future, recent graduates must start taking over the donating and fund-raising. Considering the high proportion of board members and benefactors who graduated in the 1940s and 1950s, this will soon become urgent.

As soon as Linwood finished the training program at Bank of America and became an assistant branch manager, he joined SSP as a mentor. Now he counsels and pays part of the tuition for Raymond Bernardez, a 2006 freshman at Rice. Raymond lives in the South Bronx with his mother and admits that "I'm rough around the edges, just like Mr. Sessoms was, but he's helping me get through it. At my middle school, there were big gang problems, but not here. He tells me how he turned his life around and gets fervent about it. I got some DTs and failed three subjects on my first report card, but I'm doing better now."

"When I first met Raymond, like most guys from inner city, his dreams were to play basketball, or be a rap star, or a big time actor," Linwood recalls. "My goal is to show him and other young men that there's much more. I'm taking Raymond to a college, so he can see what it is and acquire the drive to get through Rice. I want him to see that he doesn't have to be a sports star to have fun. Lots of kids around the country have narrow perspectives and see only what's in the neighborhood. But it doesn't take millions of dollars to make it out of the 'hood. My job is to do what my sponsor and others like Gober did, and show him that he can be a regular guy and live comfortably. Raymond was amazed to see my apartment and learn that I live alone. I grew up in the projects, and he can make it too if he stays focused." Fulfilling a fatherly role for Raymond has helped Linwood improve his relationship with his own father.

Raymond visits Linwood at his office in the Empire State Building, reinforcing the notion that disadvantaged black males can succeed. It doesn't hurt that Linwood's counseling sessions sometimes include going to Knicks or Nets games together.

At five feet three inches tall with a thin physique, Raymond still claims that he's going to play in the pros, "but I have a lot of doubters."

"I tell him to pursue a university education—just in case," Linwood chuckles. By taking Raymond to games, Linwood is also showing him how most people make it to the NBA: by establishing a career that pays enough to buy tickets. "Education is the real slam dunk."

———

Throughout this book, I've tried to present an accurate picture of the everyday struggles of students, teachers, and administrators at an inner-city

Catholic high school. Rice was far from perfect, and the staff made its share of mistakes. Rather than diminish the school, I firmly believe that telling its story "warts and all" is valuable for two reasons.

First, the fact that Rice and other similar schools can succeed in educating the most difficult demographic despite scant resources as well as underpaid teachers and administrators is a powerful argument for applying the Catholic school model to urban public schools. Perhaps no school can overcome challenging socioeconomic factors entirely. But Catholic schools complete the important task of empowering the deprived to become productive citizens; historically it has always taken several generations for any group to achieve equity in the mainstream. What is especially reassuring is that a high proportion of urban Catholic students prove immediately capable of graduating from top colleges and go on to become professionals, business owners, and leaders.

How much better could public schools perform if they embraced the lessons on display every day at Catholic schools? At least they could do as well, as proven by the Achievement First charter schools in Connecticut and New York, for example. Here, direct instruction, uniforms, order, and focus on basic skills for all students—regardless of background or beginning level—bring them up to proficiency with amazing efficiency. Perhaps when these grow into K–12 facilities, as planned, they will surpass neighborhood Catholic schools, given the advantage of their greater resources.

Meanwhile, big-city school districts spend the most money and achieve the worst results. In response, wealthy businessmen such as Bill Gates and Eli Broad have been pouring billions of their own dollars into public education in recent years. And now, dissatisfied with the results, these philanthropists are sinking another sixty million dollars into a campaign to place education high on the political agenda of the 2008 presidential race. But clearly it doesn't matter how much focus or funds public schools attract until the right model is adopted. If the foundation is not solid, what can be built but bigger and better ruins?

The second reason for presenting Rice's blemishes is that this makes a convincing, prima facie case for public support. Given their long track record and how much they accomplish with so little, it is obvious that funding urban Catholic schools would yield positive results. It can't be said strongly enough that for Rice Men, and millions of youngsters in their situation, there is no alternative to failing public schools other than Catholic schools and a much smaller number of other denominational schools, as well as a few secular private academies with low tuition. Surely ideology should be put aside to support the fulfillment of this urgent public mandate until public education catches up. Regardless of one's position on vouchers, tax credits, and so on, I cannot imagine what argument could trump the immediate needs of children trapped in poverty and social dysfunction. It is morally repugnant to the point of criminality to deny a child his or her birthright by sticking to an absolutist—in truth, secular fundamentalist—view of the separation of church and state.

The only certainty here is that people who fight against public funding for inner-city Catholic schools would never condemn their own children to the public schools they so readily consign those children to. In fact, politicians, union officials, public school administrators, and so on, usually send their kids to Catholic, elite private, or high-functioning public schools in affluent neighborhoods.

Once this monstrous hypocrisy is set aside, all stakeholders can work together to find solutions. There is no reason to make permanent the voucher programs that could prop up the urban Catholic schools struggling to stay solvent. In fact, the need for such public support might be short-lived if the Catholic school model were adopted. Certainly there is room for experimentation with other approaches that offer promise, but the fundamental commitment needs to be to what works.

Public support for urban Catholic schools pays huge dividends for taxpayers. Despite the often used canard that vouchers drain resources from public education, the truth is that school-choice programs, even those providing full vouchers, spend less per student than public schools. A recent study calculated that from 1990 to 2006, publicly funded school-choice programs saved state budgets $22 million and local public school districts $422 million.[3] Much of the money was, and all could have been, put back into public schooling.

Nationwide, Catholic schools save taxpayers over $20 billion, after calculating what it would cost to educate their students in the system public.[4] What could possibly be wrong with a fraction of that going back to urban parochial schools in some manner, which would constitute a sound public investment? Catholic education has paid its civic dues many times over.

Catholic schools could also save the billions of public dollars spent on at-risk students who might otherwise become a burden to taxpayers for much or all of their lives.[5] A Texas study calculated that each year's class of dropouts cost the state $377 million in lost revenue, plus increased Medicaid and incarceration costs. In addition, dropouts are far more likely to rely on other public-assistance programs, such as subsidized housing, welfare, and food stamps. The cost of these would add significantly to the above amount. The same study demonstrated that a modest school-choice program, which could be implemented immediately, would send about eight thousand at-risk students mostly to Catholic schools and save the state $53 million a year.

As stated at the outset, I invite voucher opponents as well as supporters into Rice High School to experience the type of school that is the most common destination for publicly funded school-choice initiatives. While evaluating these programs is beyond this book's scope, insofar as they provide well-deserved and urgently needed funding for urban Catholic schools, I support vouchers, tax credits, and so on. This is not a wholesale endorsement, but merely what seems the best approach in the current crisis.

Ultimately public school educators will decide the long-term outcome of the school choice debate. If they continue to ignore the Catholic lead in breaking the link between race, income, and academic success, their intransigence will surely fuel support for school choice initiatives. Given the amount spent on schooling in New York City, for example, not only could vouchers allow children access to a better education at private schools, but every youngster's financial security could also be assured. Each student could receive a $10,000 voucher, and the other $10,000 that normally would be spent on public education could be invested in the child's name, K–12. Then students would not only graduate at much higher rates, but become millionaires by about age forty-three. If these funds were allowed to grow until retirement, every student would eventually leave the workforce with almost five million dollars, and without personally putting aside one penny. This assumes a 5 percent return on investment and doesn't include the normal increases to education costs that would increase yield.

Of course, there are many considerations and interests that would weigh heavily against this proposal becoming policy, but the popularity of school choice initiatives shows that taxpayers increasingly reject the notion that schooling must be both publicly funded and publicly run. Obviously, better use could be made of education dollars. Public officials often forget that they are entrusted with money and children, both of which belong to taxpayers.

At present, there aren't enough seats available at private schools to accommodate more than a tiny fraction of public school students. But public policy could move toward resolving this in the long run. For example, in 2007, the Utah state legislature passed a universal voucher law that allows every student to attend the public or private school of their choice by

2020. Shortly after the law passed, opponents of parental choice mounted a campaign that forced a referendum in November 2007. Voucher opponents, funded primarily by teachers' unions nationwide, ran an effective—and arguably deceptive—ad campaign and won the referendum. This victory didn't defeat the voucher law, but killed spending on its implementation.[6]

And so the war rages between the education establishment—which includes most school district officials, education school professors, the teachers' unions, and most politicians who are supported by the unions—on the one hand, and school choice advocacy and citizen groups, and a small yet growing number of entrepreneurs, university professors, and politicians, on the other. Urban Catholic schools find themselves in the unenviable position of being caught in the middle of this struggle for control over the half trillion dollars a year spent on public K–12 education. Given that teachers' unions have hundreds of millions of dollars in union dues at their disposal, Catholic educators need to be extremely wary of their participation in any public program.

In 2006, the Ohio state legislature instituted the EdChoice program, which will eventually provide up to 14,000 vouchers to get low-income students out of chronically failing public schools. But shortly after being elected as the new governor that November, Ted Strickland announced plans to terminate EdChoice, as payback to the teachers' unions for getting him elected. Strickland didn't have the support in the state assembly to carry out this threat, but no doubt the unions will offer substantial contributions in future campaigns to assembly candidates who will further their objective.

"A large enough political constituency has developed in recent years, so that it will be very difficult for politicians to cancel these programs," Dan Lips, an education analyst at the Heritage Foundation, said in an interview. As of September 2007, 22,500 urban Milwaukee students are eligible for school vouchers, with over $110 million being spent. In Arizona, a program allows taxpayers to receive a dollar-for-dollar state tax credit for donations to private organizations distributing vouchers. In 2005, almost 70,000 taxpayer donations funded 22,522 scholarships.[7]

Lips was hopeful that any move against these programs would spark massive protests and counter the union-backed politicians. Maybe so, but after two decades of fighting for school choice, only 150,000 of the nation's fifty million public school students (or less than 0.003 percent) receive public support for private school tuition. Also, only 25,000 (of the 150,000) students receive tax-funded vouchers, and voucher proposals have been defeated in five consecutive referenda, most recently in Utah. The voucher movement is certainly stalled, and other initiatives are not making significant headway.[8]

For Catholic schools, public funding will never be sufficient or secure. Schools in Washington, D.C., for example, are closing despite the voucher program. Voucher amounts never come close to equaling the actual cost of educating students at Catholic schools.

More importantly, public funding can be withdrawn at any point. Consider what happened in Canada in the late 1990s. Catholic schools received substantial financial support from seven out of ten provincial governments; among them, Ontario, Alberta, Quebec, and Newfoundland funded the schools entirely. Then Newfoundland and Quebec withdrew funding, which led to the immediate collapse of the parochial systems.

After generations of complete reliance on government, Canadian Catholic educators became complacent. Their schools lost the capacity to survive on their own, which was especially poignant in Quebec where the vast majority of students have attended Catholic schools since confederation in 1867. In recent years, there have been preliminary discussions aimed at doing the same in Ontario. Decades of public funding have made the Catholic system so similar to its secular counterpart that a plausible case can be made to taxpayers that they shouldn't have to support both systems. American Catholic educators would be best served by accepting public support when it's offered, but neither rely on it nor allow it to dictate compliance with unwanted regulations.

Perhaps the education landscape will change as a new black leadership emerges that is more supportive of alternative educational opportunities. For example, Cory Booker, the thirty-eight-year-old mayor of Newark, New Jersey, and a Democrat—who has been cited in the *New York Times* as a promising presidential candidate in the near future—advocates charter schools and corporate tax credits for contributions to a fund that sends public school students to private institutions or transfers them to better public districts.[9] Booker also supports vouchers, but shies away from the term to avoid alienating the teachers' unions. He also declares that he takes Malcolm X's "by any means necessary" approach to education. Booker is interested in any model and means that will help students trapped in dozens of schools in Newark that fail miserably despite spending $17,000 per year per student.

Most African American voters favor vouchers, which is significant since blacks vote as a bloc and so hold the balance of power in many congressional, most gubernatorial and senate races, and in presidential campaigns. Black leaders could call for vouchers, unlimited charter schools, or any combination of initiatives, and both political parties would compete to meet these demands, in spite of the education establishment's influence. Indeed, Hispanic leaders hold even more sway, if they act together, since the Hispanic population is growing rapidly.[10]

However this plays out in the coming years, Catholic educators need to solve their schools' basic fiscal problems themselves. This means aggressively seeking private funding sources, both philanthropic and congregational. Professional marketing has been adopted with positive results at several dioceses, such as Newark, New York, and Memphis, but is still rudimentary. The Church has been slow to advance in this critical direction, and there is scant institutional history of doing so. Soliciting donations and promoting enrollment requires a well-financed, expert approach to telling the Catholic school story on the national, state, and local levels.[11]

Even so, the task is overwhelming. Typically, Catholic schools keep no records of the millions of their graduates who would be their most likely sources for contributions. Still today, as Catholic schools mount development efforts, they neglect maintaining contact with last year's seniors and have no way of tracking them down in later years when they could become benefactors.

In New York, the Inner-City Scholarship Fund, Patrons Program, and other archdiocesan efforts successfully engage philanthropists, and such initiatives could be expanded. The social bang for the buck dwarfs all other charities, and in philanthropic terms, the number of bucks needed is relatively small. But as Brother Walderman points out, there is tremendous competition among causes for the attention of philanthropists.

Neglected both in New York City and nationwide is an underutilized source of billions of dollars for the schools. Sunday collections used to pay for about two-thirds of school costs, but now account for only 12.5 percent.[12] There's no reason why parish contributions can't be increased to solve the present crisis. As discussed at the end of chapter 17, Catholics give five times less than Protestants, yet other than recent Hispanic immigrants, they are no less affluent.[13] They have been able to get away with lower donations because Catholic parishes are about eight times larger than non-Catholic congregations and so are much less costly to run.[14]

Considering that 80 percent of parish donations are given by 20 percent of churchgoers, there is plenty of room for improvement. Of course, many of the 80-percenters don't attend regularly, but they could still be inspired to make school donations. In fact, engaging them in a campaign might bring them back, since the project carries such obvious worth. There are dozens of studies attesting to Catholic school efficacy, and every diocese can introduce its flock to the students who need their help and to thousands of recent success stories among graduates. At the price of a Starbucks cappuccino per week—or $3.50—Catholic households could raise $3.9 billion to cover the gap between tuition and cost at every Catholic school in the country.

The main problem is that the Church has not challenged parishioners in recent decades. "Catholic contributions in the early sixties represented about two percent of their income, roughly the same as Protestant contributions," wrote Father Andrew Greeley. "Between 1965 and 1985, that proportion fell in half and has hovered around that level ever since."[15] If Catholics gave at the same level as Protestants today, the Church would take in $34 billion a year in collections, instead of $6.6 billion. If $17 billion were pumped into the schools, tuition could be kept affordable at all schools and eliminated entirely from those serving the underprivileged. In addition, there would be money to build new schools, which represent both an historic opportunity for the Church and a growing need.

Worth noting is that at the height of revelations of priestly sex abuse and the Church hierarchy's complicity in negligently reassigning these criminals, often to continue molesting children, it was widely reported that Catholics would withdraw their support in disgust. But a study showed that instead, parish donations increased across the country, other than in Boston where the prelate was guilty of the most egregious mismanagement of ordained sociopaths.[16] Catholics are resilient and will rally around their Church despite failings of its leaders.[17] Now these leaders need to take cues from their flock and step forward together to save Catholic education.

Since the 1960s, the Catholic population has doubled, while school enrollment dropped 60 percent. Given the decline in birthrates, to regain their 36 percent share of school-aged Catholic children, the Catholic system would have to increase the number of seats by 75 percent. But the Church hierarchy has yet to recover from the post–Vatican II loss of religious teaching orders. As a result, constructing enough schools in the suburban areas where middle-class Catholics have moved is long overdue, and this has contributed to declining rates of church attendance and donations.

Since the nineteenth century, Catholic schools have functioned as the Church's engine, lifting impoverished immigrant groups to unimagined prosperity. The schools, more than any other institution, made the Catholic Church into the country's most powerful denomination. Yet many in the hierarchy have developed a distaste for the schools in recent decades, according to Father Greeley, and even see them as competing for the funds they need to run parishes and dioceses. This is not to disparage the many priests and bishops who labor heroically to save the schools. But sorely lacking has been coherent national leadership on the most important question facing Catholics. Inculcating the next generation will determine the Church's future, and the schools are needed for this now more than ever, given how secular and inimical to religion the mainstream culture has become.

In 1990 the United Sates Conference of Catholic Bishops issued a pastoral letter calling for financial support to make it possible for all Catholics who want to send their children to parochial school to do so by 1997. The bishops looked to both the public and private sectors for financial solutions. However, initiatives in the public realm have achieved minimal success, and the Church is only beginning to engage the private sector professionally. Hundreds of schools closed, mostly in urban centers, because although well-intentioned, these efforts lacked Archbishop Hughes's fiery determination. He battled for public funding, and today's bishops continue to do so, but Hughes went forward with unflagging tenacity to do nothing less than build entire institutional systems.

That fierce resolve is sorely lacking today for the most part. It is no coincidence that the decline of church attendance has paralleled school closings and the weakening of Catholic identity at most of the remaining schools. What happens, Jesus asked, when salt loses its saltiness?[18] The warning in Revelations is clear: "Because you are lukewarm, neither hot nor cold, I will spew you out of my mouth!"[19]

From a financial perspective, it should be much easier to face today's problems even though they are likely to get worse. Already 35 percent of Catholic schools have waiting lists, and in many areas, more than half the schools don't have enough seats for applicants. More importantly, as Dr. Catherine Hickey, the New York archdiocese's secretary for education, told me, there are many poor Catholic parents who petition schools for financial aid but can't be accommodated. Most of these are Hispanics, whose children constitute only 11 percent of the Catholic school students, far less than their 40 percent overall share of the Catholic population. Because of higher Hispanic birthrates, this percentage will grow significantly in the coming decades. The Hispanic population is estimated to increase from 35.6 million on the 2000 census to 102.6 million by 2050.[20] How will the Church accommodate this massive surge of Catholic children, mostly from financially challenged families? Are they somehow less worthy than their European predecessors? Should less effort be expended to give them a Catholic education?

"We shall have to build the schoolhouse first and the church afterward," said Archbishop Hughes over 150 years ago. "In our age the question of education is the question of the church."[21] That is no less true today and will become increasingly so. But will Catholics take up the challenge to once again exceed their comfort zone and provide a Catholic education to all congregants and others who want it for their children?

This is a matter of grave public concern. Public education's track record with the disadvantaged has been abysmal for decades. How will this new wave of immigrants and their children be assimilated? So far not well, and the cost of not doing so is enormous. A recent study showed that immigrant households, both legal and illegal, headed by low-skilled adults—meaning without a high school diploma—cost taxpayers almost ninety billion dollars a year in government benefits and services.[22] This doesn't include incarceration costs, nor the enormous expenses associated with crime victims. Without massive advances in mainstreaming low-skilled immigrants, this burden will increase, along with the nonfiscal social costs associated with poverty, dysfunction, and Balkanization.

It is predicted that the United States will increasingly become a Catholic country. The question is whether the nation will absorb and integrate new arrivals properly, along with the enormous task of responding to the needs of the existing underclass. In coming decades, will the United States resemble Mexico or Canada (44 percent Catholic), as the percentage of American Catholics doubles from its current 23 percent share of the population?[23] Fortunately for the nation's benefit, the Catholic Church continues to put enormous effort into educating disadvantaged Catholics as well as the children of non-Catholics, and schools like Rice repay the special debt owed African Americans for previous exclusion.[24] The most conscientious approach for all citizens would be to back urban Catholic—and other denominational—schools with public funds, while at the same time lobbying public educators to adopt the Catholic model. As this adoption of the Catholic school model within public institutions takes place, those who oppose public funding of religious institutions can withdraw their support for schools like Rice. But in the meantime, if this implementation takes generations, disadvantaged children shouldn't have to bear the disastrous consequences of ineffectual public schooling or be turned away from parochial schooling due to their family's lack of funds.

On the other hand, this change might not take so long. A rigorous curriculum was established in public schools in Massachusetts over the last decade, along with a focus on effective instruction. As a result, Massachusetts improved more than any other state on the NAEP tests. This doesn't comprise the entirety of the Catholic school model, the elements of which bear repeating: all students, regardless of their ethnic background, social class, family problems, or future plans, and regardless of their scholastic level entering high school, are taught basically in the same way. Other factors include a demanding curriculum, high expectations, discipline, school safety, a high level of parental involvement, a dedicated faculty, and a learning environment imbued with moral values.

It should be noted that parochial schools are open for visitors who would like to learn firsthand about inner-city education and the Catholic school model. The message that urban Catholic schools have been delivering successfully for generations to inner-city youth is expressed best by a graduate of a Christian Brothers high school. "I'm not comfortable being preachy," said Kareem Abdul-Jabbar, "but more people need to start spending as much time in the library as they do on the basketball court."[25]

INTRODUCTION

1. There are two teaching orders referred to as Christian Brothers. The first was founded in 1679 in France and is officially known as the Brothers of the Christian Schools. Members of this order arrived in the United States in 1846. Today they are usually called the De La Salle Christian Brothers or Lasallian Christian Brothers. The other order, whose official name is the Congregation of Christian Brothers, was founded in Ireland in 1802 by Blessed Edmund Rice. This order did not come to the United States to establish schools until 1906. To distinguish themselves from their Lasallian counterparts, they are commonly called the Irish Christian Brothers. Rice High School is affiliated with the latter order.

2. Elizabeth Bernstein, "The Price of Admission," *Wall Street Journal*, April 2, 2004. An amazing 41 percent of Saint Ann's graduates gain admission to ten of the country's most exclusive colleges, including Harvard and Yale.

3. Jay P. Greene and Marcus A. Winters, "Leaving Boys: Public High School Graduation Rates," *Civic Report*, no. 48 (Manhattan Institute, April 2006). A debate developed between Greene and Lawrence Mishel, president of the Economic Policy Institute, who published a book (Lawrence Mishel and Joydeep Roy, *Rethinking High School Graduation Rates and Trends*, Economic Policy Institute, Washington, D.C., 2006) with higher high school graduation rates. However, Greene and Winters's findings are more in line with other reputable reports, such as Daniel Losen, Gary Orfield, and Robert Balfanz, "Confronting

the Graduation Rate Crisis in Texas," The Civil Rights Project, Harvard University, October 7, 2006; Gary Orfield, Daniel Losen, and Johanna Wald, "Losing Our Future: How Minority Youth Are Being Left Behind by the Graduation Rate Crisis," The Civil Rights Project, Harvard University, February 25, 2004; and Daria Hall, "Getting Honest about Grad Rates: How States Play the Numbers and Students Lose," The Education Trust, June 2005.

4. See Samuel G. Freedman, "A Teacher Grows Disillusioned after a 'Fail' Becomes a 'Pass,' " *New York Times,* August 1, 2007.

5. David Gelernter, "One Nation: A Cheer for These Books about America," *Wall Street Journal,* June 30, 2007.

6. David Firestone, "Giuliani Sees Catholic Schools as Model for City," *New York Times,* August 5, 1995.

7. Diane Ravitch, *Left Back* (New York: Simon and Schuster, 2000), pp. 15–18.

8. In 2006 the performance of New York City public school students on the statewide tests remained virtually unchanged. In May 2007 the headline of a *New York Times* article by David Herszenhorn read "New York Eighth Graders Show Gains in Reading" (May 23, 2007). Reading proficiency for eighth graders improved from 49.3 to 57 percent. A month later, a *New York Times* article by Jennifer Medina proclaimed "City Students Lead Big Rise on N.Y. Math Tests" (June 13, 2007). Results showed that over 65 percent of the city's students achieved grade level—according to the test, which is the rub.

9. National Center for Education Statistics, "Mapping 2005 State Proficiency Standards Onto the NAEP Scales" (NCES 2007–484, U.S. Department of Education, Washington, D.C., 2007). This federal report shows that standards of reading and math proficiency vary widely state by state. In addition, standards change from year to year. This reinforces that the NAEP provides the only reliable assessment of K–12 student achievement.

10. National Assessment of Educational Progress, "Trial Urban District Assessment: Reading 2005" (National Center for Education Statistics, February 2006). Typically, NAEP scores are much lower than those on state tests, and correspond more accurately with graduation rates. Of the third of New York City's minority students who finish high school, only 20 percent of these are ready for college (see Jay P. Greene, "Public High School Graduation and College-Readiness Rates: 1991–2002," Education Working Paper, Manhattan Institute, February 2005). This corresponds far more accurately with NAEP's low competency levels, in contrast to the 60 percent proficiency rate that, for example, New York State's reading test indicated. Also, in large cities, the proficiency rate on NAEP's fourth-grade reading test was 44 percent higher for girls.

11. National Assessment of Education Progress, "Trial Urban District Assessment Results at Grades 4 and 8: Reading 2007" (National Center for Edu-

cation Statistics, November 2007). See also National Assessment of Education Progress, "Trial Urban District Assessment Results at Grades 4 and 8: Mathematics 2007" (National Center for Education Statistics, November 2007). New York City's public school students averaged 25 percent proficiency in reading at the fourth grade level (with black students at 15 percent and Hispanics at 16 percent) and 20 percent at the eighth grade level (with black students at 11 percent and Hispanics at 13 percent). In math, New York City's public school students averaged 34 percent proficiency at the fourth grade level (with black students at 20 percent and Hispanics at 26 percent) and 22 percent at the eighth grade level (with black students at 10 percent and Hispanics at 14 percent). The fourth grade math results showed a significant improvement from 2005, which hopefully will persist. However, public school students consistently perform worse in the eighth grade. As well, on the NAEP "12th-Grade Reading and Mathematics 2005" (http://nationsreportcard.gov/reading_math_grade12_2005), high school seniors averaged only 23 percent proficiency in both reading and math. These results included private school students, indicating that public school students attained proficiency at significantly lower rates and that minority public school students at best performed at the same rates as in the eighth grade.

12. The 2007 NAEP results showed that Catholic schools averaged 44 percent proficiency in reading at the fourth grade and 53 percent at the eighth grade levels. Catholic schools average almost identical proficiency levels in math and reading on both grade levels as private schools. See www.ncea.org/news/NAEP2007Results.asp. According to "Student Achievement in Private Schools: Results from 2000–2005" (http://nces.ed.gov/nationsreportcard/pdf/studies/2006459.pdf), "Black students in Catholic schools had higher average scores than Black students in public schools in all subjects and grades, except in grade 4 mathematics and grade 4 writing, where the apparent differences were not statistically significant."

13. Douglas N. Harris, "High-Flying Schools, Student Disadvantage, and the Logic of NCLB," *American Journal of Education* vol. 113, no. 3 (May 2007), www.journals.uchicago.edu/AJE/journal/issues/v113n3/113302/113302.text.html. This study showed that public schools enrolling poor minority students have a 1-in-300 chance of posting consistently high test scores.

14. Anthony S. Bryk, Valerie E. Lee, and Peter B. Holland, *Catholic Schools and the Common Good* (Cambridge, Mass.: Harvard University Press, 1993), p. 24.

15. John Kuo Wei Tchen, "Quimbo Appo's Fear of Fenians: Chinese-Irish Immigrants in Antebellum New York," in Ronald H. Bayor and Timothy J. Meagher, eds., *The New York Irish* (Baltimore: The Johns Hopkins University Press, 1996), pp. 125–152.

16. Ronald B. Mincy, *Black Males Left Behind* (Washington, D.C.: Urban Institute Press, 2006).

CHAPTER ONE

1. Per Archdiocese of New York.

2. Gail Russell Chaddock, "U.S. Notches World's Highest Incarceration Rate," *Christian Science Monitor,* August 18, 2003.

3. The "Blessed" honorific means that Edmund Rice has been recognized by the Church for the holiness of his life and is being considered for canonization as a saint.

CHAPTER TWO

1. However, just like any lay Catholic male, a brother may seek ordination as a deacon and perform some priestly duties—and of course ultimately seek the priesthood. Typically, teaching brothers are too absorbed in their education vocation to take on the religious duties of an ordained ministry. See www .askacatholic.com/AAC_AnswerDirectory/Answers_to_Questions/2006 _09SeptemberQuestions/2006SeptemberDeaconBrotherAndPriest.cfm.

2. David Moniz and Tom Squiteri, "Frontline Troops Disproportionately White, not Black," *USA Today,* January 21, 2003.

3. In 2007, All Hallows High School was named one of the fifty best Catholic high schools in the country by the Catholic High School Honor Roll. See www.chshonor.org.

4. Per Ed Flood, who started teaching at Rice in 1963.

5. Per the Archdiocese of New York and the Diocese of Brooklyn.

6. Dale McDonald, "United States Catholic Elementary and Secondary Schools 2006–2007" (National Catholic Education Association, 2007).

7. By this I don't mean to imply that there was no racial prejudice in Canada. There was racial conflict in Nova Scotia, for example, after both free black United Empire Loyalists and the slaves of white Loyalists moved there in the years of the American Revolution. Without a plantation economy, slavery never became a large institution in Canada and was abolished in 1834. When I grew up, there were so few blacks in most of the country that discrimination was seldom an issue.

8. Salim Muwakkil, "The End of Race?" *In These Times* (Institute for Public Affairs), July 21, 2003.

9. The average cost per pupil for fiscal year 2000–2001 was $10,513, per the New York City Department of Education's Web site: http://schools.nyc.gov. For a prediction of increased spending per pupil, see New York State Department of Education, Division of Budget Operations & Review, http://schools.nyc.gov/ offices/d_chanc_oper/budget/dbor. Including the billions of dollars spent on debt service, construction and renovations, and pension benefits, the actual per-student cost for the 2006–07 school year was $16,000. This will soon approach $21,000 per student, as the resolution of the Campaign for Fiscal Equity lawsuit with the state will pump an additional $4.7 billion per year into the city's schools. See Jacob Gershman, "City, Albany Mull a Funding Swap on Schools, Health," *The New York Sun,* September 20, 2006.

10. New York State United Teachers Web site: http://nysut.org/standards/students_graduation.html.

11. See Abby Goodnough, "How Grades 4 and 8 Fared on Tests," *New York Times,* October 15, 2000. These are the 1999 results. There were significant gains on the fourth grade statewide test in both English and math in 2005. But on the eighth grade level, over two-thirds of the city's black and Hispanic students failed the math test, and three-quarters failed the statewide English test. Results were significantly worse for minority students in other urban areas across the state. See "Summary Report on the 2005 Results of the State Elementary and Intermediate English Language Arts Assessments (Grades 4 and 8)," on the New York City Department of Education Web site.

12. Mayor Michael R. Bloomberg, who was elected for his first term in 2001 and his second in 2005, has made reforming the city's high schools a central part of his plans to improve public education. But as Sol Stern points out in "City's Pupils Get More Hype than Hope" (*City Journal,* Winter 2006), Bloomberg's overall education goals are not being met, and only a third of the city's students graduate with a Regents diploma. Less than 10 percent of minority students do so, and less than half of these are black and Latino males.

13. Robert Rector and Rea Hederman, "Income Inequality: How Census Data Misrepresent Income Distribution" (A Report for the Heritage Center for Data Analysis, September 29, 1999). The report states that "Today, the standard of living for the average American is nearly seven times higher than it was 100 years ago, after adjusting for inflation. The large gains in prosperity have affected all Americans, including low-income groups. At present, workers earning the minimum wage comprise the lowest-paid 2 percent of all employees. Yet today's minimum wage worker earns more, in real terms, in a single day than a low-skilled worker earned in an entire six-day workweek at the turn of the century. In other words, today's minimum wage worker earns more in eight hours than a low-skilled worker earned in 70 or more hours a century ago." This is referenced by two endnotes. The first reads: "Per capita GNP in 1900 was $246. See U.S. Bureau of the Census, *Historical Statistics of the United States: Colonial Times to 1970, Part 1* (Washington, D.C.: U.S. Government Printing Office, 1975), Series F1–5, p. 224. Prices adjusted by the Consumer Price Index (CPI-UX1). See *Historical Statistics of the United States,* Series E 135, pp. 210, 211, and *The Economic Report of the President* (Washington, D.C.: U.S. Government Printing Office, February 1999), Table B-62, p. 398." The second endnote reads: "Jacob Riis, writing around 1890, described low-skilled workers earning $1.75 for a six-day week. After adjusting for inflation, this comes today to about $31.50 per week, or $5.25 per day; the typical workday would have been at least 12 hours. Minimum wage workers today earn $5.15 per hour, or $41.20 for an eight-hour day. See Jacob A. Riis, *How the Other Half Lives* (New York: Dover, 1971), p. 184. *How the Other Half Lives* was first published in 1890." Therefore, it's reasonable to conclude that the working poor and working class in the 1940s

and 1950s were at least as poor as their counterparts today. Of course, poverty isn't merely about the standard of living. As a May 26, 2001 *New York Times* article (Louis Uchitelle, "How to Define Poverty? Let Us Count the Ways") asks: "Is a ghetto family impoverished because of its crime-ridden surroundings and poor schools, although the family has enough income to rise above the official poverty threshold?" No doubt, these factors make it more difficult for the lower classes to improve, but in material terms, the poor were poorer in past generations.

CHAPTER THREE

1. According to the annual school reports for A. Philip Randolph High School, a zoned public secondary school in Harlem with about 1,300 students in 1999–2000 and 1,900 in 2004–05, about 60 percent of the students qualify for the free lunch program. According to Brother Walderman, the same is true at Rice High School. The latest report—for 2005–06—is available at http://schools.nyc.gov/SchoolPortals/06/m540/AboutUs/Statistics/default.htm. For an account of violent and potentially violent incidents during one day in New York City's public schools, see David Herszenhorn, "Schools Report Gun Incidents and Assaults," *New York Times,* December 11, 2003. Also according to a recent study (Lisa Snell, "School Violence and No Child Left Behind," Reason Foundation, January 2005), school violence nationwide is grossly underreported.

2. Mary Gibson Hundley, *The Dunbar Story: 1870–1955* (New York: Vantage Press, 1965).

3. Stacey Vanek Smith, "A Renewed Harlem. But a Renaissance?" *The Christian Science Monitor,* May 30, 2003.

4. Ralph Ellison, "Harlem Is Nowhere," *The Collected Essays of Ralph Ellison,* ed. John F. Callahan (New York: Modern Library, 1995), p. 321.

5. The order of classes in the six-day cycle is periods A through H on days one, three, and five. On the even days, the sequence reverses and is shuffled as follows: H, G, D, C, F, E, B, A. On all days, the ninth period is the extended school period (ESP). Because this system is confusing, references to class periods are usually made by their order in the school day—first period, second period, and so on—except for ESP. When reference is made to a class period by its letter, this normally indicates a group of students: for example, Hebinck's H-period English class, which she teaches during first period one day and last period the next.

6. Per several interviews with Adam Robinson over the course of writing this book.

CHAPTER FOUR

1. Lynette Holloway, "Low Pay and Retirements Aggravate Teacher Shortage," *New York Times,* January 5, 2000. The figure cited, $31,910, includes the pending slight increase at the time.

2. Mary Frances Taymans and Christopher Scalise, "Dollars & Sense: Catholic High Schools and Their Finances" (National Catholic Education Association, 2007).

3. Per Ron Davis, the spokesman for the United Federation in New York City, September 2000.

4. Per Ron Davis, April 2007. Between 2000 and 2007, the average salary of a public school teacher rose to $62,300. Meanwhile the average salary at Rice increased to $42,000. Not only do public school teachers now make 50 percent more, by virtue of the newest contract, but they can top out at over $100,000 after twenty-two years. At Rice, teachers can now earn up to $79,000, but the only one to get to this level was Ed Flood after forty-four years. Few teachers make over $50,000 at Rice.

5. Per the Archdiocese of New York and Diocese of Brooklyn. For the 2006–07 school year, elementary school tuition averaged $2,600.

6. There is a $20,000 gap between Rice's average salary and that of teachers at the city's public schools in 2006–07. So matching salaries for twenty-six teachers would cost $520,000.

7. The average SAT scores at Rice have risen to about 860 on the reading and math sections from 2000 to 2007.

CHAPTER SIX

1. http://womenshistory.about.com/od/quotes/a/mary_bethune.htm.

2. www.cookman.edu/subpages/Founder_of_College_2.asp.

3. "Six Sons in Service," *The Shelby Daily Star*, June 20, 1945.

CHAPTER SEVEN

1. Harry K. Wong Publications, "The Effective Teacher," www.effectiveteaching.com/product/tet.htm.

2. I conducted a written survey of the 950 students at Bishop Loughlin Memorial High School in Brooklyn, New York, as I wrote the book proposal. Overwhelmingly the students cited discipline as the main reason they chose to attend the school, indicating that they felt safe from physical or verbal attacks, and that they could focus on their school work as a result.

3. Interview with Dr. Hilbert Stanley, who was executive director of the National Black Catholic Congress (NBCC) from 1991 to 2002 and currently serves as chairman of the board of trustees for the Morgan State University Foundation. One of the NBCC programs that Dr. Stanley oversaw was the African American Catholic High School Consortium.

4. Clarence Edward Beeby, *The Quality of Education in Developing Countries* (Cambridge, Mass.: Harvard University Press, 1966). See this book for a discussion of fundamentals of educating the poor from an international perspective. Beeby was the director of New Zealand's Education Department, before becoming

ambassador to France and the chairman of UNESCO's executive board. See www.unesco.org/publications/ThinkersPdf/beebye.PDF.

5. Advocates for Children of New York, "Leaving School Empty Handed: A Report on Graduation and Dropout Rates for Students Who Receive Special Education Services in New York City" (June 2, 2005), available at http://www.advocatesforchildren.org/pubs/2005/spedgradrates.pdf. Out of the 111,078 special education students who left school during the eight school years from September 1996 and June 2004, 11.84 percent earned regular (or local) diplomas. Only 512 of these students earned Regents diplomas.

CHAPTER EIGHT

1. Baltimore Catechism #3, Third Plenary Council of Baltimore (1891 version), lesson 6, question 278, available at www.baltimore-catechism.com/lesson6.htm.

CHAPTER NINE

1. Genesis 2:15–18, in *The New American Bible,* Catholic edition (New York: Thomas Nelson Publishers, 1971).

2. Roger Scruton, "Modern Manhood," *City Journal,* Summer 1999.

3. Susan S. Lang, "Working mothers, and particularly single mothers with jobs, are helping reduce U.S. child-poverty rate, Cornell study finds," *Chronicle Online* (Cornell University), November 28, 2005, available at http://www.news.cornell.edu/stories/Nov05/child.poverty.ssl.html.

4. Robert Rector, Kirk A. Johnson, and Patrick F. Fagan, "Understanding Differences in Black and White Child Poverty Rates" (A Report for the Heritage Center for Data Analysis, May 23, 2001).

5. Steven A. Camarota, "Illegitimate Nation, An Examination of Out-of-Wedlock Births among Immigrants and Natives" (Center for Immigration Studies, May 2007), available at www.cis.org/articles/2007/back507.html.

6. "New York City HIV/AIDS Annual Surveillance Statistics 2005," New York City Department of Health and Mental Hygiene, available at http://www.nyc.gov/html/doh/html/dires/hivepi.shtml. Citywide, African Americans account for 53 percent of the HIV diagnoses and Hispanics 28 percent. However, few cases are diagnosed among thirteen- to nineteen-year-olds, regardless of race or neighborhood.

But in Harlem, Washington Heights, the South Bronx, and other predominately minority areas, the HIV rate rises precipitously among twenty- to twenty-nine-year-olds. Since otherwise normally healthy teenagers can live for several years without symptoms after being infected, it is probable that many are contracting HIV while still in high school (per Daniel Gordon, research scientist at the Bureau of HIV/AIDS Epidemiology, Division of Epidemiology, New York State Department of Health).

7. Centers for Disease Control and Prevention, "Dear Colleague Letter on CDC's Heightened Response to the Ongoing Crisis of HIV/AIDS among African Americans," March 8, 2007, http://www.cdc.gov/hiv.

8. Guttmacher Institute, "Facts on Sex Education in the United States," http://www.guttmacher.org.

9. Per interview with Father Greeley, June 5, 2007.

10. Dinesh D'Souza, "A World without Racial Preferences" (American Enterprise Institute for Public Policy Research, January 1, 2000), available at www.aei.org/publications/pubID.9735,filter.all/pub_detail.asp.

CHAPTER TEN

1. Advocates for Children of New York, "Leaving School Empty Handed: A Report on Graduation and Dropout Rates for Students Who Receive Special Education Services in New York City" (June 2, 2005), available at www.advocatesforchildren.org/pubs/2005/spedgradrates.pdf.

2. Hebinck Zernike, "Study Points to Racial Slant in Special Education," *New York Times,* March 3, 2001.

3. Per Al Widziewicz. The average combined SAT score at the end of the year was about the same. While some scores went up, students who were reluctant to take the test in May 1999 eventually did so and scored in the lower ranges.

4. Susan Edelman, "City Kids Drop Back Further on SATs," *New York Post,* September 3, 1999. To access "The College Board, National Reports 1996–2006," go to http//www.collegeboard.com/about/news_info/cbsenior/yr2006/reports.html. From 1999 to 2006, religious schools increased their mean score to 1060, at three times the rate of public schools, which edged up to 1014.

5. "College Board National Reports." These scores are for 1999. For blacks, the combined math and verbal SAT scores increased slightly to 860 in 2000 and 863 in 2006. For Hispanics, it was about 916 in 2000 and 918 in 2006. Please note that the College Board reports the scores for Hispanics in three groups (Mexican or Mexican American, Puerto Rican, and other Hispanic or Latin American), so the mean scores given here for Hispanics are approximations.

6. Theodore Cross and Robert Bruce Slater, "Black Student College Graduation Rates Remain Low, But Modest Progress Begins to Show," *The Journal of Blacks in Higher Education* (Winter 2005/06), available at http://www.jbhe.com/features/50_blackstudent_gradrates.html.

7. "Bowen urges 'class-based affirmative action,'" *Inside UVA,* vol. 34, issue 8 (April 23–May 27, 2004).

8. Stephan Thernstrom and Abigail Thernstrom, "Racial Preferences: What We Know," *Commentary,* February 1999.

CHAPTER ELEVEN

1. There was discussion between principals and the New York Archdiocese's education department during the 1999–2000 school year about whether the passing grade would be 55 or 65. After consulting with the state department of education, it was resolved that the passing grade would be 55 for an indefinite period. Then raising the bar was delayed so that students starting high school in 2005 would be the first required to pass the Regents at 65 (two exams). For 2006 freshmen, it would be three Regents exams at 65, then four for 2007 freshmen, and then all five for 2008 freshmen. See http://www.insideschools.org.

2. In 2005, according to http://www.nacme.org.

3. Society of Women Engineers, "NACME: Thirty Years. Thousands of Stories," *SWE Magazine*, vol. 50, no. 1, Winter 2004. NACME is not the only such program. See Samuel G. Freedman, "Challenges for Black Colleges' Brightest in the Lab," *New York Times*, July 18, 2007.

CHAPTER THIRTEEN

1. Luke 14:28, *The Holy Bible, New International Version* (Grand Rapids, Mich.: Zondervan, 1984), www.ibs.org/niv/index.php.

2. Jacques Steinberg, "Nation's Schools Struggling to Find Enough Principals," *New York Times*, September 3, 2000.

3. Jennifer Medina, "What It Will Take to Recruit Principals: A Lot," *New York Times*, February 26, 2003. The principal shortage has become so severe that New York City's schools chancellor launched a recruiting campaign and is seeking candidates outside the area. But suburban school districts and what many would consider more attractive areas across the country are also advertising for principals.

CHAPTER FOURTEEN

1. Nicholas Lemann, "The Origins of the Underclass," *Atlantic Monthly*, June 1986.

2. The Children's Defense Fund, "State of America's Children Yearbook 1994," http://www.childrensdefense.org.

3. Police Department, City of New York, Compstat, vol. 14, no. 22, June 3, 2007. Weekly crime statistics available at http://www.nyc.gov/html/nypd/html/precincts/precinct_025.chtml. From 2001 to 2006, rates for major crime (murder, rape, robbery, assault, burglary, grand larceny, and grand larceny auto) fell another 21 percent. Also see Todd Zeranski, "NYC Is Safest City as Crime Rises in U.S., FBI Says," Bloomberg L.P., June 12, 2006, available at http://www.bloomberg.com.

4. Patrick J. Harnett and William Andrews, "How New York Is Winning the Drug War," *City Journal*, Summer 1999.

5. Per interview with retired Detective Sergeant Lou Savelli, April 30, 2007.

6. See Dr. Vincent E. Henry, "Compstat Management in the NYPD: Reducing Crime and Improving Quality of Life in New York City" (129th International Senior Seminar Visiting Experts' Papers, United Nations Asia and Far East Institute for the Prevention of Crime and the Treatment of Offenders), available at www.unafei.or.jp/english/pdf/PDF_rms/no68/07_Dr.%20Henry-1_p100–116.pdf. Compstat is a crime-fighting management tool that involves technology, communication, and weekly meetings at headquarters demanding precinct and borough accountability for crime rates. The term "Compstat" is shortened from the name of a computer file called "Compare Stats" (or, statistics).

7. George L. Kelling, "Crime Control, the Police, and Culture Wars: Broken Windows and Cultural Pluralism" (Perspectives on Crime and Justice: 1997–98 Lecture Series, National Institute of Justice, November 1998).

8. Ibid.

9. Thomas Sowell, "Race, Culture and Equality," *Forbes,* October 5, 1998.

10. Heather Mac Donald, "Diallo Truth, Diallo Falsehood," *City Journal,* Summer 1999.

11. Heather Mac Donald, "New York Cops: Still the Finest," *City Journal,* Summer 2006.

12. Heather Mac Donald, "Time for the Truth about Black Crime Rates," *City Journal,* April 2, 2007. Mac Donald notes: "Though blacks, 24 percent of New York City's population, committed 68.5 percent of all murders, rapes, robberies, and assaults in the city last year, according to victims and witnesses, they were only 55 percent of all stop-and-frisks."

13. Per interview with Professor David Kennedy, April 2007. According to the National Youth Gang Center, less than 10 percent of murders are gang-related. See National Youth Gang Center, "National Youth Gang Survey Analysis" (2006), available at http://www.iir.com/nygc/nygsa.

14. Sudhir Venkatesh, "The Financial Activity of a Modern American Street Gang," in Sudhir Venkatesh, Richard Curtes, and Charles H. Ramsey, *Looking at Crime from the Street Level* (Research Forum, National Institute of Justice, November 1999).

15. Federal Bureau of Investigation, "Crime in the United States: 2005," available at http://www.fbi.gov/ucr/ucr.htm.

16. Reuters, "Murders, Robberies Drive Up U.S. Violent Crime Rate," June 4, 2006, available at http://www.cnn.com/2007/US/06/04/usa.crime.reut/index.html. It is noteworthy that while violent crime increased significantly in 2006 for the second year in a row nationwide, it continued to decline in New York City. In 2007, for the first time since the NYPD began keeping reliable records in 1963, the number of homicides fell below 500. That marks an almost 80 percent decline in seventeen years. See Chris Mitchell, "The Killing of Murder," *New York Magazine,* January 7, 2008.

17. National Youth Gang Center, "National Youth Gang Survey Analysis."

18. James Q. Wilson and Richard J. Herrnstein, *Crime and Human Nature* (New York: Simon and Schuster, 1985), p. 281.

19. Robert Warshow, "The Gangster as Tragic Hero," in *The Immediate Experience: Movies, Comics, Theater, and Other Aspects of Popular Culture* (Garden City, N.Y.: Doubleday, 1962), pp. 85–88.

CHAPTER FIFTEEN

1. Per Barbara Keebler, director of communications, National Catholic Education Association.

2. In 1993 Notre Dame University founded the Alliance for Catholic Education (ACE) program that currently places 175 teachers in a two-year service program teaching in urban Catholic schools as they earn a master's degree in education. In 2000 the University Consortium for Catholic Education (UCCE) was founded to extend this approach and today consists of fourteen Catholic colleges and universities (including Notre Dame) placing 400 teachers in under-resourced Catholic elementary and high schools. UCCE operates in thirty-two states, not including New York. The program also upgrades curriculum to ensure rigorous academic standards, trains principals, and helps with marketing and fundraising efforts. The ACE program was mentioned by one of the principals at the African American High School Consortium meeting in December 1999, but there was no involvement with the program at that point.

3. Andrew M. Greeley, *The Irish Americans: The Rise to Money and Power* (New York: Harper & Row, 1981), pp. 1–8.

CHAPTER SIXTEEN

1. Charles R. Morris, *American Catholic: The Saints and Sinners Who Built America's Most Powerful Church* (New York: Random House, Times Books, 1997), p. 314.

2. William J. Stern, "How Dagger John Saved New York's Irish," *City Journal*, Spring 1997.

3. Luc Sante, *Low Life* (New York: Vintage Books, 1991), p. 48.

4. Alan M. Kraut, "Illness and Medical Care among Irish Immigrants in Antebellum New York," in *The New York Irish*, ed. Ronald H. Bayor and Timothy J. Meagher (Baltimore: The John Hopkins University Press, 1996), p. 156.

5. Thomas Keneally, *The Great Shame* (New York: Random House, Nan A. Talese, 1998), p. 134.

6. William McFeely, *Frederick Douglass* (New York: W.W. Norton, 1991).

7. Barry Schwartz, ed., *White Racism* (New York: Laurel Leaf Books, 1978).

8. Sante, *Low Life*, p. 113.

9. Frederick Engels, *The Condition of the Working Class in England in 1844* (London: George Allen and Unwin, 1952), p. 91.

10. Dinesh D'Souza, *The End of Racism* (New York: The Free Press, 1995), p. 137.

11. Graham Hodges, *Slavery, Freedom & Culture among Early American Workers* (Armonk, N.Y.: M.E. Sharpe, 1998), pp. 109–110.

12. Charles Loring Brace, *The Dangerous Classes of New York and Twenty Years Among Them,* 3rd ed. (New York, 1872), pp. 26–27.

13. Tyler Anbinder, *Five Points* (New York: The Free Press, 2001), p. 208.

14. William J. Stern, "What *Gangs of New York* Misses," *City Journal,* January 14, 2003.

15. Timothy J. Gilfoyle, *City of Eros: New York City, Prostitution and the Commercialization of Sex, 1790–1920* (New York: W.W. Norton, 1994), p. 345.

16. Allan Nevins and Milton Halsey Thomas, eds., *The Diary of George Templeton Strong,* vol. 2: *The Turbulent Fifties, 1850–1859* (New York: Macmillan, 1952), p. 57.

17. Fredrika Bremer, *The Homes of the New World: Impressions of America,* trans. Mary Howitt, 3 vols. (New York: Harper and Brothers, 1853), letter 39; available at http://digital.library.wisc.edu/1711.dl/History.BremrHemme.

18. Edward T. O'Donnell, *1001 Things Everyone Should Know about Irish American History* (New York: Doubleday Broadway Publishing Group, 2002), no. 195 about British historian Edward A. Freeman.

19. Henry Louis Gates, Jr., *America behind the Color Line: Dialogues with African Americans* (New York: Warner Books, 2004), p. xvii.

20. James Alan Fox and Marianne W. Zawitz, "Homicide Trends in the U.S." (U.S. Department of Justice, Office of Justice Programs, Bureau of Justice Statistics, 2007), available at http://www.ojp.usdoj.gov/bjs/homicide/homtrnd.htm #contents. Regarding interracial homicide, 8.5 percent were black on white in 2005, and 3.5 percent were white on black. Since Hispanics are counted as white for the most part, the differences in population create the 12:1 ratio.

21. William Julius Wilson, "When Work Disappears: Societal Change and Vulnerable Neighborhoods," in Peter Kivisto and Georgann Rundblad, eds., *Multiculturalism in the United States, Current Issues, Contemporary Voices* (Thousand Oaks, Ca.: Pine Forge Press, 2000), pp. 219–28.

22. Lemann, "Origins of the Underclass."

23. Gates, *America behind the Color Line,* p. 8.

CHAPTER SEVENTEEN

1. Saul K. Padover, *Thomas Jefferson on Democracy* (New York: Appleton-Century, 1939), p. 89.

2. Diane Ravitch, *The Great School Wars: A History of the New York City Public Schools* (Baltimore: The Johns Hopkins University Press, 2000).

3. Stephan Brumberg, *Common Schools, Uncommon Faiths: Religious Conflict and the Shaping of American Education* (New Haven: Yale University Press, 2007).

4. Ravitch, *The Great School Wars,* p. 49. Ravitch quotes from a report given

to Archbishop Hughes by a committee of prominent Catholics in the summer of 1840.

5. Brumberg, *Common Schools, Uncommon Faiths.*

6. Kraut, "Illness and Medical Care among Irish Immigrants in Antebellum New York," p. 165.

7. Brumberg, *Common Schools, Uncommon Faiths.*

8. Schwartz, *White Racism,* p. 42.

9. Stern, "How Dagger John Saved the New York Irish."

10. Rev. Msgr. Florence D. Cohalan, *A Popular History of the Archdiocese of New York* (Yonkers, N.Y.: U.S. Catholic Historical Society, 1983), p. 89.

11. Stern, "How Dagger John Saved New York's Irish."

12. Ibid.

13. Vizard, "In Yonkers, an Archive for the New York Archdiocese." See also the New Advent Catholic Encyclopedia at www.newadvent.org/cathen/01691a .htm and www.newadvent.org/cathen/11020a.htm, and an independent Web site at www.catholic-hierarchy.org/diocese/dnewy.html.

14. McDonald, "United States Catholic Elementary and Secondary Schools 2006–2007."

15. Morris, *American Catholic,* p. 123.

16. Cohalan, *A Popular History of the Archdiocese of New York,* p. 90.

17. William J. Stern, "Once We Knew How to Rescue Poor Kids," *City Journal,* Autumn 1998.

18. Lawrence A. Cremin, ed., *The Republic and the School: Horace Mann on the Education of Free Men* (New York: Teachers College, 1957), pp. 84–97, http:// usinfo.state.gov/usa/infousa/facts/democrac/16.htm.

19. John Taylor Gatto, *The Underground History of American Education: A Schoolteacher's Intimate Investigation into the Problem of Modern Schooling* (New York: The Oxford Village Press, 2001), p. 20.

20. Ravitch, *The Great School Wars,* p. 82, quoting Thomas Boese, *Public Education in the City of New York* (New York: Harper Brothers, 1869).

21. Matthew Josephson and Hannah Josephson, *Al Smith: Hero of the Cities* (Boston: Houghton Mifflin, 1969), p. 89.

22. Morris, *American Catholic,* p. 111. As Morris chronicles, Paul Cardinal Cullen transformed the Catholic Church in Ireland in militant fashion, in stark contrast to the lax Catholicism and poor Church attendance that had previously been the norm. In North America, many prelates followed suit, including Archbishop Hughes and Rochester's Bishop Bernard McQuaid, for example, making this conservative and practical mold the one that ultimately predominated.

23. See the cartoon on the cover of *Harper's Magazine,* December 9, 1876. The caption reads, "The Ignorant Vote—Honors Are Easy" (available at http:// www.yale.edu/glc/archive/971.htm).

24. Richard Jensen, a retired University of Illinois history professor, takes

issue with the historical claim of systematic job discrimination against Irish Catholics (see "No Irish Need Apply: A Myth of Victimization," available at: http://tigger.uic.edu/~rjensen/no-irish.htm). Perhaps generations of Irish Catholics have exaggerated their perceptions of prejudice, but most sources chronicle significant anti-Irish Catholic bigotry.

25. Kraut, "Illness and Medical Care among Irish Immigrants in Antebellum New York."

26. Ravitch, *The Great School Wars,* p. 405.

27. Harold A. Buetow, *Of Singular Benefit: The Story of Catholic Education in the United States* (New York: Macmillan, 1970), p. 179.

28. Buetow, *Of Singular Benefit,* section entitled "The School Controversy," pp. 170–176. Also see chap. 3, "The Grand American Catholic Compromise," in Morris, *American Catholic.*

29. Morris, *American Catholic,* p. 194.

30. Buetow, *Of Singular Benefit,* p. 225.

31. Morris, *American Catholic,* p. 268.

32. Gail Foster, "Historically Black Independent Schools," in *City Schools: Lessons from New York,* ed. Diane Ravitch and Joseph P. Viteritti (Baltimore: The Johns Hopkins University Press, 2000), pp. 298–99.

33. Joel Schwartz, "Where Dr. King Went Wrong," *City Journal,* Winter 2002.

34. Ibid.

35. Ravitch, *The Great School Wars,* p. 405.

36. Number of religious sisters as of 2006 per Barbara Keebler, National Catholic Education Association. Denise McKenzie, "Lower Enrollment, High Costs Require School Closings," *Buffalo (N.Y.) News,* February 1, 2007.

37. Bryk, Lee, and Holland, *Catholic Schools and the Common Good,* p. 32.

38. McDonald, "United States Catholic Elementary and Secondary Schools, 2006–2007."

39. Sister Mary Agnes O'Brien, S.C., "History and Development of Catholic Secondary Education in the Archdiocese of New York" (Ph.D. dissertation, Columbia University, 1949), p. 163.

40. Since the 1999–2000 school year, Rice's tuition has continued to increase yearly to $5,550 for the 2007–08 school year. This is about $700 less than the national average, per the National Catholic Education Association's Web site: http://www.ncea.org/news/AnnualDataReport.asp.

41. McDonald, "United States Catholic Elementary and Secondary Schools, 2006–2007."

42. Brian L. Carpenter, "Urban Catholic Schools Excel Academically, Struggle Financially," *School Reform News,* April 1, 2005.

43. McDonald, "United States Catholic Elementary and Secondary Schools, 2006–2007."

44. Per Archdiocese of New York and Diocese of Brooklyn.

45. Pew Hispanic Center, "Changing Faiths: Latinos and the Transformation of American Religion," Pew Forum on Religion & Public Life, April 25, 2007. See also www.ncea.org/news/AnnualDataReport.asp.

46. Per Susan George, executive director of the Inner-City Scholarship Fund. This figure applies to the 2007–08 school year.

47. Per Archdiocese of New York for the 2007–08 school year.

48. Center for Applied Research in the Apostolate (CARA), Georgetown University, http://cara.georgetown.edu/bulletin/index.htm.

49. Joseph Claude Harris, "Giving USA 2007: The Annual Report on Philanthropy for the Year 2006" (Giving USA Foundation, June 2007). The number of U.S. Catholic families per e-mail from Harris. See also www.ncea.org.

CHAPTER TWENTY

1. Joe Mahoney, Tracey Tully, and Bill Hutchinson, "Jurors Standing by Their Decision," *New York Daily News,* February 28, 2000.

2. Mac Donald, "Diallo Truth, Diallo Falsehood."

3. Tom Hays, "Jurors Explain Diallo Verdict," Associated Press, February 28, 2000.

4. Sourcebook of Criminal Justice Statistics Online, "Arrests By Offense Charged, Age Group, and Race, United States, 2005," Table 4.10 (2005), http://www.albany.edu/sourcebook/pdf/t4102005.pdf. Mac Donald, "Time for the Truth about Black Crime Rates," reports that blacks account for 68.5 percent of violent crimes and yet are only 55 percent of stop-and-frisks.

5. Kit R. Roane, "The Diallo Shooting: The Echoes," *New York Times,* March 26, 1999.

6. Orlando Patterson, "Life, Liberty, and Excessive Force," *New York Times,* February 28, 2000.

7. Paul C. Vitz, "Support from Psychology for the Fatherhood of God," *Homiletic and Pastoral Review,* February 1997.

CHAPTER TWENTY-TWO

1. Edward Jay Epstein, "The Black Panthers and the Police: A Pattern of Genocide?" *New Yorker,* February 13, 1971.

2. Sol Stern, "Ah Those Black Panthers! Beautiful!" *City Journal,* Summer 2003.

3. Stéphane Courtois, Nicolas Werth, Jean-Louis Panné, Andrzej Paczkowski, Karel Bartošek, and Jean-Louis Margolin, *The Black Book of Communism: Crimes, Terror, Repression* (Cambridge, Mass.: Harvard University Press, 1999). The authors estimate conservatively that so far a hundred million people have been murdered by communist regimes worldwide.

4. Fred Siegel, *The Future Once Happened Here: New York, D.C., L.A., and*

the Fate of America's Big Cities (New York: The Free Press, 1997). Siegel, an historian, coined the phrase "ideology of riot."

5. Cohalan, *Popular History of the Archdiocese of New York*, pp. 56–57.

6. An audio recording of Malcolm X's Oxford debate is available at http://www.brothermalcolm.net/2003/mx_oxford/index.html.

7. Robert Weisbrot, *Freedom Bound: A History of America's Civil Rights Movement* (New York: W.W. Norton, 1990), pp. 28–29.

CHAPTER TWENTY-THREE

1. Ralph Ellison, *Invisible Man* (New York: Vintage Books, 1947), p. 262.

2. Ibid., p. 1.

3. Steve Estes, *I Am a Man! Race, Manhood, and the Civil Rights Movement* (Chapel Hill: University of North Carolina Press, 2005), p. 6.

4. Ralph Ellison, "The Art of Fiction," *The Paris Review,* interview with Ellison in 1954, p. 16, available at www.parisreview.com/media/5053_ELLISON .pdf.

5. Ralph Ellison, "The World and the Jug," *The New Leader,* December 9, 1963.

6. Gates, *America behind the Color Line,* p. 16.

7. Ibid., p. 13.

CHAPTER TWENTY-FOUR

1. There were 1,259 SSP students in the 1999–2000 school year, per Jane Martinez, executive director. In 2006–07, there were 1,300 students, per Lisa Cernera, the associate director of admissions.

2. Maine Public Policy Institute, "The Town Tuitioning Program: Maine's Hidden School Choice Gem," http://www.policyforme.org/info.php?s=9&ss= 16&id=13.

3. Dan Lips and Evan Feinberg, "School Choice: 2006 Progress Report" (Heritage Foundation Backgrounder #1970, September 18, 2006), http://www .heritage.org/Research/Education/bg1970.cfm.

4. Per Lips and Feinberg, "School Choice: 2006 Progress Report," and a phone interview with Dan Lips on May 30, 2007. He projected that 150,000 students would be receiving between $1,000 and $7,500 each toward private school tuition in September 2007. Most of this funding comes directly through vouchers, which are referred to most often now as "scholarships."

5. Sol Stern, "What the Voucher Victory Means," *City Journal,* Autumn 2002.

6. Some voucher programs help disabled students from a wide range of family backgrounds. Also, the Utah program potentially benefits all public school students, but students from poor families receive substantially more aid.

7. David L. Lean, "Latinos and School Vouchers: Testing the 'Minority Support' Hypothesis," *Social Science Quarterly,* vol. 85, no. 5 (December 2004).

CHAPTER TWENTY-FIVE

1. Randall S. Sprick, *Discipline in the Secondary Classroom: A Problem-by-Problem Survival Guide* (West Nyack, N.Y.: The Center for Applied Research in Education, 1985).

2. Shelby Steele, "The Age of White Guilt," *Harper's Magazine,* November 2002. Steele has expanded his views in *White Guilt: How Blacks and Whites Together Destroyed the Promise of the Civil Rights Era* (New York: HarperCollins, 2006).

CHAPTER TWENTY-SIX

1. Paul Tough, "What It Takes To Make a Student," *New York Times Magazine,* November 26, 2006.

CHAPTER TWENTY-SEVEN

1. Dr. Mary McLeod Bethune, "Last Will and Testament," available at http://www.cookman.edu/subpages/Last_Will_and_Testament.asp.

2. Theodore Roosevelt, excerpt from speech entitled "Citizenship in a Republic," delivered at the Sorbonne, Paris, April 23, 1910, available at www.bartleby.com/56/4.html#txt1.

CHAPTER TWENTY-NINE

1. In 1999, I visited the diabetic ambulatory and Hansen's disease clinics at the Staten Island University Hospital.

2. C. J. Schofield, G. Libby, G. M. Brennan, R. R. MacAlpine, A. D. Morris, and G. P. Leese, "Mortality and Hospitalization in Patients after Amputation: A Comparison between Patients with and without Diabetes," *Diabetes Care,* October 1, 2006.

3. Genesis 39:19–20, King James Bible, available at http://kingjbible.com/genesis/37.htm.

EPILOGUE

1. Per Brother Thomas Schady, associate superintendent of secondary education, Archdiocese of New York. There are four Catholic high schools in Manhattan that compete with the best private schools. In addition to Loyola, Regis is a scholarship school, and the other two are all-girls schools. The Convent of the Sacred Heart charges $29,500 and Marymount charges $27,800. All figures are for the 2006–07 school year.

2. http://www.brrice.org/AboutUs/aboutUs_brothers.htm.

3. Susan L. Aud, "Education by the Numbers: The Fiscal Effect of School Choice Programs, 1990–2006" (Milton and Rose D. Friedman Foundation, April 2007), available at www.friedmanfoundation.org/friedman/downloadFile.do?id=243. Since the Friedman Foundation supports school choice, Aud assures the reader that her study maintained scientific rigor.

4. This is the result of multiplying the total Catholic school enrollment (2,320,651) times the national average amount spent per student ($8,701); see Sam Roberts, "New York Is Top State in Dollars per Student," *New York Times,* May 30, 2007.

5. In addition, according to a recent study (Scott W. Hamilton, ed., "Who Will Save America's Urban Catholic Schools?" [Thomas B. Fordham Institute, April 10, 2008], http://www.edexcellence.net), three hundred thousand students have been displaced from Catholic schools due to the thirteen hundred closings since 1990, costing taxpayers $20 billion to educate in public schools. Over the next twenty years, another three hundred thousand Catholic school students could lose their schools, which will cost taxpayers another $20 billion. These lost seats are lost to future generations as well, meaning that taxpayers will continue to pay to educate students who would otherwise attend Catholic school.

6. Michael Coulter, "Utah Voucher Plan Succumbs to Misinformation Ad Campaign," *School Reform News,* November 9, 2007.

7. Per interview with Dan Lips.

8. Sol Stern, "School Choice Isn't Enough," *City Journal,* Winter 2008.

9. Damien Cave, "Man in the News—Cory Anthony Booker: On a Path That Could Have No Limits," *New York Times,* May 10, 2006.

10. Sam Dillon, "U.S. Data Show Rapid Minority Growth in School Rolls," *New York Times,* June 1, 2007.

11. There are some hopeful signs, as documented in the Fordham study ("Who Will Save America's Urban Catholic Schools?"): "In Wichita, Catholic schools are free to all Catholics, and the inner-city Catholic schools also offer an inexpensive option to poor non-Catholic families. The Jubilee schools in Memphis illustrate how committed church leaders and inspired educational leaders have attracted serious money from philanthropists eager to underwrite educational revival in a city whose children are stuck in public schools that have squandered tens of millions over the last decade. The recent uptick of enrollment in Denver's Catholic schools appears to result from vigorous recent efforts to market these schools to families who have more school options than ever before." There are also groups of independent Catholic schools run by religious orders, such as the Cristo Rey and NativityMiguel networks, operating in low-income areas, that are expanding successfully. Cristo Rey Jesuit High Schools (http://www.cristorey.net), begun in 1998, now educate 525 disadvantaged students in twelve high schools across country, with six more schools being planned. The NativityMiguel Network of Schools (http://www.nativitymiguelschools.org), with sixty-four schools from pre-K through twelve, run by twenty-nine religious orders and other organizations such as the National Council of Negro Women, currently educate 4,323 students in urban areas in twenty-seven states.

12. Per interview with Charles Zech, May 29, 2007. McDonald, "United States Catholic Elementary and Secondary Schools, 2006–2007."

13. According to the Pew Forum on Religion and Public Life's "U.S. Religious Landscape 2008," Catholics rank in the middle in education and income levels in comparison to other denominations. However, if Hispanic Catholics—half of whose households earn less than $30,000 per year and over 40 percent of whom did not graduate from high school—are discounted, then, as Greeley demonstrates, Catholics rank next to Jews in income and education levels.

14. Joseph Claude Harris, "Managing Growth: The Challenge Confronting Catholic Church Leaders in the Diocese of San Jose, 1990–2005" (Office of Parish and Planning, forthcoming). Nationwide, parishes raise $6.6 billion in offertory collections and another $2.4 billion through bingo, golf tournaments, and other fund-raising drives. The per-household donations referred to here make up the offertory amount.

15. Father Greeley wrote the introduction to Joseph Claude Harris, "Did Catholic Giving to Parishes or Diocese Decline in 2002?" October 2003, http://www.josephclaudeharris.com.

16. Harris, "Did Catholic Giving to Parishes or Diocese Decline in 2002?"

17. The resiliency Catholics have shown doesn't obviate the enormous damage that priestly predators inflicted on their victims and that both these failed priests and the bishops who enabled them have wrought on the Church. Now there is a presumption of guilt whenever a priest or brother is accused of sexual misconduct.

18. Mark 9:50, Matthew 5:13, and Luke 14:34.

19. Revelations 3:16, in *The New American Bible,* Catholic edition (New York: Thomas Nelson Publishers, 1971).

20. U.S. Census Bureau News, "Census Bureau Projects Tripling of Hispanic and Asian Populations in 50 Years; Non-Hispanic Whites May Drop to Half of Total Population" (U.S. Department of Commerce, Washington, D.C., March 18, 2004), http://www.census.gov/Press-Release/www/releases/archives.

21. Stern, "How Dagger John Saved New York's Irish."

22. Robert Rector, Christine Kim, and Shanea Watkins, "The Fiscal Cost of Low-Skilled Households to the U.S. Taxpayer" (Heritage Special Report, Heritage Foundation, April 4, 2007).

23. Sam Dillon, "U.S. Data Show Rapid Minority Growth in School Rolls." While African American students constitute 15.6 percent of all students, slightly above the black proportion of the population, Hispanic students make up 20 percent, indicating a much higher rate of increase.

24. Although some Catholics would argue that the Church should focus its efforts on supporting Catholic schools with predominately Catholic student bodies, thereby abandoning many inner-city schools, I believe it is imperative to keep all Catholic schools open. There is a special historical debt owed African Americans that will not be repaid anytime soon. Also, from the Catholic point of view it's just as important to teach religious truth to non-Catholics as to

Catholics. "We don't educate children because they're Catholic," declared Washington D.C.'s James Cardinal Hickey, "but because we're Catholic." For Catholics the point is moot. From the viewpoint of students at struggling Catholic schools, however, conversion to charter schools as a last resort is certainly preferable to closing them.

25. Often quoted, less often implemented. Available on many Web sites, for example, http://www.bellaonline.com/articles/art27977.asp.

INDEX

A. Philip Randolph High School
(Harlem), 424n1

Abbasse, Christopher M., 43–47, 64, 79,
95, 158, 160, 172–76, 253, 265, 349, 356,
363, 365–74, 387, 402, 405, *photo 10;*
background of, 45; classrooms
monitored by, 57–58, 101; and
confidentiality of student records, 98;
counseling of troubled students by, 92,
367–68, 397; drinking of, 110, 376; drug
dealing at Rice suspected by, 127, 263,
265, 365, 366; Dwayne and, 67–68, 140,
141; Ephraim and, 107–109, 174, 267–68,
368–70; expulsions recommended by,
266–67, 367; at graduation breakfast,
365, 367; intervention with Hebinck's
class of, 255–60; lunch periods
supervised by, 77, 98–100, 370–71;
morning inspection of students by, 43,
44, 47; Orlando's relationship with, 47,
166, 288; parent conferences with, 175,
366–67; and parents' complaints, 130,
159, 268–69; Prince and, 99, 117–18, 173,
267, 372; return to public school
considered by, 46, 350; on Rice's

academic success, 360, 361; Ricky and,
44–45, 47, 99–100, 103–6, 370–71, 373;
structure and high expectations
established by, 96; student of the month
recommendations of, 210; students'
complaints about teachers to, 63;
students motivated by, 304; as teacher,
45, 339, 383, 390, 391; thefts reported by,
74; warnings to troublemakers by, 132;
Yusef and, 262–65

Abdul-Jabbar, Kareem, 60, 417

Abednego, Iyashia, 190

Abednego, Kareem, 190

Abednego, Rasheeda, 190

Abednego, Yusef, 31, 188–96, 199, 208–9,
261–66, 281, 406, *photo 9;* Abbasse and,
262–65; drug dealing by, 188, 193,
200–201, 263, 265, 271; expulsion from
Rice of, 264–66; gang affiliation of,
191–93, 200; jobs held by, 193, 377, 406;
at Orlando's funeral, 397; Orlando's
relationship with, 188–90, 193–96,
209–12, 214, 261–62, 264–66, 270,
289–90, 317–18, 327–28, 383; at Our
Savior Lutheran High School, 270, 377,

441

Castellano, Nelson, 49, 77, 92, 171, 175–77, 256, 268, 371

Cathedral High School (Manhattan), 111

Catholic Protectory, 241, 242

Catholic schools, 387–88, 401, 408–17 *(see also specific schools);* academic efficacy of, 5–6, 10; authority of principals in, 6; behavior and dress codes in, 199; in Canada, 2, 5, 8; Catholic Universities and, 222–23; difficulty of teaching at, 347–48, 350; discipline and structure at, importance of, 95–96, 105; faculty recruitment problems of, 59; fighting in, 191; financials of, 217–19; gangs and, 206; graduation rates of, 6; history of, 235–45; instruction in faith and morals in, 116–17; lack of remediation for functional illiteracy in, 18; loss of enrollment in, 251; metal detectors absent from, 46; middle- and upper-class, 49–50; NAEP results for, 421n12; in nineteenth and early twentieth centuries, 11; nuns in, 250; patience extended to students at, 140; privately funded vouchers for, 102–3, 106, 324–25 *(see also* Student Sponsor Partners); reading scores in, 9; religious mission of, 28–29, 36; report on, 224; SAT scores at, 61, 152–53; transferring of students between, 108; tuition of, 33, 39–40, 225, 250–52, 433n39

Catholic University, 157

Centers for Disease Control and Prevention, 137

charter schools, 10, 408, 413

Chicago, 224, 247; homicide rate in, 202; reading scores in, 9

Children's Aid Society, 231, 242

Children's Scholarship Fund (CSF), 324

China, Boxer Rebellion in, 299

Chinese immigrants, 11, 190

Christian Brothers, 2, 34, 36, 106, 134, 138, 285, 302, 340, 341, 383, 400–402; Abbasse hired by, 45; African American, 273; and declining enrollment, 36, 106; De La Salle *(see* Lasallian Christian Brothers); discipline and order imposed by, 96, 390; Eastern Province

headquarters of, 221, 400; financial issues for, 217–18; founding of, 23, 225, 270, 419n1; influence on students' academic and social behavior of, 70; in Irish independence struggle, 85, 281; openness to outside influences of, 116; Orlando appointed principal by, 20, 29, 33; postsecondary liberal arts institution of *(see* Iona College); residence of, 61, 218; on Rice faculty and staff, 26, 167, 274, 288, 402 *(see also* DePiro, Brother James; Maistre, Brother Matthew; Sherlog, Brother Bill; Walderman, Brother J. Matthew); schools operated by, 28, 60, 349, 392, 401, 402, 417 *(see also* All Hallows High School); tuition charged by, 32, 250

Christian Brothers, Congregation of, 23, 85, 419n1

Christianity, 38, 138, 179, 235, 242, 302; Afrocentric, 37, 246–47; Apostolic, 144; nondenominational, 2

CHS 2000: A First Look, 224

City College, 82

civil rights movement, 81, 83, 136, 246, 299, 305, 307, 311, 377; assertion of African American manhood in, 310; connecting students to, 281–82, 284–88, 292, 294–96; legal equality and opportunities resulting from, 198, 232; loss of self-esteem in aftermath of, 316; sit-ins during, 279, 302–3; transformation of racial consciousness in, 38

Civil War, 360

Clark Atlanta University, 156

Clarkson University, 405

Claxon, Hanif, 259

Clinton, Bill, 399

Clinton, Hillary, 399

Cold War, 299

Coleman, James S., 6; *Public and Private High Schools,* 5

Colgate Inc., 129

college admissions, 8, 130, 151–58, 181, 183, 314, 361, 313, 314; athletic scholarships and, 317, 319, 320, 326–27

College of New Rochelle, 144, 147

233, 234; in New York Police Department, 272; parishes for, 238–40; poverty and crime among, 227–32; racism of, 11, 190; riots against, 298–99
Irish Christian Brothers. *See* Christian Brothers, Congregation of
Irish Emigrant Society, 239
Islam, 11, 45–47. *See also* Nation of Islam
Italian Catholics, 11, 32
Ives, Levi Stillman, 241
Ivy League colleges, 4, 154, 155, 160, 366, 405. *See also specific colleges and universities*

Jackson, Jesse, 89, 216, 276, 292
Jamaicans, 57, 175
James Monroe High School (Bronx), 191–93, 209
Jay, John, 228–29
Jefferson, Thomas, 234
Jeffries, Paul, 221–22
Jesuits, 49, 52, 127, 129, 154, 217, 240, 242, 348, 393, 401
Jesuit Volunteer Corps (JVC), 52
Jews, 4, 86, 246, 285. *See also* Judaism
Jim Crow segregation, 71, 80, 310
John Jay College of Criminal Justice, Center for Crime Prevention and Control, 201
John XXIII, Pope, 249
Johnson, Lyndon Baines, 81
Johnson, Magic, 51
Johnson, Mark, 396–97
Jones, Jordan, 276–78, 397
Jones, Langston, 64
Jones, Ray, 182, 406
Journal of Blacks in Higher Education, 155
J. P. Morgan Foundation, 219
Judaism, 179; Moorish, 107
Justice Department. *See* U.S. Department of Justice

Kafka, Franz, *Metamorphosis,* 311, 349
Keith, Robert, 323, *photo 7*
Kendrick, Bishop Francis P., 298
Kennedy, David, 201
Kennedy, John F., 246
Kilpatrick, James J., 303

King, Martin Luther, Jr., 19, 93, 247, 299, 300, 310, 316, 386–87; assassination of, 231, 279, 280, 286, 294–95, 386; "I Have a Dream" speech of, 1, 81, 278; at Morehouse College, 156, 248
King James Bible, 235
Kipling, Rudyard, 138
KIPP Academies, 10
Kryzewski, Mike, 180
Ku Klux Klan, 39, 82, 294
Kwanzaa, 297

Laboy, Lorenzo, 273, 275
Lancasterian system, 243
Lane, Paris, 171, 204, 208, 318, 326–28, 365–66, 371–72, 389, 403–4
Lange, Blessed Mother Elizabeth, 225
Lasalle Academy (Lower East Side), 124, 224–25
Lasallian Christian Brothers, 123, 193, 241, 224, 242, 243, 349, 419n1
Lasch, Christopher, 247
Latin Kings, 205
Latinos. *See* Hispanics
Lebanese Americans, 45
Lee, Duane, 111, 120, 123
Lemann, Nicholas, 197
Lewis, Eunice, 103, 172, 173, 175, 176, 275, 368
Liberia, 401
Liburd, Calvet, 397
Lil' Kim, 213
Lindhart, Aston, 160, 161, 175, 297, 301, 336–37
Lips, Dan, 411
Longmore, Spencer, 303–4, 334–35
Lopez, Dionedes J. (D.J.), 62, 172, 174
Lopez, Felipe, 326–27
Los Angeles: gangs originating in, 192; homicide rate in, 202; reading scores in, 9
Louima, Abner, 272, 280
Louis Armstrong Middle School (I.S. 227, Queens), 321
Loyola High School (Manhattan), 393
Loyola University, 327
Lutheran Church, 13, 18, 37, 86–87, 222, 223, 270, 280; Missouri Synod, 274

National Catholic Education Association, Elizabeth Ann Seton Award, 292
National College Athletic Association (NCAA), 319, 327, 405
National Council of Negro Women, 82
National Endowment for the Humanities, 45
National Guard, 288, 294
National Honor Society, 291
National Oceanographic and Atmospheric Administration, 331
National Opinion Research Center, 246
National Science Foundation, 332
Nation of Islam, 45, 216
Native Americans, 168, 222
Navy, U.S., 93, 359, 406
Neal, Derek, 5–6
Newark (New Jersey), 412; Diocese of, 240, 413
New Bethel Way of the Cross Church of Christ (Harlem), 144
New Direction Middle School (Harlem), 147
New Guinea, 401
New Orleans, Catholic schools in, 126, 128, 137–38, 221
New Testament, 133
Newton, Huey, 300, 315
New York, State University of. *See* State University of New York
New York Archdiocese, 20, 239–40, 251, 272, 302, 403, 413, 415, 425n5, 428n1; Office of Black Ministry, 273
New York City, 128, 221, 410; black independent schools in, 246–47; Board of Education, 6, 86; Commission on Charity, 240; crime rates in, 198–99, 429nn12,16; death and arrest rates for gang members in, 201–2; Department of Small Business Services, 396; graduation rates in, 5; Irish immigration to, 226–29, 237 (*see also* Irish Catholics); Parks Department, 145; parochial school attendance levels in, 249; privately funded voucher programs in, 324 (*see also* Student Sponsor Partners); public schools in, 3–4, 9, 40, 46, 235–36, 240,

242, 288, 332, 420n8, 422n9, 423n12, 426n5, 428n3. *See also specific schools*
New York Daily News, 271
New York Police Department (NYPD), 199–202, 213, 404, 429n16; and brutalization of Louima, 272, 280; Citywide Anti-Gang Enforcement, 202; fatal shootings of black suspects by, 271–72 (*see also* Diallo, Amadou); Holy Name Society, 274–75; Manhattan North, 204; Street Crimes Unit, 200, 282
New York Post, 60
New York State Bar, 218
New York State Board of Regents, 40
New York Times, 4, 6, 56, 64, 273, 412, 420n8, 423–24n13
New York Times Company Foundation, 219
New York University, 8, 63, 283, 405
Nicene Creed, 178
Nichols, Omar, 127
Nixon, E. D., 310
No Child Left Behind, 10
Notre Dame University, 154
Nunez, Ed, 172–74
Nutty Professor, The (movie), 210
N-word, 288; banning of, 69–70, 105, 278–79, 397

Oakland (California), 297
Oblate Sisters of Providence, 225
O'Connor, John, Cardinal, 250, 274–75
Ohio, voucher program in, 324, 411
Old Testament, 178
100 Blacks in Law Enforcement Who Care, 275
Ortega, Jose, 203–4
Orwell, George, *Animal Farm,* 347
Our Lady of Mercy School (Bronx), 108
Our Saviour Lutheran High School (Bronx), 270, 289, 290, 377, 383, 394
Oxford University, 231, 299

Palestinian intifada, 45
Parks, Rosa, 294–96
Passion of the Christ, The (movie), 404
Patrons Program, 251–52, 413

Text: 11.25/13.5 Adobe Garamond
Display: Perpetua
Compositor: Binghamton Valley Composition, LLC
Indexer: Ruth Elwell
Printer and Binder: Maple-Vail Manufacturing Group